TWO
CHARLESTONIANS
AT WAR

TWO CHARLESTONIANS AT WAR

The Civil War Odysseys of a Lowcountry
Aristocrat and a Black Abolitionist

BARBARA L. BELLOWS

LOUISIANA STATE UNIVERSITY PRESS
BATON ROUGE

Published with the assistance of the V. Ray Cardozier Fund

Published by Louisiana State University Press
Copyright © 2018 by Louisiana State University Press
Manufactured in the United States of America
FIRST PRINTING

DESIGNER: Michelle A. Neustrom
TYPEFACES: Minion Pro, text; Esther, display
PRINTER AND BINDER: Sheridan Books, Inc.

LIBRARY OF CONGRESS CATALOGING-IN-PUBLICATION DATA

Names: Bellows, Barbara L., author.
Title: Two Charlestonians at war : the Civil War odysseys of a Lowcountry
  aristocrat and a black abolitionist / Barbara L. Bellows.
Description: Baton Rouge : Louisiana State University Press, [2018] |
  Includes bibliographical references and index.
Identifiers: LCCN 2017049364| ISBN 978-0-8071-6909-4 (cloth : alk. paper) | ISBN
  978-0-8071-6910-0 (pdf) | ISBN 978-0-8071-6911-7 (epub)
Subjects: LCSH: Pinckney, Thomas, 1828–1915. | Barquet, Joseph H. |
  Charleston (S.C.)—History—Civil War, 1861–1865. | United
  States—History—Civil War, 1861–1865—Biography. | Confederate States of
  America. Army—Biography. | United States. Army. Massachusetts Infantry
  Regiment, 54th (1863–1865)—Biography. | Charleston (S.C.)—Biography.
Classification: LCC E467 .B45 2018 | DDC 973.7/457—dc23
LC record available at https://lccn.loc.gov/2017049364

The paper in this book meets the guidelines for permanence and durability
of the Committee on Production Guidelines for Book Longevity
of the Council on Library Resources. ♾

CONTENTS

ILLUSTRATIONS & MAPS

ACKNOWLEDGMENTS

WRITING IS A FAMOUSLY LONELY OCCUPATION, but also one that would be impossible without the many people who so kindly and conscientiously support scholarly research in libraries and archives, who share their own hard-won knowledge and insights, as well as those who are willing to read drafts and discuss ideas. Equally important are those who goad you to finish, leave your study, and return to the business of everyday life.

My special thanks go to the staffs of the South Carolina Historical Society (especially Virginia Ellison, Molly Inabinett, Karen Stokes, and Matthew Lockwood), the South Carolina Department of Archives and History, the Virginia State Library, and the Library of Congress. Henry Fulmer and Nathan Sanders were helpful at the South Caroliniana Library, as was Autumn Bennett at the College of Charleston Library. Arthur House of the National Archives went above and beyond to help me meet a deadline by supplying a critical document in record time.

I owe a debt of gratitude to Harlan M. Greene, head of Special Collections at the College of Charleston and fount of wisdom about the history of the Carolina lowcounty, for his many years of friendship and sage advice after reading a very early (and much longer) draft. Sue Rainey, Virginia Christian Beach, and Laura Mina also read portions of the text and offered very helpful suggestions. Professor Stephen R. Wise shared research materials and his vast knowledge of the Civil War in the lowcountry on a memorable "field trip" to the site of the Battle of Honey Hill.

Roxie Minor provided invaluable IT assistance with a skill that approaches wizardry.

I am grateful to all those who helped me navigate twenty-first-century technology to secure the nineteenth-century images for this book: Mai Pham, Bridgeman Images; Becca Hiester, The Gibbes Museum of Art; Randy L. Goss, Delaware Public Archives; MaryJo McAndrew, Special Collections & Archives at Knox College; Jennifer McCormick, Charleston Museum; Celeste Wiley,

South Carolina Historical Society; and David Rosado, New York Public Library. Artist and cartographer Mary Lee Eggart provided the maps.

The editors and staff at Louisiana State University Press performed the alchemy of transforming my manuscript into this book. I appreciate the professionalism and guidance of P. Rand Dotson, editor-in-chief, and Lee Sioles, managing editor, who shepherded this project through the publication process. Kevin Brock's sharp editorial eye, knowledge of southern history, and deep well of patience made the sometimes-harrowing copyediting experience a pleasure and an education. I particularly valued the comments of the press's anonymous reader who took the time to write a thoughtful and most helpful evaluation.

Relatives of Captain Thomas Pinckney, Mary Louise "Pie" Friendly, St. George Pinckney, and Isabella Breckinridge have been gracious with their assistance. Katharine Gates, historian of the Stewarts of Brook Hill, generously supplied important background on the family of Mrs. Thomas Pinckney.

Tracking down the relatives of Sergeant Joseph H. Barquet was more challenging, but proved enormously rewarding. I had the pleasure of introducing cousins, Kimberly Tabb, Sgt. Barquet's direct descendant, with John R. Clauson, great-grandson of his elder brother, Liston.

They have kindly shared family stories, photographs, and documents with me, and have, together with other family members, worked to have a proper headstone honoring his military service installed at Barquet's unmarked grave. Many thanks go to Deb Williams of Oakdale Memorial Gardens in Davenport, Iowa for her advice and for sharing with us the cemetery's excellent records.

Working on this book reminded me of the fun of being a South Carolinian teaching Civil War courses in New England. The students at Middlebury College during those years were a genuine pleasure; some still remain friends. I have, in turn, learned from two who became historians and writers, Kate Côté Gillin and Dorie McCullough Lawson, as well as from the ever-challenging and questioning Rita M. Glavin and Tristan Phifer O'Leary, who predictably became lawyers. With me always will be the memory of Ryan Fairman Waldron '97, an exuberant son of the South, too soon taken from us.

I benefited from the advice and encouragement of friends and family over the years including Richard Chasin and the late Laura Chasin, Mary Morgan and David Callard, Ann R. Roberts, Dr. Mario F. Romagnoli, Craig M. Simpson, and Tim Ecott.

All might have been lost—or at least much delayed—if, at a critical moment near the end of this long process, Jennifer R. Nolan, Ingrid R. Rockefeller,

Steven C. Rockefeller Jr., Laura S. Rockefeller, Patricia H. Bellows, and George Bellows Jr. had not stepped into the breech and, in their different ways, provided indispensable help. They have my heart-felt gratitude.

As ever, I am thankful for Steven C. Rockefeller's zen-like patience; in this case, with having these two Civil War soldiers live with us for so long.

TWO
CHARLESTONIANS
AT WAR

PROLOGUE
The Two Roads to Coffin Island

THIS IS THE TALE OF TWO SOLDIERS. Both were native sons of Charleston—the little city that started the big war—raised one mile and two worlds apart. Captain Thomas Pinckney, rice planter and scion of one of America's founding families, fought for the Confederacy with the 4th South Carolina Cavalry. Sergeant Joseph Humphries Barquet, a brick mason and son of a *gens de couleur libre* from Saint Domingue, fought for the Union with the 54th Massachusetts (Colored) Infantry. They were born during the 1820s along the squall line of history, where one world was dying while another was coming into being. The era of the plantation slaveholder had begun its wane, but that of the free man of color with political ambitions was only a dim glimmer on the far horizon. Neither man has had his story told before.

I came upon this anomalous pair quite by accident and just at the one moment in time when their paths crossed on Morris Island, a wispy bar of shifting sand in Charleston Harbor known locally as "Coffin Island." During the course of my research for a biography of Josephine Pinckney, poet and novelist of the Charleston Renaissance, I thumbed through the unpublished Civil War memoirs of her father. They began with a justification of secession and ended predictably with a rant about the long-term pernicious effects of Republican Reconstruction, but the account of his 1864 imprisonment on Morris Island as one of the suffering "Immortal 600" intrigued me.[1] That his guards were black soldiers from the 54th Massachusetts Infantry—still stranded there more than a year after their brave but disastrous attack upon Battery Wagner—added interest.

But what particularly engaged my curiosity was Pinckney's account of Joseph Barquet. The sergeant was not one of the captain's regular guards, but he showed up at his tent in October 1864 and introduced himself as a native Charlestonian. A student of history who closely followed public affairs, Barquet had many questions to ask and right away began peppering the surprised and delighted Pinckney with inquiries about Charleston politics and politicians past and pres-

1

ent. Pinckney immediately "located" the light-skinned man as a member of the small, interrelated, and "respectable" class of "free mulattos, chiefly of French, Spanish and Portuguese extraction." These artisans and mechanics, caterers and seamstresses, he reflected, composed the city's useful working class and the elite among the free people of color.[2]

Pinckney held the view of most antebellum Charlestonians of his class that the upper tier of blacks shared some common interests with the white elite, especially that significant portion who owned slaves or hoped to.[3] This assumption had been reinforced by his understanding of events around the rumored Denmark Vesey plot, which had occurred before either he or Barquet had been born but would significantly transform the landscape of their youth, albeit in very different ways. "Back in the year 1822," Pinckney recalled, "a serious insurrection planned by the negroes of this city, . . . was nipped in the bud in consequence of information given by one of this class, who were not favorably disposed toward the freed slaves being put on an equality with themselves, hence they occupied a useful place in our body politic and were granted some consideration in consequence."[4]

But this sunny evaluation of the relationship between free blacks and the white elite omits the critical background role played in that dynamic by the Haitian Revolution, a historical juggernaut of dizzying complexity that began with a seemingly spontaneous slave rebellion in August 1791 resulting in massive loss of life and property. The reactions of two of Pinckney's ancestors are illustrative. Charles Pinckney, the captain's cousin some generations removed, was serving as governor when the shocking news arrived. He understood that the Carolina lowcountry had many of the same vulnerabilities as that French colony and understood the implications for South Carolina. The state's "profusion" of slaves dwelled among whites at approximately the same ratio of ten to one in its plantation areas, such as the Santee District north of Charleston. Knowing Charlestonians too "slept at the foot of Vesuvius," Pinckney predicted that "a day may arise when they may be exposed to the same insurrection." Rather than acknowledging that the slaves (many native Africans) may have been driven to revolt when some random act of cruelty ignited the dry timber of their unrelenting misery, Charleston's leaders concluded that French abolitionists were to blame for the slave uprising and the subsequent freeing of the colony's slaves in 1793.[5]

After the 1822 Denmark Vesey scare, Captain Pinckney's grandfather, Major General Thomas Pinckney, blamed the plot, at least in part, on "the example of

St. Domingo" and argued that free blacks should be banished from the city lest they too imbibe that "indiscreet zeal in favor of universal liberty" and form a subversive fifth column. Likely referring to the bloody conclusion of the revolution in 1804 when Haiti won its independence and General Jean Jacques Dessalines, after crowning himself emperor, had ordered the massacre of about four thousand whites (whether slaveholders or not), Pinckney cautioned that emancipation in South Carolina would result "in a war of extermination to their white fellow-citizens, their wives, and children." These warnings from the venerated Pinckney cousins, which lodged in the memory of white citizens for a generation and more, provide perspective on the divided mind of the city toward those people of color living outside the strictures of slavery.[6]

But in Pinckney's recollection, for all their historic differences, these two sons of Charleston greeted one another as lone travelers meeting accidentally in a foreign country and finding that they actually had much in common. From his perspective in 1864, the captain felt a greater connection to Barquet than to many of the unsavory, rabidly racist Confederates drawn from the southern lower classes with whom he was imprisoned. In contrast to those of Barquet's own New England officers, who assumed that most of their men were runaway slaves or northern reprobates, Pinckney understood the great diversity that existed among peoples of color and, from his own experience, had no doubt that among the black race were individuals of intelligence and bravery.

Sergeant Barquet, in turn, was comfortable enough with Pinckney to share an account of his own travails in the "free" states, where he experienced neither justice nor equality, and also his worries about the inferior segregated education available to his children despite the taxes he paid. He also expressed his sadness over the prisoner's unnecessary privations and offered to bring him some fresh food (at some personal risk), waving away, as any southern gentleman might, the captain's offer to pay. Pinckney recognized Barquet not only as a man of standing with a history, a family, and a separate tradition of his own, but also as one with whom he shared fundamental human values.[7]

The two soldiers' conversation about Charleston took place as the old city's civilian population was under siege by Union artillery. Both Barquet and Pinckney still had friends and relatives living along its narrow streets. The Charleston of their childhoods, they knew, would soon be, like their lost youth, only a memory. What the future would bring, whether it was the reelection of President Abraham Lincoln, the outcome of the war, or the fate of the slaves, was as unfathomable to them in the autumn of 1864 as the secret of the Sphinx.

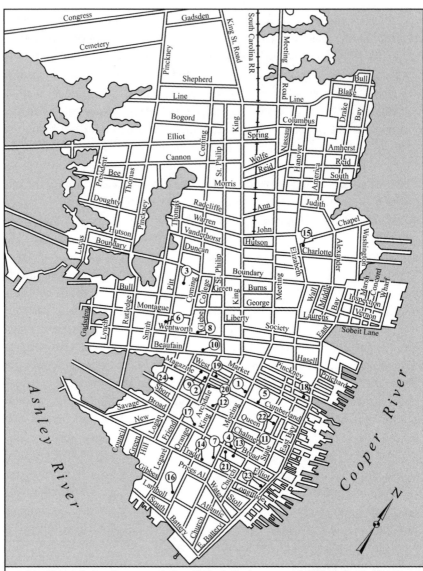

1. John Pierre & Barbary Barquet
2. Margaret Bellingall
3. Brown Fellowship Society
   Graveyard
4. City Hall
5. Cumberland Methodist Church
6. Hagar Cole
7. First (Scots) Presbyterian
   Church
8. Grace Episcopal Church

9. Cornelia Tunno Harrison
10. Richard Holloway
11. (French) Huguenot Church
12. Joseph Humphries
13. Jehu Jones Hotel
14. Eliza & John Lee
15. Caroline Pinckney & C.C.
    Pinckney Jr.
16. Edward Rutledge Pinckney
17. Colonel Thomas Pinckney

18. Pinckney Family Mansion
19. Charles Pinceel
20. St. John's Lutheran Church
21. St. Michael's Episcopal
    Church
22. St. Philip's Episcopal
    Church
23. Adam Tunno
24. Workhouse & Jail

Charleston in 1830

* * *

LONG AFTER THE JOSEPHINE PINCKNEY biography went to press, unbidden thoughts of these two soldiers began to inhabit my imagination. I tried to ignore them. Library shelves already groaned with Civil War biographies. I had learned that compared to the mountain of government documents and official correspondence generated by the statesmen and diplomats among Pinckney's august ancestors, the Confederate captain's surviving papers, beyond his reminiscences, scarcely constituted an archival molehill. The chance of picking up the tracks of a well-traveled black brickmason-cum-abolitionist seemed discouragingly remote as well.

Nevertheless, an image of Pinckney with unruly full beard, gaunt and lanky, sitting cross-legged in the sand with the trim Barquet—one, wan and emaciated in ragged, filthy Confederate gray; the other, swarthy and squared away in Union blue—became fixed in my mind like a nineteenth-century *tableau vivant* or a Matthew Brady photograph. Providing the background to their brief separate peace, I could imagine the flap of canvas in the harbor breeze, the boom of cannons, the buzz of mosquitoes, and the aching clarity of Carolina's October light reflecting off the churning gray waters of Charleston Harbor. Over time, perhaps because I too am Charleston born, they drew me in. I began to think of these two free men, simultaneously enemies and fellow sufferers stranded together on Coffin Island, as a symbolic allegory of the long-fraught, yet interdependent, relationship between the races on Charleston's narrow peninsula.

Puzzling over the two roads that brought these men to Morris Island, I found myself walking all over the city, mentally mapping out the locations where their journeys began. The site of Thomas Pinckney's birthplace, an urban villa on Elizabeth Street in a leafy section of the Charleston Neck, required a mile hike from downtown St. Philip's Episcopal Church, where members of both the Barquet and Pinckney clans worshiped. The Pinckney family seat, a mansion built overlooking the harbor by Thomas's great-grandparents Eliza Lucas and Chief Justice Charles Pinckney, had once reigned over upper East Bay Street, a few blocks north of what later became the city market. Just five minutes away from that site, if walking purposefully, is the spot where Joseph had been born. He had lived with his parents, John Pierre and Barbara Tunno Barquet (both umbrella makers), and his six brothers and sisters in a brick house on Meeting Street near Horlbeck Alley. Up and down this busy thoroughfare bisecting the peninsula lived John Pierre's friends from the exclusive Brown Fellowship Society, with membership limited to prosperous mixed-race freemen. Tinsmiths, barbers, and shoemakers all earnestly plied their trades in shops interspersed among doctors' homes and lawyers' offices. Along the narrow intersecting alleys lived slaves and free blacks of the poorer class. Proximity bred both fear and familiarity between the races—as well as an inevitable level of contempt and reaction. And yet blacks and whites have somehow lived together on the narrow Charleston peninsula since the seventeenth century. It is a world and a culture they built together, one that produced both Thomas Pinckney and Joseph H. Barquet.

The elements of Barquet's varied and revealing life that I have pieced together comprises the first full-length biography of a black soldier from the famous *Glory* regiment of Hollywood fame and provides a rich, nuanced understanding of the challenges faced by the survivors among the "Famous 54th" Massachusetts. The misbegotten assault upon Battery Wagner depicted in the film was just the beginning, rather than the end of their story. Born in 1823, Joseph Barquet grew up as part of a small, tight-knit community of free mixed-race urban artisans often referred to as the "colored elite." As an intelligent light-skinned youth of relative privilege with a good education, he felt elevated above most blacks, free or enslaved, and considered himself as French, identifying with the European ancestry of his father, a native of Saint Domingue. Complicating his self-understanding was his mother's father, a wealthy Scot, who contributed to the family's material well-being from the profits of the slave trade, the foundation of his first fortune.

By his early twenties, the ambitious Barquet could see no real future for himself in the city of his birth, with its sagging economy and repressive laws governing free blacks. Craving greater freedom and a bit of adventure, he left Charleston in 1846 for years of travel that first took him south to Mexico, then north and west of slavery, providing a panoramic view of the free black experience in nineteenth-century urban America. The unexpected and racially motivated hardships, dangers, and rejections he encountered during his odyssey at first stoked his anger, then taught him humility. The surging river of African Americans' great struggle swept up Barquet in its powerful current and over time washed away his feelings of superiority to the dark skinned, the enslaved, the poor, and the illiterate. He took the cause of the chattel as his own, believing that racism had its roots in slavery. Barquet mastered the windy oratory so popular in Charleston during his youth as well as the principles of the Constitution so venerated there, becoming known as "a colored Demosthenes" by the time he had settled in Illinois about 1850. With a flair for words and a good grasp of the sectional debates tearing at the heart of the nation, Barquet left a trail of letters to newspaper editors expressing his frustration at constantly being denied the rights of a native citizen that often penetrated to the heart of the matter. One written in 1855 to a Galesburg journal protesting the western states' discriminatory "Black Laws" posed its question directly: "What have we done to engender such malicious hate from our fellow man in the State—in the country at large?"[8]

In contrast to the peripatetic seeker Barquet, Thomas Pinckney's life story is a study of intense localism, resistance to change, and longing for lost glory. Judge Henry A. M. Smith's preface to Pinckney's memoirs described his close friend as a man deeply "attached to his native soil and the life among his own people" who never lost his passion for "the charm of his country's emerald rice fields, the majesty of her great pine forests, the golden spread of her wide marshes, and the glamour of her many waters." Never fully embracing Confederate nationalism, Pinckney established a home guard to protect the Santee River plantations of family and friends in 1861, a unit later integrated into the 4th South Carolina Cavalry. His identity can hardly be separated from his deep connection to his iconic ancestors, who were present not only at the creation of the Republic—three kinsmen signed the US Constitution—but also at the founding of the Carolina Colony in 1670. In a nod to their influence, George C. Rogers Jr. dubbed his golden-age history of the colonial capital, from the 1720s to the 1820s, *Charleston in the Age of the Pinckneys*.[9]

Captain Pinckney's biography fills in the neglected chapters of a dynasty in decline. His birth in 1828, the same year as the death of his venerated grandfather and namesake, statesman and diplomat Major General Pinckney, coincides with the twilight of the plantation aristocracy and marks the point when historians switch their focuses to the Age of Democracy and the rise of two Carolinians of humbler origins, Andrew Jackson and John C. Calhoun. Captain Pinckney's stern and domineering father, C. Cotesworth, signed the Articles of Nullification in 1832 but lurched in an entirely different direction the next year. Renouncing politics in favor of religion, he became a pioneer in the controversial Christian paternalism movement that encouraged slaveholders to introduce the Gospels to plantation slaves. Advocates also urged the kinder treatment of slaves, replacing raw power over a captive people with the model of the extended family, the patriarchal master acting as a father to his childlike dependents.

The chronicle of the iconic Pinckney family, whose heroic deeds, political machinations, strategic marriages, acquisitions of sprawling estates, and dynastic aspirations might have been imagined by some American Trollope. Only a Tolstoy, though, could have conjured the family's breathtaking descent after the Civil War. As Tom's sister Caroline Pinckney Seabrook declared, "Did ever such universal ruin descend on a people at one blow in the history of the world?"[10]

Thrust into military service just as he was on the cusp of achieving his life-long ambition to run the ancestral rice plantations on his own, Pinckney was fated instead to be among those planters having to reinvent their operations using laborers in recent transit from slavery into freedom. The political revolution wrought by Radical Republicans in 1867 had profound effects upon those living in districts with large black majorities. Pinckney distanced himself from the racist violence and corruption of Reconstruction politics and struggled in a tragic and Sisyphean attempt to maintain his life on the land as government policies and changing markets made that impossible.

Pinckney never saw Barquet again after their one meeting and never benefited from the fresh food he promised to bring. But the captain was nourished by the sincerity of the sergeant's regrets about his unnecessary suffering and the chance to reminisce about their hometown. Within days, Pinckney was transferred to yet another prison. Forty years later, when he wrote his memoir, Pinckney still remembered his candid conversation with Barquet and that man's "soldierly bearing." A uniform had indeed made all the difference and equalized the social space between the aristocrat and the artisan.[11]

I FRAME PINCKNEY AND BARQUET's dual biography in alternating chapters, rather with the idea of continuing the back and forth of their Morris Island conversation. When first beginning this project, I was reminded of two books that broke new ground during the civil rights movement and benefited from rereading them. Robert Penn Warren's *Who Speaks for the Negro?* (1964) challenges the argument that there can be one voice that speaks for African Americans by underscoring the great diversity of thought and opinion that has historically existed among them. James McBride Dabbs's *Who Speaks for the South* (1965) outlines the long, often contentious, history of blacks and whites together shaping the culture of the South and the importance of personal relationship between the races.

To the extent possible, I let Pinckney and Barquet speak for themselves. Both men struggled to have their competing versions of the Civil War experience consecrated in the national memory. Their choices, their opinions, their missteps, and their self-justifications are theirs, not mine, and are part of the historical record of a particular time and a particular place. I did make a few editorial judgment calls, such as omitting Pinckney's claim that Barquet referred to him as "Sire"—this surely did not happen. Whether Barquet could have really said that his youthful years growing up among his family and the free community in Charleston were, as Pinckney reports, the "happiest years of his life," skeptical readers of the following chapters may decide for themselves.[12]

In emphasizing their shared humanity and the intersection of their lives, I do not mean to suggest a false equivalency between their experiences. Although tragedy stalked Captain Pinckney, and at times his suffering was profound, his trials bear no comparison to Barquet's life as a black man in nineteenth-century America who could find no place—North or South, East or West—to call home, where his talents might be respected and his own complex history valued.

More complicated than mere symbols or representative men, Barquet and Pinckney were deeply human, thus inevitably flawed. They made mistakes and disappointed as they navigated without charts in the eddying political currents after the Civil War. Back in their home states of Illinois and South Carolina, the soldiers were both affected by the political battles over citizenship, the franchise, and the organization of free labor as leaders of the Republican Party debated how best to retain the hegemony they had enjoyed when the southern states were out of the Union.

One particularly valuable insight that comes from this pairing is the chance to compare how differently Reconstruction played out for blacks in Republican strongholds in Illinois and other midwestern states as opposed to those in South Carolina and other bastions of the Democratic Party. To the detriment of his own economic well-being and his family's security, Barquet became a loyal soldier of the Republican Party and was outraged when illiterate former slaves were enfranchised before he was and when the civil rights of black men and women in the North drifted so quickly off the party agenda, replaced by the demands of American industrial capital. One of the haunting, unanswered questions about Barquet's story is how his life might have been different had he chosen to stay in South Carolina, where he still had family connections and would have had a chance to become part of the Reconstruction government, an opportunity always denied him in Illinois.

I will confess that I have probably violated the biographer's first rule and developed too much empathy for my subjects. Perhaps too, I have indulged in rather old-fashioned storytelling at the expense of more probing analysis because I have so enjoyed my time with both of these men and their families and wanted to share the details of their lives lest they be lost.

Read together, the stories of Sergeant Joseph H. Barquet and Captain Thomas Pinckney are reminders that the course of history does not move in a straight line to a fixed, inevitable point, but its twists and turns are almost always unexpected and never simply a matter of black and white. In Civil War history, particularly, every story has more than two sides.

I

JOSEPH'S STORY
Sunshine and Shadow

JOSEPH H. BARQUET WAS BORN on September 10, 1823. It was the worst of times. His parents, John Pierre and Barbara Barquet, no longer cherished the same hopes for his future as they had for their other four children. Even though they owned their Meeting Street home and possessed greater security than the majority of Charleston's free people of color (and a significant portion of the white population too), they felt ill at ease and vulnerable to forces beyond their control. Economic stagnation had settled upon the city like dust in an abandoned house. Dwelling in an ether of social suspended animation—neither slaves nor citizens—the Barquets never knew from one year to the next what new (and to their minds, irrational or simply punitive) restrictions might be inflicted upon them by South Carolina's legislature. The rising tide of antislavery sentiment in the nation and the South's declining power in Congress had thrust the state's leaders into a defensive state of mind.[1]

Since the birth of their fourth child in 1821, the Barquets felt that their community had lost ground. The 1820 state law prohibiting all manumissions without special legislative approval dashed the hopes of their friends who had been saving every penny to buy family members out of bondage. With the exception of those fortunate ones emancipated by their owner's will, enslavement had become a life sentence.

Free blacks in Charleston could still legally marry, freely associate, and travel. They could participate in the economy by owning property, investing in bank stocks and city bonds, loaning money at interest, and making contracts. Whatever wealth they accrued could be passed on to their children. Their participation in civic life was restricted to petitioning the legislature and bringing lawsuits in certain situations. In short, they possessed privileges rather than constituted rights. Those thin threads separating their status from that of the slave majority were anchored to windward only by the indulgence of their fair-weather friends among the city councilmen and state legislators.[2]

Whenever white Charlestonians lay sleepless in their beds, free blacks also tossed and turned. When city leadership began calculating the value and safety of staying in the Union, as they did during the 1820s, free blacks began calculating the value and safety of staying in Charleston. Friends of the Barquets already had started moving to northern cities, such as New York and Philadelphia, that had long-established free black communities.

In 1822 tragedy knocked the precarious racial equilibrium of the city out of kilter. Given the incomplete and corrupted nature of the existing historical record, no one can say with 100-percent certainty that Denmark Vesey, a freed carpenter in his fifties, actually masterminded a rumored slave uprising against Charleston. By the same token, no one can say with 100-percent certainty that the complex, nefarious plot of which he was accused ever existed beyond a "grotesque fantasy" in the minds of the scores of slaves forced to give testimony under intense pressure. The narrative that evolved contained elements of the popular gothic-horror novels of the day. Vesey's conspiracy was conflated with elements of the Haitian Revolution and said to have involved the collaboration of masses of slaves from the town and country intent on randomly murdering whites (with particularly evil intent toward women), torching the city, and liberating all those in bondage, with the leaders fleeing to Haiti afterward. In some versions sympathetic Haitians, acting in black solidarity for the cause of freedom, would come to Charleston to participate in the slaughter.[3]

What no one disputes is that in July of that year, Vesey and thirty-four of his accused co-conspirators were publicly hanged after being found guilty in a secret trial. Consequently, the bonds upon the enslaved were tightened, while the free people of the city became less free.

The story of Denmark Vesey told around the Barquet dinner table during Joseph's youth surely differed from the current interpretation, which holds him up as an iconic freedom fighter. From that free family's perspective, the hero of 1822 was not the man who wanted to burn Charleston, but rather the man who wanted to save it—their longtime friend, tinsmith William Pinceel.[4]

It cannot be strictly proven, but it is unthinkable that, on the evening of May 22, Pinceel would not have dashed the one long block up Meeting Street from his Queen Street workshop to the Barquet home, anxious to share some inflammatory, possibly dangerous, news. Earlier that day Peter Francis Desverney, an enslaved man whom John Pierre knew as well, had come to him in a panic of indecision. While he idled at the harbor's edge after finishing his Saturday shopping, Desverney reported, an enslaved man of his acquaintance had whispered that a massive conspiracy of city and country slaves was preparing to rise up to "shake off our bondage." When asked if he wanted to join, "horror struck" Desverney said "no," turned on his heels, and left lest he be seen and later connected with the possible trouble to come. Desverney's question to Pinceel was now whether he should tell his master, Colonel John Cordes Prioleau, what he heard or stay mum.[5] In contrast to most slaves, Desverney had received permission from Mrs. Prioleau to marry in St. Philip's Episcopal Church, where she attended services and he had been baptized. He wanted at all costs to protect his wife, a freewoman of color, and their two little children, who by law took their mother's status and were also free.[6]

The two men could see danger in both choices. The white community, they understood, was like a sleeping tiger: any hint of caballing slaves, the slightest breaking of a twig of intrigue, could arouse indiscriminate fury, blind slashing and tearing of all within reach. Pinceel told Desverney "with great earnestness" to tell the truth. This he did. Colonel Prioleau later took him to city hall to testify, and Desverney set the wheel of fate in motion, although in truth he reported merely smelling smoke, not actually seeing a fire.[7]

Both Pinceel and Desverney received rewards for their commitment to public safety. Illustrative of the divided mind of the city toward free people of color, though, just before the official account of intendant James Hamilton, *Negro Plot*, went to press, a "vide" was inserted into the text ostensibly correcting the original version that praised Pinceel's wisdom in advising Desverney. The new version, betraying the constant fear of collaboration between free and unfree blacks, has Desverney turning first to the teenaged "young master" for guidance, thus placing "the fidelity of the slave who first gave the intelligence of the intended insurrection, on much higher ground."[8]

When he first heard about the possible slave uprising, Pinceel would have been particularly anxious to alert John Pierre Barquet since as a "French negro" born in Saint Domingue, he could become a suspect in any plot. Neither man had anything to gain and everything to lose by violence; given their histories, they held no romantic notions about the virtue of the enraged, uneducated mob. Both knew firsthand that whatever noble goals and justified anger might inspire the first pitch of a torch or toss of a rock, riots usually ended up causing suffering to innocents in their paths rather than righting any wrongs. They also understood the complex social divisions among peoples of color, free and enslaved, and were familiar with the exaggerated high talk animating the urban grapevine. Every slave, they acknowledged, craved freedom. An enormous chasm loomed, however, between their wish for liberty and their willingness to do murder. But if a well-orchestrated slave revolt actually was brewing in the lowcountry, Barquet realized from his experience of violent revolution in Saint Domingue that free people of color, the well-to-do *gens de couleur libre*, especially those with slaves, would be among the first targets.

Legislation enacted during 1822 and 1823 in the wake of the Vesey panic transformed the legal contours of the state. The Barquets suffered from the reimposition of a burdensome capitation tax (basically a levy for being black and free), and the knowledge that at any time they might be stopped and demanded to show proof of their freedom. Other laws diminished free blacks' ability to associate in any numbers, while any leaving South Carolina could never return for fear that they would bring with them revolutionary ideas espoused by northern abolitionists. For much the same reason, black seamen, who also could read the night sky and had knowledge of paths of escape, were to be jailed while in Charleston. Every free black man had to have a white "guardian," who would testify that they were free, of good character, and not a danger to the community. Knowing his vulnerability, Barquet strove to avoid all appearances of impropriety and enlisted auctioneer John W. Payne to vouch for him. Payne would never be suspected of abolitionist sentiments, for at his auction house he rang his gavel down on large lots of slaves with the same regularity as he did fine Philadelphia-made furniture.[9]

Two months after Vesey's execution, the premonition of danger from the West Indies that had so preoccupied white Charlestonians during the summer of 1822 was realized, though in a quite different way than they had imagined. Late on the night of September 27, startled dreamers awoke to a nightmare. Were those the sounds of black Jacobins banging at the door and breaking glass, some wondered. No, it was the wind, howling like a thousand banshees. The most destructive hurricane in a century had blown up from the Caribbean and murderously pummeled the Carolina coast in "an awful exhibition of the elemental war" and as a fitting coda to that summer of hell. Great gusts rocked houses back and forth, broke window glass, ripped off roofs like tissue paper, and lifted wooden piazzas up and away. Boats in the harbor crashed and splintered like children's toys as they were hurled against the shore. All around the Barquets' house, buildings were damaged; theirs could not have escaped. The storm mauled the handsome city hall, only a few of blocks away. No structures, humble or grand, were immune from the gale's indiscriminate furies. The next day black and white bodies alike were found crushed under fallen houses; others dotted the beaches up and down the coast. All told, hundreds perished.[10] The lesson that might have been learned was that on that narrow peninsula where the races lived in such physical proximity, any harm that came to one would come to all. No one was exempt from the brutal forces of nature—or history.

THE FOLLOWING SEPTEMBER, 1823, Charleston was mercifully spared another storm. The Barquets' fifth child, Joseph Humphries, was safely delivered into an increasingly anxious world. They named him in honor of another close family friend, Joseph Humphries, a well-respected Queen Street tailor of Scottish descent who in 1803 had helped found the Minor's Morality Society to aid orphans of the free black community.[11]

Young Joseph's childhood in Charleston would be a mixture of sunshine and shadow. Not a slave, but not altogether free, not black, but also not white, he dwelled in the shade of differences ever searching for his place. His parents taught him the proper racial etiquette about what he could wear, how he should carry himself, when to avoid eye contact, when to yield the sidewalk to whites, and where he was permitted to go. The newly built pleasure gardens at the tip of the peninsula were off-limits to him. The rules were not so very different from what John Pierre would have learned as a young *gens de couleur libre* in Saint Domingue before the revolution. But his parents also taught their son self-respect.[12]

Joseph enjoyed the one element that makes all the difference in the complex equation of human happiness—he was loved. He grew up feeling himself a person of worth, even potentially of power. He had the benefit, not common in the larger world of free blacks, of living with two parents, who were always accessible. They worked together making and repairing umbrellas in a little shop adjacent to their house at 113 Meeting Street, on a busy thoroughfare in the heart of town. No matter what unkindness, hostility, or even danger lurked outside the sturdy brick walls of their home, once inside, the Barquets could lock the doors and enjoy their own haven in a heartless world.

By 1827, seven children filled the Barquets' two-story house with laughter and tears, fun and games, and the inevitable conflicts of family life. With a new addition born every two years, the little Barquets stood like stair steps. They bore the names of close friends and relatives, reflecting their diverse family tree: Margaret Campbell (1815), Mary Louisa (1817), Carolina Eudora (1819), Liston Warren (1821), Joseph Humphries (1823), Bissett (1825), and Edod or Edouard (1827).[13]

Since their 1814 marriage, Barbara and John Pierre Barquet had woven themselves into the small circle of mixed-race families sometimes referred to as the "colored elite" or even "aristocracy," an upper caste of mixed-blood men and women often with French, British, or Portuguese ancestry. These were relative terms only. "Petite bourgeois" perhaps better reflects their modest living circumstances and their aspirations for their children. The term used is not as important as the understanding that in their minds ethnicity, class, religion, or caste often trumped race in the formation of their identity.

At the time of Joseph's birth in 1823, the population of Charleston hovered around 25,000 residents, with whites making up close to 43 percent; slaves, 51 percent; and free blacks, 6 percent. The Barquets belonged in the upper quadrant of the literate and propertied free people of color. The majority of free blacks suffered from the multiplied effects of intense poverty and illiteracy as well as the lack of stable families, training or skills, and any contacts in the white world of authority and power. Many fell into bad habits of drinking, prostitution, and crime that eventually landed them in the workhouse and gave evidence to those slaveowners who complained that such people endangered the public safety and corrupted the morals of the enslaved.[14]

With women also having opportunities in the city for paid work, the two-parent household emerged as the free blacks' engine of economic advancement, with the family as their core social unit. Joseph would never in his adult life enjoy the same financial security that he did as a child. As the artisans and mechanics, seamstresses and caterers of the city, the most skilled enjoyed some comfort; a few reached affluence through thrift, skill, and prudent investments. Those who could afford to buy slaves to bolster their earnings did so. Some treated their slaves as family (which, indeed, sometimes they were), while others considered them as chattels to be sold or even mortgaged when need mandated. Throughout Barquet's childhood and youth, his mother owned as many as ten slaves whom she hired out in the city, receiving their wages in return.[15]

Joseph first tried to sort out his complex genealogy when he came of age and began to ask the question "Who am I?" His elder brother, Liston, described their father as "French, from Hayti" and their maternal grandmother, born enslaved, as "a negro," which was by the definition of the time a stateless person. By federal law, even American-born blacks were then legally classified as "persons of

African descent," a species of foreigner who, unlike freeborn white aliens, could never be naturalized into citizens.[16]

By embracing their French heritage, the Barquets could claim a national identity. Using the French language and forms of address as they did in their household gave the children cachet in their community. That their father belonged to the independent urban artisan class and did not use the common Gullah language—a sort of Esperanto of necessity forged among enslaved Africans from different regions—further distinguished them from the black majority in the city and created a massive gulf with those bondsmen laboring on the outlying plantations. As late as 1860 William Ellison, Stateburg gin owner and slave master as well as the Barquets' longtime family friend, still referred to Joseph's brother as "Monsieur Barquet."[17]

By presenting himself as French, Joseph Barquet could transcend, in his own mind at least, American racial particularism and adopt as his inheritance the Enlightenment traditions of France and the democratic impulses of the Haitian Revolution. Though barred from citizenship in the United States, Joseph considered himself a citizen of the "Atlantic World" and always took comfort in remembering that in Haiti, for all its multitude of troubles, he would be a member of the ruling race. In his later life he began to spell his name "Barquette" and often claimed the world's first black republic as his birthplace.

To his children, John Pierre's early life in Saint Domingue was swathed in mysterious romance. Born free during the 1780s, he hailed from the area around Môle Saint-Nicolas in the rather forbidding mountainous northwest coast. The town rests at the tip of a craggy limestone promontory known as Cap Saint-Nicolas, fifty miles across the water from Cuba. Dubbed the "Gibraltar of the Americas," the cape juts out into the Windward Passage, the surging highway of commerce that links the Atlantic to the Caribbean. The Môle's glory was a well-protected, nearly unassailable harbor ringed by a beautiful fine-sand beach that offered sailing ships shelter from blustery trade winds. Merchant vessels of all nations regularly stopped there for fresh water.[18]

According to family legend, John Pierre's family was involved in the shipping trade. Their surname, uncommon in Saint Domingue, may have its origins in the Haute-Normandie region of France, where the village of Barquet still exists. Le Havre, its nearest port, served as an important link in the West Indian trade. During the seventeenth century, the name "Du Barquet" or "Barquet" appeared occasionally among fleeing protestant Huguenots as well as among

Roman Catholics who settled in "Acadia," then a French colony in northeastern Canada. When the British drove the Acadians out of their territory in 1763, some of the most desperate settled around the Môle.[19]

Wherever their origins, John Pierre's French relatives intermingled with the local population and other Europeans in the little settlements hugging the narrow northern coastlines of the rugged peninsula, making their livings on the margins of Saint Domingue's booming sugar economy on small farms, as artisans, or from the sea. In 1769 an evocative advertisement for a Congo-born slave who ran away from Saint Louis du Nord described the man as wearing an iron collar around his neck stamped with "Barquet." In 1778—roughly around the time of John Pierre's birth—a young Acadian man reportedly died on a farm owned by a Mr. Barquet outside of Jean-Rabel, a town northeast of the Môle known for its active smuggling trade.[20]

So long the object of desire among France's enemies, Môle Saint-Nicolas became a very dangerous place during the French Revolutionary Wars. The British attacked in 1793 and with relative ease occupied the naval station there for almost five years as a base from which to launch their invasion of Saint Domingue. Competition by all combatants over this strategic port was fierce, and the Môle suffered as a cockpit of fighting during the Haitian Revolution. Fearing for their children's safety, at some point John Pierre's parents arranged passage for their four sons on four separate vessels bound for four different ports, or so the legend goes. Each reportedly had a placard secured by a string around his neck stating his name, destination, and probably a responsible person from the refugee diaspora to contact. The United States had remained neutral in theory during the European wars that roiled the Atlantic trade, but daring Charleston captains (many of whom were sympathetic to the British) were among those from other American ports who continued the profitable commerce with Saint Domingue, risking intervention by privateers, trading with whichever side was in power at the time.[21]

In Charleston John Pierre found an established community of French-speaking refugees seeking a place of safety from the excesses of both the French and Haitian Revolutions; a few had been victims of both conflicts. They gravitated to the narrow rooms and cheap rents on the fringes of one of the city's oldest neighborhoods, radiating outward from the French Huguenot Church at the corner of Queen and Church Streets. Huddled in cafés with cups of strong brew and delicate pastries, the dispossessed shared stories of their past lives and nourished themselves on memories of the worlds they had lost.[22]

Barquet first appeared in the public record in 1807, seemingly already well established. The city directory lists him with two addresses (41 Meeting Street and 39 Queen Street) and identifies him as an umbrella maker, a typical trade among French immigrants. On his lathe he also made walking sticks and fire bellows. Barquet may possibly have been part of the large contingent of refugees from Saint Domingue that went to New York, where he did his apprenticeship with the firm of Martinot and Roe. The company in 1807 opened a Charleston manufactory at 25 Queen Street, producing umbrellas and parasols for the wholesale and retail trade while also offering repairs in the "neatest manner."[23]

John Pierre's 1807 induction, along with William Pinceel and Joseph Humphries, into the Brown Fellowship Society, a mutual benefit and burial society founded in 1790, suggests that he was well known by then, for membership was a rite of passage for future leaders among Charleston's free people of color. Candidates for this organization, which also encouraged "public spiritedness" among the "free brown" community, were screened according to the content of their character as well as the (light) color of their skin. The society enjoyed the imprimatur of the white elite and had a historic link to St. Philip's Episcopal Church.[24]

The ability to pay hefty initiation fees and regular dues to maintain the work of the society limited the number of eligible candidates as did the requirements of European ancestry and being free. Having been a slave or being married to a former slave did not disqualify, nor did being a slaveowner. "Decent, peaceable and orderly" behavior was expected both inside and outside their meetings. Only children who were "heirs in law," legitimate offspring of married members, would be eligible for orphans' benefits or for apprenticeships.[25]

Criticized, then and now, for not being more inclusive, the organizers developed a rationale for admitting only mixed-race free men. Banning whites as well as blacks, a descendant of one founder recalled, closed both the "front door" and the "back door" of the society, thus creating an environment of "social equality among ourselves . . . each contributing a like proportion to the compact." Sharing the same values and status in life, the men found a congenial place of safety in one another's company—discussions of religion or politics were banned—with "just enough friction to keep things lively."[26] Within the society, Barquet and Pinceel would enjoy the status of "military men," both having served as buglers with Captain Richard Howard's detachment of the South Carolina militia when British warships threatened Charleston during the War of 1812.[27]

The craftsmen and mechanics of the Brown Fellowship Society dared to hope in the early days of the Republic that by *acting* like good citizens they might one day actually have the opportunity to *be* good citizens. In pursuit of their goals of economic advancement and rigorous civic engagement, black property owners leaned against racial barriers, pricked at the logical inconsistencies of their status, and fully exercised their limited legal rights.

Although the optimistic members of the Brown Fellowship Society in retrospect seem like dancers on the deck of the Titanic, those who lived through the changes of the eighteenth-century revolutions understood that "race has a history" (to use John G. Garrigus's apt phrase) and that identities and attitudes could change. After the overthrow of the *ancien régime* in France, the world seemed highly malleable to man's best desires, even perfectible. Anyone, it seemed at the dawn of the American republic, could dream the revolutionaries' dream that society was no longer divinely ordained, with every person born into a fixed station for life. During those first heady decades, the definition of "an American" persisted as a topic of passionate debate. Some among Charleston's "colored elite" even speculated that eventually their lighter-skinned descendants would evolve into a new American people who would be "like Jews among the Gentiles" or a *tertium quid,* a distinct middle estate.[28]

In contrast to so many southern-born blacks such as Frederick Douglass, who grew up enslaved and never in his youth knew a man of color who was not a slave, John Pierre's friends provided young Joseph with models of aspiration and achievement, even in the face of the stiff headwinds to their success. Joseph had contact with the older generation, who retained cosmopolitan worldviews, were actors in their own lives, headed their own families, and owned their own time, their own businesses, their own homes, and in numerous cases, their own slaves. A son of hotelier Jehu Jones, he knew, in 1826 had even become the first black student to attend Amherst College. Belief in the possibility that the world could be changed—even in the face of so much evidence to the contrary—was a critical aspect of Joseph Barquet's intellectual heritage from his early years in Charleston. Indeed, the formal toasts at the society's anniversary dinners in his father's day always looked to the future: "May the members of the Brown Fellowship grow in greatness as we grow in age. . . . May the members be illuminated with wisdom as the stars illume the firmament. . . . May the rising generation be blessed through this institution."[29]

In 1808 John Pierre set out on his own future as a married man and as a father to a rising generation. In a ceremony held in St. Philip's Church, he took as his wife a young woman of French extraction named Mary. In 1809 they returned there for the christening of their first son, John Pinceel Barquet. William

Pinceel served as godfather; a young family friend, seventeen-year-old Barbary Tunno, as godmother. Six months after Mary's death in childbirth in March 1814, John Pierre married Barbary, who brought to their union a dowry, slaves, and a home on Archdale Street.[30]

THE JOURNEY THAT Barbary Barquet took to her wedding day could scarcely have been more different from that traveled by her new husband. Unlike John Pierre, who was born free, escaped the turmoil of the Haitian Revolution, and became an independent craftsman, Barbary was born enslaved in 1792. Her mother, a plantation-born slave, had been swept up in the vortex of violence between the Tories and the Whigs in the Carolina lowcountry during the American Revolution. In the war's bitter aftermath, the fates of both women hung in the balance of a business negotiation between two rival Scots.

Much that is written about the lives of slaves in eighteenth-century America involves speculation, and piecing together the narrative of Barbary Tunno's life is no exception. Peggy, her mother, was likely born about 1768 in Saint Bartholomew's Parish south of Charleston and grew up on a 600-acre rice plantation on an area of high ground locally referred to as The Horseshoe near Jacksonborough. Peggy's mother would have been among the twelve house servants brought by the wealthy widow, Elizabeth Nash Eberson, to her 1767 marriage to Scotsman Robert Ballingall. With no resources except his training as a plasterer, seventeen-year-old Ballingall had fled the poverty of his Aberdeen home in 1754 for Charleston, a town where numerous Scots had prospered. With hard work and assiduous application to business, he clawed his way up in the fluid society of colonial South Carolina to find moderate success as a factor and small-scale planter. His alliance with Elizabeth, though, elevated him into the more rarified world of the Carolina-born gentry.[31]

Married just at the time when the higher taxes of the Townshend Acts inflamed the Carolina colonists, the politics of empire began to intrude upon the Ballingalls' happiness almost immediately. The household slaves observed the changing dynamics and the crosscurrents of political discord eddying through the home with growing interest. Coming in and out of the dining room, passing around venison roasts and sweet potatoes, they caught snatches of heated conversations punctuated with unfamiliar words such as "nonimportation," "associations," "loyalty oaths," and "confiscation." One word the eavesdroppers focused on was "liberty." What they did not comprehend was liberty for whom.

Back in their quarters, though, they generated their own freedom narrative. Black evangelists, secretly trained in the nearby dark cypress swamps by unorthodox Scottish minister William Burnet, had surreptitiously spread the word among local slaves that God would deliver from bondage all who truly believed in him. Combining this message with the snippets of news picked up in the plantation house, the story evolved through many retellings that it was King George III who was sending his Moses to free them.[32]

In 1776 "war" echoed throughout the Ballingall household and in homes throughout the parish, and the names of remote places such as Lexington and Concord entered the slaves' expanding vocabulary. Actual battle between the organized military forces of the Americans and British, though, was slow in coming to the southern-most colonies. Members of Elizabeth's family professing their solid and fervent support for the cause of American freedom included her sister, Mary Nash Ford, and her husband, Tobias, of neighboring Woodford Plantation as well as their cousin Isaac Hayne, a leader among the wealthy planters.[33]

For domestic harmony and his own protection, Ballingall remained silent about his loyalty to the king until January 1779, when the British occupied Savannah and rumors began flittering along the plantation grapevine that the redcoats had crossed into the province and were headed their way. For their part, many servants thought the prophesized time of liberation might be close at hand. The first of the lowcountry's 3,000 wartime runaways began silently moving through the swamps on moonless nights and appearing like apparitions at British camps. But Brigadier General Augustine Prévost, leader of the British foraging "expedition" from Georgia, was no Moses. Although some generals, such as Lord Dunmore (the last royal governor of Virginia), had seen the strategic value in liberating slaves, emancipation was never a war aim of either the British or the Americans. Prévost's was not the messianic army of the Lord, but one of plunder and destruction. The soldiers under his command brazenly seized black runaways to sell in Georgia or, worse, to ship off to traders in the West Indies, where their lives would be brutishly short.[34]

In May Ballingall volunteered to ride with Prévost and direct the British troops to the plantations of leading revolutionaries of the parish, including that of young Major Thomas Pinckney on the Ashepoo River, so they might ransack and burn them. For these sins, he was captured and jailed by the Americans. With the successful British siege and occupation of Charleston in 1780, he was released from prison. Recognizing Ballingall as a man of integrity with a good military mind rare among the colonials, British general Lord Cornwallis granted him a commission as colonel of the Colleton County Loyalist Militia and an appointment as magistrate and justice of the peace over a large, lawless territory. Assigned to a panel charged with sorting out the conundrum of how to best deal with runaways, he endorsed the idea of keeping the slaves of the rebels and promising that if they contributed to the king's cause, they would be freed at the end of the war. The Loyalists' slaves should be returned to their owners if they promised not to punish them. When Thomas, one of the runaways from Ballingall's own plantation, was brought back by the soldiers, the freedom hopes of his other servants dimmed.[35]

Over time the revolution in South Carolina degraded into a civil war between local partisans of each side. Months after Cornwallis's formal surrender at Yorktown on October 19, 1781, the sheer momentum of the violence kept the war going throughout the next spring. Lowcountry slaves inevitably became part of the spoils lusted after by Tory and Whig alike. In May 1782 Ballingall disbanded his Colleton militia and spurred his horse for the only remaining place of safety—the walled city of Charleston—riding for his life. His dust probably had not yet settled upon the road when his neighbors fell upon his house and plantation buildings, looting and pilfering with abandon and carrying away his slaves across their saddles. Those servants and his other property, however, now belonged to the province of South Carolina.[36]

In January 1782 the South Carolina assembly, confident that victory was within their grasp, had met in exile in Jacksonborough to map out the last stages of the war. Judged among the worst offenders against the colonial cause, Colonel Ballingall was listed among the "public enemies" to be banished forever and their property confiscated.[37]

Although Ballingall protested that when his wife died in 1780 she left all her slaves and other property to their five-year-old daughter, Eliza Mary, and his was only a life interest, auditors refused to differentiate. His heart hardened at the news that everything of material value in his life—his new home, his books, his plantation, his church pews, his investments, his slaves, his wife's entire estate—would go to the highest bidder. The action left father and child destitute.[38]

Only for reasons untold and yet unknown, Ballingall contrived to hold back one young house servant from the auction block "on the pretense of having sold her." Presumably this was the teenaged Peggy, whose mother and other family members would have been swept away from her in the sales. No evidence suggests that he favored her because she was his daughter; throughout her life Peggy was generally described as "black." Had he wanted to spare her the fate of an unprotected girl sold to the highest bidder, Ballingall, as one of the three "commissioners of claims" sorting out the various applications from slaves professing to have aided the king's cause, simply might have added her name to the list of the 1,500 granted freedom and transportation away from South Carolina. He could have written a certificate for her as he did in 1782 for Phillis Thomas, "a free Black Woman," giving his permission "to go from hence to the island of Jamaica or elsewhere at her own option." Peggy too might have been among those freed blacks clutching their belongings and joyously scampering aboard British ships for a new life of freedom in Nova Scotia or some other British possession. Perhaps Ballingall may have not felt at liberty to give away his daughter's only remaining asset, but the enterprising Scotsman probably had another plan in play in Peggy.[39]

Most plausibly, young Peggy had been the caregiver of his motherless child, and Ballingall wanted her to remain as a familiar presence when he left for Scotland. Rather than make Eliza Mary share his "poverty and distress" in Scotland, he placed her in a Charleston boarding school, where a child having a slave in attendance was a common practice; her mother's relatives living in the city could also watch out for her. Ballingall left his daughter in 1784, not knowing how he could possibly pay her £50 annual school fees. When he arrived in London, the few guineas that jingled in his pocket would not even pay his passage back home.[40]

Years later an embittered Ballingall brooded in the austere, windswept landscape of Drumgley, just north of Dundee. Playing over and over in his mind were the series of tragedies and, to his thinking, injustices, that had brought his three-decade sojourn in South Carolina to such an ignoble end. In his late forties he had had to start over, trying to secure credit and scratch out a living as a merchant in Scotland's grim economy. About 1790 he received an unexpected communication from Charleston. Breaking its seal must have been like opening a Pandora's box of painful memories.[41]

The letter was about Peggy. Charleston merchant Adam Tunno wanted to buy her and the two little children she now had. The elder was about three years old, with the traditional slave name of Hagar. The younger, a mixed-race boy, bore the Scottish name Owen—Tunno's son, Ballingall surely guessed. This was a familiar story with Scots far from home, he knew.[42]

During the British occupation of Charleston from 1780 to 1782, Ballingall had gotten to know Tunno and his brother John, natives of Dunse and raised in Kelso, County Fife. John's former business partner, Robert McKenzie, was then serving under Ballingall as a lieutenant colonel of the Colleton County loyal militia. Shocked by the American victory, John and McKenzie had gotten caught in the same snare of confiscation and banishment as Ballingall. Adam, though, having quickly grasped the better part of valor and loyalty, had skillfully tacked his way through the changing fortunes of the Revolution, shifting his allegiances as adeptly as he trimmed the sails of his trading vessels to catch the prevailing winds and slipped out of British-occupied Charleston just in time to avoid capture by their vindictive foes in 1782.

Ballingall was still in the city when Tunno returned some time the following year. Anti-British passions had already started to cool, and Tunno was forgiven his past treasons because he possessed what few in this city of rebels could obtain: letters of credit in London as well as links to the slave trade, which had reopened after the war. He also brought back his brother's ledgers to track down those rebels who owed him money and took over his business interests. After applying for American citizenship, he was ready to begin the next chapter of his life in the world's newest republic.[43]

Desperate like so many others facing banishment before their affairs could be settled, Ballingall might well have turned to Tunno, who acted as an agent for other Loyalists returning to Great Britain, to be Peggy's informal guardian in his absence. It is quite possible that it was through Tunno or his lawyer, Samuel Prioleau, that Ballingall executed his subterfuge to save Peggy from the auction block. Some years before, Ballingall had assisted Prioleau in perpetrating a legal ruse that allowed an enslaved woman named Jane to purchase her own freedom. When Eliza Mary rejoined her father in Scotland about 1789, Peggy could have stayed among the numerous slaves that Tunno and another brother, William, owned.[44]

Ballingall knew that the Tunnos lived as young lords in the wide-open seafaring city that was Charleston after the war. Both traveled a great deal to the West Indies and East Florida, buying and selling slaves and pursing their various mercantile interests. Ballingall possibly just shrugged at Adam Tunno's involvement with Peggy, or he may have been incensed at a violation of trust or the crossing of lines of respectability so important to the Scots. In any case, he likely seized the opportunity to extract some benefit from Tunno's desire to free his son from slavery. Before their trans-Atlantic transaction was resolved and recorded, Peggy gave birth to Tunno's daughter, Barbary, in 1792, necessitating another round of negotiations that were—no doubt after spirited haggling—settled only in 1800. Finally in 1795, Ballingall agreed to a purchase price of £180 sterling for Peggy and her older children, accepting in 1800 £217.10 in an agreement that did not mention Barbary by name but simply granted Tunno ownership of any future children Peggy or Hagar may have. Owen died young, probably before 1803, when Tunno filed an official declaration that Barbary was a free person of color and that he was her legal guardian. No record exists proving he legally emancipated Peggy or Hagar, but they both came to be considered free.[45]

By the time of Barbary's birth, Adam Tunno was well on his way to becoming one of the wealthiest men in war-ravaged Charleston. The resumption of South Carolina's slave trade in 1783 fueled his first fortune. He was among the outsiders with cash, credit, and good connections who reaped the benefits of the local planters' long-repressed demand for slaves to expand their profitable rice operations after the war. Around 1786, he formed a partnership with James Cox with diverse interests, with a specialty in fine Madeira wine from the West Indies. After the Revolution, Tunno scavenged the cash-starved lowcountry, buying confiscated Tory properties at bargain prices, brokering the sales of confiscated slaves, and opening a store selling long-coveted, once-embargoed British goods on credit. Within a decade he joined those Scots dominating the credit system of South Carolina, as planters found finance an increasingly distasteful undertaking. In a testament to his power, music-loving members of the pro-British Federalist Party, including Thomas and Charles Cotesworth Pinckney, made an exception to their exclusion of men in trade and invited Tunno to join the St. Cecilia Society. Of course, he owned their meeting rooms.[46]

In 1787 Tunno purchased a three-and-a-half-story Georgian house located at what is now 89 East Bay Street on Charleston's "Rainbow Row," fronting the harbor. At the time, this was a busy commercial district, populated by prosperous Scottish merchants.[47] Following their common practice (and one that the planting classes denounced as déclassé), Tunno based his enterprise in his home. He maintained an office and counting house on the first floor and probably entertained with his famous wine parties on the second floor. He had a special stone-lined cellar built to store his treasure trove of old brandies, rare Madeira, Canary Island "sacks" or sherries, and French Burgundies. Always close at hand for customers and friends were good supplies of "social wine" and porter.[48]

Tunno's property ran westward for the depth of the long city block to Bedons Alley (a narrow lane of mixed repute) and was a confusion of buildings, storehouses, a slave yard, and quarters that in 1800 accommodated at least twenty-five servants. Either Peggy was not free, or she did not live on the premises, for no census from 1800 to 1830 reports any free people of color living there. Peggy may have lived in a nearby location, perhaps the brick house owned by Tunno abutting his property that came to be known as 2 Bedons Alley, later transferred to her. This might be where she resided with her children. Perhaps she acted as Tunno's housekeeper, for she does not seem to have pursued a trade or craft.[49]

Precisely how Peggy and her children fit into the geography of the worldly Tunno's affections is as much a puzzle as how they fit into the geography of his establishment. No conclusive evidence exists, however, to impose a scene of Victorian domesticity upon their relationship as has been suggested, or to project that they were either actually married—interracial marriage was legal in South Carolina until 1865—or that Tunno considered Peggy his de-facto wife.[50]

What may be said about Tunno's relationship to Peggy and Barbary is that he performed what he understood as his duty toward them in accordance with long-established norms of the Scottish diaspora and kept them in the upper range of comfort enjoyed by the free people of Charleston. For those Scots forced by circumstances to migrate over the globe, clan and reputation remained the cornerstones of all business and personal relationships. Success continued to depend on access to their intricate global networks of shared information, credit, markets, and goods well into the next century. Tunno's leading purveyor of fine sherry, for example, was particularly concerned about the character of merchants selling its products. Charleston's large number of mixed-race families named Deas, Purvis, Inglis, McKinlay, and Humphries were established mostly in the more fluid pre-Revolutionary era.[51]

The experience of Tunno's two younger brothers illustrates the range of tolerance. Thomas Tunno had three daughters with two different black mistresses—one free, one enslaved—while on family business in Saint Augustine. Before returning to Charleston to marry a wealthy young woman whose father did business with his brothers, Thomas emancipated his enslaved children (although never acknowledging them) and provided some future security for his daughters and their mothers. William Tunno, in contrast, crossed the line. While living in Charleston, he left his well-born wife (with strong Scottish connections) and three children to run off with a mulatto woman with whom he had a daughter. In a demonstration of full-blown Caledonian wrath, his five surviving brothers on both sides of the Atlantic pronounced William "dead" and vowed never to speak his name again or acknowledge that he or his children had ever lived. The various Tunno children in England were told nothing of any of their American cousins, white or black.[52] After William died in 1824, having never recovered financially from the schism with his brothers, Adam Tunno could not deny the obligation of blood and provided for his brother's daughter, Cornelia, in much the same way as he did his own child, Barbary.[53]

In 1806, during a stagnant time in the Carolina trade, Tunno purchased two pieces of Charleston property and arranged with his lawyers to have "Peggy Bellingall" (in freedom she had taken a variant of her former master's surname) listed as the nominal owner of record; she signed with her mark. Tunno paid $1,500 in "Spanish milled dollars" for a large parcel, 50 feet by 120 feet, on the southwest corner of Archdale and West Streets. Once part of the bucolic old Mazyck lands outside the city wall, by 1806 the institutional life of Charleston had expanded to the area, with three churches on Archdale and on nearby Magazine Street the city jail and the workhouse. Wedged in the remaining lots were corner stores, many run by Germans, and narrow wooden houses inhabited by free blacks and slaves. Tunno also paid £230 sterling to Joseph Morton, a slaveowning drayman, for a second property a few blocks away on Pitt Street, between Montague and Wentworth Streets, not far from the burial ground of the Brown Fellowship Society.[54]

Over the years, Tunno would use trusts to transfer bank stocks, slaves, and other real property to Barbary and to Peggy, often listing his lawyers as principles in these transactions. Peggy shared her portion with her other daughter, Hagar Bellingall Cole, as well as Hagar's array of children and grandchildren. Sometime later, in acknowledgment of her evolving status as a property owner, matriarch of a sprawling family, and woman of standing in the free community, Peggy adopted the name Margaret Bellingall.[55]

Barbary, now going by Barbara, and John Pierre's first two children—Margaret Campbell and Mary Louisa—were born when the couple lived in a house on the Archdale Street property. In 1818, when Barbara was expecting her third child, Adam Tunno began looking for another home for the growing family. He submitted the high bid on 113 Meeting Street and placed it in trust for Barbara and her children (specifically excluding John Pierre from an interest).[56]

As the children came of school age, they attended the Colored Children's School on Beaufain Street, founded by Thomas Siah Bonneau, who believed that education was the frontline in the "war against the deadly enemy of the Rational Being, Ignorance." In 1830 Bonneau also started a small library on the premise that in the battle to liberate minds, books had more potency than bullets. He and his wife, Jennet, a former slave, became close friends of the Barquets and the couples acted as godparents to one another's children. Upon Bonneau's death in 1831, his protégé, Daniel Alexander Payne, took over his classes and then opened his own academy on Anson Street, an easy walk from the Barquets' home.[57]

Slight, bespectacled, and scholarly, Payne gained the reputation as the most dangerous man in town, replacing the treacherous Denmark Vesey in the imaginations of Charleston city officials, who now saw the great threat to their dominance as the black population tapping into the tree of knowledge. Despite a century of legal prohibitions, even slaves managed to acquire sufficient skills to clerk in stores and perform other "work not to their station." Enamored in his youth with the liberating violence of the Haitian Revolution, Payne had once wished to be a soldier, slaying the enemies of that black republic, but his study of history convinced him of the impotence of brute force to effect real change. In a soft voice he almost whispered his subversive rhetoric drawn from the Bible, the Declaration of Independence, and the Constitution of the United States. The only difference, he repeatedly told his rapt students, between a master and a slave is "superior knowledge." His favorite text, *The Columbian Orator*, was a classic anthology of great works proclaiming human freedom that was widely used by early nineteenth-century teachers dedicated to forging an American identity and educating the citizenry.[58]

Payne's passion for learning worked like a flint to ignite wonder in young minds. He taught smatterings of literature and grammar, mathematics, geography, botany, and biology, depending on what books he was given or was able to find. To keep those sparks aglow, he also encouraged his students to dream and locate themselves in the rolling stream of time. Of Scottish descent himself, Payne loved romantic tales of heroic deeds from all cultures and convinced his students that they too were the heirs of great civilizations. Joseph's time with Payne deeply affected the young man. When grown and longing to change the world, Barquet rejected the temptation to be a saboteur carrying a torch in the night. Raised regarding William Pinceel as the "Paul Revere" of Charleston, he never lost his admiration for his boyhood idols, Crispus Attucks and sailmaker James Forten, patriots of the American Revolution, and Haitian general Toussaint-Louverture, who urged his followers to think in terms of nationalism rather than racialism.[59] These were all men who did not take vengeance into their own hands but sought legitimate means to right historic wrongs.

In 1834, when Joseph Barquet was twelve years old, South Carolina passed a law banning the teaching of black children, free or slave, by any teachers, white or black. "Heart-broken" at what this law meant for him and for his "defenseless race," Payne closed his school in May and departed for Philadelphia, determined to enter the ministry. As soon as he left, the city's concern about black education receded, and most teachers and students carried on, although discreetly.[60]

NOT LONG AFTER PAYNE LEFT for Philadelphia in 1835, John Pierre died. Barbara then undertook the task of helping her children find their life's work. Later, she did not hesitate to advise them about selecting their life partners as well. Until her death in February 1846, she remained very much the family matriarch, for she controlled the family finances. Even as adults, her children still resided chockablock under her roof at 113 Meeting Street.

The five Barquet children who married while still in Charleston chose appropriate spouses from among the prominent and propertied families associated with the Brown Fellowship Society, as had long been the plan. The dense interweaving of the black elite was scarcely less complex or strategic than that of the white aristocracy. Two of the Barquet daughters trained as dressmakers and married the sons of well-known Charleston tailors of Scottish ancestry. Margaret became the wife of Joseph Penceel Humphries, son of John Pierre's great friend. In 1842 Mary Louisa married Archibald McKinlay, who had a successful Coming Street shop with his brothers, George and William, also wise real-estate investors. Carolina married a very light-skinned coppersmith, John Francis Plumeau, whose father of the same name was likely a white émigré from Saint Domingue. Barbara helped them buy a house on Charleston Neck.

First, Liston, then Edod, undertook apprenticeships as tailors under John Lee and worked in the shop connected to his Mansion House hotel (once Jehu Jones's well-known establishment), which Lee ran with his wife, Eliza Seymour Lee, one of the city's leading cooks. In 1844 Liston married the Lee's eldest daughter, Abigail, who joined him on Meeting Street. Some years later Edod married their youngest, Sarah Ann. Bissett too opted for the relatively genteel life of a tailor.[61]

Joseph took another path and learned the brick mason's craft. He probably lacked the temperament to be a successful tailor, for practitioners of that trade needed not only the deftness to sew a fine seam but also the knack of working in intimate relationship with white patrons, always smiling, always admiring, and always trying to cover their client's flaws to make their outward appearance match their inner self-conception. Although dirty and often backbreaking work, brick masonry was an ancient art once dominated by the free blacks in Charleston, that linked Joseph to the more independent world of nineteenth-century urban artisans in which his father and William Pinceel once dwelled.

And like these two friends, Barquet was a musician. He belonged to a band that accompanied the governor on his annual review of militia formations around the state to play rousing patriotic tunes.[62] While other members may have nodded off under the hot sun during long-winded stem-winders, Barquet clearly paid attention and was mesmerized by the spectacle that translated the abstract ideals of liberty he had learned from *The Columbian Orator* into concrete messages at the hustings. As a result, he received a first-class education in the power of words and how to use rhetoric and bombast to move an audience.

At these events during the early 1840s, the young man also gained valuable insights into the mind of the southern leadership, noting the fervency with which South Carolina's politicians argued that the Republic was a compact of states and worked to convince their audiences that white liberty depended upon black slavery. He no doubt heard a great deal about the contributions of the first families of the state—the Pinckneys, the Rutledges, the Middletons, and the Heywards—who were also among the founding families of the nation. In Barquet's mind the Constitution evolved as the sacred vessel of American rights. He identified politics—the sport that rivaled horseracing as a favorite among white Carolinians—as the path to greater freedom and adopted citizenship as his life's goal, boldly beginning to imagine that he too was included among "We the People." Rather than being forever the victim of politics, perpetually excluded from the civil decisions that affected his life, Barquet determined to master them.

The political rhetoric reached fever pitch in May 1846, when President James K. Polk declared war against Mexico for its resistance to the precipitous American annexation of the Republic of Texas the year before. Although a strong Unionist who could see that the addition of new territory would exacerbate the growing national tensions over slavery, popular governor David Johnson heeded the president's request for troops from each state.

When the governor asked, Barquet answered. Apparently caught up in the excitement and pageantry surrounding the recruitment of South Carolina's Palmetto Regiment, he saw an opportunity to join in a great communal adventure as one of nearly a thousand citizen-soldiers of the state. With his mother gone, Barquet had no compelling reason to stay in Charleston, where the economy stagnated and the oppression of free blacks intensified with new laws mandating that all blacks would be considered slaves unless they could prove otherwise. Whites were fleeing westward to states such as Alabama and Mississippi, even Texas. Family friends from the Brown Fellowship Society were joining the northward exodus to cities such as Philadelphia and New York, even Canada. He knew, though, from reports that the absence of slavery in the North did not translate into the absence of racism.[63]

Barquet craved acknowledgment of his manhood and believed that only by participating in war and its public commitment to the nation might he prove himself equal to the nineteenth-century masculine ideal. Volunteering with others to fight the nation's common enemy in a distant land was an adventure that appealed to the twenty-three-year-old, even if, as a black man, he would be carrying a bugle—or "French horn," as it was sometimes called—rather than a musket. At least he would not be among the numerous black servants following their masters.[64]

Colonel Pierce M. Butler, an avid nullifier when he served as governor a decade earlier, stepped forward to head the regiment. Another notable Carolinian, Captain Francis Sumter, led Barquet's Company A. Although the ten companies were headed by men with patrician names, many of the Carolina chivalry lost enthusiasm for the fight against Mexico as the time to leave for the front approached. A diverse lot ended up filling the ranks, with 10 percent of the soldiers from other states as well as nearly fifty immigrants—Irish, Germans, and even a Swede. Economic need pressed some men to enlist.[65]

The presentation of the regimental flag in December 1846 was a grand event staged in front of city hall, only blocks from Barquet's Meeting Street home. Within days, Joseph Barquet had squeezed onto one of the troop trains clattering westward. A possible intimation of what throwing in his lot with the leaders of the state establishment meant to his family may be glimpsed in an account of a dream that his brother Liston related in his journal many years later: "I left the place of rest a little before seven. . . . After dreaming about Keep Cool. Thought I saw him play the French horn, and as he was along with the Secession Boys, I bade him the last goodbye."[66]

2

THOMAS'S STORY
In the Shadow of Greatness

THOMAS PINCKNEY WAS BORN sickly and frail on August 13, 1828, during a summer of intense Charleston heat and in a year of almost unprecedented gloom. The political climate, roiled by growing sectional antagonism, sizzled as well. Dengue fever poisoned the peninsula's humid air. The population declined as greater opportunity beckoned in the western states. Charleston's once-brilliant star was clearly in retrograde. Melancholy filled the urban villa of C. Cotesworth Pinckney, scion of one of the early republic's most influential families.[1] Although Pinckney and his wife, Caroline Elliott, were both heirs to old lowcountry rice and cotton fortunes, they feared that the decline of the aristocratic old city heralded their own. Indeed, as one contemporary observer noted, "the old Stock," descendants of the notable colonial families, had nearly died out and only survived here and there "like roses in the wilderness—marking 'where a garden had been.'"[2]

The early history of Charleston had been, like that of the Venetian republic during the days of the patrician Grimanis, a history of families. The Pinckneys and their large interrelated network of kin—the Rutledges, the Middletons, the Manigaults, the Barnwells, the Izards, and the Elliotts—had risen in three generations to dominate the society, culture, and politics of their own "city-state." Harmony reigned as all agreed that Charleston existed to serve the planters' interests; commerce and finance must always be the handmaidens of agriculture. In 1828 Charleston intellectual Hugh S. Legaré suggested that the decayed eighteenth-century Venice might offer a lesson for the once flourishing nineteenth-century Charleston. Indeed, according to one historian, Napoleon conquered the Venetian republic in 1796 because its enervated leaders "knew the current of history had started to flow against them" yet lacked the will to resist.[3]

C. Cotesworth Pinckney belonged to that conservative generation hounded by time's "ever-rolling stream."[4] With every peal of St. Michael's church bells, with every turn of the calendar's page, and with every phase of the moon, the

Pinckneys, still rooted in many ways in the political culture of the eighteenth century, sensed disturbing changes in the Republic. Uncontrollable events twisted the landscape of their lives like a kaleidoscope, leaving them as disoriented as the randomly arranged bits of colored glass. They were planters in an age of capital, aristocrats in an age of democracy, individualists in an age of standardization, and slaveholders in an age of expanding liberty—truly strangers in the transformed land of their fathers.

Young Thomas was born as his revered namesake lay dying. Nothing brought home the sense that Charleston was at the end of an era so much as the passing of Major General Thomas Pinckney in November 1828. Dying after a long illness at age seventy-eight, the general was a scholar, warrior, agriculturalist, congressman, governor, member of the Society of the Cincinnati, chair of the state convention that ratified the Constitution, diplomat, and the last of the nation's Founding Fathers from South Carolina.[5]

Charleston prepared a state funeral in Pinckney's honor. The first such solemn event had marked the death of President George Washington; the most recent, three years earlier, the passing of his gifted older brother, General Charles Cotesworth Pinckney, a signer of the Constitution. The two statesmen had been born in the lowcountry, but their parents, Chief Justice Charles Pinckney and agriculturalist Eliza Lucas Pinckney, had dreams for their future on a larger stage and provided them with the same rigorous education that future British prime ministers received, beginning at Westminster School, then Oxford University, followed by legal studies at the Middle Temple, and finally military training at Caen. Born as children of the Enlightenment, the young men embraced republican ideology and, upon their return to South Carolina, took up arms in the cause of colonial self-rule and distinguished themselves during the Revolution. After the war, they moved in the powerful Federalist Party circles that orbited closest to Washington. Many thought Thomas would inherit "the president's chair" after Washington's second term, but John Adams of Massachusetts edged him out. Charles Cotesworth later made two unsuccessful bids for that high office.[6]

General Pinckney's passing in 1828, then, should have bathed Charlestonians in nationalist sentiment, but the long vigil at his bedside had seemed more like a wake for the old agrarian republic, their first love. Pinckney symbolized a glorious past when Charleston enjoyed the reputation as a cradle of liberty rather than as a Gibraltar of slavery; when South Carolina's Revolutionary heroes—Thomas Sumter and William Moultrie—were the nation's heroes, and its statesmen—

Henry Laurens and John Rutledge—its founders. Something stirred in Charlestonians' hearts when they wreathed the city in black crepe and watched the solemn cortege with a riderless horse pass during the general's funeral and burial at St. Phillip's Episcopal Church, as if some precious connection had been lost, never to return.

The birth of young Thomas as the general lay dying, however, presented a hopeful symmetry that encouraged his family to believe that somehow through this child (should he survive), their clan and the city of Charleston might return to the old greatness, even glory. Had a hooded soothsayer been summoned to the cradle of this infant prince of the city (as in fairy tales of old), he would have reeled back in horror at the unbelievable, unfathomable images of the future conjured before him: of a Charleston crowd wildly cheering as the 1788 ordinance of constitutional union was repealed unanimously by the Ordinance of Secession in 1860; of Tom, a tall soldier in gray, raising one of his grandfather's swords against the flag of the American republic; of Tom near death in a prison pen in Charleston Harbor; of Tom disinherited by the solemn force of history. In the backdrop of this vision would have been Charleston itself, blockaded, bombed, burned, and abandoned as the Four Horsemen of the Apocalypse raced away in glee.

Along the path to this fate, personal choices or historical contingencies might have deflected Thomas Pinckney and South Carolina from the road to rebellion, but had the seer been asked when the child's life course would be set, he might have pointed to the scene of a disappointed four-year-old boy in 1832, the year his family did not celebrate Christmas. That would also be the year the Union was almost lost, the Pinckneys were saved, two second sons became unexpected heirs, and the Santee River flowed into the narrative of Tom Pinckney's life.

THOMAS PINCKNEY'S FIRST YEARS were like those of an only child. His sisters—Caroline born in 1816 and Maria in 1821—coddled the delicate boy and were more like little mothers than playmates. The Pinckneys' earnest first-born, Charles Cotesworth Jr., upon whom so many hopes were already bestowed, was then a serious seventeen-year-old occupied with choosing a college and paid scant attention to his little brother's arrival. Their father's alma mater, Harvard, was out of the question since the cult of abolitionism was thought to have seeped into every textbook, every classroom, and every lecture hall of the Massachusetts school by 1828. Even South Carolina College in Columbia presented dangers to the youthful mind because its northern-born president, Thomas Cooper, had publicly questioned the historical truth of the Bible. The family agreed on the College of Charleston, an institution that had strong Pinckney connections and where Cotesworth Jr. would encounter no challenges to received wisdom. When he graduated as class valedictorian in 1832, he decided to follow in his father's footsteps and read law. But by then his father was about to take a sharp turn in a direction that would have profound consequences for the entire family.[7]

At the time of Tom's birth, Cotesworth Pinckney suffered from both a bleakness in his soul and a deep depression about the future of the South. During 1832, however, he underwent a remarkable transformation from despairing agnostic to professed Christian aflame with faith. He had, in fact, found not one, but two saviors: Jesus Christ and John C. Calhoun. Pinckney, who had lost his mother at age five, became warmly attached to his loving mother-in-law, Phoebe Waight Elliott, and enjoyed his long visits in her Beaufort home. As a pillar of St. Helena's Episcopal Church, her relentless importuning of family members to join her in its pews were rewarded when a popular revivalist, the Reverend Daniel Baker, arrived in town with his electrifying message of love and trust, forgiveness and salvation. Beaufort emerged as the epicenter of a religious awakening that swept not only South Carolina but also the whole nation. Amid this "holy atmosphere," where once-cynical sinners crowded to hear the word of their redemption—drinkers tossed away their bottles and gamblers their cards— Cotesworth Pinckney felt the "consciousness of eternity" settle upon him. He came to the firm conviction that religion was the solution to all problems.[8]

Having found his personal savior, Pinckney began his search for a savior for the South and became an acolyte of John C. Calhoun, then vice president under Andrew Jackson. Pinckney had long ties with the straight-laced Presbyterian, who possessed perhaps the most brilliant and original political mind of his generation. In response to the firestorm of southern anger caused by the "abominable" 1828 congressional protective tariff that bolstered northern manufacturing at the expense of southern agriculturalists—and also had implications for the future of slavery—Calhoun developed his theory of nullification. Arguing that imbedded in the Constitution was a remedy that allowed minority interests protection against the tyranny of the majority, he postulated that whenever Congress passed a law that an individual state deemed unconstitutional—the tariff of 1828, for example—that state had the right to hold a convention of democratically elected delegates who may vote to veto or nullify the offending act.

With the zealotry of the new convert, Cotesworth Pinckney embraced nullification as holy writ. Moving from a national perspective on politics shared with his father to a sectional one after the general's death, he joined the new States' Rights and Free Trade Party. In 1832 the three sons of General Thomas Pinckney and the three daughters of General Charles Cotesworth Pinckney—the two men perhaps most responsible for securing South Carolina's ratification of the Constitution—supported that party's successful candidate for governor, Robert Y. Hayne (a Pinckney relative through marriage), who promised to call a state convention to declare "certain acts of Congress"—both the 1828 tariff and the compromise 1832 tariff—null and void in the state of South Carolina.[9]

By the time the Ordinance of Nullification was drafted, the youngest of the general's three sons, Edward Rutledge, had died through his own rash behavior, but Colonel Thomas Pinckney Jr. and Cotesworth, delegates to the convention, pledged their "lives, fortune, and sacred honor" when signing the document that had revolutionary implications. The ordinance proclaimed with breathtaking audacity that after February 1833 no federal duties would be collected at South Carolina ports. Inflamed by the bravado of the moment, the legislature also voted to raise an army in a show of defiance and threatened that any attempt by the federal government to force payments of the import tax would result in secession.[10]

This challenge to the president may have given the sons of General Pinckney a particular pleasure. When their father had come out of retirement to serve as a major general during the War of 1812, he oversaw the southern theater of operations during the time of Jackson's great victory, which earned him the reputation as the valiant "Hero of New Orleans." Thrilled with the younger general's daring, Pinckney, whose own sons had achieved no military distinction, developed an admiring paternal affection for Jackson.[11]

Cotesworth and his wife, Caroline, who had gathered with her family in the Elliott home in Beaufort for Christmas, anxiously awaited "King Andrew's" response. When his "memorable Proclamation" denouncing nullification as "the mad project of disunion" appeared in the local press on December 15, they took it as a personal affront. President Jackson was unequivocal: nullification was unconstitutional; the Founders intended the Union to be perpetual; armed resistance to the laws of the nation was treason. In private, Jackson expressed his desire to "hang every leader . . . of that infatuated people, . . . by martial law, irrespective of his name, or political or social position." The same newspaper that brought Jackson's warning also carried a notice that Cotesworth Pinckney had been elected lieutenant governor by the state legislature, a fact of which the new officeholder had been "quite unconscious."[12]

On Christmas morning 1832 gloom hung over the Elliott household. No pine boughs decked the mantles. No one had the heart for carol singing. When little Tom bounced into the room where his large family huddled, heads together in sober conversation, his cheerful "Merry Christmas!" was met with silence. The "situation of our state" had been such an "all absorbing topic," his mother wrote Cotesworth Jr. the following day, that the adults, "feeling too deeply the crisis of our affairs," could not share his joy. Her sister Mary Barnwell Elliott summed up the general feeling of disbelief that God had not taken their side since "as a People, we were more awake to our duties to God, and less deserving of judgments than at any former period of our history." Instead of the traditional expressions of gratitude for all their blessings, the talk was almost exclusively of federal "coercion" and state "resistance."[13]

War was averted only at the eleventh hour, with face-saving compromises hammered out before the South Carolina militia fired on any federal gunboats in Charleston Harbor. The state's reckless act, distained even by sympathetic southerners, thrust South Carolina into greater isolation from the nation's political mainstream. Unionist James Louis Petigru ruefully pointed out that in the Palmetto State, "the public mind is poisoned."[14] The sense that the interests of South Carolina were no longer safe within the Union would dramatically shape the mindset of Tom Pinckney's generation. He would be raised in an environment of inflamed regional pride, political passion, swelling southern nationalism, declining expectations, contested ideals of patriotism, and wistful longing for a world he never knew.

Concluding that politics were "incompatible with Christian charity and brotherly love," Cotesworth Pinckney withdrew from public life when his two-year term as lieutenant governor was over in 1834 and gave himself over to the dictates of the Gospel as he understood them. To that end he became a leader in the movement to spread Christianity among South Carolina's slaves. Pinckney caused a stir among members of the Agricultural Society of South Carolina when, in giving its 1829 anniversary address, he argued that planters were wrong not to provide slaves access to ministers and the Holy Bible. Challenging the growing abolition movement that had gained strength during New England's own great spiritual awakening, he contended that the blessings of religion were, after all, eternal and thus "more important than freedom."[15]

Pinckney translated the "insurgent ideals" of Christian paternalism into the management of his own slaves. He agreed that rather than hammering that tired old saw that slavery was a "positive good," planters could best defend their domestic institutions by reforming them along Christian principles. Religion, Pinckney and these plantation radicals argued, had the power to transform the inherently brutal institution by making masters more kind and slaves more obedient. Enthusiasm for plantation missions was found among all Protestant denominations. At its most basic level, this approach reimagined slavery as a domestic institution based on the model of the Old Testament patriarchal family encompassing both "order and discipline as well as a sense of kindness and reciprocal affection." In contrast to past generations, who used coercion and fear to strip slaves of their sense of self and susceptible to the absolute will of the master, in the paternalist model the master saw himself like a biblical patriarch responsible for his extended family, both black and white. Under this arrangement, slaves were encouraged to look to the master for their welfare. The paternalist ideal was most fully realized in the situation, one contemporary observed, where the slave was treated "as a bondsman, but still as a man."[16]

After finding this new direction for his life, Cotesworth Pinckney became more solicitous of his children's religious development and their morals than was customary among men of his class. During the 1832 Beaufort revival, Cotesworth Jr., always anticipating his father's wishes, decided that the legal profession he had first taken up—as had his father—in preparation for a life in politics now offered neither "honor nor happiness." His announcement that he was abandoning Caesar for Christ, leaving the study of law to enroll in the Episcopal Seminary in Virginia and take up the cloth, was met with the same enthusiasm in his immediate family as if had been elected governor—or even better, archbishop of Canterbury.[17]

Young Tom had his first lesson in Christian paternalism soon after his fourth birthday when he was assigned his own "scholar" at one of his Elliott aunt's Sunday schools for enslaved children. His assignment was to teach the boy Isaac Watts's poem about Christian self-control, "Against Quarrelling and Fighting," which Tom had already memorized.[18]

Also in 1832, Eldorado Plantation, the crown jewel of the family's holdings and its more than one hundred slaves, fell quite unexpectedly into Cotesworth's hands. The timing was so propitious, he might have wondered quietly to himself if the shocking death of his thirty-two-year-old half-brother Edward Rutledge that September might not have been a divine intervention allowing him to work out his destiny as a Christian master. A bachelor, Edward was being hailed as the successor to his brilliant father while standing for reelection as a state senator from the district. But just then he displayed inexplicably poor judgment by ignoring all warnings from concerned friends against overexerting himself and sleeping for three nights during the late summer in the Santee swamp, soaked by black water most of the time. As a result, fever set in and took his life quickly. His niece, Rebecca Lowndes Rutledge, had been so startled by reports of his "imprudence" that she wondered if he sensed somehow that "his time had come, and all that he did tended to that end."[19]

With his brother's death, Cotesworth Pinckney took over management of Eldorado and laid out his plan to make the plantation a canvas upon which to exhibit Christian paternalism in action. In 1833 he reported to his elder son, who was then deep in his theological studies: "We find the [Methodist] missionary is joyfully received here by the negroes & they express much gratitude to your Father for having procured them such a blessing. Whether their lives evidence the good they profess to desire from his labors, we have not yet had an opportunity of judging." On the matter of black preachers, Cotesworth Pinckney did not disapprove on principle but thought those without "proper theological training" might pose a "danger" if they gained too much power over the slaves.[20]

But his evangelical experiment faced powerful resistance. Planters along both the North and the South Santee Rivers began "showing a little anxiety on the subject" of bringing preachers to the slaves. They reminded their friend that the 1822 insurrectionist Denmark Vesey had been a churchgoer and that six slaves had been hanged in 1829 for plotting an uprising in neighboring Georgetown County. Even more recently, Nat Turner's slave rebellion in Virginia had resulted in the deaths of more than fifty whites. Pinckney waved their concerns away with cavalier confidence, for he believed, as his father had, that the real danger to the lowcountry resided with literate free blacks who might spread the abolitionists' gospel of rebellion.[21]

Perhaps the most vocal and influential opponent to Christian paternalism was the "fussy and pedantic" Whitemarsh B. Seabrook, who succeeded Pinckney as lieutenant governor in 1834. Seabrook regarded white preachers tutoring slaves in the Bible stories or planters teaching Sunday schools with alarm as a practice that would inevitably erode the distinctions between white and black, free and slave. In 1833 he introduced a series of bills into the state senate that, if passed, would have made South Carolina's laws regulating its black population the most draconian of any in the South or even in the Caribbean. Some of his recommendations, however, were developed into laws placing restrictions on slave preachers, denying blacks the freedom to assemble for their own religious services, and making the teaching of slaves or any person of color a crime. Upon his election as governor in 1848, Seabrook even flirted with the idea of expelling free blacks from the state, an idea that an elderly General Thomas Pinckney had proposed in 1822 after the Denmark Vesey scare.[22]

Cotesworth Pinckney did score one signal victory over Seabrook in their battle over the religious life of slaves. In 1833 his eldest daughter, Caroline, married Seabrook's son, Archibald Hamilton, whom Pinckney then thoroughly converted to his cause. Some years later, when Seabrook sold slaves from his family's Edisto Island holdings to a Santee River man known as a cruel "sot," Cotesworth Jr. rebuked him severely. He parried his brother-in-law's barbs by pointing out that the slaves had themselves agitated for this sale so that they could return to the place they were born. "I did that matter in the fear of God and after much prayer to be directed aright," Seabrook protested, "and therefore have nothing, I hope, to be sorry for . . . [knowing] that at Santee they would- be even more in the way of the gospel than at Edisto, (because we have no missionaries) therefore after due consideration I did as I did."[23]

When young Tom Pinckney moved from Charleston to Eldorado, his future merged with the course of the ancient and unpredictable Santee River, which had flowed through his family narrative for over a century. Born of the confluence of the Congaree and the Wateree Rivers in the midlands of South Carolina, the Santee becomes of two minds about ten miles from the Atlantic, dividing into parallel channels. The North Santee and the South Santee, both yellowed with silt, empty into the largest alluvial delta on the Atlantic coast and create what was then one of the most perfect environments in the world for growing rice.

The South Santee District, about forty miles north of Charleston, had long been the home of generations of rice planters of English and Huguenot descent—the Pinckneys, Middletons, Rutledges, Mottes, Lynches, Horrys, and Shoolbreds—celebrated both for their "hereditary distinction" and their devotion to public service. Equally noteworthy were the establishments along the North Santee River of the distinguished families of the Hugers, Allstons, Waties, Trapiers, Bloomfields, and Kinlochs. Tom Pinckney's generation looked back with reverence to their forebears who "took a wilderness in hand, conquered the land, the Indians, the beasts of the forests, turned it over to us subjugated to agriculture to the use of men, free from foreign rule, [and] civilized," bringing the Santee District "into the world." The King's Highway that linked Charleston to Boston passed nearby.[24]

Like Thomas Jefferson's Monticello, carved out of the rugged western edge of Virginia's frontier, General Pinckney's Eldorado was also a sliver of civilization wrested from a forbidding tangle of dense maritime forest. Researching the latest engineering techniques developed in the lowlands of Holland and buying the most modern equipment available in Europe, he drained the "worthless" swamps, built trunks and sluice gates to control the flow of water, and ditched the lands into orderly rice fields that returned his investment many times with "Carolina gold." Out of dense piney woods his enslaved workers created broad sun-dappled lawns, interspersed with gardens laid out with indigenous plants but manicured in the formal British fashion. At the end of an avenue of live oaks, the general's chateau-style mansion sat lightly on the landscape. Inside a gracious ballroom, the well-chosen library of volumes in several languages and elegant French furnishings combined to make Eldorado seem the place where Europe and America met.[25]

General Pinckney may have asserted his dominion over the land, but he never tamed "The River." The Santee always played the cat's paw—giving, then taking away—with all who tried to claim its gifts. But Pinckney learned to live with its cunning whims. Looking so dreamy at one moment—so accommodating, so malleable, so somnambulant and heavy burdened, so willing to passively serve as a nursery for fish, a resting place for ducks, and willing highway to the sea—in an unforeseen fit of pique, the Santee could turn on a dime, canceling all bets, and become a whirling dervish of destruction, relentlessly firing off its freshets and making a folly of rice planters' dreams in a flash of destructive rage. In an instant all the tender sprigs or heavy-headed, nearly ripe stalks, so carefully tended, were suddenly ripped out of the soil, leaving no trace of all the months of human labor. Slaves too could be washed away in a sudden freshet. Watchtowers reminiscent of temples to the river gods dotted lowcountry rice fields. This land, The River would remind the planters time and again, is mine.

Pinckney and the others played this game only because rice was such a valuable crop that even when the Santee surged out of its banks and extracted a ransom of as many as three crops out of four, planters could still enjoy a profit; two good crops, and they flourished.

Caroline Pinckney fretted over the health of her young children when the family moved from Charleston Neck to Eldorado. Tom remained frail and vulnerable to the deadly swamp miasmas. So too was his baby sister, Mary Elliott, although she was born hearty in 1833, notable for her "size rather than her beauty." No one at the time knew exactly why the incidence of disease increased as more trees were cut and lands flooded to cultivate rice. Truly wonderlands in the spring, the plantations became deathtraps in the summer and fall. Even without understanding the etiology of malaria and yellow fever, planter families knew that when the magnolias began to blossom, they must steal their babies away until the first frost in early November.[26]

Despite the best efforts of his parents to keep him cosseted from harm, Tom contracted malaria during one of his seasons at Eldorado. His mother did everything that was known to do at the time to treat this mysterious illness. She wrapped the boy in blankets, kept up his strength with meat broths, and administered doses of Peruvian bark. Though he got through the crisis, Tom was greatly diminished. Malaria had entered his system and would remain with him all his life—but so would his love for The River.[27]

Pampered and excused from all chores, Tom became a dreamy sort of boy who idled his time away immersed in history books and adventure stories. Tales of Scottish chieftains embroidered by Jane Porter and Sir Walter Scott ranked among his favorites. Like every southern boy of his generation, Tom liked to imagine that he could make time stand still on the morning of September 11, 1297, when William Wallace and his small but gallant band were poised at Stirling Bridge, anxious to strike the first blow for Scottish independence against the rapidly approaching, well-mounted, and well-armed English army of King Edward I. In his childhood games the cause thought to be lost could always be won through faith, courage, and virtue.[28]

Tom grew up with fiction and family history woven together. His many relatives enjoyed lifting the small boy onto their laps to recount stories of Pinckney family derring-do during the war for American independence and describe their family ties with other legendary figures, including the Marquis de Lafayette and Brigadier General Francis Marion. Heroines as well as heroes populated the family pantheon and danced about in his imagination as he recollected tales of their bravery, sacrifice, and suffering at the hands of the redcoats.[29] Tom knew much was expected of him. Studying the portraits of his famous kinsmen and comparing them with his own reflection as he tiptoed to gaze in the ornate mirror at Eldorado, he felt very insignificant indeed.

When Tom was about eight or nine years old, his parents despaired that he would ever enjoy vigorous health at Eldorado and sent him to live fulltime in the bracing air of Pendleton Village in the northwest quadrant of the state, where both their families had summered for years. Built around a public square like a New England town, Pendleton stood as an oasis of taste and sophistication in the rolling Carolina upcountry. Around 1830 Cotesworth and Caroline had completed the final touches on Woodburn, a graceful plantation-style clapboard house built on a nearby promontory. In Pendleton the Pinckneys enjoyed the dense community of lowcountry relatives and friends who communed together in St. Paul's Episcopal Church. Social life centered around the Pendleton Agricultural Society.[30]

Tom attended the "village school," probably Pendleton Academy, which had once enjoyed an excellent reputation but had declined under the uninspired leadership of Thomas Wayland, the English-educated son of moral philosopher Francis Wayland. Among Tom's classmates were the youngest of the Calhoun boys. William Lowndes Calhoun (named for his father's political ally and Tom's uncle by marriage) was a year younger, while James Edward was two years older. Raised by their father, as he had been raised, by the immutable Presbyterian law of the strap and sent outdoors barefoot except in the very worst weather to toughen them, the rough-and-tumble Calhoun boys targeted the pampered Master Pinckney, swaddled in the heavy flannels and thick socks mandated by his absent mother. Other students joined them. In self-defense Tom would work himself into a fury, pulling and tugging at his clothes, his first struggle to free himself from the luxurious encumbrance of being a Pinckney.[31]

After his ordination in 1836, Cotesworth Jr. accepted a call to become the rector of Christ Church in nearby Greenville, South Carolina, and spent a great deal of time getting to know eight-year-old Tom. "Not deeply learned, but well-read," the minister became a mentor and surrogate for the boy. When Cotesworth's wife, Anne Randolph McKenna, died in childbirth in 1839, eighteen-year-old Maria Pinckney moved to Greenville to help her brother with his small children. Tom joined them whenever he could, and the three formed their own little family unit in the "Upper Country," celebrating Christmas 1841 together while their "distressed" mother remained at Eldorado.[32]

In contrast to his rather rigid brother, Tom Pinckney developed into an easygoing young man of the type his daughter would later describe as "sitting loosely in the saddle of life." He often took on the role of affable peacemaker in his strongminded family. Despite his perilous early start, Tom grew sturdy and strong as he pursued his passion for outdoor sports. Despite not holding, like his older brother did, the intellectual and spiritual concerns of their father, Tom did share his love of agriculture and well-bred horses.[33]

Deeply influenced by the precepts of Christian paternalism, one core conviction Tom maintained until the day he died was that his family had always been good masters to loyal slaves. In a short biographical sketch written at the end of his life, he did not portray his father as the grave, soul-saving Christian of his siblings' memory, but instead he crafted a heroic allegory in which his father was more like himself, a strong swimmer, a skilled horseman, and a protector of his "slave family." Tom recounted an event when the enslaved workers of Eldorado were busy, looking downward at their tasks in the rice fields, when a flood suddenly flashed across the low ground. All dashed to safety except one man, who shimmied up a tree as the waters swirled menacingly ever higher below him. One of the hands ran for the master, who immediately threw a saddle on his keen horse and galloped to the scene. Without hesitation, he spurred his mount into the churning water. Upon reaching the tree he gestured to the desperate man to release his death grip on a quivering limb and trade places with him. Swinging himself onto the tree, Cotesworth Sr. eased the man into his saddle and whipped the horse, which instinctively turned and made for the safety of the bank. He then leapt into the swirling water after him and, swimming against the tide with long, powerful, confident strokes, gained the shore, having fulfilled his role as both protector and savior of a dependent people.[34]

In truth, Tom and his father often clashed. A convivial fellow, he had much more in common with his uncle, Colonel Thomas Pinckney Jr. The disappointed father of two girls with no male heir, the colonel felt a special kinship with the eager nephew who bore his name. In contrast to his devout younger brother, who believed that "earthly joys are to be found principally in works of fiction," the colonel—a soldier, lawyer, planter, and dabbler in local politics—enjoyed a reputation as a "high-minded South Carolina sportsman." Popular among the city's bon vivants, he also was known for graceful and open-handed hospitality at the elegant Broad Street mansion he shared with his wife, Elizabeth Izard Pinckney. His wine cellar incited envy. A fixture at the South Carolina Jockey Club for forty years and its president for more than ten, the colonel was known for his kindness, amiability, and heart-felt renditions of the "High Mettled Racer."[35]

Like an Old Testament prophet, Cotesworth Pinckney always warned his family that pride would be their downfall. In the case of his brother, he was proven right. In a tragic entanglement of honor, patriarchy, pride, Colonel Pinckney essentially disinherited his beloved daughter, Celestine, when in contravention of his will she married her first cousin, Captain Benjamin Huger, an army officer with no home of his own or expectation of an inheritance. The colonel's fury was exacerbated by hotheaded Captain Huger's youthfully arrogant retort that he would never take a penny from him. Although both men seemed to mellow over the years, Cotesworth was not fooled. "Only religion," a commodity in short supply in his brother's household, could heal the "family breach." After the colonel's death in 1843 at Le Havre, his family—the whole legal community, in fact—was dumbstruck to read that his complicated will, written with venom and quoting Huger's insult verbatim, effectively left "Fairfield Plantation and the 120 people thereunto belonging" to his nephew and namesake, fourteen-year-old Thomas Pinckney, "and his heirs forever." Even Captain Robert E. Lee, a friend of the Hugers from Fort Monroe, weighed in, regretting the colonel's "cruel" sowing of the "apple of discord" and the "tainting" of his posterity.[36]

"My God, where is justice," exclaimed the widowed Eliza Izard Pinckney when she learned that under some circumstances their townhouse, bought in part with her marriage settlement as well as their Pendleton home, might also revert to Tom. In January 1846, the South Carolina Court of Appeals granted her desire to retain a life interest in Fairfield, but Cotesworth Pinckney pushed his son's interests in the plantation to their fullest extent, constantly arguing about her share of the crops and goods produced on the place. The whole affair poisoned their relationship.[37]

The colonel's legacy also brought young Tom into conflict with his father. In 1845 the seventeen-year-old Pinckney announced that he was not going to college but instead planned to prepare for his life on the land. He had long set his heart on living the independent life of a rice planter on his ancestral acres as the master of slaves, who too had dwelled on the Santee for generations. Keenly aware of the temptations Charleston society offered to wealthy young men without sufficient occupation, Cotesworth Pinckney thundered in response, "No!" Neither of his own brothers—Colonel Thomas or Edward—who both knew they were to inherit family plantations, had been willing to submit themselves to academic discipline, and neither finished their college educations. He would not be moved from his insistence that Tom must get the classical education of a gentleman and then study for a profession. No man could master The River without first mastering himself.[38]

Tom Pinckney enrolled without enthusiasm in the University of Virginia in 1846 during a rare time when the prestigious school was in desperate need of applicants. The year before, pistol-packing students had staged a violent protest over the school's strict regimen, and nearly half of the student body had been dismissed in response. Many students nevertheless returned. Campus distractions combined with deficiencies in Tom's early preparation and his relaxed study habits to make his academic life at the university a struggle for the young man, who "never cared to be brilliant."[39]

Letters from Pinckney's affectionate parents always paired gentle admonitions to work with assurances of "our united love." His father criticized the tortured grammar in Tom's replies and warned him that unless he mastered their "Mother Tongue," his letters would give no satisfaction to either his correspondents or himself. His mother directed him to seek out and "attend lectures on the evidences of Christianity" and arrive a half hour early to be assured of a seat. Even his little sister Mary Elliott, who excelled in her own studies at Miss Bates's school in Charleston, urged him to bear down in Latin and begin attending lectures on Greek literature. To help conquer his difficulty in public speaking, he forced himself to join the Jefferson Literary and Debating Society.[40]

Eager to please, Tom struggled diligently, but the same letters from home urging greater industry at his lessons were also full of family news, making him intensely homesick. He longed for frosty mornings in duck blinds along the Santee and agonized over missing important family occasions that the Pinckneys celebrated with such style. During the winter social season in Charleston, for example, his parents sometimes brought an entourage of eighteen, black and white, from the Santee to stay in the Victoria Hotel on King Street.[41]

The biggest news, though, besides the Pinckneys' banner year in rice, was his father's sale of their Pendleton farm and the purchase of Rest Park, a 1,150-acre cotton plantation on Hilton Head Island in the Beaufort District for $6,500. Tom's sister Caroline Seabrook and her husband planned to live at Rest Park with their children and employ the Pendleton slaves there. His elder brother would also have an interest in the operation.[42]

For a new summer home, the Pinckneys bought several hundred acres near Flat Rock, North Carolina, adjacent to Beaumont, where Caroline Pinckney's younger sister, Mary Barnwell Elliott, and her husband, rice planter Andrew Johnstone, escaped Annandale, their Georgetown County plantation, during the sickly season. The little mountain village already had attracted enough low-country families of fashion to enjoy a reputation as "Little Charleston." The summertime refugees built showplaces on tracts obtained from cash-starved hardscrabble farmers who later deeply resented selling their ancestral lands to flatlanders for a mess of pottage.[43]

After two years in Charlottesville, Tom eagerly returned to Charleston and (less eagerly) enrolled in the Medical College of South Carolina. Bending to the implacable pressure from his father, he chose a profession that would let him pursue his love of the natural world and also had practical application on a plantation. Cotesworth Pinckney, who had "not the smallest genius for attending the sick," approved of his son's choice as a useful as well as fashionable course of study. Sons of some of South Carolina's first families, including Tom's uncles Francis Kinloch Huger and Ralph Emms Elliott, had trained as physicians before becoming planters. Pinckney's cousin R. F. W. Allston had studied "physic" as a way to avoid the high costs of doctor's bill for his family and slaves. And a founder of the Medical College and the school's professor of anatomy, John Edward Holbrook, was married to another cousin, charming and well-educated Harriott Pinckney Rutledge. Beaufort born but raised in Massachusetts and trained at the University of Pennsylvania, Holbrook was one of America's few professional zoologists and a naturalist of international renown.[44]

Like everything in southern society during Pinckney's formative years, medical education was affected (and diminished) by the imperative not to challenge the slavery system. The death of Calhoun in 1850 silenced one of the last moderate southern voices, and his state funeral—the first since that of General Pinckney—also carried a portent for the future. Reflecting the South's growing intellectual isolation, the scientific debate current in the 1850s focused upon whether human beings had singular origins—*homo sapiens* all—or like all other mammals, multiple origins, was carried out in the context of the theoretical implications for slavery. Another hypothesis bandied about was "medical singularity," which suggested that the uniqueness of a southern practice demanded that southern doctors train at their own regional schools.[45]

Pinckney's studies gave him an adequate background in natural science but very little training in the actual art of healing. So much of his work had been among the dead, with their putrid smell and corrupted flesh: skinning, peeling, cutting, and probing poor diseased creatures often retrieved from pauper graves. An avid hunter, Tom was used to blood, but this was different. After a dissection the students shoved the remaining bones and bloody gore unceremoniously down a hole in the basement "dead room."[46]

In 1850, with his formal studies behind him, Tom still felt, like many new graduates, ill-prepared for the actual practice of medicine. Before the formulation of the germ theory, even experienced doctors had an extremely limited repertoire of diagnoses and treatments. The contents of a physician's bag had slightly expanded since the Revolutionary War, when General Thomas Pinckney had assembled his medical box. A young doctor could scarcely offer his patients a better prescription for sore throats than cousin Harriott Pinckney's special remedy of spoonfuls of plum jelly or sips of port wine.[47]

Wanting also to postpone as long as possible the tedium of a journeyman doctor's life, Tom implored his father to let him undertake some further training. Always leery of sending his son into the path of sin, Cotesworth Pinckney reluctantly approved his plan to attend lectures at the College of Physicians and Surgeons, a Presbyterian-run school that strictly forbade professors from separating religious and moral precepts from scientific study and was affiliated with the City University of New York. He knew as well that New York, unlike Boston, still welcomed southerners. New York was about business, and cotton was still king. That Dr. Samuel H. Dickson, a family friend and formerly one of Tom's professors, had recently accepted a position in the medical department there and could keep an eye on the young man was no doubt persuasive.[48] For his part, Tom looked forward to spending more time promenading around Washington Square, the militia parade ground near the university that had recently been transformed into a park in the heart of Greenwich Village. To fit in, he might even trade in his frockcoat for the more fashionable "sack suit" and add a four-in-hand tie.

Tom Pinckney boarded his steamer for New York with a light heart and expected smooth sailing. He longed for the churn of the open sea, its expansive vistas, and freedom from his father's scrutiny, his mother's fretting, and the relentless drumbeat of sectional politics. With engraved calling cards in his pocket and letters of introduction in his valise, the young man also considered his journey north a chance to broaden his social horizons. Little did he realize, however, that the time he spent cultivating acquaintances in New York would prove more providentially useful than any medical knowledge he would pick up, for these northern friends would one day save his life.

3

"WHAT HAVE WE DONE...?"

JOSEPH BARQUET RETURNED to Charleston in December 1848 after mustering out of what remained of the Palmetto Regiment. After a rough trip to Vera Cruz, the "Palmettoes" had wreathed themselves in glory and were the first to raise their regimental flag over Mexico City. But it was overall an inglorious war, an adventure filled more with boredom than danger, the men paying a terrible price for a victory few would remember. More than four hundred of them never returned. Disease took the majority, though the rate of desertions too was high. Their colonel, Pierce M. Butler, died at Churubusco. The regiment was disbanded at Mobile, Alabama, during the last week of June 1848, the men told to find their own way home.[1]

Charleston was a lonely place for Barquet when he returned, with no mother to greet him. He walked into a family feud. His sister Margaret and her husband, Joseph Humphries, one of Barbara's executors, had taken the position that as she was the only survivor of the children alive when Adam Tunno put the Meeting Street house in trust for his daughter and her issue, the family home belonged to her. Liston had taken exception to her theory and had brought a lawsuit to force its sale and a division of the proceeds among all of Barbara's heirs. He also questioned why the other executor, his father-in-law John Lee, was taking so long to liquidate his mother's estate. The controversy created strife for their youngest brother, Edod, who still worked with Lee.[2] Liston stirred this dispute from the distance of New York, where he had taken Abigail and their young daughter to squeeze in with her brother, John Lee Jr., and his wife, Mary Hanscome, in their Hudson Street apartment while he looked for any work he could find.[3]

After all he experienced during his Mexican venture, Joseph had little tolerance for either the domestic bickering or the oppressive atmosphere of Charleston and decided to head for New York as well while he considered his next move. He knew that, by law, he could never return to the city of his youth. If Bissett, still unmarried, did not travel with him at this time, he too left Charleston soon thereafter.

Straining for his first glimpse of Manhattan from the undulating deck of his steamer, Joseph would have seen a vista remarkably reminiscent of his hometown. The steeple of Trinity Episcopal Church dominated the skyline, as St. Michael's did in Charleston. The confluence of the East and the North (now the Hudson) Rivers with the Atlantic Ocean formed New York's majestic harbor in much the way that the Ashley and the Cooper melded together in Charleston's beautiful bay. In 1849 both ports were crowded with vessels heavy-laden with cotton, the "king," it seemed, of both Charleston and New York. By some calculations, forty cents of every dollar generated by the southern cotton crop jingled in the tills of New York merchants, drowning out the still small voice of conscience; these profits, like those of Charleston planters, were ineluctably tied to slavery.[4]

Historically, New York had an ambiguous relationship with slavery and race. During the colonial era, more slaves had lived in New York City than in Charleston, although they made up a smaller percentage of the population. Emancipation advocates met strenuous resistance after the American Revolution; the last slaves were not liberated until 1827. By that time the state legislature and the city council of New York had erected legal roadblocks denying blacks most of the rights of citizens, barring them from large sectors of the economy, and segregating the races in public places. Delegates at the 1846 state constitutional convention voted against the enfranchisement of black men.[5]

When Barquet disembarked from the ship and strode among the wonders of Wall Street, he could sense right away a different energy at work from Charleston's somnambulant business district. The buildings were taller, the pace quicker, the streets more crowded, and the majority of passersby had "foreign" faces rather than black ones. Immigrants, not slaves, did the heavy work of the harbor, moving cargoes to various wharves, storehouses, and auction houses, and jealously guarded their monopoly. Particularly arresting would have been posters of grinning white men with cork black on their faces and kinky wigs on their heads advertising the minstrel shows, which featured characters such as "Jumpin' Jim Crow" that had originated in New York but not yet found popularity in the South.

The standard rules for blacks newly arrived in New York urged caution when moving about the city, never asking for directions nor looking lost, lest they be singled out as a target for muggers or worse, opportunistic slave catchers. After his experiences in the past two years, Barquet would have moved with confidence even in these unfamiliar surroundings. One concern, though, was that he knew no white person here who could vouch that he was a freeman.[6]

Life in New York had proved a struggle for Liston as bespoke tailoring work was hard to find. The sewing machine had not yet been patented, but ready-to-wear clothes were already becoming widely available and increasingly affordable as more and more European immigrants—men, women, and even little children—labored in New York sweatshops or did piecework at home, stitching for their livelihood in sunless tenement rooms. Members of the New York upper crust were not comfortable dealing with blacks in shops, but the well-mannered, neatly dressed Liston could pass for white and eventually found a position cutting cloth in the workroom of a gentlemen's tailoring shop along Broadway.[7]

Even in Joseph's stonemason world of callused hands and grimy overalls, rivalry for work proved fierce. In the accelerated, competitive American economy of the 1840s, the artisan classes, white and black, suffered from the same ever-present threat of displacement and redundancy. In Manhattan the Irish had staked out their claim upon the building trades, and within that universe brick masonry—considered a skilled craft in Charleston—was perhaps the most highly contested and "heavily sweated" occupation. Burly men from County Cork would shove aside blacks even for the backbreaking job of hod carrier on construction sites. Project bosses encouraged animosity within the labor pool as they sought to cut costs in every way possible, even contracting for convict laborers who could, with new technology, produce more-or-less-standard results in dressing cheap materials.[8]

Joseph Barquet eventually landed a place working in a downtown confectionary. He may have had some past experience. In Charleston and probably in New York too, refugees from Saint Domingue often specialized in making French-style chocolates and other sugary treats. Barquet rented a room at 246½ Greenwich Street, in what had once been a fashionable neighborhood along the Hudson River, now devolved into a slum of vermin-infested boarding houses; a magnet for the dangerous demimonde. Starving poet Edgar Allen Poe had tried to write there for a while, but between the noise of late-night brawling and the stench of aging clams and catfish from street vendors, his muse had fled—soon after so did he.[9]

As had so many of his young Charleston friends, Barquet came to New York desperate to experience "the full fruition of Political Intellectual and Physical *Manhood.*" Discouraged by his failure to find work appropriate to his skills, this setback made him more determined to pursue his true purpose in going to New York: the quest for personal liberty and citizenship. Barquet realized—as had his former teacher Daniel A. Payne, who eventually became a leading black abolitionist—that in New York "heroism and consequent fame offered their laurels to any young man of talent and intelligence who might be willing to become the fearless and successful opponent of American slavery, and the eloquent defender of liberty and human rights." Payne's powerful message that slavery was a human tragedy that entrapped whites as well as blacks attracted the attention of wealthy New York businessman Lewis Tappan, who invited him to work as a traveling spokesperson for the American Anti-Slavery Society. After Payne declined, believing that God had called him to preach the Gospels, Tappan hired another man from the South who had an even more intimate experience with slavery, Frederick Douglass.[10]

Barquet had not been long in Manhattan when Douglass's new journal, *The North Star*—an allusion to Polaris, the constant light that led runaway slaves through the night to freedom—first came off the press. Inspired by William Lloyd Garrison's antislavery newspaper *The Liberator,* Douglass published articles about politics and the most pressing issues of the day. Barquet admired him for his advocacy of equal rights for free blacks in the northern states as well as the abolition of southern slavery. Douglass's four-page weekly, written by black men for black readers, opened up a new world for Barquet, who had long been in love with words and oratory. One of the editors, abolitionist William Cooper Nell, had Charleston roots. His father, William Guion Nell, was a freeborn Charlestonian who had served a seven-year apprenticeship in the fashionable tailor shop of the Barquet family friend Jehu Jones before going to sea as a steward and ending up in Boston.[11]

In New York, Barquet was exposed to the many different strands of antislavery and reformist thought percolating in America. During the 1820s, the radical wing, which had sympathizers from both races, began agitating with religious fervor for the immediate abolition of slavery; challenging those who favored a more gradual approach, including advocates for the colonization of free blacks in Africa. During the 1840s, the coalition between white and black abolitionists began to fray. The emphasis upon moral uplift was one area of contention. Barquet radiated toward the strain of black abolitionism that branched off from the mainstream to focus on grassroots politics. That the rising Democratic political machine of the city stood ready to shepherd newly arrived immigrants into jobs and eventually into the polling booth infuriated American-born blacks. Another black-abolitionist tack that appealed to Barquet was the effort to organize a skilled-black working class distinct from the large numbers of freemen trapped in servile occupations. Reading and debating the varieties of black thought at mid-century proved exciting for Barquet and validated his core conviction that native-born men of color had the potential to be equal in intellect, courage, and morals with all other Americans.[12]

ONCE IN NEW YORK, Barquet remained mum about his Mexican War experience with the Palmetto Regiment. What had been for him an assertion of manhood and patriotism had rapidly devolved into a flashpoint of sectional controversy as antislavery advocates painted the conflict as a blatant attempt by southerners to seize more territory and spread plantation agriculture. Repeated attempts in Congress to link funding of the war to a provision that slavery would never exist in whatever lands might be acquired in the peace treaty never succeeded, but they did set the stage for a national debate and ultimately the Compromise of 1850, which would have major implications for Barquet's own career.

Once he had some distance from Charleston, Barquet began to explore the complex, tangled nature of his own moral universe. A survey of his mother's estate, which also provided insight into the finances of his grandmother, forced him to admit that he had been as much a beneficiary as a victim of slavery. All his life Joseph felt himself superior to the slaves his mother had bought, sold, or hired out to pocket their earnings to benefit her own family. Realizing her three eldest sons would eventually be leaving Charleston, his mother had changed her will to stipulate that the slaves once bequeathed to them would be sold instead and the proceeds divided among all the children.[13]

Despite his growing revulsion against slavery, Joseph accepted his portion of the $1,350 brought by the sale. Her other assets that totaled nearly $5,000 were mishandled by her executors as Liston learned when he initiated an investigation into her estate. He managed in 1850 to force the sale of the family home sold at auction. Adam Tunno's good friend, lawyer and artist Charles Fraser, made the winning bid of $3,000. By the time that all the numerous Charleston lawyers involved extracted their fees and court costs were paid, each Barquet heir received only $380.96.[14]

Even so, capital from their mother's legacy transformed all the children's lives. Margaret and her extended family moved to Philadelphia. Edod remained in Charleston, continuing to work as a tailor in John Lee's shop, and bought a house for his wife and son in a largely white neighborhood on Greenhill Street. Bissett and Liston eventually would open their own tailoring shops in New York.[15]

But Joseph had another plan and went west. Perhaps hoping to cleanse ill-gotten money through good purpose, he left New York, not just to change his life but also to change the world. He set off on an errand, not exactly into the wilderness, but to Cincinnati, Ohio. Likely working with the small New York branch of the evolving "Underground Railroad" that assisted runaway slaves in their journey to freedom, he had three people under his wing when he traveled. Bending to intense political pressure from abolitionists, Ohio was one of the few states of the old Northwest Territory that in 1849 had somewhat relaxed its strictures against black settlement within its borders.[16] What he learned was that white southerners organized race relations around slavery, northerners around segregation, and western settlers around exclusion, having vowed that theirs would be the white man's republic and passing laws designed to prevent black immigration.

Cincinnati evolved as an entrepôt of freedom in the longing imaginations of enslaved people, the promised land where the North Star led them. Harriett Beecher Stowe, who once lived in the city, captured that desperate faith in *Uncle Tom's Cabin* (1852), with her harrowing description of the enslaved Eliza clutching her baby while hopping across the Ohio River on ice floes, the slaver's hounds snapping at their heels. Conscience-stricken masters and mistresses from states, including South Carolina, that prohibited emancipation could bring their slaves to Cincinnati for manumission.[17]

By late summer 1850, Barquet had found work as a bricklayer and was living in another unsavory neighborhood of taverns and rooming houses by the levee in Cincinnati's Fourth Ward, a section of town called "Little Africa." The black population in the city had exploded from less than 500 in 1810 to more than 3,000 in 1850. The 1850 census identifies a Connecticut-born woman and a child as Barquet's wife and six-year-old daughter, but they soon fade out of his story without explanation as does the thirteen-year-old mixed-race boy also listed as part of the household. Whatever the true nature of their relationship, Barquet was soon on the road again, apparently alone, and radicalized by a shocking turn of events.[18]

Barquet left Cincinnati in the wake of passage of the Fugitive Slave Act in September 1850, which sent a wave of terror through every black community in the North. An inflammable and highly contentious provision of the Compromise of 1850, engineered in part by Illinois senator Stephen A. Douglas, the Fugitive Slave Act was intended to diffuse sectional tensions but instead ignited a firestorm of catalyzing northern protest. The law reaffirmed the constitutional provision that federal authorities in every state of the Union were required to return runaway slaves to their rightful owners and levied heavy fines on those who refused to cooperate. The essential assumption of the act was that any black person anywhere may be considered a slave until they could prove otherwise. Individuals accused of being runaways enjoyed no legal protections, such as the writ of habeas corpus, and could be legally kidnapped by slave catchers or federal marshals.

Barquet, who was rapidly gaining a reputation as a rousing antislavery orator, headed for Milwaukee, where he teamed up with another stonemason, William Harlan, also recently arrived from Cincinnati. Since Wisconsin had only become a state in 1848, they had set out on a mission to educate Milwaukee's small, but vulnerable, population of 100 blacks about the possible dangers they faced from the new legislation. Barquet was the keynote speaker at their initial meeting on October 7, 1850. The local press sympathetically covered the event, which attracted a large crowd, and printed Barquet's speech in its entirety.[19]

Drawing on the style of southern oratory he had had learned in his Charleston youth, Barquet began his speech quietly, then steadily built to a crescendo as he laid out the facts of the desperate times in which they now lived. His first theme was of racial solidarity. In comments that signified how far he had evolved in his own thinking, Barquet urged all present "to forget everything like feelings of animosity, forget that you were freeborn, forget whose parents wore chains, all differences between you; remember only the hour that has arrived when you, one and all, are called on to do your duty to yourselves and your brothers. Springing from one race, let us make common cause, one with another; let us shield one another; let us die for one another." Living free in the North, he emphasized, did not mean they were safe. Slaveholders could "rush even unto our hearthstones and tear from our fond embrace, the children of our loins, yea, the wife of our bosoms," just as if they were fugitives. Since "the blood of Nubia is in our cheeks," all were vulnerable; "the fangs of the bloodhound [are] not particular as to [their] prey." The only way to counter this overwhelming force, he argued, was to unite, for "nature teaches us that wolves hunt in packs to protect themselves." The crowd stirred as Barquet hit his stride. "Gentlemen, before you tonight, I pledge my life to come forward at any time, and redeem my word." Returning to one of his favorite allusions, he admonished them to "be ready, sharpen your swords by the midnight lamp, be in the saddle by the first streak of day. If your liberty is worth having, it is worth a life to preserve it."

At the same time Barquet encouraged his rapt listeners to ban together, he also charged them to remember, "We are Americans by birth." "How heart sickening it is to reflect upon our situation," he observed, "that the land of our nativity refuses us her protection, while she holds out her widespread arm[s] to receive [foreign] fugitives, lovers of liberty and republicanism." As a last resort, since "the [American] eagle no longer protects them under the shadow of her wings," he proposed (mixing his metaphors) sending their enslaved brethren to Canada, "in the direction of the North Star," where they would be sheltered "under the tender clutches of the British lion." With a big finish designed to bring his audience to their feet, Barquet called the Fugitive Slave Act a pyrrhic victory for slaveholders and shouted out: "Remember then, that bayonets may be called upon to uphold such abominations for a time, but surely as the love of freedom swells the hearts of mankind, surely as sweet freedom, once tasted, can never be forgotten, the end of that triumph will be terrible."[20]

Energized by Barquet and other persuasive, though more measured, speakers, the group unanimously adopted resolutions condemning the Fugitive Slave Act, vowing to do all in their power to rescue their enslaved brethren when possible, thanking the Wisconsin legislature and the state's congressmen for voting against that unjust bill and applauding the newspapers that editorialized against it. The crowd booed when those states supporting the odious law were called out, including "Old Virginny, Nullifying South Carolina, and Disunion Georgia."[21]

For a while Barquet enjoyed a supportive community and a good base of operations in Milwaukee. By March 1851, he had started a whitewashing and "wall coloring" business—an undertaking that afforded him maximum mobility—at the corner of Wisconsin Street and Post Office Alley. His brother Bissett may have joined him for a while. Within the year, though, he was making his way to Chicago to play a larger role in the great abolitionist drama unfolding in Illinois. Riding the rails across the broad expanse of prairie always generated in first-time passengers the same excitement of liberation from time and place as an ocean crossing. The sensation of boundlessness, of space to live unimpeded, was, Barquet soon found out, but a mirage. The narrowness of political vision in Illinois stood in bitter contrast to the vastness of its plains.[22]

Even though Illinois had entered the Union as a free state in 1818, slavery was deeply imbedded in its culture, particularly in the southern counties bordering Missouri, Kentucky, and Tennessee, and was not outlawed until 1845. About the same time, the state legislature passed a set of "Black Laws," eerily reminiscent of the slave codes of South Carolina, designed to discourage African American settlers. The laws stipulated that any black or mixed-race person moving into Illinois had to have a certificate of freedom, register with the state, and post a $200 bond to insure that they would not become a burden to their community. Those caught without proof of freedom or the $50 to pay a fine could be sold into slavery for an unspecified length of time. These laws restricted all aspects of life for free blacks by banning interracial marriage, denying their children access to public schools, limiting their right of assembly, forbidding their service in the militia, and disallowing their testimony in court. After living under this regime for a few years, Barquet described the Black Laws as sadistically designed to wound black people "at every point thought vulnerable."[23]

Chicago was just shedding the rawness of a frontier outpost when Barquet arrived in 1852. No police force yet patrolled its muddy, unpaved streets. Regular mail service had only commenced in 1845. As in Milwaukee, the black population constituted only 1 percent of the 30,000 inhabitants; of those, most were mixed race. Aside from a smattering of the West Indian born who had traveled up the Mississippi and arrived a decade earlier, almost all were newcomers to the Windy City. Quite a few among them were emancipated or self-emancipated slaves who had slipped into town under the cover of night and moved quietly in the shadows.[24]

Barquet lived in Chicago's boisterous Third Ward, where the rents were low and the black population congregated. At first he found lodgings on Madison Street in a rowdy neighborhood populated with petty thieves, prostitutes, pimps, and gamblers fresh off the riverboats. By 1854, he had moved to Randolph Street, near a popular saloon, the first owned by a black man. The dubious clientele lurking around the tavern engaged in frequent fistfights and shootouts and earned the area a reputation as the "Hair-trigger Block."[25]

Everyone had a story in Chicago. For self-protection, many had crafted several different narratives of their lives and went by a number of different names. In Barquet's case he played down his southern roots in favor of the cachet of his Haitian heritage. Jean Baptiste Pointe du Sable, a trader of African and French extraction and probably from Saint Domingue, had opened a trading post along Lake Michigan about 1780 and was widely hailed as Chicago's founding father. Some of Barquet's new friends came to believe that he too was Haitian born.[26]

In April 1852 Barquet described himself in a letter to Frederick Douglass as "one of the laborers in the field of our progression and elevation" working in Chicago. These "sentinels of freedom, standing on the outposts," he wrote, could "almost hear the moanings of the slave as borne on the zephyr across the Prairie State." The heartbeats of the black-rights movement in Illinois were John Jones, a skilled tailor and dry cleaner, and his wife, Mary. Light skinned and relatively prosperous, the couple served as a bridge between the various all-white and all-black antislavery societies. With the skill of a diplomat, Jones helped find common ground among those who wanted the total and immediate abolition of slavery across America, those comfortable with slavery where it existed but not its spread to the western states, and those in the free black community who were particularly focused on the repeal of the Black Laws.[27]

The Fugitive Slave Act united the disparate black community of Chicago. Members of the Quinn African Methodist Episcopal Chapel, organized in 1847, formed the Liberty Association to "promote a general dissemination of the principles of Human Freedom" and practiced what they preached by formulating strategies to help runaways reach Canada. A vigilance committee posted volunteers all over the town, ready to send up an alarm whenever those odious "low white" slave catchers prowled the back streets and alleys with their sniffing hounds. The specter of crying men, weeping women, and bawling children wrenched out of their hiding places and sent back to slavery had the unexpected consequence of also rousing the ire of white Chicagoans, many of whom joined the conspiracy against slave catchers. The town rapidly gained a reputation among southerners as "a sinkhole of abolition."[28]

Barquet reveled in the opportunity to do meaningful work. During the years since he had left Charleston, he had undergone a transformation in his self-understanding. In his youth he identified himself as "French," a class apart and a caste above local blacks. In Charleston, as in most slave societies, the light-skinned and the dark-skinned people were, as writer William C. Nell had observed, "as the Jews and Samaritans of Scripture [and] had no dealings one with another." In contrast, Barquet found a perverse equality in Illinois. All blacks in that state, he soon learned, were judged by whites to be equally inferior and subjected to equal discrimination. If barriers to fellow feeling and racial unity, such as class, skin color, previous condition of servitude, and even religion, did not disappear entirely in this melting pot of shared oppression, they lost their sharp edges. Over time Barquet accepted the truth of Douglass's words: "We are one people in general complexion, one in common degradation, and one in popular estimation. As one rises all must rise, as one falls, all must fall."[29]

Through the tireless abolitionist press, which coordinated activities among isolated communities, Barquet kept abreast of events affecting people of color across the nation. In December 1851, he helped raise funds for the defense of the "Christiana sufferers," more than thirty Pennsylvania blacks accused of treason for their armed resistance to a federal marshal holding a warrant to arrest fugitive slaves. After developing a friendship with former Douglass protégé, Henry O. Wagoner, a self-educated staff member of the *Western Citizen*, Barquet began submitting occasional letters to this newspaper, the official organ of the state's Liberty Party. He also sharpened his wits in verbal combat with other black abolitionists who held a variety of divergent views. One of the most frequent and heated debates pitted the assimilationist argument, which Barquet supported and encouraged blacks to fight for their rights as Americans, against the emigration advocates, such as H. Ford Douglas and Martin Delany, who contended that the United States was already a lost cause and urged resettlement in Latin America, Africa, or the West Indies. Douglas, an "anti-slavery emigrationist," sought to destroy slavery, which was the basis for racial discrimination. Delany represented a black-nationalist school of thought within the emigration camp that contended blacks must form their own separate self-governing nations to prove their ability to govern.[30]

In 1852 Barquet wrote Frederick Douglass with his ruminations about the Fugitive Slave Act. Raging against the law or deeming it unconstitutional was fruitless. Whenever his friends suggested that this odious piece of legislation was patently unconstitutional and would necessarily be struck down, or that the moral outrage of the nation would force its repeal, or that it was simply unenforceable, Barquet would object. Although he personally found the law loathsome, he argued that it was indeed within the government's powers under the Constitution. Its passage in Congress by a majority vote had further endowed the act with the sanction of the people. From his years of close observation, Barquet understood the inflamed political culture of South Carolina, which saw the Constitution as a firewall against the abolitionist movement. "The law would be sustained at all hazards," he predicted, including by "bayonets." He proposed that "a prophet must arise" and turn the tables on the belligerent southerners by attacking the act as a purely constitutional violation of states' rights. "Oh, how I feel my inability," he confessed, to be that prophet and to make that argument he had heard so often in South Carolina. Barquet believed that the legislature in a state such as Pennsylvania should assert its inalienable right, superior to that of the federal government, not to hunt down slaves. Perhaps he suggested that Douglass might use his magazine "to enlarge upon this subject."[31]

Although unconvinced that he should take up the cudgel of states' rights,

Douglass did agree to come to Chicago. In December 1852, he spoke at a mass meeting organized by Barquet and his friends in the Colored Literary and Debating Society. He attacked a problem closer to home and denounced the insidious Black Laws of Illinois that rendered "colored citizens defenseless and stigmatized." In advance of the meeting, Barquet undertook a speaking tour of his own in the northern part of the state to generate interest in the cause. Drawing from the speech, he wrote a letter to the *Western Citizen,* adopting a burlesque tone in complaining that those laws designed to block blacks from entering the state "beats hard, very hard against Sambo." "I wish to annex myself to a wife, but the community in color is scarce in our market. . . . If we go from home to import one, the dear creature will be sold" in Illinois. What was the solution, then, if the "black gals" were shut out, "why we must take the white ones, that's all," even if the law also prohibits interracial marriage. "But, sir, to be serious," Barquet stated that his real aim was to raise awareness. He believed that the prediction made by supporters of colonization that an equalization of the races would lead to a war of the races had been realized in the Fugitive Slave Act. "A government that would legislate away the freedom of one mean inoffensive citizen, would not be too good to raise an army of extermination." He also brought up the philosophy of the late Robert Y. Hayne, South Carolina's governor in 1834 when the law against teaching free blacks was passed and teacher Daniel Alexander Payne was driven from Charleston, "who said that no State could of a right expatriate its inhabitants, but laws so hard in their bearing could be enacted that would drive them away." He warned in a hyperbolic flourish that slavery was being planned for the freeman and that the war of extermination has come.[32]

In 1853 Barquet attended a state convention in Chicago called to address the "forlorn condition of the colored citizens of Illinois." The model for this meeting was series of "national colored conventions" in which John Jones, Douglass, and Delany had all honed their political skills as they began to engage in serious debates about the future of black America. The Illinois meeting attracted a cross-section of "self-made men"—printers, carpenters, blacksmiths, clergymen, grocers, tailors, and housepainters—who believed that the problems facing their race were not inherent in America but were, like sin, susceptible to change. They adopted a question devastating in its simplicity: "Why are we singled out and made the subject of laws so cruel and so degrading and so contrary to every principle of Republicanism?"[33]

Treading carefully, wary of white reaction to large gatherings of blacks, the opening statement was tempered: "we feel keenly our wrongs, still we come together, we trust, in a spirit of meekness asking only for 'fair play,' and that the rights of all citizens be extended to black Americans." Believing that the widespread poverty, illiteracy, and immorality among people of color was the source of white prejudice, and admitting that their leaders had "too long remained supinely inactive, and apparently indifferent to our oppressed and degraded condition," the resolutions of the convention were largely focused upon "our great work of redemption" and guided by the principal that "God helps them who help themselves."[34]

At the convention Barquet was in his element and seemed to be everywhere at once. He introduced a successful motion creating a committee to study the role of mechanics in the black community and sat on the business committee. At the meeting of the education committee, Barquet engaged in an "animated discussion" with Douglass about the "gross and flagrant violation of justice" in Illinois towns where taxpaying black parents had to send their children to inferior segregated public schools. In his grand finale Barquet delivered "a most eloquent and convincing speech" condemning all colonization schemes to locate people of color away from their American homeland. The convention's statement of purpose echoed Barquet's sentiments—and perhaps his words—and played on William Cowper's 1795 antislavery poem, "The Task": "We are Americans by birth and we assure you that we are Americans in feeling; and in spite of all the wrongs which we have long and *silently* endured in this country, we would yet exclaim with a full heart, 'Oh, America! With all thy faults, we love thee still.'"[35]

Laying out the problems of the black people in Illinois was easier, of course, than coming up with solutions. Most of the convention's proposals, such as the idea of raising private funds to build an alternative school system, were aspirational pipe dreams since few had any money to give. Unable to accept that the white majority of the state would wish such pain and hardship upon free blacks, a hopeful contingent proposed the formation of the Illinois State Repeal Association to take their case directly to white voters. Although falling short in achieving concrete goals, the convention provided a venue where ambitious, committed men such as Barquet could meet in a supportive environment, exchange ideas, and gain practice in the art of politics. The *Chicago Tribune* noted that in contrast to most political meetings, the delegates to the "Convention of the Colored Citizens" proved exceptional for their mastery of Robert's Rules of Order and their "courtesy, urbanity, and kindness towards each other."[36]

After the Chicago convention, thirty-year-old Barquet could look back with pride upon his achievements since leaving Charleston eight years earlier. In New

York the cause of abolition had come to consume his life with all the power of a religious conversion. Wrapping himself in the mantle of freedom, he had traveled the country and become a popular evangelist for this cause. In Milwaukee, he had consulted with Congressman Charles Durkee, a member of the antislavery Free Soil Party and later the abolitionist wing of the Republican Party, about how best to defeat or circumvent the Fugitive Slave Act. Now he had shared a stage with the rising star Frederick Douglass and challenged Martin Delany on the matter of black emigration to Africa.

The year 1853 also proved a landmark on the personal front. After finding his life's work and a home, he found his life's partner and soon started a family. His twenty-one-year-old wife, a mixed-race woman named Maria, had come west from Pennsylvania. In 1855, after the birth of their first child, Horace Ward, Barquet moved his young family south to Galesburg, a college town with that rare reputation as a good place for a black man. In 1857 the Barquets' second child was born; Joseph named their daughter Barbary, after his mother.[37]

Founded in 1836 in the old "Military Tract," a huge territory larger than the state of Massachusetts originally set aside for veterans of the War of 1812, Galesburg was not a typical prairie settlement but the setting for a dream. The town actually grew up around Knox College, a western outpost of eastern evangelical thought established by George Washington Gale, who had also been involved with the creation of Lane Theological Seminary. Gale hoped to replicate the success of his New York–based Oneida Institute, which trained religious young men for the rigors of missionary work by pairing an emphasis on academics with manual labor. He and his followers had been swept up in the Second Great Awakening, a religious revival that had deeply touched Americans during the 1820s and early 1830s. Initially focusing on moral regeneration, keeping the Sabbath, piety, and temperance, the later introduction of abolition caused a rift with southern evangelicals but also caused many to examine ways to bring their domestic institution more closely in line with Christian teaching. Devout students at Knox College founded the first antislavery society in Illinois.[38]

Galesburg proved a good choice for Barquet, who quickly assumed the leadership of its very small black community, and surely played a critical role in channeling the ever-increasing traffic of runaway slaves flowing across the Missouri border to safe houses. The college town was well known for its hospitality to fugitives. Once the rail line to Chicago was completed, the runaways could, with some assistance, simply board at the depot and ride north toward freedom in relative safety.[39]

From a practical point of view, Galesburg offered Barquet the opportunity to ply his masonry skills as homesick New Englanders, nostalgic for the look of permanence displayed by their hometowns and concerned with the danger of fire and "wood famine" on the prairie, banned log cabins in favor of brick and stone. To boost his chances of success, Barquet also continued to offer wallpapering, whitewashing, and plastering.[40]

Upon his arrival in February 1855, Barquet wrote a long letter to the *Galesburg Free Democrat*—the text probably drawn from his 1853 convention speech—introducing himself to the community. Although he touched on all the issues that concerned him, he focused on the threats to black Americans of the widespread support for colonization. If free black people were seduced into leaving the United States for Africa, he argued, "the door of knowledge" would be forever shut to "our posterity." He unveiled the hypocrisy of those religious leaders who would not condemn the degrading institution of slavery but who criticized "the degraded negro of our country who could be men [in Liberia]" but refuse to go. "Alas! for our friends, heaven save us from them," Barquet countered. "If the Americans esteem us so highly, and wish to give us this great blessing of self-government, should they not have us near them to see the wonderful change that would be produced upon us? But no." Black people, they say, are "good for naught here," he bemoaned, and "distance lends enchantment to the view / And turns the niggers to statesmen, too." "Our country, . . . our birth land," he lamented, "has turned us out of its protection. . . . [W]e are told to be ready to remove for Africa." Barquet then posed the question that was not merely rhetoric, but one that tormented his soul: "What have we done to engender such malicious hate from our fellow man in the State—in the country at large?"[41]

Over the next several years, Barquet joined abolitionists across the nation as they soberly considered the direction of the country. In 1859, when he delivered the annual West Indian Emancipation Day speech at Gale's home, he abandoned the usual platitudes about how the 1833 abolition of slavery in the British colonies pointed to the inevitable liberation of America's enslaved people. Instead, Barquet unleashed an hour-long harangue "full of burning eloquence," denouncing the recent US Supreme Court decision in *Dred Scott v. Sanford* that Scott, a slave, had no standing to bring a suit in federal court, thus mooting his claim that after being transported to a free state, he was liberated. More pernicious still was the court's ruling that the federal government had no right to make laws regarding slavery in the unorganized territories of the West. Barquet's lament that blacks now had no place of safety and no rights that whites were obliged to respect was praised by the local press as the product of "deep, thorough, historical research" that had "seldom if ever been equaled in the State."[42] Barquet, who had since the days of his Charleston youth revered the US Constitution as the repository of human rights, now feared that the entire nation was becoming South Carolina.

On October 7, 1858, a blustery cold day, the people of Galesburg experienced another exhibition of high oratorical theater when Illinois's incumbent Democratic senator, Stephen A. Douglas, squared off against his challenger, the relatively unknown Republican nominee, Abraham Lincoln. Barquet surely crowded in with the thousands of spectators gathered to hear them speak from the raised platform outside Knox College's Old Main building. Douglas, condemned for his formulation of "popular sovereignty," or letting the voters in each new state determine whether to be a slave or free society, stumbled badly before the Galesburg audience. Lincoln gave a strong performance, realizing that the crowd was largely sympathetic to the new Republican Party and its "free men, free soil, free labor" ideology, even if they knew little about its candidate.[43] Barquet knew that the canny Lincoln often played to his audience and had in other debates referred to blacks as an "inferior race."[44] Neither Lincoln nor the Illinois Republican Party had passed Barquet's litmus test of publicly opposing the state's Black Laws. That was of no practical concern, of course, since he had no vote.

His feeling of desolation, that the fate of the black man played no role in the arc of history, caused the true believer Barquet to at last give up on the United States in 1859. Still refusing to emigrate to Africa, he gathered his family and his trowels, jointers, and edgers in preparation to leave for Haiti, his father's homeland. Just at the time when he had been at his lowest ebb and most discouraged about his future, General Fabre Nicholas Geffrard, who had recently come to power in yet another military coup in that strife-ridden nation, had invited American blacks to settle in his country. In May, Barquet attended a local meeting with others from nearby towns attracted to the idea of a new start under a black government. At the end of the general discussion, Barquet offered a resolution that won near-unanimous endorsement: "Whereas; We believe the time has arrived in our dark history for us to choose between exile and slavery, and that [since] our longer remaining in this country cannot loose[n] the chains of our bond brethren nor ameliorate our own condition . . . we will accept the former. . . . We believe it the duty incumbent on every young man of color to make Hayti his future home."[45]

An editorial in the *Galesburg (Semi-Weekly) Democrat* endorsed the growing sentiment for emigration among the local black population and was overly quick to bid them a fond farewell. Haiti, the *Democrat* conceded, was perhaps the best place for blacks after all: "*There* is a chance for political advancement; *here,* none. *There* they will be equal in all respect to their fellows; *here,* for a generation to come, at least, they will be regarded as an inferior race, a lower caste, made to be 'hewers of wood and drawers of water' to their white brethren. This is the present aspect of their case. We wish it were different, but are constrained to state the facts as they are, and frankly own that if their case were ours, we should turn with longing eyes to the Republic of Hayti."[46]

When several hundred black midwesterners traveled to New Orleans and sailed for Haiti, Joseph Barquet was not among them; for some reason he changed his mind. Perhaps he realized the instability of the military government there or he learned that General Geffard was not offering American blacks asylum so much as luring them to his country to cultivate cotton, a crop he assumed they all knew how to grow and that Haitians disdained to plant. At some point as he was debating the move, Barquet learned that his wife was expecting their third child and could not risk a sea voyage to an unhealthy land. His shaky finances likely contributed to his final decision.[47]

In September 1859 Barquet hired a Galesburg legal firm that specialized in investigating real estate titles to prosecute his claim to bounty land based on his service in the Mexican War. He was either still probing ways to escape Illinois or more likely hoped to sell his claim to speculators, as most veterans had. In March 1855 Congress had expanded eligibility for these grant programs awarding 160 acres of land in the public domain to all those mustered in for service to the military, including militia, musicians, wagon masters, and clerks, even Indians as if they "had been white men." Although he had lost his certificate of honorable discharge, Barquet was sure he would be listed as a private on the muster roll of Company A in Colonel P. M. Butler's South Carolina regiment and took an oath to that effect. The rejection of his application because his name never appeared on the quite randomly maintained rosters of any of the South Carolina companies, in which volunteers were routinely signing up, dropping out, deserting, being sent home with injuries, or dying, deepened his sense of alienation in America.[48]

While Barquet awaited the results of his application, an event of enormous magnitude rocked the delicate equilibrium of the nation. In October 1859, abolitionist John Brown, who had been implicated in the murder of slaveholders in Kansas, organized a small band of blacks and whites to attack the federal arsenal at Harpers Ferry, Virginia, to secure weapons for a bloody slave uprising. Within two days, US Army colonel Robert E. Lee had forced Brown's surrender and took his band into custody for treason, a hanging offense. The news troubled but did not surprise Barquet. The old man had been a frequent visitor to Chicago while guiding fugitive slaves to Canada and often spent time with Barquet's friends. The Joneses regularly provided Brown with a bed but found him an unsettling guest, particularly when a strange, faraway look clouded his eyes and he lapsed into periods of rambling speech. Brown evinced no interest in John Jones's strategies to overturn the Black Laws but spoke in apocalyptic terms of fire and blood about his own plan "to take the war to Africa" by inciting slave rebellion in the South. The down-to-earth Mary Jones confided to her husband that Brown seemed "a little off" on his approach to the slavery question.[49]

On December 2, the night of Brown's execution in Charlestown, Virginia, Barquet spoke with great feeling at a memorial service at Galesburg's African Methodist Episcopal church. The "prevailing sentiment," as recounted by the local Democratic newspaper, was that while the black abolitionists felt "sympathy and respect" for Brown's "philanthropic and heroic impulses," they condemned his violent actions as detrimental to their cause.[50]

Barquet undertook a small rebellion of his own in 1860. Just as his eldest son, Horace Ward, was approaching school age, the Galesburg Board of Education mandated that "Colored" and white children could no longer attend school together and must be segregated. This decision reflected the changing demographics of the town. Increasing numbers of runaway slaves chose to stay in the Galesburg at the same time that many of those committed to an open and tolerant community died off. An influx of immigrants from Ireland, Germany, and Sweden added their own prejudices to the brew. Ashamed that he could not provide his son with even the good basic education he had enjoyed in South Carolina, Barquet lashed out. As the secretary of the Galesburg African Literary and Debating Society, he was loud in his public condemnation of school segregation. In June 1860, he denounced the directors of a public school near Galesburg who had indignantly marched into a classroom intent on purging a child rumored to have "colored" blood. Staring at the rows of little upturned faces, the embarrassed men were unable to pick out the offending child from his white classmates and withdrew in furious embarrassment.[51]

The excitement of national politics overcame local disputes as the two sons of Illinois competed for the presidency that year. Robert and Thomas Hamilton, editors of the New York–based *Weekly Anglo-African*, to which Barquet was an occasional contributor, anticipated politics as usual as far as race issues were concerned. One editorial warned that the Republicans who "cry humanity to the world" were actually more dangerous in their deception than the unabashed proslavery Democrats, for when "it is clearly in [the Republican's] power to do anything for the oppressed colored man, why then they are too nice, too conservative, to do it." Another editorial predicted that the Republicans would be no more willing than the Democrats to sacrifice the Union to uplift the black man. They drew no comfort from Lincoln's campaign slogan, "Vote Yourself a Farm," which tried to sidestep the slavery issue yet telegraph his support for free homesteads in the unsettled western lands.[52]

The election of the Republican Lincoln, who did not appear on the ballots in ten Deep South states, provided the catalyst to South Carolina's secession on December 20. Knowing the passion and pride of that state's politicians, Barquet was scarcely surprised. The issues that had propelled his home state out of the Union had been festering since his birth. In the months to come, as other southern states followed the Palmetto State's lead, Barquet resented his impotence to act more keenly than ever. When the Confederates fired on Fort Sumter on April 12, 1861, and loyal Knox College students threw down their books to answer President Lincoln's call for volunteers, he was left behind. No one of "African descent" might join the army, even to fight this slaveholders' rebellion.

With the commencement of the great war between the states, Barquet agonized over what this conflict meant for him and for all free men of color banned from military service. Should he just agree with his friends in the barbershops and feed stores around Galesburg that this was a white man's war? Was it even possible for a black man to be a patriot, to love a country that did not love him back? In 1855 Barquet had written that the United States was merely the "birthland" of black people, not really "our country." The heart of the matter was whether America would ever truly be their home or whether they would always be merely a "people within a people," sojourners with no possibility of entering fully into public life.[53]

For years Barquet had followed the debate about patriotism in the pages of the black press. Before losing faith in America and advocating emigration, Virginia-born man-of-many-talents Martin Delaney had asserted that the "so-called" free black people of the United States, those "indefatigable enemies of oppression, and friends of God and humanity," must surely be counted as patriots, for true patriotism required an "impartial love," not just for all the laws but also for every person in a country. Frederick Douglass, who anticipated a day when blacks might be amalgamated into the American nation on terms of equality, insisted that patriotism or "true loyalty" was devotion to the national ideals of freedom and equality rather than rigid adherence to a particular government or its politicians.[54]

Barquet knew in his heart what he must do. If President Lincoln called, he would answer. He had been preparing for this moment all his life—and with all its faults, he loved America still.

"Cap and Môle St. Nicolas, Isle St. Domingue, ca. 1808." Birthplace of
John Pierre Barquet. *Courtesy of the Schomburg Center for Research in Black Culture,
Photographs and Print Division, New York Public Library Digital Collections.*

Adam Tunno (1754–832) in 1827. Watercolor on paper miniature by Charles Fraser (1782–1860). *Courtesy Cincinnati Art Museum, Ohio; gift of Mr. and Mrs. Charles Fleischman III/Bridgeman Images.*

Bishop Daniel Alexander Payne (1811–1893), ca. 1852. *Courtesy of the Schomburg Center for Research in Black Culture, Manuscripts and Archives Division, The New York Public Library Digital Collections. 1900.*

Liston Warren Barquet (1821–fl.1904), ca. 1890. A New York tailor, poet, and elder brother of Sgt. Joseph H. Barquet. *Courtesy of John R. Clauson.*

General Thomas Pinckney (1750–1828) in 1818. Water color on ivory miniature
by Charles Fraser (1782–1860). *Courtesy of The Gibbes Museum
of Art/Carolina Art Association.*

Colonel Thomas Pinckney Jr. (1780–1842), in 1801. Water color on ivory miniature by Edward Green Malbone (1777–1850). *Courtesy of The Gibbes Museum of Art/Carolina Art Association.*

Captain Thomas Pinckney (1828–1915), ca. 1861. *Private Collection.*

The Reverend Charles Cotesworth Pinckney Jr. (1812–1898), ca. 1840.
Courtesy of the South Carolina Historical Society.

4

GENERAL PINCKNEY'S SWORD

AS MOST OF THE NATION anxiously awaited the result of the presidential election on November 6, 1860, Dr. Thomas Pinckney spent the day packing boxes and helping his elderly parents close up their mountain home at Flat Rock for the winter. Naturally, the election attracted their interest, but the four-way contest seemed strangely remote, as if it were happening in a different country.[1] This disconnection stemmed in part from the fact that South Carolina remained the only state retaining the eighteenth-century practice of having its legislature select presidential electors as well as that the Pinckney family was no longer a force even in state politics. In 1828, the year of Tom's birth, two South Carolinians—Andrew Jackson and John C. Calhoun—successfully ran on the Democrat ticket for president and vice president. The Pinckney family knew these men personally and felt powerfully invested in the outcome of their race against incumbent John Quincy Adams, whose father had succeeded President George Washington in 1796, a position that General Thomas Pinckney had been widely expected to win.[2]

By 1860 the center of political power had shifted to states west of the Appalachian Mountains. Now two candidates ran from the state of Illinois: Senator Stephen A. Douglas, nominated by the northern wing of the Democrat Party, ran a national campaign, whereas Abraham Lincoln, standard-bearer of the newly formed Republican Party, did not appear on the ballot of any southern state. South Carolina's electoral ballots, Tom Pinckney knew, would surely go to the candidate of the southern Democrats, John C. Breckinridge, the sitting vice president from Kentucky. A fourth candidate, Tennessean John Bell, carried the banner for the anti-secession Constitutional Union Party.

The Pinckneys learned the shocking news of Lincoln's election on their journey home. The winning candidate had evaded direct questions about slavery and promised to maintain the status quo, but the slogan of his new party, which incorporated antislavery and abolitionist enthusiasts, was "Free Soil, Free Labor, Free Men." At each stop on their winding way home—by wagon, stage, and train—the Pinckneys grabbed every newspaper they could find. Anxiously they traded them back and forth until the whole family became "able politicians," shaken, according to Tom's sister Mary Elliott, out of their former "dross of indifference." No headline, of course, arrested the attention of the family more than that emblazoned across William Barnwell Rhett's *Charleston Mercury* on November 8: "The tea has been thrown overboard, the revolution of 1860 has been initiated." That a president could be elected without one southern vote validated the warnings of the firebrands urging disunion. Learning that "secession" had already emerged as the "watchword" in the state capital, the Pinckneys too "took fire" and were swept up in the excited frenzy by the time they reached the Santee.[3]

In December 1860 Charleston seemed an unlikely little city to start a big war. Before the American Revolution, the Carolina lowcountry enjoyed the greatest wealth of all the colonies of British North America. Once the thriving crossroads of the Atlantic, electrified by the friction of new ideas bumping into old, the "Queen City of the South" had nearly a century later come more closely to resemble a staid dowager, decorated with a few gaudy baubles from the recent cotton boom, rather than young Athena. Now a little hard of hearing, the genteel old lady preferred the quiet unexamined life, isolated from the political and intellectual mainstream, content to doze on a piazza while other American ports (even languid New Orleans) buzzed with purpose.[4]

Like Charles Dickens's jilted bride, Miss Havisham—introduced to Americans in an 1860 serialization of *Great Expectations*—Charleston seemed to have withdrawn from the world, still dressed in her bridal finery and closed up in her ruined mansion, stopping all the clocks at the moment of her disappointment. Once holding her haughty head high with Boston, New York, and Philadelphia as her nearest competitors, Charleston never regained her footing after the 1828 decline, plummeting from an 1830 ranking of sixth in population among US cities to land with a humiliating thud at twenty-second place in 1860. Concomitantly, the number of South Carolina's delegates in the US House of Representatives dropped ominously during these years from nine to four (none from Charleston), making Washington seem a more distant and hostile place. The time when Charleston could stamp her pretty foot and declare that the Senate would not discuss slavery, making silence fall within the hallowed hall, had long passed.[5]

Time also had its way in the planter districts outside of the city. The Pinckneys' plantation, Eldorado, once a seat of the aspiring American nobility where Greek scholar General Thomas Pinckney welcomed the great and the good, had by 1860 moldered down to the status of a "sweet old place" in need of a new roof.

The Pinckneys too had mellowed a bit into a life of comfort rather than style, eliciting fond admiration as a fine old country family rather than one brimming with brilliant promise as in generations past. Tom's parents had both reached their allotted three score and ten. His mother, Caroline, was as ever "affectionate, trusting and unsophisticated." His father, Cotesworth Sr., continued grave and pious. Since renouncing politics in 1834, only rural pursuits and the Society for the Promotion of Religion in South Carolina had occupied his interest.[6]

In 1860 Cotesworth Pinckney Sr.'s holdings at Eldorado consisted of 338 acres of high-quality rice land and 1,250 "inferior acres" worked by about eighty-five slaves. As executor of Colonel Thomas Pinckney's conflicted estate, he also had responsibility for ninety-six enslaved people, although his brother's widow, Elizabeth, still lived on the property, and their disputes still continued. Tom helped his father with the plantation as well as with the Santee lands that had belonged to Cotesworth's sister, the long-widowed Elizabeth Pinckney Lowndes, who had died in 1857.[7]

With the news of South Carolina's secession on December 20, Cotesworth Sr. rejoiced that God had indeed heard his fervent prayer. Once again enjoying moral clarity, the old passion returned with the resurrection and (in his mind) vindication of the nullification movement, the "spirit of '32." Abandoning his earlier caveat, he proclaimed, "all men are divided at this time into three parts, 'body, soul and politics.'" "Delighted with the state of affairs," the elder Pinckney comforted his daughters and grandchildren, who worried that secession might mean war. He waved away such fears. No shots would be fired, he assured them, because of the "self-evident" constitutional right of secession: "We are to be the most glorious people and prosperous country." South Carolina's revolution would enjoy God's grace as had the American Revolution. Throughout the month of January 1861, the Pinckney household at Eldorado got into the spirit by reading Washington Irving's *Life of Washington* out loud in the evenings.[8]

Unwilling to challenge his father, Tom Pinckney nevertheless believed him wrong. Secession meant war. He sided with his brilliant uncle, William Elliott III of Beaufort, who also saw disaster, not rainbows, at the end of the secession frenzy. Cotesworth Pinckney had always viewed the world in terms of sin and salvation, black and white, while Elliott perceived its shadows and shadings, from time to time playing the role of Greek chorus when "Sister" Pinckney's husband veered too far off course. Elliott, who had been Pinckney's roommate at Harvard, agreed that the southern states had the Constitution and justice on their side, but he also understood that the underdeveloped southern economy lacked the financial institutions and industrial capacity to sustain an armed conflict against the northern states. And too, as a practical matter, his properties—eight plantations in all—and those of the Pinckney family were mostly scattered along the coast and extremely vulnerable to attack.[9]

Fully aware for years of the darkening clouds of sectional discord, the ever-optimistic Tom had always believed that somehow another rabbit could be pulled out of the hat of congressional compromises—he still did. Had secession come a couple of years earlier, he might have welcomed a break in the monotony of a medical practice that chiefly consisted of pacing the pavement of the notoriously unhealthy city in his tight boots, going from a house with measles to a house with whooping cough. In the last years yellow fever had been showing up much too often. Only the "éclat" of the winter social season, with its horseraces and balls, broke the monotony of his humdrum bachelor's life. Those special occasions were, he complained, "like angel's visits, few and far between." In 1858 Tom withdrew from society altogether to mourn his sister, Maria Henrietta, who had died while accompanying their father and Mary Elliott on a trip to Paris.[10]

By 1860 thirty-two-year-old Tom still had not taken a bride despite his family's pressure to produce another heir. Warnings against young flirts chasing him for his money made him wary. Pressure to take a wife "within the family," or at least within the narrowing confines of his class, also limited his options. He placed his hopes on regular visits to the White Sulphur Springs resort in Virginia, patronized as much for its reputation as a marriage mart for children of the national elite as for its healing waters. But an alliance on the perfidious side of the Mason-Dixon line with an old Boston or even Philadelphia family now could not be considered. A bride from one of the founding families of Virginia, though, might be just the thing. Even a very wealthy wife from a newer family might do.[11]

In January Tom had believed that he was at last poised on the cusp of his youthful dreams of becoming a rice planter. His apprenticeship, under his father's critical eye, had lasted longer than his medical studies. The successful cultivation of rice—being able to "read" the soil and the tender plants and knowing when to flood the fields and how long to let them dry—was exacting, as much art as science. Mistakes were costly. His parents deeded over to him Eschaw Grove Plantation, 245 acres of pineland once belonging to his grandfather about twenty-two miles up the meandering South Santee River from Eldorado. This acquisition, coupled with his interest in Fannymeade Plantation on Minim Island in the North Santee, made him now feel a man of parts and of standing within the family and planter community. He went heavily into debt buying slaves to work his own land.[12]

Now with secession, his excited father urged Tom to toss aside his plough-shares—figuratively, of course—and pick up one of his grandfather's swords. The general had bequeathed a sword to each of his sons with the strict command that it should "never be drawn in a private quarrel and never remain in their scabbards, when their country demanded their service."[13]

As Tom Pinckney tested the heft of this curved-blade relic from another conflict—one fought in defense of the nascent American republic—he contemplated the general's words and felt the weight of history. Since secession, did he have a "country" any longer? Endorsing an abstract constitutional right such a state's right to withdraw from the Union was one thing, bearing arms against the United States quite another. Tom, of course, considered himself a patriot, but at the end of December 1860, he had no country to love. The new "Independent Sovereignty," as he called the Republic of South Carolina, did not even have an official flag; the proposed Confederacy was yet unborn. According to reports, Mississippi and Alabama would soon secede and ally with the Palmetto State. But what about a state such as Virginia, where he had attended college and for which he had great affection? As aristocratic as South Carolina and equally devoted to states' rights, the Old Dominion still remained with the Union.[14]

The premise asserted by South Carolina's secession that the United States was no more than the sum of its parts caused the question "What is our country?" to be debated on every street corner North and South. A *Harper's Weekly* article published the week of Lincoln's inauguration identified the central dilemma for Tom Pinckney, whose sense of himself was so deeply connected to his grandfather's contributions to the founding of the American republic: "How much country must a man love to be a genuine patriot?" The nation stood divided over two points of view: "One says you must love the whole country under the nation's flag. The other—it is enough to love your own state." Following that logic, the article concluded, "one person might say loving one's own county is sufficient, another, his own town, and still another, the farm of his birth."[15]

Tom Pinckney's heart, in truth, belonged to Eldorado, Fairfield, and the surging South Santee River—the land he loved. Yet he also understood his life as little more than another chapter in the continuing saga of the Pinckney family. Now that narrative was about to take a dramatic turn. Nothing convinced him of that fact more poignantly than the dissonant sight of his enslaved men digging rifle pits on the willow-draped river-facing lawns of Eldorado, his grand-

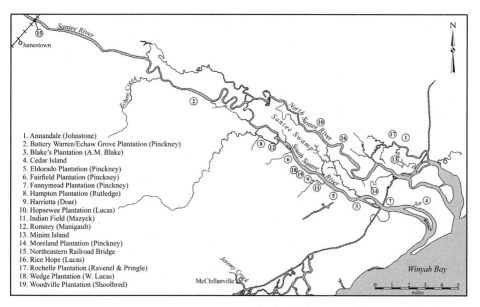

1. Annandale (Johnstone)
2. Battery Warren/Echaw Grove Plantation (Pinckney)
3. Blake's Plantation (A.M. Blake)
4. Cedar Island
5. Eldorado Plantation (Pinckney)
6. Fairfield Plantation (Pinckney)
7. Fannymead Plantation (Pinckney)
8. Hampton Plantation (Rutledge)
9. Harrietta (Doar)
10. Hopsewee Plantation (Lucas)
11. Indian Field (Mazyck)
12. Romney (Manigault)
13. Minim Island
14. Moreland Plantation (Pinckney)
15. Northeastern Railroad Bridge
16. Rice Hope (Lucas)
17. Rochelle Plantation (Ravenel & Pringle)
18. Wedge Plantation (W. Lucas)
19. Woodville Plantation (Shoolbred)

Santee River Delta in 1860: Pinckney Family Properties
and Selected Other Rice Plantations

father's monument to civilization and grace. This defensive work was done at the request of Governor Francis Pickens. Not long afterward, Pinckney allowed the state to build a battery on a point of Eschaw Grove, a critical part of the defense of the nearby and strategically important railroad bridge across the Santee.[16]

As a physician Pinckney had been exempted from any militia service, but with his family connections he could have his pick of any lowcountry, high-society volunteer formation, with their gold braids, polished boots, and white gloves. All was silence among his family when he announced his plans to enlist as a private in a new Georgetown County cavalry company, specifically raised for coastal defense and headed by Captain Arthur M. Manigault, a planter and commission merchant who had been an officer in the Palmetto Regiment during the Mexican War. The unit assembled in a muster field sixteen miles and two river crossings away. His niece Carrie Pinckney spoke for them all with her loud complaint, "I do not at all like the idea of Thomas Pinckney being a private."[17]

After attending a meeting of the parishes of Saint Stephen's, Christ Church, and Saint James Santee later that month to organize their own defense, he became excited about the possibility of raising his own independent cavalry to protect more particularly the land he loved. Becoming "completely engrossed in military affairs," Tom began recruiting friends and neighbors for a unit that would become variously known as the Santee Mounted Rifles, Saint James Mounted Rifles, and (after his unanimous election as its captain) Pinckney's Company of Independent Riflemen.[18]

His new venture with the home guard met with tut-tutting around the home fires. Mary Elliott Pinckney doubted whether Tom's captaincy satisfied "Mamma's ambitions." It did not. Caroline was every bit as ambitious as her husband to revive the glory of the Pinckney name. In an ideal world she might have dreamed Tom would form the "Pinckney Legion" along the lines of a similar unit organized in 1861 by Columbian Wade Hampton, which had the grand if unworkable plan of bringing artillery, infantry, and cavalry together under one command. Pinckney turned down an invitation to join those audacious men who correctly predicted that Hampton's Legion would be an incubator of generals and future politicians. Theirs was not to be a defensive force, its members boasted, but a killing machine whose "steps are to be turned northward" when the anticipated fighting in Virginia commenced. When casualty reports arrived in June 1861 from Bull Run, Virginia, site of the first major battle of the war, showing that only 160 of the 627 men who galloped into the fray behind Hampton were still standing—the colonel himself survived a blast of Yankee shot to the face—Pinckney felt convinced that he had made the right decision, despite the continued barbs from the women in his family. His uncle, William Elliott, despondent over the war, instructed his sons to join one of the home guards.[19]

Eighteen-year-old Cotesworth Pinckney Seabrook, son of Tom's sister Caroline, emerged as the family hero. Widely admired for his intelligence, manly tenderness, and Christian virtue, "Pinck" immediately left his studies at the University of Virginia and rushed home upon learning of South Carolina's bold gambit. He enlisted right away as a private in the elite Washington Light Infantry, a perfect fit for the peerless young man. One of the oldest militias in the nation, the "WLI" was named in honor of the first American president, whose own "peerless character" his confidante General Thomas Pinckney was also said to share. The association was made to order, like the young man's fine blue-gray uniform.[20]

After the Rev. Cotesworth Pinckney's twenty-one-year-old son "Charley" heard of South Carolina's secession and the rumors of war while studying in Bonn, the father did all he could to discourage the young man from coming home. He came anyway.[21]

Caroline did approve of the officer slate Tom chose for his mounted rifles, for he recruited close kin among the Cordes, Alston, and Mazyck families. Although one was a doctor and another a teacher, all had substantial holdings along the Santee. Some even had a smattering of militia training, but Pinckney candidly admitted that his officers were still basically "civilians with little knowledge or experience in military matters."[22]

Although later historians would be perplexed, Pinckney was not at all surprised when volunteers, some who owned no slaves and others no property, emerged from the piney woods or off the river to enlist at his cavalry muster. All manner of men—young, old, backwoodsmen, stockmen, fishermen, overseers, turpentine gatherers, and yeomen farmers, some with their cousins, brothers, or neighbors—mostly from around Saint James Santee District rode in on their farm horses or mules with shotguns or even flintlocks across their ersatz saddles; the inevitable "Yankee marauders" were their enemies too.

The Pinckneys and other plantation families of the Saint James Santee District had never forgotten that the black-to-white ratio of their population was about ten to one, the same as Saint Domingue at the outbreak of the bloody revolution in 1791, and had quite consciously cultivated whites of all ranks as a matter of security and good politics once the franchise was expanded. Northern or European visitors to the great homes along the rivers often expressed surprise that overseers attended the local chapel with the planters, their homespun brushing up against silk, all united under the liturgy of the Episcopal Church.[23]

The state militia law demanding service by all white men had also reinforced personal relationships between the classes. At the regularly scheduled musters, planters, wearing their father's or grandfather's old moth-eaten officers' uniforms and ill-fitting plumed hats, seldom pressed the privates to do more drilling than they cared to. With that business wrapped up, they spent the rest of the day together engaged in horseraces, drinking, and general merriment. At election time candidates for the state house of representatives (the only branch elected by popular vote) competed for votes with barbeques and spirited punches. Politics on the Santee were always local. Tom Pinckney believed that the long tradition of inclusion reassured the volunteers of 1860 that the planter community would continue to look after the needs of their families when they went off fighting to protect the land they all loved.[24]

Despite all the election-year rhetoric about the great democracy of white men, at the muster of Captain Pinckney's independent company, the truth of the vast gaps between the white classes was evident. Overcoming his unpromising start at birth with plentiful healthy food and the ability to escape the worst of the swamp fevers, Pinckney grew to be over six feet tall, strong and straight like an oak. Many of his less-privileged recruits, however, suffered from deficient diets and their lifelong exposure to the unabated heat and toxic miasmas, growing to be young men as spindly as pine saplings, pockmarked, bow legged, and sunken cheeked. Pinckney's younger sister, Mary Elliott—seldom diplomatic in her observations—reiterated her disappointment in his choice of service with her observation that she did not really relish having these "fever-shaken, mosquito-bitten wretches" as compatriots in this new republic, tactlessly expressing her doubt that they could defeat more-fit northern soldiers "from better climes."[25]

Tom's family misunderstood him. Knowing that he could never be like his grandfather, he imagined himself more like Francis Marion, the Swamp Fox. And looking at his rough-hewn men, he did not see the bottom of the gene pool, as had his sister, but the grandsons of Marion's storied "irregulars," who during the American Revolution had galloped through the same woods and lowlands of the Santee to win independence. Though poor in worldly goods, many of these new defenders of South Carolina had the blood of old Hugue-not families flowing through their veins. They gave Pinckney respect, though not obeisance. He came to love them for a certain innocence, or even nobility, common to men who lived so close to the earth. Despite later receiving offers of promotion and service in more-prestigious units as the war went on, Pinckney kept his vow to stay with his "troopers," and they (mostly) stuck with him. In those first months after secession, when the viability of South Carolina as an independent nation was in question—inspiring James Louis Petigru's memora-ble 1860 quip about being "too small for a republic and too large for an insane asylum"—Pinckney came to look upon his men and his company as his country, and he gave them a patriot's devotion.[26]

During the secession winter of 1860, that exciting four-month interlude between South Carolina's withdrawal from the Union and the firing on Fort Sumter, war remained strictly theoretical and thus almost enjoyable. After five other states of the Lower South also declared their independence and made common cause with the Palmetto State, a festive, almost euphoric, air enveloped Charleston. Its streets looked like Paris during the palmy days of the French Revolution, with citizens all wearing their politics on their sleeves or collars or hats as red patent-leather stars, blue cockades, and palmetto rosettes became all the rage. Mary Elliott stitched little palmettos onto the shirts of the family's soldiers and made them knapsacks. Tom's father enjoyed himself thoroughly, having "attained the desire of his heart." He built a fortification at their summer home on Cedar Island at the mouth of the Santee and bought a seven-shot revolver.[27]

When Tom went to Charleston in January to get kitted out in his new uniform and pick up supplies for his men, he paid a call at the Pinckney mansion on East Bay Street, where George Washington had once visited. In "high spirits" he presented himself to his cousin, the family matriarch Harriott Pinckney, for her approval. Frail at age eighty-five and venerated by the community as "the last of the old world Pinckneys," she was nevertheless steeled with the outraged militancy of Joan of Arc. Having with her sister, Maria, been among the staunchest supporters of nullification in 1832, she had been waiting for this assertion of states' rights for nearly thirty years.[28]

Few examples illustrate the unreality of the time, and failure to recognize the profound meaning of secession, than the most popular parlor game of that season—contriving a new flag for the Confederate nation. In February 1861 the newly minted Captain Pinckney joined a tea party hosted by the children of banker and lawyer Christopher G. Memminger in their spacious Beaufain Street home. Memminger, full of high spirits after his recent appointment as the Confederacy's secretary of the Treasury, challenged the group to come up with a replacement for the "Bonnie Blue Flag," now that a single star would no longer do. He promised to present their idea to the Confederate Congress, which was assembling in the capital of Montgomery, Alabama.[29]

Captain Pinckney's idea won. He suggested a blue field emblazoned with the Southern Cross, a constellation in the southern sky that guides storm-tossed sailors to safety in much the same way that Polaris, or the North Star, is a fixed point for north-bound travelers. He remembered that Congressman Robert Winthrop of Massachusetts had used this metaphor in his 1850 funeral oration to describe Calhoun's role as a beacon for the South.[30]

One of the most thoughtful among southern skeptics, William Elliott confessed that what kept him up at night was "the incompetency of the men—now having our fortunes and lives in their keeping." Pinckney, in fact, worried that he and his fellow officers were not military leaders yet worthy of their men and their potential sacrifice. He began taking lessons in the art of war. Henry W. Moran, an Irishman who had served in an English regiment of light dragoons before coming to Charleston, offered daily classes in saber combat at the city market. He attempted to teach real-world lessons of swordsmanship, but most of his students grew impatient with his emphasis on the protective "guard" and wanted instead to perfect their thrust and slash.[31]

The image of the long-limbed Pinckney earnestly trying to master classical European maneuvers with an eighteenth-century broadsword—wielding and slashing with the right hand while keeping the left hand stationary as if holding the reins of a charger—provides a poignant vignette of how poorly prepared the Confederacy was for the war ahead. American cavalrymen generally favored the short, straight-bladed sword popular with the British in India during the 1857 Sepoy Rebellion. Even though his instructor and the other men viewed Pinckney's inherited sword as a curiosity, the inexperienced captain clung to it as if it were Excalibur alive with the magic of the past.[32]

Pinckney eventually had to admit that organizing and imposing military discipline upon untrained volunteers was beyond his abilities. An equally inexperienced friend, Christopher Gaillard, who captained the independent Santee Light Artillery, joined with Pinckney to petition Governor Pickens in September 1861 to place their companies and others that might be raised in their district under the command of Major Edward Manigault, a veteran of the Mexican War. After a great deal of lobbying, their request was granted.[33]

Major Manigault's irregular regiment mustered at McClellanville, the closest approximation of an urban center in the parish, though really just a planter's summer colony with about a dozen houses. Strategically located on Jeremy Creek about seven miles from the South Santee River, McClellanville offered the advantage of a relatively healthy environment and easy access to the inland waterway for those with knowledge of the intricate web of inlets and sandbars. Incorporated into the camp was a lot that Pinckney had bought in 1860 with the idea of building a bachelor's retreat. Instead of lounging in a hammock and enjoying the ocean breeze as he had then imagined, his time was consumed with the mundane duties of his rank, ordering subsistence stores of bacon, coffee, sugar, candles, hard bread, reins for mule, halters for horses, and salt licks.[34]

Manigault proved a stern taskmaster. When he took charge, he put a stop to the enlisted men's casual movement in and out of camp at their convenience. He subjected all ranks to the discipline necessary to transform rank civilians into soldiers. When the men were allowed to elect their commanders and officers under the Conscription Act of April 1862, they replaced Manigault, much to Pinckney's displeasure, with the "easy-going, inefficient" Major Stephen Decatur Miller Byrd, a surgeon and state legislator from the Williamsburg District.[35]

As predicted, Federal warships ominously appeared off the coast by the end of May 1861, lurking in the deep water as part of President Lincoln's naval blockade of the South's key ports and charged with keeping supplies from coming in and cotton and rice from going out. If the conflict was not soon resolved, the navy would have to invade the state to establish a coaling station. The Federals intermittently swarmed the beaches and inlets in small boats, testing the vulnerabilities around Bull's Bay and making Pinckney's job of patrolling the area nearly impossible. Whenever the weather and tides were advantageous, raiding parties landed at vulnerable sites and deserted houses, looting and burning at will. By the time Confederate pickets could relay a message to Pinckney in McClellanville and a patrol arrive at the site of the incursion, all that remained were boot prints around smoldering ruins of a cotton gin inland or a salt works on the shore.

The slaves somehow always knew when the Federals were approaching. Many appeared on the beach, offering to serve as guides, and left with them on the next tide. Despite Pinckney's warnings that the Yankees were not saviors but "negro stealers" planning to sell the runaways in Cuba, had he not ordered all small boats pulled out of the water and guarded, he knew the slaves would have stolen them and rowed out to the fleet at night.[36]

Pinckney was partially right. The Federals' mission was not to liberate slaves, but to destroy the Northeastern Railroad bridge that crossed the upper reaches of the Santee not far from Pinckney's Eschaw Grove property; the Confederates' primary job was to protect it. Built in 1840, the railroad replaced the old Santee Canal that had linked the port of Charleston with the cotton fields of the up-country. Not only did the railroad provide communications between Savannah, Charleston, and Richmond, but it also could transport lowcountry rice to the ever-hungry Confederate soldiers at the front.[37]

Notorious blockade-runners also used the railroad bridge as a dropping off spot. The daring seamen offloaded Bahamas-bound cotton from train cars onto shallow-draught vessels that on dark, cloud-shrouded nights could slip out via Alligator Creek, gain Bull's Bay, then shoot pass the Federal blockade into the Atlantic. If successful, these missions reaped fortunes for their investors. Once Pinckney provided armed protection to one of these heavily burdened ships after it grounded on an oyster bank until the tide rose and released it to the open sea.[38]

Battery Warren, an earthen fortification completed in 1862 on Eschaw Grove Plantation, provided the last line of defense for the railroad bridge. The Confederates' secret weapon, though, was the Santee, that twisting turning snake of yellow water mined by nature with sandbars and shoals that would never let Federal gunboats pass.[39]

On November 7, the months of waiting for the Federal invasion ended. Captain Samuel F. Du Pont directed the largest naval force ever assembled to that time against Port Royal, meeting only perfunctory resistance. The enemy now had a base of operations in Beaufort District, where the Pinckney and Elliott families also had extensive holdings. Most fled in advance of the attack and were despondent after General Robert E. Lee, then commander of the Department of South Carolina, Georgia, and Florida, later inspected the area. He concluded that, given the numbers of Federal troops and extent of their naval resources, the Confederates had no hope of reclaiming the port and the adjacent sea islands. The blockade of the coast, Lee predicted, was going to be a harsh fact of life for the Confederacy.[40]

The invaders also swept up 2,000-acre Pinckney Island in their net. Owned in 1861 by General Cotesworth Pinckney's surviving daughter, Harriott, and slated to go to Tom's father upon her death, the island had been abandoned hastily by its white overseers after hearing of the Federal flotilla's arrival; they left more than 200 slaves entirely on their own. Almost immediately the workers organized themselves into a community and divided up tasks. In January 1862 diarist Mary Boykin Chesnut spread a rumor that on Pinckney Island "the negroes had been reinforced by outlaws and runaways" who had been "laying supplies, getting in provisions, electing a king &c &c."[41]

CHRISTMAS EVE 1861 found Captain Pinckney shivering, lonely and despondent, at the McClellanville encampment when he suddenly heard singing in the distance. Lifting the tent flap, he saw a long torchlight procession of carolers snaking around the camp, spreading what joy could be mustered in time of war. When they stopped to serenade him, Pinckney recognized the soldiers of Captain John A. Wagner's German artillery. He had been deeply impressed with the intelligence and efficiency of these men, who could turn their hand to any task, whether milling rice or making halters and girths for their artillery horses from the ratline removed from abandoned ships. On Christmas Day the Germans invited the Santee River troopers to their "jollification" of music and skits. As a special treat, two former circus clowns performed their old routines.

Few of Pinckney's men had ever seen a circus. They stared in amazement at the antics of the clowns in their ersatz costumes, especially a soldier dressed as a woman. When the jokes would finally "strike in," Pinckney recalled that the men "would turn round and almost split their sides with laughter."[42]

From his encampment Pinckney was still able to help oversee the family's various properties.[43] His responsibilities increased in February 1862, when his father, understanding that the army planned to shift manpower southward in anticipation of a Union attack upon Charleston or Savannah, began the process of relocating his family and the core of his workforce to the interior. Having waited too long, given the massive exodus from the coastal areas, all they could find was a dilapidated six-room house on a worn-out farm at Cokesbury, a stronghold of Methodism about a mile from Hodges Depot in Abbeville District, that cost a princely $9,000 in Confederate currency. By March he had orchestrated a departure from the halls of Eldorado that took on the dimensions of a major military movement and would cost an additional $10,000. Finally, a team of workers packed and shipped the contents of their barns to Cokesbury to feed about a hundred slaves from Santee and another hundred from Rest Park Plantation on Hilton Head during the winter months.[44]

By keeping the slave families together for the trip inland, the Pinckneys (unlike many of their neighbors) encountered no serious resistance to their plans to leave the Santee. The great gloomy unknown looming over them was when they could return to Eldorado and what they would find when they did. "Maum" Clarissa stayed behind as chatelaine, with the plantation house and barn keys entrusted to her care. Her father had served as General Thomas Pinckney's body servant during the War of 1812 and as his plantation manager in peacetime. Her son, James Broughton, the youngest of three children, took on his grandfather's position for the young captain at McClellanville. Crippled by a childhood gunshot wound and unfit for military service, Augustus Shoolbred, from neighboring Woodburn Plantation and close friend of Tom's since youth, promised to oversee the day-to-day operation of the Pinckney properties.[45]

Reports of slaves fleeing the Santee plantations in great numbers as soon as their masters and mistresses left for safety poked a hole in the planters' "equanimity" that all would remain as they left it. "Times and slaves have changed since the revolution," Mary Elliott Johnstone warned her family; "we must not be surprised at losing everything." In mid-December 1861 she sent word to her mother at Oak Lawn Plantation not to trust her servants to bury her valuables (as would have been her inclination) because "the darkies all think this is a crisis in their lives that must be taken advantage of, and would tell the Yankees anything they wanted to know for $10."[46]

At the end of June 1862, Pinckney's pickets reported five Federal vessels steaming up the South Santee. He dashed with his squadron and some artillery to the river, thinking to fire upon them from the bluff at Fairfield Plantation, but the steamers carried too deep a draft and the next afternoon went aground across from the rice fields of Eldorado. Seeing his chance, Pinckney called upon Captain Gaillard at Battery Warren to bring his rifled gun, sent word to Major Byrd that he needed infantry and the 32-pound guns from the base camp, and set the slaves at the unprotected Blake plantation to constructing earthworks from which the guns might blast the Federals like sitting ducks as they retreated out of the channel. Byrd arrived with infantry but did not order them to engage the enemy. To Pinckney's intense fury, the major refused to put his men at risk in defense of a private home and countermanded Pinckney's order for the construction of gun emplacements. Gaillard and his men arrived with their gun in a great flurry and managed to get off one successful round before the rising tide liberated the enemy vessels.[47]

That night a hundred Confederates bedded down "under the venerable roof of Eldorado" fully anticipating another visit from the invaders. The next morning Pinckney watched with a spyglass from atop a mill loft at nearby Indian Fields Plantation while the Yankees returned, guns blazing, shelling every building in sight. One round crushed a brick arch supporting the front steps of Eldorado. Seeing they were preparing to land at Arthur Blake's Washo Plantation, Pinckney and his men hurried to intercept them. They engaged some scouting parties, but the major force escaped, returning the next day under cover of a "vigorous cannonade." At Washo they burned down the main house, a threshing mill, and a barn with the year's crop of 55,000 bushels of rice, then stole away with five hundred of Blake's slaves. An elderly enslaved man the raiders had dangled from a tree in an unsuccessful attempt to scare out of him the secrets of the family's buried wealth opted to stay behind.[48]

All the slaves who had escaped to the invading army or had been seized during plantation raids were "corralled" on North Island, where the Federal fleet had their base of operations. Union authorities had not yet decided their status. Meanwhile, Confederate forces kept a keen eye out for opportunities to recapture them. Pinckney surveyed the area to see if the inlet separating the island from Debidue Beach might be crossed by cavalry. Consulting Captain

John H. Tucker, commanding an independent company that called themselves "Marion's Men of Winyah," he secured a guide who knew these waters well. They discovered that the inlet was ten feet deep in parts and that the Federals had a warship that could circumnavigate the island and intercept any attackers. Pinckney thought it just as well that no lives were lost "encumbering ourselves" with the runaways. Federal forces would soon realize the burden of being liberators.[49]

In the late summer of 1862, Pinckney obtained leave to see his family, who still continued their customary sojourns to the summer home at Flat Rock, where fourteen slaves—a family of three generations with five children—lived as a permanent staff. Caroline and Archibald Seabrook relocated to Piedmont after Rest Park Plantation was swept up in the Federal occupation of Hilton Head. One evening the Pinckneys gathered with their cousins, the Johnstones and the Means, for a "picturesque" outdoor service conducted by Tom's older brother, the Reverend Cotesworth Jr. A reading table draped with the Confederate flag served as an altar, where "the parson" read Scripture by candlelight. The congregants sang and prayed in the dark night, their still-hopeful faces illuminated by a bonfire. Among their prayers was that Great Britain would grant diplomatic recognition of the Confederacy.[50]

Prayers for victory later gave way to prayers for preservation when, in the winter of 1862, the dark angels of typhoid and diphtheria visited every household in the Pinckney family circle. Pneumonia, a common occurrence among the slaves who threshed rice in close spaces, also ravaged the quarters at Cokesbury, claiming a great many of the old and young unaccustomed to the colder climate of the upcountry. Caroline fretted over the slaves' lack of shoes, and "on those rare occasions" whenever she got a piece of cloth, her daughter Mary Elliott related, she wanted to have it cut out and stitched up into carpet slippers that same day "for the last ragged negro she saw." The food stores brought from the Santee had been nearly consumed by April 1863. With no fertilizer, the depleted soil of their refuge yielded only fifteen bushels during that year's harvest, forcing Cotesworth to draw down his cash reserves to feed his family and more than 200 slaves. His daughter, Caroline Seabrook, had added her brood to the household, fearing the lawlessness that swept over Flat Rock from plundering deserters. Trying to make ends meet, the Pinckneys experimented with setting up looms for the enslaved women to weave cloth and instructed the carpenters in making jabots, such as European peasants wore; all with little success. Failing in his attempts to raise cash by hiring the able-bodied men out to work on the railroads, the aged Cotesworth endured the agony of having to choose which thirty slaves he would sell at auction that the others might live.[51]

LATE IN 1862 the Confederate government reshuffled its command system and, in the interest of greater efficiency, ordered all independent companies—those created outside of the militia system—to be organized into regiments. In December Pinckney's Saint James Mounted Riflemen lost their independent identity when Byrd's 6th Battalion of Infantry was dissolved, and they became simply Company D of the thousand-man 4th South Carolina Cavalry, headed by Pinckney's cousin Benjamin Huger Rutledge. Formerly the captain of the Charleston Light Dragoons and having little battlefield experience, Colonel Rutledge had leapfrogged over senior officers who lacked his polish and connections. Among these were Major William P. Emanuel, a Jew of German extraction and Citadel graduate from Marlboro District who had been part of the defenses of Georgetown, and Lieutenant Colonel William Stokes of the 2nd Carolina Cavalry, formerly a Saint Bartholomew Parish farmer.[52] General P. G. T. Beauregard praised Rutledge as having "no superior as a volunteer cavalry officer," "volunteer," of course, being the key word. Whatever his deficiencies, Rutledge certainly looked the part of a colonel with his waxed moustache and aristocratic profile that mirrored the way lowcountry Confederates still imagined themselves. Beauregard also had recommended Pinckney for promotion to major, but the captain declined, opting to stay at the head of his company of Santee men, despite the pleasure his promotion would provide his mother.[53]

Rutledge's Regiment of Cavalry, as it was initially called before becoming the more mundane 4th South Carolina Cavalry, was made up of two battalions of four companies each and the two independents. This consolidation threw together men from all over the state. Pinckney met up with his old acquaintance from his schooldays in Pendleton, John C. Calhoun Jr., who served with the upstate men in Company C; both were now living out the consequences of their fathers' earlier political enthusiasms. Although merged into a new command structure, the original companies stayed intact, maintaining their unique identities and loyalty to the officers from their own county. The great diversity among the white men of the state became apparent. Pinckney's "backwoodsmen" suffered under the withering scorn of Rutledge's Charleston Light Dragoons, who looked down upon them as a "country company" mounted on draft animals chafed by homemade saddles.[54]

The regiment's first posting was at Pocotaligo, near Union-controlled Port Royal in Beaufort District. Rutledge's assignment was similar to Pinckney's on the Santee, defending the object of the Federals' desire: in this instance the Charleston and Savannah Railroad bridge over the Pocotaligo River, a depot, and the parallel telegraph lines that provided an indispensable link between the two port cities. Recognizing that nothing could be done to reverse the enemy occupation of Port Royal, General Lee had been absolutely adamant that his forces must not give up one inch of ground on the mainland or allow Federal vessels to gain entry to the rich plantation districts along the lazy tributaries flowing into Saint Helena Sound. The surrounding land was low and swampy like that around the Santee River and thick with cypress, tupelo, and gum trees, but the slow-moving black water of the Combahee River, its banks layered with impenetrable bushes and undergrowth, was more benign. Theoretically navigable for about forty miles into some of the state's richest rice lands, the Combahee could be treacherous for the inexperienced since logs frequently blocked the channel. The addition of Confederate torpedoes (that is, mines) compounded the hazard.

At Pocotaligo Pinckney felt confident in his new commander, Brigadier General W. H. T. Walker, known as "Live Oak" Walker for his gallant and creative defense of the railroad bridge in October 1862 against overwhelming numbers of determined Union soldiers.[55] With his headquarters, "Little Canaan," based on Huspar Creek, the captain and his company maintained a picket line from the Combahee River to Mackey's Point at the head of Port Royal Sound. The most critical part of their territory followed the Coosaw River, about thirteen miles long and a mile wide, which divided the mainland from the Federal stronghold on Beaufort Island. Although sometimes mocked because they held a defensive position close to their homes, Pinckney's men found that always being on the *qui vivre*, always knowing the enemy was close—at the Port Royal ferry videttes could hear the conversations of their Union counterparts nearby—was both mind numbing and exhausting, with none of the exciting bursts of adrenaline that lifted the tedium of those in active engagement. Federal pressure was as constant as the incessant buzz of mosquitoes and biting midges that tortured men and beasts in the swamplands. Forays of Union saboteurs, such as the unexpected trio of the telegrapher, the chaplain, and the escaped slave who tapped into Confederate communications, kept Pinckney's men and the camp's tracking dogs busy. Sickness also took a heavy toll. Every man was required to take four grams of quinine a day to ward off malaria.[56]

Pinckney's tenure at Pocotaligo had thus far provided him with few war stories with which to regale his family on home leaves. His only real coup was charming a pair of young northern women, who had crossed by ferry under a flag of truce, into revealing to him some information about troop movements on Beaufort Island. The sole remarkable event involving gunfire had been his prideful tale of shooting four squirrels in one day with his Colt Navy revolver when food supplies had run low.[57]

On June 2, 1863, however, the nature of the war changed in the middle of the night. Pinckney awoke to the sound of an alarm. Knowing what this meant—a Federal vessel had penetrated up the Combahee—he leapt into action. Alerted by a *New York Tribune* article claiming that black troops on the Carolina coast under Colonel James Montgomery would soon be part of an expedition "different in many respects from any heretofore projected," the 4th South Carolina had been put on "increased vigilance," with orders to meet any raid with "boldness and confidence," to "cut off the enemy's line of retreat, and to charge all foragers at a gallop."[58]

Pinckney dispatched a message to General Walker at Pocotaligo requesting instructions and in turn received orders to lead a battalion of cavalry and a battery of artillery at top speed to the south side of the river. Another officer took a force of equal size along the north side. The majority of Colonel Rutledge's regiment, however, was encamped sixteen miles away from the miasmic river in the healthier environment among the pine trees and sandy soil of McPhersonville, an old summer refuge.[59]

Once again Pinckney tried to do battle on horseback with a moving ironclad target, an eighteenth-century knight brandishing his sword at an industrial-age foe. At the time, Pinckney assumed the flotilla was headed for the railroad bridge but soon realized that Montgomery had another purpose. The boats made stops along the way, seemingly by appointment, where hundreds of slaves with bundles and babies, chickens and pigs, appeared when the boats drew near, clambering aboard with the help of soldiers. Those left behind put up quite a racket. Major Emanuel was awakened at his camp at Green Pond, a critical point on the axis running between Charleston and Savannah. Later blamed for insufficient familiarity with the local terrain, he did not reach the landing sites until the boats were steaming away, riding low in the water with their human (and animal) cargo. Infuriated by the sight and by his impotence to reach them with his single piece of field artillery, Emanuel used poor judgment and rashly pressed his men into the range of Union snipers.[60]

Embarrassed by the Combahee Raid, one Confederate officer accused the Federals of acting "more as fiends than human beings," in disregard of all rules of civilized war, and staging an action "designed only for plunder, robbery, and destruction of private property." The officers in Pinckney's regiment were unnerved to realize that the enemy clearly had spies who informed them of "the character and capacity of our troops" and the locations where they would encounter the least opposition. They must have had guides as well.[61]

Plantation owner William C. Heyward stated that his remaining servants told him that the raiding party, made up entirely of black soldiers with one white officer, came up his causeway and with seeming premeditation split off, one group ready to burn his house and the others to torch his mill. In their wake every building on the place was a pile of ash; only the slaves' quarters were spared.[62]

Pinckney surveyed the area and found that the Yankees had burned everything they had not been able to carry away, destroying four plantation houses and six rice mills. "Up and down the river" were the devastating scenes of "smoking ruins and naked chimneys" that Pinckney had feared he would one day behold along the Santee. Confederate officials laid the loss of slaves squarely at the doorsteps of the planters who, hoping to squeeze the maximum profits from their Combahee operations and unwilling to assume the expense of relocating, had ignored the many official warnings to remove their laborers to the interior.[63]

As soon as the captain learned all the facts of Colonel Montgomery's raid, he understood that the nature of the war had fundamentally changed. This had not been a "military raid," rather it was an "abolition raid," scooping up seven hundred to eight hundred slaves and employing the tactics of John Brown, once a comrade-in-arms of the colonel during the antislavery war in "Bloody Kansas." In this "mortifying" act Montgomery had "taken the war to Africa." In an article for the *Charleston Mercury,* "Finis," one of the victims of the raid, described watching from a hiding place in the woods as the black soldiers burned his house (and his classical library of 3,500 volumes inside), his mill, his barns—everything: reflecting on the "roaring of the flames, the barbarous howls of the negroes, the blowing of horns, the harsh steam whistle, and the towering columns of smoke, . . . here, I thought to myself, is a repetition of San Domingo."[64]

5

AGAINST WIND AND TIDE

IN EARLY APRIL 1863 Joseph Barquet was bound for glory on a crowded east-bound train. He was going to war. No longer a spurned patriot bowed by the unrequited love for his country, Barquet prepared to give his heart to a great cause—or rather, three great causes: restoration of the Union, killing off of slavery in the South, and striking a blow against racism in the North.

Since the firing on Fort Sumter in April 1861, Barquet had begun closely following the war news from Washington. By early 1862 he could detect some signs of stress beginning to appear on the edifice of opposition to black enlistment. The massive casualties from the early Confederate victories discouraged reenlistments among those Union troops with three-month contracts. Rumblings for a negotiated peace accelerated among President Lincoln's Democratic opponents. That Great Britain might officially recognize the Confederacy as a legitimate government emerged as a real possibility.

Seeking to diminish the advantage that slave labor afforded the Confederates in terms of performing heavy labor, digging ditches, and building fortifications, Congress passed the expedient Confiscation Act and the Militia Act on July 17, 1862. Together these laws allowed runaway slaves making their way to Union lines to be deemed "contraband of war" in some cases and used in similar supporting roles for Federal operations, rather than being returned to their masters per the previous policy. Rather than being considered soldiers, these "persons of African descent" would be employed by the army in noncombat roles. Despite much official resistance, these men were issued uniforms, but unlike other soldiers the clothing cost was deducted from their monthly pay, which was three dollars less than for a white private.

Barquet noted this with some interest but became quite excited in September 1862. In a carefully constructed proclamation, President Lincoln took the war to a different level by announcing that all slaves in areas still in a state of rebellion on January 1, 1863, would be "forever free." Knowing this would have no immediate effect on slavery in the South or even in "border states" such as

Kentucky aligned with the Union cause, he did find an obscure paragraph that black leaders seized upon as having revolutionary import. On that same date men "of African descent" would be eligible to enlist as soldiers in the Union army and navy. This was the chance Barquet had been waiting for. He agreed with Frederick Douglass that the full rights of citizenship could never be denied to a black man with "the eagle on his button and the musket on his shoulder."[1]

By March 1863, some of the best and the brightest of America's black abolitionists had begun recruiting for the Massachusetts Volunteer Infantry, the brainchild of the Bay State's governor, John A. Andrew. Andrew invited free black men from across the United States to join what he imagined would be "the most important corps to be organized during the whole war." Although three other black regiments, consisting mostly of former slaves, had already been raised in Union strongholds in Louisiana, South Carolina, and Kansas, the 54th would be the first regiment composed of free northern men.[2]

Barquet and his compatriots fell into a whirlwind of activity, beating the drum to attract recruits. In Chicago Martin Delany ran an enlistment office in John Jones's Dearborn Street dry-cleaning establishment and urged skeptics to seize this once-in-a-lifetime opportunity. Not entirely giving up his ideal of black nationalism, Delany had, perhaps under the influence of the Zouave craze, begun to imagine the creation of a separate division of black warriors modeled on the "corps d'Afrique," which fought for the French in Algeria.[3]

In Galesburg Barquet mustered all his considerable powers of persuasion to convince thirteen men from the tiny black population to join him in the great adventure of their lives. He repeated Governor Andrew's assurances that every black enlistee would enjoy respectful treatment from their white officers and receive the "same wages, the same rations, the same equipment, the same protection, the same treatment, and the same bounty, secured to the white soldiers." The promise that blacks would be eligible for some officer ranks particularly interested Barquet. For those men unmoved by the chance to walk in the footsteps of the world's great liberators, the enlistment bounty of fifty dollars and the promise of fourteen dollars a month was persuasive. William Tims, a barber, and Joseph H. White, a hostler, both signed on. Barquet just took the word of the nine young laborers—mostly in their twenties and newly arrived in Galesburg—that they were free and enlisted them too. The Union may have been an abstract concept without a great deal of meaning to these men, but the relationship between a rifle and freedom was clear; shooting at slaveholders without retribution was equally unambiguous.[4]

Barquet was the only married volunteer from Galesburg and the oldest by quite a bit. His wife, Maria, would have been a rare woman had she not questioned the wisdom of a forty-year-old father dashing off to war when she was expecting their fourth child. As his little children pulled at his pants leg to prevent him from leaving, Barquet surely must have considered all the different meanings of loyalty. How would his family cope without him? The Black Laws, which affected them directly, remained intact and unaffected by the ideals of the war. In fact, a month after Lincoln signed the Emancipation Proclamation, six Missouri contraband had been arrested by local officials in the western Illinois town of Carthage for not having posted the requisite security bonds and were sold at auction back into slavery.[5]

Barquet, nevertheless, got on the train, no doubt telling himself that what he did, he did for them. Joseph and Maria's conflicted leave-taking was repeated in train stations across the northern states as fourteen hundred black men from as near as Boston and as far as Michigan answered Governor Andrew's call; volunteers came from Canada and the southern states as well. Extra trains had to be added to the Boston and Providence line to accommodate the sudden popularity of Dedham Station, the nearest stop to Readville, where the 54th Regiment was based at Camp Meigs. New England men had filled its first companies in early February. By the time Barquet's Illinois contingent arrived around April 13, Company H was receiving recruits. Two more companies, I and J, would be incorporated into the regiment. Disappointed latecomers were directed to the second black regiment, the 55th Massachusetts.[6]

Forty-six-year-old New Yorker Sergeant Peter Vogelsang of Company H noticed Barquet and his friends as soon as they strutted into camp. The Galesburg contingent had rendezvoused in Chicago with about eighteen men from other Illinois towns and arrived together. Some among them wore flashy uniforms of short jackets, baggy pants, sashes, and oriental headgear modeled on those of the exotic French Zouaves in Algeria. Vogelsang remembered Barquet as one of the Zouave lieutenants. The other lieutenant was Joseph D. Wilson, a Chicago-area farmer who had been a member of Elmer Ellsworth's civilian militia of Zouaves that had captivated the Windy City and the entire Northeast with their precise and athletic system of drills based on West Point manuals. They had made soldiering look deceptively fun as, quickly and quietly as cats, they would fall to the ground, load their rifles, fire, turn over on their backs, reload, and fire again, then jump, run, and form human ladders.

The Zouave captain was Chicago housepainter John H. W. Collins, "a remarkably well-drilled and soldierly man" who may also have been part of Ells-worth's troupe or perhaps a member of a black independent militia unit that had been organized in Chicago. Collins had expected to become an officer and was furious when he learned that the policy had been changed; Secretary of War Edwin M. Stanton overrode the governor's declaration, claiming that while the country would struggle to accept blacks in uniform, it would absolutely reject having them placed in positions of authority over whites. Moved by "purely pa-triotic" motives, Collins accepted the highest rank possible of orderly (or first) sergeant of Company H; the rank of regimental sergeant major had already been given to Frederick Douglass's son, Lewis.[7]

At the same time Governor Andrew was turning down capable black men for leadership positions in the 54th, finding experienced white officers will-ing to risk their careers on the very uncertain and generally unpopular exper-iment of transforming black men into soldiers proved excruciatingly difficult. The Confederate government's warning that any white Union officer captured while leading black soldiers would be immediately hanged for fomenting slave insurrection—captured enlisted men would be sold as slaves—further damp-ened enthusiasm for this enterprise. Andrew's dual agenda of using the 54th as a vehicle both for showcasing the abilities of black men and for exhibiting the leadership talents of the white New Englander, further complicated recruitment efforts. In addition, he hoped to add an abolitionist to the pantheon of heroes emerging out of the Civil War. Naturally then, to this end he looked not to West Point, but to Harvard. His choice for regimental commander, Captain Robert Gould Shaw, was the fair-haired scion of a class that once led the nation and should, in the governor's opinion, lead it again. Not only had Shaw displayed military capability with the well-regarded 2nd Massachusetts Infantry, with his breeding and excellent personal character, the twenty-seven-year-old was "the very type and flower of the Anglo-Saxon race."[8]

When he reluctantly accepted the position with the 54th, Shaw rose mete-orically from a captain, with oversight of a hundred men—many his boyhood friends—to a colonel, with responsibility for a thousand black men. The 54th became known as a regiment where promotion came easily for officers with the right profile. Philadelphian Norwood Penrose Hallowell, the son of a wealthy Quaker merchant, served as lieutenant colonel and second in command. He and Shaw filled the officer corps with family and friends. Five had no prior military experience, while of those who had served in other units, only five had held commissions.[9]

At camp the officers and the new recruits viewed each other askance. Each wondered if the other could be trusted with his life. Lieutenant Cabot Jackson Russel, the newly recruited commander of Barquet's Company H, confided his doubt that black men could be soldiers to Colonel Thomas Wentworth Higginson, a family friend and militant abolitionist from Cambridge who had served as commander of the 1st South Carolina Volunteers, the first federally sanctioned black regiment. Deeply sympathetic to the cause of the slave (he was said to have slept beneath a picture of the martyred John Brown), young Russel feared that black men were too "awkward" and "dull of apprehension" to be effective military men. Higginson who believed "intensely human" the best description of the dusky soldiers, assured him, "it can be done."[10]

Private Barquet surely harbored doubts of his own about eighteen-year-old Lieutenant Russel. The fun-loving, underachieving cousin of the Cabots and the Lowells had failed out of Harvard during his first year and had been filling his time with travels in the West when news of Fort Sumter brought him home. Taking orders from an inexperienced teenager surely proved difficult for Barquet. The white officers could be overbearing in their interactions, always monitoring, hectoring, and correcting, yet in their hearts never expecting very much. Barquet was neither blind to their smirks nor deaf to their insults, but he knew the whole world was watching. Antiwar Copperheads and conservatives in the Democratic Party were poised, ready to capitalize upon any hints of insurrection, resistance to authority, display of bad morals, or poor performance that would prove what an irresponsible, quixotic experiment the Republicans had undertaken in trying to make soldiers out of black men.[11]

Russel found his recruits "tractable" and eager to master the art of soldiering, even if it meant drilling in the snow. Company H quickly learned the manual of arms "by imitation" and took pride in their growing precision and speed. Deaths among their comrades from the influenza epidemic that swept through the camp put "a terrible strain" upon the men, but through their dedication they made Lieutenant Russel look good. Before long the young man was wondering whether *he* was worthy of his men. With guidance from Colonel Shaw, Russel rose to the occasion and ultimately became a painstaking and effective drillmaster. After two months he was promoted to captain.[12]

On May 28, 1863, led by mounted police and a drum-and-fife corps, Barquet stepped smartly into history along with more than eight hundred black soldiers of the 54th Massachusetts united under their regimental colors. The city officers were alert; warnings had gone around that the "roughs of Boston" planned to attack the parade. Marching down State Street to the strains of martial music, eyes front, the soldiers moved through pockets of sounds: antislavery groups cheered wildly, Democrats hissed, Irish navvies booed. One onlooker quipped as the well-muscled black men passed, "there goes a million dollars." Black men and women of Boston, not wanting to attract too much unwanted attention to themselves in this highly charged crowd, stood proudly silent as they took in the almost sacred meaning of this long blue line of black men.[13]

All his life, it now seemed, Barquet had been preparing for this moment. That he did not even know where the awaiting ship would take him added to the existential poignancy. He had, as all soldiers must, relinquished his individualism and merged himself into this martial machine, this mass of men moving toward their mutual fate. The heroic stories from his school days and the republican rhetoric during his teenage years at South Carolina militia parades found full expression as he moved straight-backed into time, into a new era that merged with the past. He was a freedom fighter, a Christian crusader, an American conqueror, a Haitian liberator. He was neither a vengeful man of hate and with murder in his heart, nor a saboteur with a torch, but rather a man of courage, a man with a country, a flag, a uniform, a rifle, and a duty to do. He was the avenging angel of the Constitution, the sworn enemy of rebels, nullifiers, and secessionists. With every footfall, Barquet savored the Christian hope and Homeric glory of the work before him. With these good men and true, he would mend the great flaw in the Republic. The men of the 54th, his comrades in arms, had become his country. When Barquet caught his reflection in the shining panes of a shop window, he saw the man he had always wanted to be.

Upon reaching Boston Common, the 54th passed in review before a distinguished assembly including Governor Andrew, whose own dream was also coming true. After an hour of receiving congratulations from the town, the men of the 54th made straight for the Battery Wharf, already feeling rather heroic. With a soldier's faith, Barquet boarded the new troop transport *DeMolay* and headed into his future.

Had one plan been followed and the 54th been taken first to New York to parade up Broadway as an encouragement for the enlistment of black men in that city, Barquet might have had the pleasure of marching before his three brothers—Liston, Bissett, and Edod (who had arrived in 1858)—gathered proudly in Union Square. In the end, though, Colonel Shaw and his staff had considered it best to get the men right on their way while this jubilant spirit lasted. Drinking and desertion had already become a problem in the 54th as it had with all units.[14]

Once underway the *DeMolay* became a rollicking vessel of nervous antic-ipation. For the most part, the men huddled in groups singing and chatting, speculating where they might be headed; most guessed the Virginia front.[15] On June 3 though, Barquet found himself back on the waters off South Carolina, but this time saw a wall of fifteen Union blockaders lurking outside of Charleston Harbor with a stranglehold on the city's trade. Continuing southward through the night, the *DeMolay* arrived in Beaufort just before daybreak on June 5. Barquet was shaken from his torpor by a most remarkable sight. Piling out of the *John Adams* berthed nearby were more than seven hundred "genuine contraband" at the dawn, quite literally, of their freedom. The men of the 54th pressed alongside the rail to better see this mass of men and women, and their many children, still in their field suits of dirty gray, clinging to pigs or chickens snatched in haste. High-spirited black troops of the 2nd South Carolina Volun-teer Infantry (African Descent), most not so very long out of slavery themselves, shepherded them along and joyfully toted their own cache of "moveables" sim-ilarly "liberated" from plantation mansions afterward put to the torch. Barquet would later learn that he was witnessing the fruits of Colonel Montgomery's raid up the nearby Combahee River.[16]

Barquet spent his first night back on South Carolina soil under the open sky without a tent in an abandoned cotton field about a half mile inland. All night long he engaged in a relentless and losing battle against the mosquitoes, sand gnats, biting ants, and midges. At daylight he awoke to the landscape of his youth—green marsh alive with herons, ancient live oaks heavy with moss. Perhaps a bit of the lowcountry had stayed with him over the years. His Charles-ton teacher, the Reverend Daniel Payne once recalled that for many years af-ter moving to the northern states, the Carolina landscape would come back to him in his dreams: "sometimes I was sailing into it and sometimes I was flying out of it."[17]

The professional bearing of the 54th contrasted with the more relaxed atti-tudes of the "contrabands" of the 2nd South Carolina and attracted attention wherever they went during their short stay in Beaufort. An article in *The New South*, a weekly newspaper edited and published by the Federal occupation forces at Port Royal, commented that until the 54th came to town, the dirt streets of Beaufort had never been trod by "so many free born colored people" since the Indians camped there before "the ancestors of the chivalry founded it." From the first, the educated, squared-away free men marching under the Massa-chusetts flag felt embarrassed by the rather slapdash appearance and attitudes of the recently freed slaves put, perhaps precipitously, into the same uniform they wore. They also resented that the white officers from other units treated all men of color with the same disrespect.[18]

Knowing that the rebel stronghold guarding the rail line at Pocotaligo was just across the river, the 54th anticipated some serious soldiering on their second day in enemy territory. Instead they were once again handed shovels and sent to reinforce fortifications. In response to Colonel Shaw's request for more active engagement, on June 6 Montgomery ordered the 54th to board the *DeMolay* again bound for Saint Simons Island, Georgia, where they formed a brigade with Montgomery's 2nd South Carolina Infantry, men they had first seen returning home with plunder from the Combahee plantations.[19]

To men of the 54th, the Gullahs of the 2nd, with their thick undecipherable patois, were as exotic as Bedouin. The freeborn and the newly freed viewed one another warily. The men of the 2nd were very black, with no obvious traces of white blood, and intensely disliked "dom bloc Yanks," who returned the favor. The teaming of the two regiments proved a mistake and underscored the army's inability to understand the vast gulf dividing freemen of color and slaves, city men and field workers, volunteers and conscripts. Most of 2nd South Carolina were drafted from the hordes of slaves, who had made their way to freedom behind Union lines, resented being separated from their families, and pressed into hard labor. The distinctions between their colonels, however, were also dramatic. The refined, idealistic Shaw differed in every way imaginable from cynical James Montgomery, a wiry and wrinkled abolitionist who learned the art of guerilla war with John Brown in "Bloody Kansas" and thought the only way to end slavery was to burn down the plantations. Believing the freed slaves had no meaningful concept of a nation, Montgomery led erratically by carrots and sticks, rather than by appeals to patriotism. He motivated by alternately cajoling, promising freedom in one moment, and threatening, putting a gun to their heads in another.[20]

For their first outing, Montgomery took his improvised brigade to the ghost town of Darien, Georgia, once a thriving port now emptied of its white civilian population. In clear violation of protocol, he released the men to loot and plunder at will the homes, stores, and the church, before setting fire to the town, even though it was of no strategic use to the Confederates—except perhaps as a convenient spot for blockade runners. The first newspaper accounts about the activities of the 54th Massachusetts described this wanton destruction of the private homes and churches by the "cowardly thieves" of the regiment. Eyewitness reports in the *New York Times* described how the "accursed Yankee-negro vandals came up yesterday with three gunboats and two transports," rampaged with torch and turpentine, and left a "plain of ashes and blackened chimneys" with milk cows shot dead in the dirt streets. One report claimed that the soldiers shot a slave woman who refused to leave with them. Colonel Shaw later claimed scruple and horror at Montgomery's decision, but he apparently did not stop his own officers from furnishing their quarters with antiques hefted by their men from the parlors of civilians. Captain Russel of Company H would also denounce the raid as "some Kansas ideas about retribution which hardly belong to civilized warfare," but he sent his little sister "a pretty sampler" yanked off the wall of a southern child's room by one of his men and presented to the captain as a gift.[21]

Resentment proved more prevalent than swamp fever during the subsequent weeks of inactivity on remote Saint Simons Island and later on Saint Helena. Even the men of Company H, once so anxious to do their nation's bidding, succumbed to the malaise of boredom and skepticism about their mission. Broken promises about receiving equal pay eroded their trust in the white officers and thrust the ranks into a gloomy mood. Stymied by their screen of evasion and easy lies, Captain Russel could never "find the bottom" of the problems in camp, whether he asked harshly or softly. Pickets fell asleep on duty "just as if they did not care." Guards left their posts "if the notion to have some oysters struck them." Russel agonized over the necessity of busting a corporal for his second stealing conviction but could find no alternative to "punishing the whole time," though he knew it did no good. "If Colonel Shaw has two or three shot," the desperate young captain wrote his father, "it will do more to bring the men to their senses than anything else." At some point, though, camp dynamics began to improve, possibly through the intervention of Barquet and the black sergeants. Russel regained his equilibrium, and by the end of June the captain came to believe that he "had them fairly well in hand"—that was until payday came at the end of June.[22]

Secretary of War Stanton had once again overruled Governor Andrew by declaring that all men "of African descent" must receive the same wages. Colonel Shaw was furious. He understood that a fair day's pay for a fair day's labor was at the heart of a black man's understanding of liberty. In high Brahmin indignation, Shaw protested that he "would refuse to allow them to be paid," and if the War Department did not reconsider, he would demand that his men be mustered out of service.[23]

Murmurs about the pay issue nearly morphed into mutiny when, during the first days of July, a rumor swept through the 54th that the muskets issued them in Readville would be taken away and exchanged for pikes, the infamous weapons wielded by the enslaved followers of John Brown at Harpers Ferry. Captain John W. M. Appleton of Company A confirmed that the "authorities" planning the attack upon Charleston had proposed that as the first step, the "colored regiments armed only with pikes" should be transported to Morris Island, one of the first line of defenses for the harbor, and ordered to attack the Confederate positions at Batteries Wagner and Gregg "with no chance to retreat left to them." Colonel Shaw again protested that those who supported the idea of the pikes clearly had in mind "a means of annihilating the negro troops altogether."[24]

Around midday on July 8, however, an urgent order from Captain Russel wrenched Barquet from his lassitude. In one hour's time Company H must be prepared to leave camp with light packs of a day's rations, waterproofs, and bedrolls. They were to be included in a major land-and-sea action that was being planned against the city's formidable harbor defenses. During a late afternoon downpour, Barquet squeezed into one of two small steamers assigned to transport the 54th. At the last minute, and only because of Shaw's importuning, the regiment had been cast to play a minor walk-on role in an unfolding drama. About noon on July 9, Joseph Barquet crossed the bar back into Charleston Harbor for the first time in nearly twenty years. The transports dropped anchor off Union-controlled Folly Island, whose tip was nearly within shouting distance of narrow Morris Island, a critical position in the Federal offensive against Charleston.[25]

Early the next morning Brigadier General Quincy Adams Gillmore launched the first phase of his offensive against the city with an attack on Morris Island. Although an insubstantial-looking bar of shifting sand and marsh less than four miles long and no more than a thousand feet wide at any point, Morris Island was at the head of the shipping lane and desirable as the perfect location from which to attack Fort Sumter, the seemingly indestructible midchannel nemesis of the Union ironclads and lynchpin of Charleston's coastal defenses. The Confederates, of course, had endowed the island with heavy firepower at Battery Gregg, which stood vigil on Cummings Point (only three-quarters of a mile from Fort Sumter), and Wagner. This irregularly shaped fortification, a masterpiece of design extending approximately three hundred feet north to south and six hundred feet east to west, was actually several forts in one. About nine hundred men could withstand enemy shelling under the deep cover of its sand-topped bombproof shelter. Built of earth and the sinewy palmetto logs that gained a mythic reputation during the American Revolution for absorbing British cannon fire, Wagner (initially called a "battery" before the completion of its back wall) loomed large on the landscape of Morris Island and in the psyches of those Union generals in the Department of the South desperate for a victory—any victory.[26]

By the end of the day on July 10, Brigadier General George Strong had successfully captured about three-quarters of the island as instructed by Gillmore's orders, a remarkable achievement overshadowed by what was to come the next day. Yet the Confederates still controlled Batteries Gregg and Wagner despite relentless and damaging Union artillery fire. But rather than press his advantage in the waning light, Gillmore decided to postpone the frontal assault until the next morning, confident that total victory was at hand. Surprised at the lull in fighting, the Confederates seized the unexpected opportunity, audaciously reinforced their positions, and handed the overconfident Union forces an unmitigated disaster the following day. Of the 1,700 men led by General Strong on that foggy dawn, 339 men became casualties: 49 killed, 123 wounded, and 167 missing.[27]

The 54th was with Brigadier General Alfred H. Terry's 5,000-man division on the small tip of James Island, trying to create a distraction, when they heard the news of Strong's defeat. On July 16 Barquet's Company H was among those assigned picket duty on the northern section of Sol Legaré Island near the old Legaré plantation at Rivers' Causeway, right in the rebels' den. This complex of marsh and rivers made the men feel confined, vulnerable. Captain Russel, scanning the horizon with his binoculars looking for signs of trouble, worried that his men might not hold up under fire. The month before, during the time of troubles on Saint Helena Island, he had written his father that if his men were challenged in combat, "I guess they will fight."[28]

At dawn on the morning of July 16, Russel found out what Company H could do. Confederate Brigadier General Johnson Hagood had contrived a complex plan to reclaim the entirety of James Island. One element of his strategy involved sending Brigadier General Alfred Holt Colquitt with more than 3,000 men across Rivers' Causeway, cutting off the 10th Connecticut (part of Stevenson's brigade) and trapping them between Grimball's Landing and the Stono River. The attack came as almost a complete surprise to the pickets of Company H, one of three companies from the 54th on duty that night. In the face of this highly motivated mass of Confederates crashing through their lines, some of the men ran away or surrendered, but for the most part the troops of Company H showed "stubborn courage." Bearing the brunt of the action, they stood their ground in a fury of hand-to-hand combat. Once alerted to the attack, Shaw ordered the remainder of the regiment camped nearby to the field, where they delayed the Confederate assault long enough to allow the 10th Connecticut to slip away. Refusing to be moved, Company H transformed a likely rout into an orderly retreat in the face of a superior force; they left the scene in a "double-quick run," firing as they went. Captain Russel was ecstatic. His men no longer ducked reflexively at rifle fire and "fought like demons." One of them even saved his life: Private Preston Williams, a Galesburg man, gracefully intercepted a Confederate saber aimed for Russel with his rifle and then shot its wielder in the neck.[29]

Of the forty-six Union casualties, forty-three belonged to the 54th. One of the lost was a young member of the Holloway family, part of the Barquets' circle in Charleston. "A brave intelligent Christian soldier" and nephew of Daniel A. Payne, Corporal Charles Holloway had been a student at Wilburforce College before enlisting in Company K. He reportedly killed three Confederates before he fell. Beyond the killed and wounded, learning that some members of the regiment had been taken captive made their comrades' blood run cold, knowing that the Confederates had threatened to sell captured black soldiers into slavery.[30]

Within hours after the skirmish, the 54th was on the move. Before leaving James Island, the regiment received the praise of General Terry and the thanks of the 10th Connecticut. Colonel Shaw let the men see a bit of his pleasure. When he first arrived in South Carolina, he had told Colonel Higginson that since the "matter of courage" among black soldiers had not been settled, he wanted to find a situation where he could place them "between two fires in case of need, and so cutting off their retreat." The men's good showing in action at Grimball's Landing two nights earlier had, Shaw believed, not only settled the question of courage but also "wipe[d] out the remembrance of the Darien affair." His conviction that the 54th had nothing left to prove makes his later fateful decision even more difficult to understand.[31]

Night was still close upon the black troops when they began making their way through the marshes separating James Island from Coles Island. A causeway had been repaired earlier with new planks, but a summer storm raged as they made their getaway from Confederate territory, soaking their uniforms and skimming the boards with slick mud. In the dark, footing was treacherous. Resembling an army of blind tightrope walkers, over seven hundred men in single file picked their way for four miles along a half-mile path of one or two greasy planks, then over narrow dikes. Clouds blocked the moon. Only when lightening flashed briefly could the men see where their steps were falling. Their trek took almost eight hours, by which time the adrenaline of the battle had ebbed away, leaving them spent. Whenever the line stopped to wait for the rear to catch up, the men simply "dropped down" in the mud, where they lay for "uneasy catnaps" using each other for pillows.[32]

By dawn they reached their rendezvous on Coles Island. The beach was empty with no transport in sight and offered no food, water, or shade to soldiers who had lived for a week, without tents or dry clothes, on coffee and hardtack. Now even that was gone. The danger of a Confederate attack kept everyone on edge the whole day. Around 11:00 P.M. the chug of a workhorse steamer was heard just as lightening once again brightened the sky. For five hours small boats plied the roiling waters, carrying seven hundred hungry, rain-soaked men to their waiting transport for the short ride to Folly Island. Exhausted, they half-walked, half-dozed while hiking back to the next rendezvous point six miles away. On the morning of July 18, the 54th arrived at Pawnee Landing on Morris Island and was sent on another two-hour trudge.[33]

The men regained the spring in their step, though, when they heard the cheers of white soldiers as they passed their camps en route to their own. The action at James Island was the first concerted effort of black and white soldiers east of the Mississippi, and it had been a success. The white troops hailed the 54th for saving the 10th Connecticut, for standing their ground, for meeting the rebel charge with hot lead, and for being fellow men-at-arms. In his official report General Terry would give the regiment the public approbation Shaw had so hoped for, complimenting the men's "steadiness and soldierly conduct" in absorbing the "brunt of the attack."[34] When the main body of the 54th arrived at General Strong's headquarters, visibly "worn and weary," Colonel Shaw was waiting with an announcement that the general was incorporating them into his brigade and giving them the "honor" of leading the frontal assault upon Battery Wagner; the regiment would leave for the battle straightaway. Beaten down and disbelieving, Barquet set off with the 54th on a dune-sheltered interior road toward the Confederate position. None of the men had had a thing to eat since their early morning hardtack-and-coffee breakfast.[35]

About six o'clock on the evening of July 18, 624 men of the 54th Massachusetts moved into formation on the beach. Although the decision to replicate the unsuccessful charge of July 10 was deeply flawed, Brigadier Generals Strong and Truman Seymour's choice of the 54th for the lead made military sense. The regiment was the only one with enough men to form the column of two wings with five companies each as Seymour had wanted. Although these men were exhausted, they were efficient and healthy; undiminished by years of heavy combat, injuries, and disease as were the other regiments; and their officer corps was basically intact. In the back of their minds, the generals may have decided that given the men's chances of survival, their condition made little difference. Their second choice, the 6th Connecticut, had been in the war since September 1861 and, after its participation in the devastating attack of July 10, could field only three hundred men. Instead, the 6th would follow and support the 54th; behind them was the 48th New York.[36]

Captain Russel marched Company H into position on the far left of the second line of the column. This was a dangerous position on the marsh side, exposed to the flanking fire from the Confederate guns of James Island. Barquet's friend George Stephens was with Company B, anchoring the opposite side toward the ocean and warily watching the incoming tide. Colonel Shaw positioned himself at the head of the first column, which would march behind the national colors; Lieutenant Colonel Hallowell took command of the second column. Sergeant Charles Lennox of Company A tightened his hold of the regimental standard. The order "Fix bayonets" echoed across the beach.[37]

As the vanguard of the charge, the 54th was instructed to run at the south-facing side of the behemoth before them, with a 250-yard area of vulnerability between Vincent's Creek and the ocean. Once the men rounded the marsh, they were to somehow scale the parapet and subdue what was promised to be minimal Confederate resistance. Their weapons were loaded, but not capped, since this was expected to be a battle fought at close range, hand to hand, with clubbing and bayonetting. Inexplicably, Shaw's men had not been supplied with tools to cut wire barriers, to help scale the thirty-foot parapet, or to spike the guns once in the fortification. The need for these would have become obvious on the first attempt.[38]

The next order was for the 54th to lie down in the sand and make as low a silhouette as possible while the other regiments took their place in the formation. Barquet eased down and tried to squint at Battery Wagner across the marsh, falling into shadows at the close of the day. The encircling moat shimmered as the incoming tide began to inch up its banks, giving the whole prospect a mirage-like quality across the shadow-streaked sand. The simple wall of earth, 250 yards wide, offered no place of safety.[39]

During his half-hour wait on the ground, with gnats and mosquitoes buzzing around his head and working their way into his eyes, ears, socks, and shoes, Barquet surely wondered about the twists and turns of his life that had brought him here. He had been in the service less than ninety days and had received minimal training and maximum fatigue duty. He knew nothing of General Strong, nor had he exchanged as much as a pleasant word with any of those white soldiers supposedly supporting the 54th in the regiments from Maine, Rhode Island, Connecticut, and New York; they too were fighting in "made-up brigades." Except for the salute of some soldiers that day after their action on James Island, white enlisted men had, in fact, scarcely hidden their disgust at seeing black men wearing the same uniforms as themselves.[40]

If Barquet was full of uncertainty about the white soldiers in blue, he surely understood those men in gray inside that fort from his experience with the Palmetto Regiment in Mexico. He knew that sons of Charleston would be at their guns, hearts beating, ruthless in defense of their city. Knowing the white aristocracy of the city as individuals and as a class, Barquet realized that they were predictable in their wild unpredictability. Manning the guns were the grandsons of the nullifiers and sons of the fire-eaters who had led South Carolina out of the Union all alone. These troops, he likely believed, would never surrender that position and would fight until the last among them was dead.[41]

Barquet likely intuited that some of Charleston's old "brown elite" would be wielding muskets with the rebels in this fight as well as some slaves improbably resolute behind their masters. Some of his old school chums, inheritors of their family's businesses, real estate, and slaves—perhaps members of the Brown Fellowship Society—may well have taken the side of the aristocracy against the abolitionists, for they too had something to lose. This was a more complicated war than his earnest officers realized. Perhaps a few of those fellows with whom he had played in the militia band so long ago were scanning the beach and might find him in their sights.

The mood in the ranks around Barquet was usually light hearted and jocular but grew solemn and quiet when the first cannon shot passed overhead. Then General Strong, all dash and flair, yellow kerchief at his neck, rode up on a prancing gray. He reminded the men that the honor of the 54th Massachusetts was at stake and calmly explained that more than 9,000 artillery shells had been plowed into Wagner, now looking deflated and vulnerable. The enemy was quiet, and no response to the Union insults had been heard for hours, he assured them.[42]

All eyes then fell on Colonel Shaw, splendid in silk sash and high black hat, slight shoulders aglitter with the silver eagles of his rank, as he assumed his position at the head of the first column. He would reveal more of himself to his men in the next half hour on the beach than in their several months together. Shaw moved among them, speaking to them softly, telling them of the importance of what they were about to do, of what they already had done, and of how thousands would hear the story of the brave black regiment. As he passed Company H, Barquet might have been close enough to see the paleness of his cheeks as he spoke, the slight nervous twitch at the corner of his mouth, or a hint of a tremor in the hand that held his cigar, his jeweled ring reflecting the dying light of day. At that moment, when his youthful humanity had shown through his godlike reserve, his men loved him all the more, for they too were scared and unusually quiet. They might have imagined that he was seeing them for the first time as individuals, not just as a mission, and even that he loved them back just a little. Hearing his promise to pick up Old Glory should the flagbearer fall made them forgive him everything.[43]

The preliminaries over, everyone was on edge, coiled, ready to spring up and charge. Shaw checked his gold watch: 7:45. He lifted his beautifully chased sword. The men held their breath until the colonel brought the blade down with flair: "Forward 54th." The soldiers let out a "tremendous scream" and moved off in "quick time," following the flag. Confidence grew with every footfall even as they advanced into the dark toward the great silence.[44]

Inside Battery Wagner 1,620 rebels were playing possum. The Yankees were expected. When the monitor USS *Keokuk* sank off Morris Island in 1862, the Confederates had salvaged its codebook, and thus they had full knowledge of the impending attack and probably knew about it before Colonel Shaw did. Their lookouts had seen the siege batteries go up. During the night, reinforcements— five companies of the Charleston Battalion, fierce in their devotion to their city, as well as North Carolina infantrymen—had quietly glided in a flotilla of small boats through the night, all stealth, hushed silence, and muffled oars.[45]

For the amount of Federal firepower expended that day and into the night on the resilient sand fortification, the Confederates had actually lost amazingly few men, though the interior was in ruins. By midday on July 18, a deadly projectile from either land or sea flared toward them every other second. About nine hundred unwashed men, cramped one upon another, huddled under the bomb- proof, insulated by ten feet of sand. The conditions approximated hell in the July heat. They had no food or water all day and waited through the breathless dark.[46]

As the moment drew near, Georgia artillerymen ripped off the protective coverings from eleven cannons, a landside mortar, and two seaside guns. The two field pieces on the beach were readied as were the supportive heavy artillery at Battery Gregg, a small work on Cummings Point three-quarters of a mile north of Wagner that protected the Confederates' landing wharf from seaward attack.[47]

When the distance between Battery Wagner and the 54th shrank to one mile, the order "double quick" echoed through Strong's brigade. At his age Joseph Barquet would have been breathing hard in the humid night air, heavy with the scent of rain. Running through the darkness, the hollowed sand and rifle pits tripped the men up and broke their rhythm. The order to halt came a hundred yards before the walls. If the original formation had held, Company H would have been among those most affected by the intrusion of the marsh into their path and had to somehow squeeze into the merging mass of men trying to filter through the narrow defile, or pass. Men on the far side of the column were forced into the knee-deep rising tide. Once through this bottleneck, they had to veer left toward the tidal moat encircling Wagner.

At about the fifty-yard point, Colonel Shaw gave the order to move forward. Fierce musketry began to rain down upon the assaulting troops from the heights of the fort. All became a chaos of confusion when the Confederate howitzers outside the fort were joined by the big guns from the outlying batteries. Some Union artillerists had been slow to follow a ceasefire order and mingled their shells with those of the enemy. After 150 men fell in the first few minutes, the 54th staggered backward. Some panicked and sought escape.

But Colonel Shaw charged ahead through the heavy fire up the slope of the wall, accompanied by a heedless wave of glinting bayonets, determined to enter the fort. Captain Russel followed close in Shaw's wake, rallying Company H to follow him through the moat. Barquet was perhaps still with them, charging through the shallow water, the bodies of his fallen comrades cushioning his way like so many stepping stones over the submerged sharpened palmetto spikes.[48]

Sergeant William H. Carney of Company C grabbed Old Glory when its bearer fell and, although shot three times, beat off rebels who tried to grab the standard; he was just able to hold up the flag when the retreat was sounded.[49] As various members of the 54th were making their way out of the position, as dangerous an undertaking as the initial charge, Federal troops began firing upon them, thinking the black soldiers were running away from the fight.[50]

Somehow, Barquet survived, one of the 400 men of the 54th who staggered back to their camp, shattered by their experience, by what they had seen and what they had done. The survivors moved about like lost souls. Colonel Shaw, their ambassador to the white world, was missing and presumed dead, as was Captain Russel. Federal forces suffered about 1,515 casualties. The 6th Connecticut also lost its colonel and about 35 percent of its men. The 48th New York too lost half of its men and all but two of its officers. The 54th was devastated, losing 272 men—34 killed, 146 wounded, 92 missing—and fourteen of its twenty-two officers. Nine of Barquet's comrades in the company had been wounded, one captured. Barquet was promoted; all of the company's sergeants had been rendered unable to serve.[51]

With the dramatic death of Colonel Shaw, public attention was focused on the brave Boston Brahmin rather than his brave black soldiers. The mythmaking around Shaw began immediately after the battle, with sensational accounts of his burial, the magnanimity of his grief-stricken parents in leaving his body among those of the black soldiers ("his niggers," the press kept unnecessarily repeating), and later their contributions in support of the restoration of the town of Darien. New Englanders quickly gained control of the narrative of Battery Wagner, shifting the emphasis from the folly of the charge and the irresponsibility of sending raw recruits into such an impossible situation to the heinous nature of the Confederates.[52]

Barquet was canny enough to realize that had the politically savvy abolitionist press not beat the drum over Colonel Shaw's death and elevated *him* as a martyr for freedom, the terrible tragedy at Battery Wagner would have been just one more terrible tragedy in a tragic war. The pointless loss of scores of black soldiers on a small island in South Carolina would have scarcely registered in light of the Union victory following the three bloodiest days in American history at Gettysburg just weeks earlier.[53]

After losing more than 2,000 men, a third of his force, General Gillmore paced the beach like Captain Ahab, haunted by his twin defeats at the hands of the Confederates. Battery Wagner, sitting squat and defiant on the horizon, had, in fact, become the white whale in the mind of this talented engineer and siege master. Unwilling to be defeated by a rebel-built pile of sand and logs, Gillmore became so obsessed with the destruction of Wagner that he lost sight of his original goal of disarming Fort Sumter so that Union ironclads might be able to penetrate into Charleston Harbor and take the city.[54] With his reputation at stake and Washington demanding results, Gillmore vowed that as a last resort he would dig his way to victory. He calculated that via a series of parallel trenches, he could push his guns right up to the rebels' front door and blow them to hell.

The siege of Battery Wagner began on July 20. The 54th's survivors were ordered to lay down their rifles and pick up their shovels. All pretense of training or drilling was thrown out the window to allow them more time for digging. The task was a marathon undertaking. The black regiments that made up 10 percent of the siege force would perform 50 percent of the heavy fatigue work. When Barquet lifted his first load of heavy sand, Battery Wagner was 1,350 yards away. The digging of trenches four feet wide and two feet deep went on for fifty-eight days under constant Confederate fire through the worse of the summer heat and the sickly time of year, requiring more courage and sheer fortitude than any three-hour adrenaline-fueled charge. The soldiers also filled 46,000 bags with sand, filled hundreds of gabions with rocks, and built eighty-nine gun emplacements. With Drummond calcium lamps and ships in the harbor illuminating their path, shovels rose and fell with a grunt and a groan day and night. Their clothes, soaked with sweat and burned by the sun, rotted right off their backs. As the laborers moved within range, Rebel sharpshooters picked them off like turkeys at a holiday shoot. More than 1,900 men reported sick, and so many died that officers finally had to ban all funeral music because the constant sound of the muffled drums had a dreadfully depressive effect upon the soldiers. Through it all, the digging continued so systematically that from a distance the Confederates thought the Federals had devised excavating machines.[55]

Barquet spent the weary hours in the company of "Messrs. Shovel and Spade" making mental notes as he dug a trench to nowhere, considering the relative unimportance of Battery Wagner in the larger scheme of the war. He wrote a parody for the *Weekly Anglo-African* illustrating how quickly former slaves had mastered the language of artillerymen and the engineers. In the sap lines on Morris Island, he wrote, "men born and reared on Southern plantations who never saw a gun can now talk as glibly as you please of planes, augers, ranges and distance, and the entire military vocabulary is becoming familiar to them." He recounted a supposed conversation between two "contraband" about the relative potency of the small mortars. "Sam, 'Coehorn mortar trow shell great range; to fetch him, reb wastes much powder.' 'Ah!' Jim, 'Coehorn mortar wus den grape and schrapanel; grape shell come straight in trench—de odder bound to go ober.'" "What a fund of information these men have gained, and what a grand school for the soldier is opened to them!" Barquet observed with irony. "Eight hours out of thirty-six toiling and laboring in the face of death, shell from front and flank, Minnie bullets [*sic*], grape and shrapnel plunging, whizzing and plowing up the earth on all sides."[56]

Adept at the graveyard humor that kept the men going, Barquet also described a scene from the nighttime sap work as the trenchers inched toward their destination. The men of Serrill's 1st New York Engineer Corps, who oversaw the trenching operation, had done little to hide their resentment at having to interact with blacks. In his description Barquet resorts to some stereotyping of his own by making the Irish lieutenant clearly tipsy. After designating some men as "miners" to dig and others as "sappers" to carry, the Irishman gave them simple but morbid instructions about how to proceed under fire: "No. 1, you're kilt! No. 2, you take his place. No. 3, you're kilt. No. 4, you must take his place." He promised that if they worked hard, by the next morning, "we'll be in the gates of Fort Wagner and the jaws of death and hell." Unhappily, four men (one from the 54th) were killed that night and others wounded, but at dawn they were close enough to the enemy's rifle pits to hear an "indignant" rebel shout out, "You black Yankee sons of b——s intend to bury us in sand, don't you."[57]

This proximity also allowed Union soldiers to capture sixty-three Confederates from their rifle pits. Barquet was surely not surprised that among them were five free men of color. Two were sharpshooters wielding "neutral" rifles smuggled in from Britain, and another was described by Corporal James Gooding as "a rebel at *heart*" and a slaveholder who "held himself aloof from his misguided brethren" of the 54th like a "lord to his vassals."[58]

On September 7 Battery Wagner fell, not with a bang or even a whimper. Two days earlier the sappers had reached the moat under cover of heavy artillery fire. While Gillmore was studying how best to stage the third assault against Wagner and administer the *coup de grâce* to his nemesis, rebel deserters approached Union lines and reported that the Confederates had abandoned Morris Island during the night. Somehow, a thousand rebels, their wounded, and their slaves had slipped away across the water while Union forces slept. The charge laid by the last Confederate out of Wagner failed, marking their departure with only a fizzle. Instead of a large crater as planned, the rebels bequeathed Gillmore a charnel house of unbelievable carnage, of stink and rot, of spent shells and sharp bits of metal, and of body parts—man and mule—disinterred by the blasts of big-caliber shells and strewn about, with a head here and a leg there.[59]

The Confederate command knew Morris Island was lost after the first assault in July, but General Beauregard, spearheading the defense of Charleston, had ordered his officers to hold on as long as possible. By extracting the maximum losses among the Federals there, he also diverted their energies away from Fort Sumter, the centerpiece of the harbor defenses. By refusing to surrender even in the face of sure defeat, the Confederates had forced the land siege that nearly sucked the lifeblood out of the sappers. General Gillmore's anticlimactic message to Rear Admiral John Dahlgren, commanding the supporting Federal fleet, read: "The whole of Morris Island is ours, but the enemy has escaped." The general had neutralized Morris Island's four thousand acres of sand, taken Battery Wagner by "peaceful possession," and captured the small but strategically located Battery Gregg at Cummings Point. His hope to score a trifecta on September 7 and overwhelm the much battered and beaten Fort Sumter failed because of a poorly coordinated small-boat attack.[60]

Nevertheless, Gillmore had secured a prime piece of real estate from which to launch a large-scale artillery attack upon Charleston and to soften the well-fortified city for an invasion. Many men of the 54th brushed their uniforms and polished their boots in anticipation of the "grand ball" to come. The nation began waiting for news of the fall of secession's birthplace. But *when* the general would make his move, all Federal officialdom wanted to know. In the meantime, artillery fire from the unmolested Confederate positions on Sullivan's Island and James Island roared on unabated. In the end, rather than conducting a full-throttle naval assault and risk losing their valuable ironclad monitors on a target of dubious strategic value, the Federals decided to starve and pound the proud old lady into submission.[61]

General Beauregard had been warned. For over a month Federal engineers had been tapping into their impressive stores of Yankee ingenuity and constructing a battery in the soupy marsh between James Island and Morris Island sufficiently stable to support the 16,500-pound weight of an ominous-looking Parrott rifle as well as its carriage. Nicknamed the "Swamp Angel," this huge gun was the nineteenth-century equivalent of a weapon of mass destruction that could, they believed, deliver its massive 150-pound payload 7,900 yards, setting fires on the streets and rooftops of houses of Charleston. On August 21, Gillmore alerted Beauregard that if he did not withdraw from Fort Sumter and his remaining positions on Morris Island, the Federals would unleash an artillery attack that, he intimated, could be of biblical proportions. Beauregard replied the Federals could have Fort Sumter whenever they could take it. So, long before dawn on August 22, Union artillerymen made their calibrations based on the towering steeple of St. Michael's Church and unleashed the Swamp Angel's shells—lethally laced with "Greek fire" (an ancient predecessor of napalm)—arcing into the heart of a sleeping city. Thus, began a record 545-day siege upon the population of Charleston, which also included Union prisoners of war.[62]

After hearing this news, Herman Melville wrote his poem *Swamp Angel,* which conflated the deadly threat from the giant gun—"There is a coal-black Angel / With a thick Afric lip"—with the specter of the black avengers, both poised on Morris Island and ready to attack Charleston as the twin avatars of retribution. "Is this the proud City? The scorner / Which never would yield the ground / Which mocked at the coal-black Angel / The cup of despair goes round."[63]

What Melville did not know, but Joseph Barquet did, was that neither the Union high command nor the wartime government had the heart for a frontal attack upon Charleston that would not be strategically worth the probable high losses. Although the city remained on alert until December, Sergeant Barquet realized that there would be no invasion when, in mid-September 1863, he and Sergeant Major Lewis Douglass were among the first in the 54th granted month-long furloughs. As the exhausted Barquet packed his gear for his first trip home in six months, one grim reality muted his joy: He scarcely had a cent to his name. Taking the high road with most of the regiment, he had refused all compensation since July rather than accept the unequal pay of "men of African heritage." To buy his railroad ticket, he applied to the quartermaster for an advance of eighteen dollars on his theoretical back pay. In the course of his long journey—first north on a military transport, then west by rail—Barquet surely weighed how best to explain to his wife why he was coming home emptyhanded, how his personal honor as a man and the honor of his regiment trumped feeding his three children. Seven dollars a month, she may have argued with some justice, was better than nothing. Barquet had taken the train to Chicago, where Maria may have gone to be part of a more supportive black community and where she might more easily find work. If he would transfer to one of the black regiments formed in Illinois, she could qualify for the state aid to soldiers' families denied her by Massachusetts. The wives of some men from the 54th had been forced into beggary or worse, their children taken away to a workhouse or indentured. (Early in 1864 Barquet would receive news that his fourth child, James, had been born, a mixed blessing at this uncertain time.)[64]

"What had been the point of it all?" was a question frequently asked by the northern press as well as by some in the War Department in the fall of 1863 about the long, costly struggle for Battery Wagner; surely it was a question asked by Barquet's wife to her husband. The Confederate flag still waved over Fort Sumter; Charleston was damaged but undaunted. In making his case for the larger importance of his service and her sacrifice, what could Joseph tell Maria that the 54th had achieved in South Carolina? The regiment had answered the two persistent questions about black men: yes, they could fight and fight bravely; and yes, they would work and work hard. The 54th had inched the door to military service a bit wider for black men, although its record had not entirely tamped down the debate about the wisdom of having black men in blue uniforms. They needed a decisive victory.

Barquet returned to Morris Island in mid-October to find that once the men of the regiment no longer had enemy fire and imminent death to concentrate their minds, a multiheaded hydra of old animosities had reemerged and seized hold of them. On its face the primary issue was about money. Not long after the war was over, a *New York Tribune* article speculated that the difference in pay between white and black soldiers was so outrageous and wrong on its face that perhaps the actual intention must have been to cause black troops to mutiny.[65] The men blamed everyone from President Lincoln and Governor Andrew to their own officers. Champions emerged, like a "wealthy Republican merchant" from Massachusetts who arrived with a sack of money, anxious to make up the difference in wages and make the public-relations problem go away. In December 1863 Barquet sat on a committee of sergeants that met with both officers and enlisted men to consider the various proposals. The committee just said no and stood on principle. That principle was, according to Barquet, that the government had made a contract with the soldiers of the 54th, and while they would not accept any payment other than that agreed upon, he and his fellow soldiers would fulfill their end of the bargain until mustered out.[66]

The other dynamic was that while the men of the 54th and 55th Massachusetts wrote letters and fought for their own increased wages, they did not take up the cause of the "contrabands" or former slaves, who had been enlisted under the 1862 militia act that clearly mandated lower pay for "men of African descent" and had expected them to be laborers in uniform rather that soldiers. Inevitably, for their argument to succeed, the northern men had to make painful and invidious comparisons between themselves and the freedmen in terms of superior education and training. Part of their purpose in fighting this war was to explode the rigid connection in the white mind between color and servitude.[67]

Barquet's friend Sergeant George Stephens, a regular correspondent to New York's *Weekly Anglo-African,* asserted in one of his letters from Morris Island that the 1862 act referencing "men of African descent" could not apply to the 54th and 55th because "there is no proof that any of our fathers are African." "What surprises us," Corporal Gooding, wrote in a letter to his hometown newspaper in Massachusetts, "is that the government won't recognize the difference between 'volunteers in good faith' and 'a class thrown upon it by the necessities of war.'" In early 1864, when the *Weekly Anglo-African* published an opinion piece supporting their campaign for equal pay, Barquet wrote a letter to the editor describing its effect: "What a stir Mr. Anglo you made in our camp. Had the shell from the bushwhackers fallen in the Quartermaster's big tent, the stir could not have been greater. Everyone wanted to read about the 54th in the weekly and commenced grabbing for it: 'Hand it in here.'"[68]

Class divisions among the black soldiers came to a head over plans to celebrate New Year's Day 1864. An energetic "rubbing of ideas" foreshadowed future conflict over black identity and how best to memorialize the meaning of their participation in the Civil War. Toward the end of 1863, Barquet and some other "noncommish" began polling the men to see what festivities they might enjoy. The "radicals" of the regiment, composed largely of "the class whose service is the root of the peculiar institution," as the freedmen among them were tactfully called, insisted that the first anniversary of the Emancipation Proclamation must be the centerpiece of any event. They wanted a petition to that effect signed by all black soldiers so that their commanding officers would see unity among them "irrespective of class." Most of these radicals had participated in a mass gathering in Beaufort on New Year's Day 1863, during which the assembled crowd of enslaved people expressed unbounded joy when a manifesto from Brigadier General Rufus Saxton was read, stating that by the grace of "our Heavenly Father" and Abraham Lincoln, they were declared "forever free." Afterward they danced, sang, and enjoyed a feast of roasted ox.[69]

Barquet, though, thought it too early to declare America's triumph over slavery since black men and women remained in bondage, not just in the Confederacy but also in border states such as Maryland and Kentucky. Emancipation depended on battlefield victory for the Union, an outcome still in doubt. He agreed with Frederick Douglass that the most important date in the history of their race was still August 1, 1833, internationally celebrated as "the colored man's day" in commemoration of Great Britain's abolition of slavery and liberation of 800,000 souls in its West Indian colonies, a milestone of morality achieved by reason rather than military might.[70]

After negotiating a compromise, Barquet—a veteran impresario of numerous British Emancipation Day events in Galesburg—agreed to help orchestrate the Morris Island New Year's Day events. The officers of the camp and special civilian guests would be invited for a day of speeches, entertainments, and solemn commemoration. The Emancipation Proclamation would be held up as a step in the right direction. Freedom would be hailed as a cherished goal rather than an established fact. The celebration went well and included the Musical and Vocal Club singing everyone's favorite song, "Year of Jubilee."[71]

Barquet delivered one of the main addresses. In "high spirits" despite the bitter winter winds blowing off the ocean, he mounted the dry goods box that served as a stage, looked about him, and quoted from Sir Walter Scott's *Rob Roy*: "What means this sea of upturned faces." The patriotic 54th's battle at Battery Wagner, he predicted, would be heralded as the black man's Bunker Hill, just the beginning of a revolution.[72]

Speaking with passion about the evolving concepts of the rights of black men, he noted the irony of celebrating Emancipation Proclamation Day on the "soil of the nullifiers." Knowing well the tempestuous battle over nullification in Charleston, he conceded that many excellent southern men had been forced by public pressure to embrace the "monster secession," and perhaps considering his own family history, he might have added that they had also been trapped by the "monster slavery." Challenging the commonly held view that all southern slaveholders and (by association) all Democrats were evil, he reminded his audience that neither party had a monopoly on public virtue. When black soldiers became voters, as he hoped they soon would, he advised them against blind allegiance to those Republican politicians who claimed to be the black man's best friend. Many elected officials, he cautioned, only adopt "the abolition platform . . . for political power, or to gain some advantage over their fellows."

Just as the sergeant shifted into high gear, approaching the crescendo of his "impassioned harangue," the box upon which he was standing gave way. Regaining his footing and not missing a beat, he continued from the wreckage with the familiar gag, "Gentlemen, I admire your principles, but I damn your platform." When the laughing subsided, more-cautious speakers followed from a safe place on the ground. At the end the camp chaplain offered a prayer, and the assembly joined hands to sing the "John Brown Song," presumably in one of its less profane versions. The ceremony concluded with a "three times three" in honor of Colonel Shaw, with "each man covering and uncovering," a "flourish of bugles, rolling of drums, and drooping of colors." Then the crowd tucked into a particularly Yankee treat of baked beans and Indian pudding.[73]

ON JANUARY 29, 1864, Joseph Barquet rejoiced as the 54th and 55th Massachusetts prepared to leave Morris Island and all the ghostly sadness of that wretched place. His regiment was at last reconstituted after its tragic losses of the previous summer, with 124 enthusiastic new recruits and a new cadre of officers, mostly good men in search of promotion in contrast to their original officers, who were deeply committed to the cause of abolition and of the black soldier. Believing they were headed for a new start, their past came back to haunt them. Rather than being attached to Major General William T. Sherman's massive military machine that had just vanquished Atlanta or heading north to the action in Virginia, the men were headed to Florida to be brigaded once again with the erratic and reviled Colonel Montgomery and his 2nd and 3rd South Carolina Infantry. Their mission to interrupt Confederate supply lines to the breadbasket of Florida, ordered by General Gillmore, was to their horror to be led by the rash General Seymour, who had been so sanguinely wrong about the assault upon Battery Wagner and bore much responsibility for that disaster.

After making small, successful raids on soft Confederate targets from his base in Jacksonville, General Seymour disobeyed a specific directive from Gillmore not to take his men deeply into the interior or engage in offensive action. On February 20, Seymour let himself be lured into a trap near Olustee Station without his full complement of troops. While out on an open, marshy plain in an area called Ocean Pond with pine trees as the only cover, he encountered wily Confederate brigadier general Joseph Finegan's force of about 5,500 battle-hardened men and sixteen cannons. By 2:30 in the afternoon, the carnage was so extensive and the situation so dire that the desperate Seymour at last called in Montgomery's brigade, then stationed, as usual, on picket duty in the rear. In a moment rife with déjà vu, Colonel Edward N. Hallowell ordered the 54th forward at double time into the breach.

The Battle of Olustee, rather than the doomed charge upon Battery Wagner, actually reveals the true spirit of the 54th. A letter by Sergeant Barquet, describing his experience with his usual verve, paints an accurate picture of that engagement. He began his account with General Seymour rushing madly to the rear, shouting "noble 54th, come up, for God's sake, save my army; save the honor of the nation!" In response: "Did we stop to ask questions, our families starving at home, our country refusing to recognize us as a part of her defenders, no pay, no protection if made prisoners? No!" Racing off in the heat and stifling humidity, he described how the men threw off their packs and "everything but what we stood *in* . . . , our race, our honor, our God from his blue temple, said *forward,* double quick! For two miles we ran, here comes the 54th! We formed and back came the rebels; our cannon gained. But the fire is too hot; every horse killed." The Confederates had "Indians" in the treetops who picked off the officers. The 1st North Carolina Colored Infantry, he claimed, only got off two rounds before fleeing, leaving the 54th fighting alone "for three mortal hours." "It was the retreat in which we suffered most," he related. "What a total rout would be I would not like to see, for a retreat, covered and in good order, is truly bad enough." Flashbacks had already begun to haunt him. When "we cool down from our frenzy the mind reverts to the scenes just before transpired." Closing his eyes, he could see one "poor devil lying down, not dead, both legs broken," when cannon fire "cuts the top from a tree, down on this already mangled body," crushing "the last spark of life." In another instance that stayed with him, a "poor fellow" whose throat was cut by a shell fragment was left behind but "crawled on all fours" and caught up to the regiment. After three hours of combat, only the 54th, having no order to retreat and with ammunition nearly depleted, remained on the shadow-darkened battlefield. With the rest of the army withdrawing to the rear, Barquet wrote, "we fight with our face to the foe, receding step by step, until God sent us night." The black soldiers watched as southern women came out to remove their dead in the dark. All during that time they could both see and hear trains bringing fresh Confederate troops to the field.

Barquet claimed that during the course of the engagement, the regiment covered 102 miles in 108 hours. Half the men were barefooted as the 54th intrepidly marched toward the enemy "through briars and thornes," from 8 o'clock to 4, 20 miles, fought five hours, and retreated 20 miles by the next morning. "We could not help our wounded; we did not bury our dead." At one point, when the flagbearer tripped over a log, Barquet boasted, "I caught the flag" and "saved the colors." Although "a shower of balls hail'd we came out all right."

"A great fault rests somewhere," Barquet concluded, when good men were "slaughtered in a poor country that no one seemed to know anything of or care about." "How much grief and care, how much we suffer, how many poor wounded for life, how many killed in this cause, that the country may be saved! And the refusal to do us justice! Contractors grow fat and saucy—we grow poor. Truly God cares for us; no grumbling, do you hear without we are trampled. We do our duty. Governor Andrew spoke prophecy when he said the colored people of the nation were to be elevated by their conduct. I can see prejudice clearing around us, we are known from others; let our boys beg a piece of meat or tobacco—'he belongs to the 54th, he must have it; don't you take less than your pay, boys,' comes from all sides. . . . Here comes the fighting black cusses, three cheers for the 54th; let them through." Barquet ended the letter: "I have lost flesh, but am well. Thank God."[74]

The sergeant's evaluation of the 54th's great leap in reputation after the Battle of Olustee was confirmed by one of the black men from the North Carolina regiment, who wrote, "Some of the white regiments are requesting to be brigaded with black regiments." From this soldier's perspective, the 54th was the "most intelligent and . . . interesting" of all the black regiments, and "to see them in line, nearly twelve hundred strong (before the late fight) makes a man with one drop of black blood thank God and take courage." A correspondent for a Charleston paper later observed, "the Yankee darkies fought like devils."[75]

"The colored regiments stood in the gap and saved the army," according to another newspaper report. By the time it reached a point of safety, the 54th had suffered eighty-six casualties; three officers and thirteen men were killed. In addition, thirty-nine horses and six pieces of artillery were lost by the Federals. In relative terms Seymour's operation might well have been the costliest of all Union defeats. To the general's great discredit, 26 percent of his troops did not return to camp: 1,355 men were killed or wounded and 506 captured or missing in the devastating scene of carnage. Self-abnegating to the end, survivors from the 54th wearily loaded up about three hundred of the battlefield injured on idled railroad flats. When the steam engine "refused to do its duty," Barquet was among those who hitched themselves up like horses with ropes and vines and for ten miles took turns pulling their moaning comrades away from the field.[76]

Their devastating episode at Olustee shattered the regiment's confidence in General Seymour and their other commanders. Being left alone with dwindling supplies of ammunition and no orders to withdraw, one officer later concluded, meant that either the regiment had been forgotten or "its sacrifice was considered necessary."[77]

The 54th's drumbeat for black officers, another of Governor Andrew's broken promises, began in earnest. While remaining for two more months under General Seymour's random and overbearing discipline in Florida—he frequently threatened execution for minor offenses—discontent grew. A Massachusetts man from Barquet's company, Thomas D. Freeman, complained that in Florida they were "not soldiers but Labourers" who spent their days building batteries, hauling guns, cleaning bricks, and clearing land so that other regiments could set up camp. Since the black soldiers basically received nothing for all they did except their board and the occasional "crack over the head" from an officer's sword, Freeman asked his brother to find out if "a man could not sue for his Discharge."[78]

In mid-April 1864 the relief the regiment had felt upon leaving Florida transformed into anger after landing back on remote Morris Island, a place that some had come to regard as more of a work camp that a military posting. Peacemakers such as Sergeant Barquet could do little to tamp down the escalating sense of outrage, for he shared it. A campaign of passive disobedience by the troops pushed even their most sympathetic officers to the breaking point. When one soldier refused to stand guard, the exhausted Colonel Hallowell snapped. He grabbed the man and put a pistol to his head but caught himself before firing. Shocked at his own behavior, the Quaker patrician realized that unless some of the grievances were resolved, the 54th should be mustered out before a real catastrophe occurred. Disgusted with the politics of his command, Hallowell longed to leave South Carolina and transfer to the Army of the Potomac to fight what he considered the real war to save the Union.[79]

To diffuse the escalating tensions, the regiment was split up, with the various companies assigned to three outposts from which they were to observe enemy movements. Their one compensation was advanced artillery training and the accompanying satisfaction of achieving proficiency in this soldierly skill. Otherwise, the stagnation of activity that summer gave Barquet and his friends time to continue their letter-writing campaign to the northern press. In August 1864 one man assigned to the Folly Island outpost sent an anonymous letter to the *Christian Recorder* accusing white officers of acting as if "a negro stunk under their noses." Barquet, serving on steamy Black Island as part of the defense of Lighthouse Inlet, penned a humorous piece published in the *Weekly Anglo-African,* a popular vehicle for black soldiers' protest, about the poor food supplied to this small hummock amid the marsh, though he did not reveal his location. Writing in the spirit of fun, he signed his own name.[80]

Toward the end of August 1864, Gillmore's provost marshal, Captain Thomas Appleton, arrived on Black Island and confronted Barquet. He whipped out a copy of the published letter and demanded an explanation. Barquet remonstrated that it was meant only as a comic satire indulging in the soldier's historic lament about the very hard hardtack and coffee with plenty of salt but no sugar. At the end of the long hot summer, Appleton had had enough of complaints and of the black soldiers using the press to pursue their own goals. He convened a field court-martial against the earnest sergeant for "conduct prejudicial to good order and military discipline." On August 24 Barquet stood before a panel chaired by Appleton. He pled "not guilty" to the accusations that he had attempted to sow disaffection among the troops or tried "to create in the mind of its [the newspaper's] readers a false impression in regard to the quantity and quality of rations issued by the Government to the troops in this District." He had fabricated nothing, he said, and only told the simple truth. The hardtack was indeed old and stale, and the coffee salty because their drinking water was brackish during high tides. He had no sugar because someone had stolen his personal supply bought at a dear price from the sutler.[81]

The only witness in Barquet's defense was the commander of Company H, Captain Charles E. Tucker, who swore that the sergeant "obliged his orders as faithfully as any man could." After a year of working with the accused, Tucker could affirm his steadfastness as a soldier and could categorically deny all charges that he was a troublemaker. The opposite was in fact true: "He has always worked with me to keep up the discipline of the company. He is a man whom I never heard utter any complaint whatever." Barquet threw himself "on the forbearance of the Court," denying any "spirit of malice or insubordination" and pleading that he had "at all times striven to do my duty as a good and faithful soldier." The court found him guilty of both charges but, "believing the accused to have acted more from thoughtlessness than from any intention of wrong," was lenient in his sentence. Barquet only received an official reprimand from Colonel Hallowell. Still, this was a bitter blow.[82]

Barquet's comrades expressed outrage on his behalf. On August 26, the day after his judgment was handed down, another sergeant from the 54th wrote an angry letter to the Boston-based antislavery journal *The Liberator*. Having learned from Barquet's hard lesson, the author left his complaint unsigned, but Sergeant Francis Fletcher of Company A—an early and ardent recruiter for the 54th—was suspected. Moving beyond the pay issue, he made the point that without black commissioned officers to speak for them, black soldiers would never really be treated fairly. Perhaps with Sergeant Barquet in mind, the writer emphasized that black soldiers keenly felt the need for other men of their race "to be represented on Court Martials where too many of us are liable to be tried and sentenced." "We need men we can understand and who can understand us," he wrote with eloquence, and "whose hearts are loyal to the rights of man. . . . We want to demonstrate our ability to rule, as we have demonstrated our ability to obey. In short, we want justice."[83]

Within a few days after receiving his reprimand, a likely subdued Barquet learned that a congressional compromise had, in theory, been reached granting wage parity and retroactive compensation to black soldiers, though only for the 54th and 55th Massachusetts. Before a black soldier could receive his pay, however, he had to take an oath that he had been a free man on April 19, 1861, the official line holding that this was necessary to parry charges made by the Confederates that the Union was enlisting runaway slaves and thus fomenting a slave revolt. Barquet was outraged at this echo of the Fugitive Slave Act. Even as soldiers in the US Army, every black man was apparently considered a slave unless he could prove otherwise. He took a "Quaker oath" contrived by Colonel Hallowell to give some cover to those who had secured their own freedom a little later. Most did swear "that they owed no man unrequited labor," even though they thought it a final insult to crown their injury.[84]

Standing on the beach and surrounded by rebel guns, Barquet reflected on the trials of his life since leaving his family and home in Charleston nearly twenty years earlier. It seemed like a lifetime ago. Once believing his posting on Morris Island was the first step to real freedom, the place now felt like a prison of unrelenting labor and brooding hostility. Surrounded by the sea, buffeted by gales, and rained on by Confederate fire, he was experiencing the harsh truth of abolitionist William Lloyd Garrison's observation that "Our Free Colored Brethren" must struggle "against wind and tide," for "adversity has 'marked you for his own.'"[85]

6

DEATH AND REBIRTH
IN THE DRAGON'S DEN

IN THE LATE SPRING OF 1864, after two years on the *qui vive* along the remote Combahee River and insulated from the real war, Rutledge's regiment was at last on the move. By May 21 Captain Pinckney was riding at the head of his company, the hoof beats of his stallion, Stonewall, tapping out the tedious miles along rough North Carolina roads leading the men toward Richmond. Once regarded as the theater of war where reputations were made, the Virginia front had become widely feared as the "dragon's den [with] plenty of footsteps going to it, but none returning."[1]

Everything had changed for the regiment in early December 1863. For months after Union forces secured the entirety of Morris Island the previous September, General Beauregard had expected a direct attack upon Charleston and had gathered a defensive force to protect the city. By December, though, he had concluded that the Yankees would not send an invasion force across the mined harbor while Fort Sumter was still in Confederate hands. The dreaded Swamp Angel by then had burst after only thirty-six firings. Nevertheless, the pounding of the lower peninsula had continued with more-modest weapons, while besieged Charlestonians—black and white—moved out of range and carried on.[2]

Over the years, maintaining a significant presence near Union-occupied Beaufort District made less and less strategic sense, although as the casualty lists grew from operations outside the state, enlistments in the various coastal units grew. The Federal offensive against Morris Island had shifted the defensive center of gravity from Port Royal, near Pinckney's Pocotaligo base, to Charleston Harbor. Since Colonel Montgomery's successful raid, the major occupation of Pinckney's regiment had become staunching the steady drift of slaves fleeing the plantations along the Combahee River; they may as well have tried to stop the flow of the river itself. An embarrassing lapse at Cunningham's Bluff on November 24, 1863, brought Rutledge's command unwelcomed attention when a brazen raiding party of black soldiers nearly succeeded in liberating twenty-seven slaves belonging to planter Daniel Heyward.[3]

With the end of the drama in Charleston Harbor, Major General Wade Hampton III, recovering from the wounds he had received at Gettysburg five months earlier, began militating to have the 4th South Carolina Cavalry, along with the 5th and 6th Regiments, attached to his division that for years had done extremely hard service with General Lee's Army of Northern Virginia. Having put his own sons in danger—one would be killed and another wounded—Hampton had no patience with influential lowcountry parents who protested against having their own boys transferred from their cozy postings to the coming showdown in Virginia, where most believed the war would be won or lost.[4]

In March 1864 the long-dreaded orders arrived. The 4th, 5th, and 6th South Carolina Cavalry would form the core of a new brigade under Brigadier General Matthew C. Butler and attached to the Army of Northern Virginia. An Edgefield County lawyer whose uncle, former governor Pierce M. Butler, had died leading the Palmetto Regiment during the Mexican War, he had joined Hampton's Legion as a cavalry captain in 1861. Butler's courage and audacity in battle had propelled him rapidly through the ranks, though taking a heavy toll upon his command. At the brutal battle at Brandy Station the previous June, he had lost a foot (and his favorite horse) and was still recuperating when Rutledge's command was instructed to make haste to Virginia.[5]

Later that month Pinckney met with General Hampton, a family friend, to discuss the details of his regiment's integration with Butler's reconstituted brigade and mobilization to Virginia. Hampton stressed in the most emphatic terms the need for speed. General Lee anticipated that when Lieutenant General Ulysses S. Grant, fresh from major Union victories in the western theater, took effective command of the Army of the Potomac on the first of May, he would concentrate his forces against Richmond. Lee wanted every available soldier at hand to defend the Confederate capital. Pinckney dutifully relayed Hampton's note of urgency to Colonel Rutledge in Pocotaligo, then left for a twenty-day furlough with his family at their Abbeville County farm in Cokesbury.[6]

Pinckney reunited with his regiment in Columbia, which had swollen to three times its prewar population as refugees from the coast flowed into the capital city. The large colony of displaced Charlestonians made him feel quite at home. Every square inch of their rented houses was crammed with displaced women, children, old men, servants, and trunks of china, jewels, and silver. Amid preparations to leave for Virginia, Pinckney was struck down by his old nemesis, malaria, and was fortunate that his cousin Harriott H. R. Ravenel and her husband, Dr. St. Julian Ravenel, who headed the Confederate Medical Laboratories, managed to find a bed for him in her crowded house. Despondent because he missed General Hampton's grand review of the troops, he was relieved that when the time finally came to set out for Virginia, he could mount his horse and lead his men.[7]

In an uneasy foreshadowing of the trouble to come, the movement of the 4th South Carolina Cavalry into Virginia had been plagued with "embarrassments" from beginning to end. Conflicting orders delayed them, then last-minute "unauthorized petitions" from planters objecting to the army's abandonment of the coastal plantation district, then inexplicably the shortage of farriers, and finally a dearth of proper horseshoes. Eventually, after slapdash assembly-line attention to their mounts, Rutledge's cavalry divided up into smaller groups and began making their way northward, leaving a trail of third-rate horseshoes behind them.[8]

ONCE PINCKNEY FINALLY SET OUT on his five-day trek to Richmond to meet up with his regiment, he began turning multiple layers of worries over in his mind. He thought of those loyal but very unsettled "backwoodsmen" following behind him. Returning veterans posted to their camp for recuperation had filled his men's heads with horror tales of battles in Virginia. The captain had promised when they innocently signed on in January 1861 "for the duration" that they would be a coastal home guard protecting their families and farms along the South Santee River. Now in all likelihood he was leading many to their deaths in a place quite foreign to them. Nothing in their training or experience this far, Pinckney knew, had prepared them for a confrontation with Major General Philip Sheridan's battle-hardened cavalry, or the rest of Grant's forces, waiting before them.[9] And was he himself ready? Nearly thirty-six years old and having grown cautious, Pinckney was too old to play the brave knight brandishing his grandfather's sword.

Should he die—a likely proposition—how would his elderly parents cope? Death had already visited their family three times in the past year. His mother's brother, the prescient William Elliott III of Beaufort, had died during a visit to Charleston in February 1863. Elliott, whose experiments with Sea Island cotton had generated great wealth for the state, had vigorously opposed Cotesworth Pinckney Sr. on both nullification and secession. Tom had been grateful for the night spent at his much-admired uncle's bedside in the Mills House Hotel just before he died in full knowledge that all he had feared about a war with the North—and more—had been realized.[10]

Almost exactly a year had passed since Lieutenant Cotesworth Pinckney Seabrook, his sister Caroline's cherished eldest son, had been buried under a full moon on the battlefield at Chancellorsville. Young "Pinck" had been his grandparents' special "prop and pride." They imagined, perhaps like the parents of Colonel Shaw, fervent abolitionists living on Staten Island, that somehow the breastplate of righteousness would protect this deeply religious young man as well. After the fighting was over, his comrades from Charleston had found his body and lovingly washed the blood from his face—he had been shot in the head—before dressing him in his uniform with sash and wrapping him in an india-rubber sheet. They carefully marked the spot, and nine days later, "Charley" Pinckney, following their directions, dug up his cousin's body and brought it home to be reinterred in the graveyard of Saint John in the Wilderness in Flat Rock. All of the family who could had attended the funeral services and a number became "excessively agitated."[11]

Having become bored with his posting with the Washington Light Infantry on languid Morris Island during the first months of 1861, the young officer had put himself in danger by enlisting with Colonel Maxcy Gregg's hard-fighting regiment in Virginia to more fully "play my part." His mother had received his last letter after learning of his death. In it he had assured her, "Have no fear for me, for I have no fear for myself." To honor his courage, Caroline Pinckney Seabrook had soldiered on, allowing herself no reprieve in her war work of assembling boxes of food for other boys at the front. Eight months later her seventeen-year-old daughter, Carrie, had died an agonizing, long-dreaded death from tuberculosis. "Sister" Seabrook stiffened her spine and, like the South itself, endured.[12]

While mulling the past and considering what the future held on his journey to Virginia, Captain Pinckney and his 250 soldiers withstood heat, dust, and hunger, then heat, rain, and hunger. When scouts brought word of "a party of Yankee raiders" headed toward Clarksville, North Carolina, Pinckney ordered an overnight forced march in an unsuccessful attempt to catch them. He later admitted to feelings of great relief at not having to "face off against two thousand well-armed Yankees" with his men, armed only with sidearms and sabers. General Hampton had shipped most of their muskets by rail. Still hoping that his cavalrymen might yet have a chance of "making their mark in the way that seems to be expected of them," the captain wrote a friend that they planned "to do our part in conquering that peace which I cannot but believe will be the result of this summer campaign."[13]

Pinckney's exhausted company finally caught up with Colonel Rutledge at Amelia Court House outside of Richmond by May 24,1864. Preparing his regiment to make an impressive entrance into the Confederate capital, Rutledge sent a terse order to the captain to keep his men in closer formation. Like most of the "country companies," Pinckney's had horses of all sizes and shapes; the nonconformity of strides made staying in line almost impossible as the jogging farm cobs fell behind the smooth broken trot of marsh tackies that were, in turn, unable to keep up with dancing thoroughbreds. Crossing the James River at the suburb of Manchester, Rutledge's regiment made a long march along Broad Street through the Confederate capital. The men stopped for the night several miles out on the Brook Turnpike, worn and rutted from the back-and-forth tromping of men as Confederate and Union troops advanced and retreated over the same hotly contested territory between Richmond and Washington.[14]

After setting up across from a schoolhouse near Brook Hill, Pinckney and Lieutenant Augustus W. Cordes took advantage of a nearby stream to wash off the dust of many miles. A genial Scotsman approached and in a light burr introduced himself as John Stewart, owner of the farm adjacent their camp. Having received their assurances that the cavalry horses would not despoil his clover field, Stewart invited the men to dinner. After meals of half-rations that translated into about a half-dozen fritters and a rasher or two of bacon—now standard in the Army of Northern Virginia—nothing could have pleased them more. Besides, the only other option was a dinner at the Exchange Hotel, location of the 4th South Carolina's headquarters, which was indifferent in quality and exorbitant in price.[15]

Stewart, a tobacco broker, flew the neutral Union Jack over his impressive three-story mansion to ward off predations from Union troops circling around Richmond and devoted part of his house to a hospital, but like so many Scots, he and his brother were devoted to the cause of southern independence. He kept open house for the Confederate high command and frequently brought home attractive, well-bred officers to meet his seven young daughters appealingly arrayed around the dining table.[16]

Pinckney's hope of accepting Stewart's invitation to return was dashed when the next day he learned that General Braxton Bragg, one of the Confederacy's eight full generals and military advisor to President Jefferson Davis, had issued a "preemptory order" that the regiment move up toward the front on the early morning of May 26.[17] Regimental inefficiency had continued in Virginia. The confusion of trying to match the cavalrymen in each company with the same-caliber rifles and then matching arms and ammunition would have been comic had it not been such a serious organizational blunder. To his further dismay, Pinckney learned that only twenty-four of the ninety-six men in his company had horses fit to ride; "Because of a shoe. . . ," the adage often associated with King Richard III's defeat at the Battle of Bosworth, probably flicked through his mind. Some mounts had lost their ill-fitting shoes, while others suffered from saddle galls. Pinckney cursed the quartermasters in Columbia who had failed to supply his men with the new-style McClellan saddle—lighter and better balanced for the business of war than even the finest English riding saddles—in time for their departure. Others, poor old plugs malnourished and never much good from the start, were broken down beyond redemption after hundreds of miles of bad roads. A shortage of horses plagued most southern cavalry outfits by that time. Even though only four hundred out of one thousand men slated for Lee's army had mounts fit for battle, Pinckney later recollected, not one would undertake to modify the order, for relentless General Grant edged uncomfortably close to Richmond despite taking heavy losses.[18]

In one of General Butler's dispatches to Colonel Rutledge, he stipulated that Captain Pinckney should stay back at the Brook Road camp and help expedite the forward movement of men and horses rather than enter the zone of battle. Butler, a savvy politician before the war who no doubt hoped to be one again afterward, had likely received a request from the Confederate government to keep the captain in a place of safety.[19]

Pinckney, however, would have none of it, refusing to be singled out for privilege, to be once again wrapped in flannels by his family. Concern for his public reputation, the chivalric code of "death before dishonor," and his genuine sense of duty to his company would not let him accept this advantage of social rank. Later recalling his decision, Pinckney immodestly wrote, "with the spirit that was characteristic of our army, I insisted that as both of my horses were in good condition, I should be allowed to go to the front with my men."[20]

On schedule, Pinckney set off on Stonewall with his attenuated company behind him. The stallion, sensing the excitement, threw his head and pulled on his bit as the cavalrymen moved off in search of the Army of Northern Virginia, the mythically powerful but imperfectly synchronized fighting machine. Within a few miles, army wagons, couriers, and road crews crowded the road. The lingering stench of putrefying horseflesh and the pitiable mounds of shallow graves hastily scraped out of the hard clay alongside the road signaled that the regiment was approaching the scene of Sheridan's raid against the outer defenses of Richmond ten days earlier. Farther along, Pinckney noted with regret Yellow Tavern, where on May 12 the bold and brilliant Major General "Jeb" Stuart had died from wounds while defending the rear of Lee's army against Sheridan's men.[21]

When the regiment bivouacked along the South Anna River, Colonel Rutledge, Lieutenant Gabriel Manigault, and Captain Pinckney crossed to the south bank in the rain to report in at General Lee's headquarters. Full of anticipation, Pinckney's heart sank at the sight of the encampment, unceremoniously plunked down in a fallow field. One large wall tent housed the general. His adjutant general and aide, Colonel Walter Taylor, made do with a smaller one. The few other single-fly tents sheltered the rest of the staff and couriers. The captain's disappointment deepened when he learned that Lee was too ill to see them. Colonel Taylor, a Norfolk native and former banker, greeted them instead and relayed the general's desire that they report the next day to Major General Hampton.[22]

The loss of Stuart had broken Lee's heart and thrown him into the terrible quandary of how to replace an irreplaceable corps commander. Under pressure to make a quick decision during a critical moment in the campaign, Lee opted to keep the ultimate power in his own hands and divide responsibilities among the three cavalry division commanders: his son Major General W. H. F. "Rooney" Lee, his nephew Major General Fitzhugh Lee, and Hampton, who also would exercise seniority when the divisions' missions overlapped.[23]

Before returning to his command, Pinckney snatched a moment to speak with some friends at Lee's camp. One was Charlestonian Major Henry E. Young, judge advocate of the Army of Northern Virginia and the general's close advisor. Another was a former classmate at the University of Virginia, Colonel Charles Scott Venable, who brought him up to date on recent events and shared a bit about Lee's current strategy to defend Richmond.[24]

Venable did not yet understand that Grant, unlike his predecessors, was not fixated on occupying the Confederate capital, but rather on destroying Lee's army and finally putting an end to the war, even if it took him all summer and cost thousands of lives. If he was not successful by the time of the presidential election in November, Grant knew full well that northern voters, already teetering in their support of the war, could turn against Lincoln and elect his challenger. The candidate from the "peace" wing of the Democratic Party, Major General George McClellan, enjoyed great popularity with the enlisted men, even though Lincoln had removed him as general-in-chief of the Union armies in 1862.[25]

Hampton's job would be to find Grant before Sheridan, head of the cavalry corps of the Army of the Potomac, found Lee. The South Carolinian must somehow anticipate and delay Sheridan's men while trying to keep his own position secret. As this complex choreography careened southward from Spotsylvania Court House to the North Anna River and then listed toward the Pamunkey River in the direction of Cold Harbor, Pinckney's regiment would take on the minor, but critical, role of probing little country crossroads for signs of the main body of Grant's infantry.[26]

In the early morning of May 27, General Hampton rode into Rutledge's camp and ordered his regiment to mount up and fall in behind Brigadier General Thomas L. Rosser's famous Laurel Brigade. Upon close examination of the "dashing-looking" Virginian, Pinckney thought him too short for cavalier status and as "swarthy" as a Louisianan. During his service with "Jeb" Stuart, though, Rosser had earned a reputation for his daring and his tactical skills similar to that enjoyed by his West Point classmate, Brigadier General George Armstrong Custer, who was rumored to be in the neighborhood with his feared Michigan Wolverines.[27]

When Hampton headed off in a southerly direction, Pinckney guessed Mechanicsville as their destination. Instead they halted at a point near Atlee's Station, where Lee's three cavalry divisions had planned to rendezvous; Hampton was nominally in charge. The station, a stop on the Virginia Central Railroad, was an inviting target for Grant's forces, which were on the move and getting closer.

As his regiment waded in through the sea of veteran cavalrymen—bronzed and tough looking as old leather, lounging about in that jaunty, devil-may-care pose of fighting men who had already been through hell and could go back if ordered—Pinckney felt their appraising eyes fall on the newcomers. After three years of service close to home, the Charleston Light Dragoons of Company K still looked like debutantes with their white gloves and drew some ironic sniggers. Eyes rolled when Pinckney's own Company D passed. His men were taut and tanned but still readily identifiable as a militia of farmers, their long Confederate-issue Enfields—single-shot muzzleloaders—gave them the incongruous look of infantry on horseback. Battle veterans always made it their first priority to snatch a shorter breech-loading Sharps carbine from the cold clutches of Yankee cavalry corpses. A glance at Pinckney's sword, with its old-fashioned curved blade, likely caused a suppressed smirk as well. Those heavy swords and long weapons made mounting and dismounting a near impossible task in the hurry of battle. The day of the audacious slashing cavalry charge, old hands in the ranks knew, was over. Under Hampton's command, much of the cavalry's fighting was done on foot, often dug in.[28]

The jests and jibes, even if meant in a spirit of soldierly fun, only added to the misery and gloom dragging down the spirits of Pinckney's company. Exhausted, far from home, disoriented, and worried about what the next day would bring, the men groaned when they finally reined up at the encampment and saw no commissary wagon in sight. Whatever his troopers ate that night, they stole.[29]

At dawn on May 28, Pinckney rose early to graze his horse in a clover field and managed to grab a few wild strawberries for his own breakfast. His men, nervous and out of sorts, were uneasy in their confusion over the chain of command. Still intensely local in their allegiance, they felt a deep loyalty to their captain and, after their year at Pocotaligo, had learned to more-or-less trust their regimental officers. Now they were somewhere in Virginia and loosely attached to General Hampton. That he was a South Carolinian was good, but the soldiers had only seen him at the review in Columbia. They had never laid eyes on General Butler, their brigade commander, and on the eve of their first major battle, he was not in camp. Major William P. Emanuel, quick to take Pinckney's safe place back at the camp in Richmond, was also missing. One of Pinckney's lieutenants, Bacot Allston, and a large detachment from Company D received orders to report to Brigadier General John R. Chambliss of Rooney Lee's Division for picket duty.[30]

Further down the chain, the command system seemed as ersatz to Pinckney as the coffee. Lieutenant Colonel William Stokes, the Branchville native, had been made temporary commander of the 4th South Carolina while Colonel Rutledge, who had little experience in leading even his own regiment in battle, had been placed in charge of Butler's new brigade. The other regiments of the brigade, the equally green troops of Colonel John Dunovant's 5th South Carolina Cavalry and Colonel John M. Millen's 20th Georgia Cavalry—partisan rangers who had been a coastal guard but had seen some action—would be thrown in with the 4th when they arrived that morning. At least Millen deflected some of the ridicule from the Carolinians when he appeared in a silk sash, looking dressed more for a review than for a battle. Pinckney did not realize that confusion also traveled up the chain as well. Colonel Rutledge was not exactly sure to which general he reported, Hampton, Rosser, or Rooney Lee, nor did he know for sure whether Millen's regiment was under his command.[31]

When the bugle sounded about 8:00 A.M., Hampton waved Fitzhugh Lee's division to the front with great flair. One of Brigadier General William Carter Wickham's seasoned Virginia regiments took the lead, traveling west on Atlee Station Road. When Rosser, his brigade positioned toward the rear, gave the word, Pinckney urged his anxious mount forward "at a rapid rate." The only impulse of riders and horses was "forward" as they entered into that state in which 4,500 men and beasts almost mystically become one column of sheer motion. Near Enon Methodist Church, General Wickham, in search of Grant's infantry, caught sight of Union pickets (Sheridan's men, he would later learn, looking for Lee's infantry) coming straight at them, traveling east. Pulling away from the main body of cavalry, Wickham gave chase and pursued his quarry to the Union line.[32]

Hampton chose an optimal position from which to engage the enemy. He established his battle line on a north–south axis across Atlee Station Road, bounded by water and marsh at either end. He ordered the cavalrymen to dismount and leave their horses in the rear. Much jostling ensued among those who knew the drill; the fourth in line held the horses, while the other three plunged into the fray. Rosser's Brigade was directed to the north of the road and Wickham's to the south. The terrain embraced heavily wooded areas, with other parts thick with the exuberant undergrowth of the late spring. Soldiers at the front of the line dug rudimentary rifle pits and threw up breastworks with whatever lay about the ground.[33]

Rather than moving up with Hampton to the front or aligning himself with Rosser, Colonel Rutledge stayed behind with the horse handlers, as did his adjutant, Lieutenant Manigault, thus further diminishing the already small ratio of officers to troopers on the firing line. Pinckney watched with concern as, under intense pressure from the enemy, Wickham's position started to weaken and his men fall back in disarray. Fitzhugh Lee then ordered Lieutenant Colonel Stokes to move the 4th South Carolina forward into the breach.[34]

Signaled by Stokes, Pinckney, encumbered by his sword, dismounted with care and handed off his horse. The regiment now numbered three hundred men. With a cheer and a (much practiced) rebel yell, Pinckney led his company as directed behind Wickham to re-form on the Confederate right. Running in his cavalry boots, his spurs jangled as he plunged forward, his grandfather's sword in one hand and his own Colt service revolver in the other. Passing through a clearing, his company suddenly appeared in the sights of Federal sharpshooters, who picked off three of their number straightaway. Stokes directed the Carolinians to dive into a low spot. There they waited, prone and vulnerable in a "hailstorm of bullets," for two hours.[35] The sweet smell of spring-ripened earth mixed with the sour odor of overripe uniforms—and of fear.

Finally, Hampton, thinking Wickham had things in hand, ordered Stokes to retire. Once again they passed through the valley of the Yankee deadeyes, leaping over fallen friends to short-lived safety behind Wickham's troopers, who were "hotly engaged with the enemy." Pinckney's men found the workaday demeanor of these veterans strangely calming. Even as stretcher bearers brought out a steady stream of casualties rent asunder and screaming in pain, Wickham's Virginians went about the business of battle efficiently, each peppering the enemy until he spent his shells, falling back, refilling his cartridge box, and then, weighted down with as much ammunition as he could carry, moving back into the fray without hesitation.[36]

The day passed with Confederate fortunes waxing and waning, attacks met with counterattacks, men moving up and falling back. Finally, Fitzhugh Lee turned to Stokes and told him once again to bring the regiment forward. Pinckney's baptism into battle was by full immersion into some of the most intense close shooting of the war. Nothing had prepared him or his men for this free-for-all in a dense wood. Rather than a field of glory, Pinckney found a forest of carnage. Bullets piercing through the dry wood crackled like the flames of Dante's inferno, hell on earth. The smell of sulfur—the scent of the devil—weighted the air.[37]

As it turned out, Pinckney's men, those haphazardly trained backwoodsmen, had an advantage in these conditions. Deadeyes with their old long-barreled muskets in the dense woods along the Santee River, this combat resembled shooting quail back home. Instead of picking their targets from the white-and-tan explosions lifting out of the hedgerows, they took aim at faces that would appear for an instant in the scrim of green, through a bush, around a tree—pop, pop. But today the prey was shooting back. The Union's new-issue Spencer repeating carbines lacked the Confederates' accuracy but could pump out seven shots without reloading—bam, bam, bam, bam, bam, bam, bam.[38]

Pinckney's problem, and that of the other inexperienced South Carolinians everyone later agreed, was that they did not know when to stop; *Dum Spiro*

Spero was, after all, their state's motto. Had Hampton been more deft in his management of the battle, less unsure in his new role, he might have been aware of the situation at the right end of the line, where Pinckney awaited instructions.[39]

Pinckney, as the second-ranking officer on the field, had command of about half of the 4th South Carolina as well as Millen's Georgia partisans and a portion of the 2nd Virginia. At some point they had become separated from Lieutenant Colonel Stokes and the rest of the men by a great yawning ravine. Placing his men in a large ditch with an embankment for breastworks, they kept up fire as the Yankees tried to ascend the hill about twenty yards before them. After several hours Pinckney observed the Confederate troops to his left falling back.[40]

Apparently, the courier with Hampton's order to disengage had been shot or become lost. Believing he had succeeded in pinpointing Grant's army, the general called for an organized withdrawal from the field. The line rolled away *ad seriatim,* like dominoes. Once Rosser's flank was exposed, he withdrew, then Wickham, then Dunovant's 5th South Carolina, then Stokes with the left wing of the 4th. Only the far right of the line—Pinckney's and Millen's men—fired on in isolation. General Custer, also ready to declare victory and call it a day, ordered two Union regiments to blaze into the thicket and snuff out those last flickers of rebel resistance.[41]

When he realized what was happening, General Hampton ordered men at "double quick march" to staunch the bleeding at the end of his line. There they found panicked, disoriented soldiers. Some were crawling out of the woods on their hands and knees; most were shattered by their experience. Hampton led them to safety as calmly as he could. Lieutenant Colonel Stokes was head-in-his-hands disconsolate, even though the general assured him he was not to blame. The silk-sashed General Millen lay dead. Someone said they saw Captain Pinckney fall, while others thought they had seen the enemy carry his body off the field.[42]

"CAPTAIN PINCKNEY IS DEAD" was the first report that his anxious family received from the battlefront. A subsequent official letter clarified his official status as "missing," warning the family of the massive loss of life at the Battle of Haw's Shop. Of the 400 men of Rutledge's regiment in action that day, 127 were killed, wounded, or captured. The Charleston Light Dragoons of Company K suffered the heaviest losses. Accusations flew as rapidly and as randomly as gunfire. Local critics felt that the gentlemen of Charleston had been sneered at and abused as "silk stockings" (and worst) for their privileged postings throughout the war, that without specific orders to retreat, they were "ashamed" to back down even when surrounded and consequently "slaughtered."[43]

Tom's sisters huddled in the little farmhouse at Cokesbury clinging to the faith that their brother might yet live. Both parents were convalescing from typhoid; his mother was judged too weak to hear the news. Letters from Pinckney's comrades began arriving at Cokesbury expressing deep regrets at the loss of so fine a man as the captain. During the course of the many difficult years to come, Thomas Pinckney sometimes wished that he had in fact fallen in a blaze of glory that day. The tale of his gallant death with his grandfather's sword still clutched in his hand would have added one more worthy chapter to his family's tradition of self-sacrificing patriotism.[44]

Instead, Pinckney had surrendered. Remaining behind to make sure that all of his men were out of the woods, he had been caught in a crossfire from front and flank and began zigzagging head down through the trees to escape. According to his account, he ran right into three men from Custer's 7th Michigan Cavalry. They leveled their carbines at him and demanded his surrender "in terms more forcible than elegant." He later learned that Lieutenant James W. O'Hear of the Charleston Light Dragoons also encountered Custer's soldiers, but he had resisted, unloading his pistols until stopped by a shot in the face. His killers then stooped to gingerly cut the gilt buttons off the dead man's gore-covered uniform.[45]

That Pinckney also surrendered his grandfather's sword to a rude Yankee officer multiplied his later remorse. After scrutinizing the "old-time curved blade," Lieutenant James Ingersoll announced that he would keep it for himself. Boasting of the superiority of the Union-issue modern straight sword, he drew out his own blade and handed it over to the captain. "It must have afforded an interesting sight to lookers-on," Pinckney remembered, "to observe us during this parley, brandishing each other's sabres."[46]

Taking some pity on his crestfallen captive, Ingersoll explained that he had a duty to disarm prisoners but promised to give back his old sword after the war was over. In his memoirs Pinckney claims that he threatened the officer that if they ever met on equal terms, they would then "settle the matter of its restitution." Lieutenant Ingersoll apparently took no notice and had him taken away. Some insolent Yankees rousted Pinckney about and led him to a holding area at the headquarters of Brigadier General David Gregg. Pinckney was treated with civility by Gregg's staff, who admired the Confederates' stubborn determination during the battle. One officer, an Englishman, offered him a welcome drink of liquor. Another irritated him with strange signs and gesticulations that Pinckney later realized was an attempt to determine if he was a brother Mason and might therefore qualify for special treatment.[47]

When the prisoners marched by General Custer's camp at Salem Church, Pinckney took macabre delight at the sight of bloodied Union soldiers laid out on the ground awaiting their turn for the surgeon's saw—"the result of our day's work on the enemy." Noting the high body count, he thought the Confederacy had won the seven-hour ordeal that came to be called the Battle of Haw's Shop, though sometimes referred to as Enon Church. Both sides suffered terribly. From a force of 4,000 cavalry, the Federals lost 365; the Confederates, 378 of their 4,500 men engaged. Sheridan may have forced his adversary off the field, but Hampton succeeded in his goal of discovering Grant's location without revealing that of General Lee, who could now confront the Army of the Potomac at a time and place of his choosing.[48]

On May 29, the morning after his capture, Pinckney and the other prisoners from Haw's Shop were shoved into formation and ordered to march. Where they were headed and how long they would be on the road, no one would say. Along the way the captain caught sight of the famed General Sheridan, whom he judged "energetic" looking if "undersized." They also passed Grant's "imposing" headquarters. The general's double-fly tent and flag had about fifteen somewhat smaller tents laid out around it with "military precision." A temporary telegraph wire looped over tree boughs, maintaining communication between headquarters and the field commanders. Different components of the Union war machine—infantry, cavalry, artillery, and ambulances—stretched out in the surrounding fields as far as Pinckney could see. Grant's soldiers all appeared young and "splendidly equipped." Reflecting on Lee's rudimentary encampment, the shoeless soldiers' short rations, and the shoeless horses' prominent ribs, he had an epiphany. "For the first time" Pinckney realized that the Confederates could indeed lose this war, that bravery and will might not succeed over the technological and material advantages of the Federal forces. Perhaps God really did favor the best-equipped battalions. Still, Pinckney discerned that deep in their souls, Grant's men were "very tired of the war" and might welcome some outcome short of unconditional surrender by the Confederacy just to stop the terrible carnage of this bloody campaign.[49]

As Pinckney entered his third day with no food and no protection from the early summer sun, his mind started to wander. A familiar voice brought him back to reality when, after being pushed and prodded into a prison "bull pen," he was hailed by his cousin Nat Barnwell as well as other comrades from his regiment. As delighted as he was to see these men of his class, he was repulsed at being thrown into the "motley" throng that included an unsavory collection of "ragged-looking Rebs," "Yankee deserters," and some impressed civilians suspected of harboring Confederate sympathies who were being paraded before the provost marshal. Nearby was a "retinue of contrabands" that Pinckney surmised "had stolen their owners' clothing, vehicles, etc. and were emigrating to the land of free love and miscegenation."[50]

One Confederate prisoner wearing an artilleryman's uniform, an object of much speculation among the guards, also excited Pinckney's curiosity. When he had a chance, he sidled up to the slight figure and, as he expected, glimpsed the smooth face of a young woman with her plait mostly hidden by a forage cap. When he asked in a whisper what she was doing in that guise, she replied, "the same as you." A scout for General Lee, she apparently slipped back and forth behind enemy lines and was held only briefly when caught. She planned when free to report to Lee's headquarters her observations of troop movements and name all the shameless Confederates who were "hobnobbing" with the Yankee occupiers. Many years later Pinckney found out that the mysterious captive was Barbara Ann Duravan, a native of Tennessee and a Confederate spy, whose identity as a woman was only discovered by the Federals when her luck ran out and she died of smallpox in the Union prison at Alton, Illinois.[51]

At one point during the prisoners' eight-day march along the slow-moving Pamunkey River, their guards allowed them to stop at a well by the side of the road. Two Virginia women came rushing up to Pinckney, tears streaming down their faces, begging for news from the front. The three pooled their knowledge, and from what the women told him, Pinckney calculated that General Hampton was now in hot pursuit of General Grant, who was maneuvering his huge behemoth of an army ever southward and would likely pass this spot. Scrounging a pencil and a scrap of paper, Pinckney scrawled a hasty message defensively explaining his situation to his father: "I am well, but in the hands of the enemy. I was commanding the right of the Reg't and we were cut off. I had no orders to fall back and held my position until we were surrounded.—Thomas Pinckney."[52]

The captain pressed the note into the hand of the one of the women and implored her to give it to the first Confederate cavalryman who passed down that road. Within a few days she had the opportunity to do so, and word of Pinckney's fate began its journey toward Hampton's headquarters, where it ultimately landed on the desk of Pinckney's cousin Captain Rawlins Lowndes, who relayed it to the Richmond office of their mutual friend, Secretary of the Treasury Christopher G. Memminger. One day not long after the Pinckney family had the chilling experience of seeing Tom's name among the "presumed dead" in the June 6 issue of the *Charleston Mercury*, an ominous letter arrived at the Cokesbury post office, where sister Caroline picked it up with the family mail.[53]

"Good news, good news, can you bear good news!" Caroline cried out as she bounded into the little grief-shrouded farmhouse waving her brother's well-traveled missive. Pinckney's elderly father, who had maintained stoic detachment while he waited and braced himself for the worst, completely broke down upon hearing the revelation that God had been gracious and spared his son.[54]

After Pinckney's capture was confirmed, his family assumed that before long he would be exchanged, as had been the customary practice. They began anew the process of searching for his name in the newspaper among the exchanged with a lighter heart that when they were scrutinizing the rolls of the dead. In her genteel innocence Tom's sister Mary Elliott wrote to a cousin that they "were actually relieved at his being in prison" since it was "safer than the battlefield."[55] But the Pinckney sisters had no concept of the horrors of a prisoner-of-war camp. No one who had not experienced the hopelessness, the filth, the disease, the starvation, and the viciousness of the guards—and sometimes of the other prisoners—possibly could.

The family members based their assumption that Tom would soon be coming home upon an exchange cartel modeled after the European-style "paroles of honor" that had become necessary after the large numbers of prisoners taken in the heavy fighting during 1862 rendered their internment impossible. The way it worked in theory was when a Confederate captain, for example, was taken prisoner, he would be briefly detained and then released to go home after taking an oath not to return to his regiment or to battle until he had received official notice that he had been "exchanged" for a Union prisoner of the same rank or (according to a complex table of equivalences) six privates.[56] The system soon broke down because Confederate soldiers generally had long enlistments or, as was the case in Pinckney's company, had signed on for the duration of the war. When these men were exchanged, they generally headed back to the front. Those Union soldiers whose initial ninety-day enlistments were nearly up by the time they were exchanged tended to stay home and not reenlist. As the war wore on and became increasingly lethal, some Union soldiers with short enlistments may well have been all too happy to be captured.

On June 7, 1864, Pinckney and his fellow prisoners, having had only two half-rations during their eight-day march, boarded the steamer *Weem*, which had just disgorged a load of cattle and mules. The footing proved tricky, but at least now he and his comrades had a roof over their heads for the first time since their capture. After passing along the heights of Yorktown, the *Weem* entered the broad reaches of Chesapeake Bay, giving Pinckney his first view of Point Lookout, a sandy peninsula at the mouth of the Potomac River. After General McClellan's ill-fated attempt to take Richmond in 1862, he had had a hospital built on the point to receive the massive number of Union wounded. A less salubrious location could scarcely have been found. The next year the Federal government established a twenty-three-acre holding depot there for Confederate prisoners awaiting parole. With the Army of Northern Virginia so close, Pinckney immediately saw the possibility that he might be rescued by a Confederate raid upon the camp. In any case, he believed that his stay in the "Officers' Prison," which was about one hundred yards across and three hundred yards long, would be brief as he would soon be homeward bound awaiting parole.[57] In truth, he was officially a dead man.

Only after his transfer from the holding pen at Point Lookout to the prisoner-of-war camp at Fort Delaware did Captain Pinckney fully realize that he had entered the darkest dimensions of the war, plumbing the deepest levels of human depravity where death was the only escape. The soldiers' war surely involved suffering and danger, but there were rules, a chain of command, a court of higher opinion, and witnesses. The press, the bane of both governments, was always buzzing about, revealing troop movements, publishing casualty statistics, caricaturing the presidents, criticizing the generals, and deflating the self-importance of the Congresses.

As a prisoner, however, Pinckney descended into a shadowy, secret place; a victim of the bitter, no-holds barred, unconditional-surrender politicians' war. President Lincoln's utter fury over secession had spilled over into his policies toward captured Confederates from the very beginning. He initially refused to even discuss a formal cartel because he did not recognize the Confederate States of America as a legitimate nation and would not negotiate any treaty with the outlaw Jefferson Davis. Prisoner-of-war conventions always assumed that soldiers were neutral actors following orders and bearing no personal blame. Lincoln insisted that the Confederates were not innocents but rebels, traitors-in-arms, and outlaws. When the first Confederate seamen were captured, the president wanted them tried as pirates. Pinckney's friend John Harleston, who later served with the Charleston Light Dragoons, had been snatched off a privateer by sailors on a Federal warship early in the war, paraded through the streets of New York City as a criminal, and thrown into Gotham's notorious "Tombs" prison along with thieves and murderers. Only threats from President Davis of "immediate and double retaliation" had saved Harleston from public hanging. Lincoln conceded the point and finally accepted a cartel when advisors warned that by taking a hard line he might reap what he sowed, that the self-proclaimed independent republics of the South could start arresting southern unionists as traitors.[58]

Pinckney's fate also became intertwined with that of the fourteen black soldiers captured by the Confederates on James Island and Battery Wagner a year earlier. The Richmond government refused to consider blacks as legitimate soldiers and would not enter into any negotiation to exchange them. President Davis engaged in a great deal of bluster about returning these men back into slavery but decided to throw the intractable question of their fate back to the individual states. Memminger, a Charleston lawyer at that time, regretted that the lack of a uniform policy on this matter forced South Carolina to come up with the "first solution" to "one of the gravest questions of the war." Acknowledging that freemen of color did possess certain civil rights, he doubted that they had lost those rights when they became soldiers. If the Confederacy went to war with Haiti, Memminger mused, "should no prisoners be exchanged?" He foresaw in July 1863 that if the state fell into the foolish trap of hanging black soldiers as insurrectionaries, "the Yankees will rejoice" and seize the long-sought opportunity to stop the exchange process. "They would rather keep one of our men than have back two of theirs," Memminger presciently surmised, acknowledging the Confederacy's food shortages, because "they know that feeding them [northern prisoners of war] would add to our embarrassment."[59]

In early May 1864, when General Grant set out on his relentless Overland Campaign to finally crush General Lee and his army, he had insisted that all prisoner exchanges be stopped. With the Confederates still fighting fiercely—long after prudence dictated they should surrender and save themselves—Grant knew that a war of attrition was his only sure option. The contest, he was among the first to admit, would not be decided by right—or even might—but by sheer numbers. Knowing his enemy well, the general worried that the rebels might just fight on "until the whole South is exterminated." Those soldiers retained in Union prisons would be of no more value to their cause "than dead men," he argued.[60]

When General Grant compared Confederate prisoners to "dead men," he spoke figuratively. Secretary of War Stanton, frustrated at inexplicable Confederate tenacity and worried about the upcoming presidential election, preferred a more literal interpretation. The only value of a rebel's life, in his opinion, had been as a pawn to trade for a Union soldier. With the end of the exchanges, what was the point in wasting resources keeping them alive? In mid-May 1864 Stanton agreed with Colonel William Hoffman, commissary general of prisons, that the vegetables, tea, coffee, and sugar regularly given to prisoners as part of the conventions of war should be cut back, not as much for the cost saving, but as a way to speed their inevitable fate—these men were never going home again. Hoffman's idea of sport became calibrating the smallest possible prison rations to just barely sustain life and the least amount of clothing to preserve minimum decorum.[61]

Captain Pinckney was swept up in the first wave of prisoners affected by this new regime. At Point Lookout, the first of the four Federal prisons he would endure over the next six months, he received one meal per day of salt pork and bean broth—and all the rats he could catch. The captain sought out fellow South Carolinians among the prisoners and squeezed his large frame into an old eight-man Sibley tent—an army discard—with some infantrymen from Brigadier General Johnson Hagood's brigade and the 20th South Carolina Infantry, both of which had served on Morris Island. Until he managed to steal some scarce wooden planks, Pinckney slept on the damp ground.[62]

The camp, a cesspool of infection, was low and marshy, with only copperas-tainted water to drink. The infrequent visitors to the island reeled at the sight and smells of 12,000 men warehoused on twenty-three acres of desolate, wind-swept ground. Soldiers of the 36th US Colored Troops (USCT), composed largely of former North Carolina slaves and new to the war, manned the palisades around the perimeter. Inflamed by still-disputed news reports that in April Major General Nathan Bedford Forrest's Confederates had committed atrocities against surrendering black soldiers of the Union garrison at Fort Pillow, Tennessee—competing claims argue that the soldiers decided to fight to the death rather than be captured—the guards rode roughshod over the rebel prisoners. Pinckney was "outraged." The situation became so tense that Hoffman, no friend to the rebels, issued a special directive restricting the use of deadly force by the "trigger-happy" guards. In early June the black troops received orders for Virginia, where they took part in the siege of Petersburg and had ample opportunity to discharge their weapons. Pinckney found that their replacements, an "invalid corps" of soldiers who had seen their share of action, demonstrated more compassion for the captives.[63]

Desperate for news of the war, Pinckney leaped up every time the cry "fresh fish" echoed through the camp and ran to the gate, hoping to find a familiar face among the newly arrived prisoners pushed blinking and uncomprehending into the pen. He was particularly anxious to find someone to contradict that "Yankee lie" being rumored around the camp that Petersburg had fallen. On June 20 the haul of new prisoners produced Lieutenant Manigault and Major Emanuel of the 4th South Carolina and Lieutenants David Gordon and William Epps, old comrades from Company D. They had been captured unharmed during a June 11–12 engagement at Trevillion Station, where, they explained with great enthusiasm, General Hampton had been at his brilliant best in another clash with Sheridan, believed to be one of the most monumental cavalry engagements of the war. Custer too had been humbled, Pinckney was happy to learn.[64]

The newcomers were equally delighted to see Pinckney alive and well. They had mourned him as lost when Manigault recognized General Pinckney's venerated sword lashed to the saddle of an officer in the 7th Michigan Cavalry. Upon later questioning by Lieutenant Ingersoll, Manigault learned Pinckney's true fate. Ingersoll inquired why the captain had put up such a fight before surrendering his sword. Manigault related the weapon's noble history, probably a mistake in retrospect, and gave him Pinckney's address where he might return it after the war.[65]

On June 22 Pinckney noticed prison clerks compiling lists describing each of the inmates, which told him they were going to be moved. Some still expected an exchange, but Pinckney, beginning to understand the new system from his interviews with other prisoners, guessed they would be headed for either Fort Delaware, on an island in the Delaware River, or Johnson's Island in Ohio. Both, he knew, were death traps.[66]

Pinckney and the other six hundred or so prisoners were quite precipitously rousted up on July 12 and hustled onto waiting transports. He had been right. Major General Custis Lee had, indeed, planned to rescue them from Point Lookout as part of President Davis's larger scheme for attacking Washington. Prison officials, however, caught wind of the plan and in haste had them taken to the middle of the channel. With no lights allowed, the men spent the night in oppressive darkness. When overcome by sleep, the "mass of sweltering humanity" stuffed in the airless, standing-room-only hold began to collapse one upon another. The long terrible night, one of the most painful in Pinckney's memory, was punctuated by oaths and curses as elbows poked eyeballs and knees jabbed ribs.[67]

Pinckney's miserable journey to Fort Delaware was like a passage on the River Styx to the underworld of the war. Located on Pea Patch Island in the Delaware River, the brooding granite hulk had been completed in 1859 as a harbor defense. Close to Washington and the Virginia theater of operations yet isolated and out of sight, Fort Delaware initially had been a convenient place to incarcerate political prisoners, particularly those outspoken civilians sympathetic to the southern cause arrested when Lincoln suspended *habeas corpus* in the case of seditious speech. With the commencement of McClellan's offensive against Richmond in 1862, the Federal government was totally unprepared to handle the resulting thousands of prisoners of war who needed accommodation. Pea Patch Island became eight acres of purgatory as clapboard shanties were thrown up slapdash, first to accommodate a thousand, then two thousand, then five thousand men outside of the fort but under its guns. A large population of prisoners from the battle at Gettysburg had suffered there for almost a year. When he arrived, Pinckney moved unbelievingly among the multitude of men in various stages of deterioration. The nearly naked bodies showed the effect of starvation diets; others, he could see, languished with highly contagious diseases in need of medical care. Torture, he soon learned, was part of life at Fort Delaware. Sadistic guards enjoyed hanging rebels by their thumbs as an amusing pastime and punished men at random. Any prisoner interfering with their sport was shot on the spot.[68]

The conditions at Fort Delaware seemed too bad not to be deliberate. As a physician Pinckney was appalled. The stinking water, he knew, harbored coliforms. The only ditch available for washing was filled with runoff from ground covered by human filth. The rations of bits of greasy bacon and loathsome soup were so inadequate that long-term inmates lost a third of their fighting weight. The lice had more life in them than the men they plagued. From time to time a sergeant would holler "rat call" as he pumped gas into the holes in the plank walls above the yard and the prisoners, desperate for protein came limping over. As the rats scurried out of their holes to escape the fumes, a pack of little terriers joyfully snatched the fleeing rodents. Whatever carcasses the dogs left behind, the guard swept to the excited men waiting hopefully below. At the end of the war, the commandant proudly showed a budget surplus.[69]

Initially the dynamics of prison life ground down all men to a rough sort of democracy of deprivation. Captain Pinckney, having been stripped of his gold watch and cash, experienced the same relative sense of destitution as those penniless captives who could scarcely tell time. Gradually, however, the inequalities of civilian life reasserted themselves as native talents, connections, and creativity once again pushed the skilled and lucky up to the surface, while men with few resources sank like stones. When Virginia infantryman John S. Swann first arrived in Fort Delaware, the "very strange state of things" among the 2,000 prisoners puzzled him. Some wore decent clothing and maintained sufficient good spirits to sing songs together and play cards, whereas others lay in their bunks "dejected, ragged, dirty and evidently suffering," even though the better off did share their food with them.[70]

Sidney Lanier, who became one of the most beloved southern poets of the postwar years, viewed his own experience as a prisoner of war at Point Lookout in terms of a death and a rebirth. Whatever the "depth" or "capability of body or soul" a soldier possessed at the time of his capture or his "death," Lanier theorized, would be the "inheritance" with which he would begin life *de novo* at his second birth as a prisoner. "In this far little world" of the prisoner-of-war camp, "which was as much separated from the outer world as if it had been in the outer confines of space," he wrote, "it was striking to see how society immediately resolved itself into those three estates which invariably constitute it elsewhere." Captain Pinckney fit into his first category of "true-gentlemenly type aristocrats" (in contrast to the "philanthropic sort" or the "insulting-obtrusive sort"), who managed to live well without working. Prison contorted the definition of the good life. The goal of every man was not "honor or luxury" but sleeping in a "cracker-box cabin" instead of the "wet, vermin infested tents."[71]

By Lanier's criteria, Pinckney, for all his genuine suffering, lived like a prince among prisoners by virtue of having a blanket and a frying pan, a utensil that made all the difference in fricassee of rat or stolen ears of horse corn. The key to surviving on the inside, he had quickly learned, was pretty much the same as on the outside—good connections. With his well-known name and genial good manners, Pinckney could beg or borrow a pen, bits of paper, and most precious of all, stamps. He began his writing campaign back at Point Lookout, where he had quickly grasped the lay of the land. He had to have money. Without credit with the quartermaster (cash was not allowed because guards could so easily be bribed), he could not buy the overpriced food from mercenary sutlers that he needed to live. All the time he had spent socializing in New York while attending (or perhaps instead of attending) medical lectures, Pinckney realized, probably saved his life during these months. He wrote everyone he knew in the North who might send him food, clothes, or a check. One letter reached his friend Harry Armstrong in New York City, who sent him twenty-five dollars. Dr. Samuel H. Dickson, Pinckney's former medical-school professor who had relocated to Philadelphia's Jefferson Medical College, was able to spare him five dollars.[72]

Cash even rained upon the captain unsolicited. In one mail he received a cryptic unsigned letter addressed in a lady's hand and bearing a Philadelphia postmark. His correspondent had seen his name among the list of prisoners at Fort Delaware in a northern newspaper and wrote asking if he was the same "Thomas Pinckney" who had once attended a country party and entertained everyone by appearing in "feminine costume." If indeed he was, he should write to a third party who would supply him with everything allowable by prison rules. Pinckney remembered the event and his own antics well and deduced that the sender must be Nellie Habersham, daughter of a Savannah rice factor. She had married a Pennsylvania man, whom she obviously did not want to know about her helping a rebel prisoner. After complying with her directions, Pinckney received a generous box of supplies (much picked over by the guards) and a check for fifty dollars.[73]

Tapping into the elaborate system of information gathered by long-term prisoners, Pinckney learned about the women's associations secretly organized in Baltimore and New York to supply Confederate prisoners with life's basics. After exploring how the system worked, he secured the name of a Miss Steuart to whom he was to write as though she was an old friend—for the benefit of the prison censors—and request what he needed. Only sheer desperation forced the proper Pinckney, who always used the term "appetite" to refer to a "stomach" in polite society, to ask a lady for underclothes. Prison authorities had caught on to the gambit but played along, freely helping themselves to care packages—they took the solicited underwear—and daring the prisoners to complain. Still, the soap and towels from Miss Steuart's package were as welcome as gold. Pinckney craved something to read and began asking friends for "any sort of trash" just to divert his mind. Receiving no replies to his letters home, he assumed that they had not been delivered.[74]

All around the letter-writing Pinckney buzzed that energetic second class of prisoner described by Lanier as "living well by laboring." Whatever skills these men possessed in their old life were resurrected in the camp. Small businesses sprung up like mushrooms in the forest. Whittlers carved crosses, rings, or useful implements such as spoons for sale. Some made their living playing cards and gambling for whatever his mark could spare.[75]

The third class in Lanier's hierarchy, the "drones" with no skills and no friends, "starved by not laboring." Some were sick or wounded, of course, but a certain number of prisoners simply gave up; the horror of it all was just too much. Those with no one to write (or who could not write) or no skills to put to use tended to stay in their bunks all day to save their strength, especially on those two days a week when they only received crackers. Sleep deprivation contributed to their downward spiral. Without warm clothes (or almost any clothes) or blankets on the cold nights, they were chilled to the bone and had to keep getting out of bed to huddle near a fire. The Virginian Swann realized that he could too could have succumbed to hopelessness had not a guard, touched by his desperate plea to trade his socks or his handkerchief for a stamp, passed him fifteen in secret.[76]

Pinckney's relative good fortune did not guarantee that he would survive his incarceration. When his thirty-sixth birthday rolled around on August 13, 1864, he believed it would be his last. In his depleted state his old nemesis malaria reasserted itself and struck him down again with fevers and chills. Ever the doctor, Pinckney had dispassionately monitored his own decline. Each day he tested his strength by walking the same route around the prison pen over ground wet with mud and slippery with human waste. Each day he weakened. Had he been at home, where his mother would have buried him in blankets and fed him nourishing broth and Peruvian bark as in years past, he might have been able to fight back, but in this cauldron of infection, he judged that he no longer had a fair chance.[77]

Pinckney's life became a daily struggle. He did not hunch up in his blanket and wish his life away, but he did confront his own mortality and tried to view his lot with equanimity. His father had always preached the moral imperative of self-control, of checking pride in good times, of being stoic in bad, and of giving oneself over to the will of God. As a Christian with rock-solid faith, he accepted that the events of history played out according to an ineffable plan and that his suffering and death would somehow have meaning. His upbringing had encouraged him to believe that he had a personal destiny. Although he had lived most of his life in deep comfort, even luxury at times, the Pinckney family narrative had actually prepared him for a life of sacrifice rather than ease. Earlier generations had been imprisoned for acting on their convictions. General Thomas Pinckney and his brother General Charles Cotesworth, as well as their younger cousin Charles, had been consigned to the horrid holds of British prison ships during their days as young patriots of the American Revolution. British officers had held Rebecca Motte a captive in her own home. The family's glory, like their salvation, had been bought with a price. Over the generations Pinckney men and women had always been willing to live or to die for their country. The only question remaining for the captain was which fate would it be for him. Now he thought he knew.

Later that day, however, good fortune did intervene in the most unexpected fashion, making this birthday his most memorable. While resting from the rigors of his daily walk, he heard a company of Union infantry march into the prison yard. Looking out the window of his plank shanty, he observed that the much-despised Commandant General Albin F. Scheopf was with them—not a good omen. Scheopf's provost marshal trailed behind him, carrying an armload of papers. Pinckney perched on the sill to see what was coming.[78]

Scheopf announced that six hundred prisoners would be transferred to South Carolina within a week. With no further explanation, the provost marshal began haphazardly picking up the rolls of prisoners listed by date of committal. He began to read out names at random, a dozen or so from one roll, then bored with that list, a dozen or so from another. Pinckney's spirit sank as the officer droned on. More than five hundred men had stepped forward when at last the captain heard the names of Lieutenants Epps and Gordon, both men of his regiment admitted with him. Pinckney held his breath—the last name called was his. He clambered out of the window where he had perched and did a dying man's version of a sprint to join the chosen. This just might be his happy ending. Perhaps, he hoped, exchanges had resumed in Charleston Harbor. At the very least he would die in the land of his ancestors.[79]

The day before his scheduled departure, Pinckney wrote to his father that he was being sent back to South Carolina. If indeed he was going to be exchanged, he promised to try to see the family before rejoining his regiment, although he admitted illness rendered him "hardly fit for the field." After a week of anxious waiting, when given the departure order, Pinckney packed his few things "with alacrity." On the morning of August 21, he stood nervously at the head of the long line of prisoners. He and Lieutenant Epps carried a biscuit box between them that contained all their worldly possessions: some extra clothing and a few eating utensils. They sang out when the roll was called. When the gates swung open, they could scarcely keep from running toward the waiting South Carolina–bound steamship, an old side-wheeler dubbed *Crescent City* impressed by Union forces after the fall of New Orleans. To ward off Confederate rescue attempts, three gunboats—the USS *Eutaw*, the USS *Dictator*, and the USS *Admiral*—formed an armed escort.[80]

The holiday mood changed abruptly when the prisoners saw their accommodations. Once a cotton freighter, the *Crescent City*'s reconfigured interior more closely resembled a slaver from middle-passage infamy than a transport ship. Instead of berths, Pinckney found a series of shelves constructed between the two decks three rows high. He and Lieutenant Gordon had quickly evaluated the situation and dove into an alcove platform under the aft hatchway with some access to fresh air. Those who followed squeezed into berths about six-feet square with two feet of headroom. The last men aboard had to crawl into stuffy dark places near the boilers, with a narrow passageway as their only source of ventilation. Everyone found the mid-August heat enervating, but those in the middle spent their entire journey poaching in their own perspiration. The only available water came from the steaming condenser.[81]

As the *Crescent City* made its way through the chop of the Chesapeake, then the churn of the Atlantic, those seasick prisoners wedged in their bunks transformed the passageways into a "state more readily imagined than described," as Pinckney delicately phrased it. He might have perished during this voyage had he not been among the fortunate officers allowed occasional access to the fresh salt air on the upper deck. A kindly old English stewardess helped sustain them by secretly passing the prisoners cold vegetables, leftovers scraped from the Yankee officer's plates.[82]

The trip proved uneventful until the night of August 24, when the *Crescent City* ran aground about forty miles north of Charleston. Pinckney awoke to the clamor of some prisoners being forced off to try to lighten the vessel. Peering out through a porthole at sunrise, the captain glimpsed with amazement the familiar lazy yellow water of the Santee delta. Observing none of the convoy ships nearby, he correctly deduced that his vessel, manned by a civilian crew, had gone off course while attempting to dodge the strong northerly currents of the Gulf Stream and had breached the infamous Cape Romaine Shoal nine miles offshore. Riding these muddy waters again was like returning to the embrace of his family. In the daylight he would be able to identify the rooftops of McClellanville, where in an optimistic moment in 1860 he had bought a cottage for himself as a refuge from the summer heat.[83]

While Pinckney was musing above decks, desperate prisoners plotted below. The ranking Confederate officers huddled together, contriving how to take over the ship. Not only did the prisoners enjoy superior numbers, but they also had experienced naval officers and engineers among them. Believing themselves "masters of the situation," the conspirators' blood was running high when they drafted an ultimatum to present to Captain James H. Prentiss. "In order to save the effusion of blood," they stated, he must turn the ship over to the prisoners. They guaranteed him a parole in return and safe conduct north. Remembering that the vessel was stranded in Pinckney's home waters, someone quietly asked him to join the group. Ever cautious, he warned that judging distances at sea was tricky and that the lighthouse—long darkened by the Confederates—that seemed so close in the moonlight was actually on Raccoon Island. The mainland, where they could connect with local Confederate units, was across ten miles of water.[84]

Prentiss refused the prisoners' "parlay" and put his men on high alert with fixed bayonets. The only action left to the Confederates was to wait for the ebbing tide and make a "desperate rush" at their captors, a move that they all knew would cost a great many lives. As the men were steeling themselves to put their plan into action, the Federal escorts hove into view. Alerted by a blockader hanging off Bull's Island that the *Crescent City* had not yet passed, the warships had retraced their course. The prisoners' hopes evaporated with every creak, groan, and jerk of the old ship as the gunboats hauled it off the shoal.[85]

When word of the approaching convoy reached Charleston, the general expectation in the city was that an exchange was finally going to occur. Instead, the ships passed farther south to Port Royal Sound, where the prisoners languished during court-martial proceedings against the *Crescent City*'s negligent pilot and a hapless lieutenant accused of conspiracy.[86] Once completed, the steamship then revved northward to Lighthouse Inlet on Morris Island. On September 7, 1864, seeing the Confederate flag still flying atop Fort Sumter, the battered and besieged guardian of Charleston Harbor, the "dead man" began to hope that he might yet have a rebirth as a free man on his native soil.

"The Old First Church of Galesburg." Reputed to be one of the "depots" of the Underground Railroad system of western Illinois. *Courtesy of Special Collections and Archives, Knox College Library, Galesburg, Illinois.*

"Storming Fort Wagner," 1890. An idealized postwar rendering typical of the popular decorative lithographs by the Chicago publishing firm of Kurz and Allison.
Library of Congress Prints and Photographs Division.

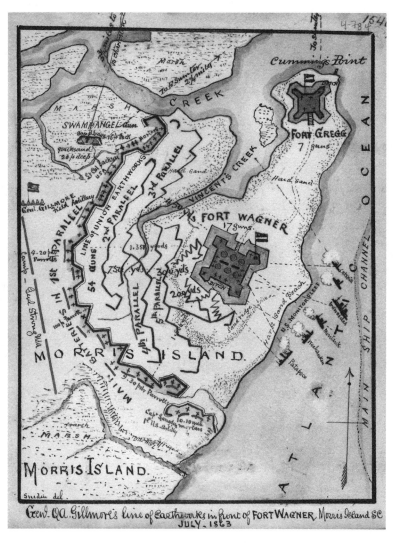

"General Q. A. Gillmore's line of earthworks in front of Fort Wagner, Morris Island, S.C., July 1863," drawn by Robert Knox Sneden. *Library of Congress, Geography and Map Division, from the collections of the Virginia Historical Society.*

"In the Trenches before Wagner." Black soldiers on Morris Island bore a disproportionate burden of the manual labor during the six-week land siege that finally caused the evacuation of Fort Wagner in August 1863. *Harper's Weekly,* August 29, 1863.

"Pocataligo Depot, South Carolina." Confederates successfully defended this critical Beaufort District link in the Charleston and Savannah Railroad until General Sherman's army swept through the lowcountry in early 1865. Sketch by Theodore R. Davis in *Harper's Weekly,* February 25, 1865. *Courtesy of The Charleston Museum, Charleston, S.C.*

"The Arrival of Two Thousand Vicksburg Prisoners at Fort Delaware."
When Captain Pinckney was incarcerated here in 1864, the prison's population
was about eight thousand. By D. Auld, *Harper's Weekly*, June 27, 1863.
Courtesy of the Delaware Public Archives.

Union Stockade on Morris Island, 1864.
Library of Congress Prints and Photographs Division.

"'Marching On!'—the Fifty-Fifth Massachusetts Colored Regiment singing
John Brown's March in the streets of Charleston, February 21, 1865." The 54th received
a similarly ecstatic reaction from the formerly enslaved people of Charleston during
their triumphant entry six days later. *Harper's Weekly,* March 18, 1865.
Courtesy of The Charleston Museum, Charleston, South Carolina.

7

THE FIFTY-FOURTH AND
THE SIX HUNDRED

ON SEPTEMBER 7, 1864, the prison ship *Crescent City* lurched to a stop at the Lighthouse Inlet wharf on Morris Island. When the hatch opened, nearly six hundred Confederate prisoners of war spilled down the gangplank of the old cotton freighter, shading their eyes and gasping for fresh air. Sardined together for eighteen days in the sweltering, dark hole of the steamer, these captives—poached and pale as ghosts—looked as if they had been regurgitated from hell.[1]

Shaky and feverish, Captain Pinckney blinked in disbelief at the scene on the overcast beach. Before him was every slaveholder's worst nightmare: Nine companies of sober-faced black soldiers, sharply dressed in blue, stood in formation on the windswept sand, rifles at their sides. Then an officer sang out, and the detachment swung into a very precise rendition of the manual of arms: "Shoulder arms . . . support arms . . . present arms," signaling "We are soldiers. . . . We are men."[2]

For those northern-born men of the 54th Massachusetts, the sight of hundreds of wheezing, wraith-like Rebels also had a surreal quality. They had been braced for the satanic southerners of their own fraught dreams. Indeed, a few of the prisoners did still have the anticipated demonic look—"dark, long-haired and fierce of aspect"—but most appeared impotent and broken. During their ordeal on the *Crescent City*, once-defiant men who had displayed "powerful nerve" on the battlefield now prostrated themselves before their captors, weeping and begging for a sip of water.[3]

To the uninitiated, these Confederates appeared surprisingly dissimilar. Among the prisoners were officers of all ranks (except general), all social classes, and a variety of ethnicities. Tall, lanky mountaineers straggled beside once-jaunty city men. Some still wore more-or-less recognizable remnants of the signature gray uniform, while others had on blue jean suits, homespun, or butternut, all reduced to rags. Their headgear was equally eclectic: straw hats, slouch hats, and forage caps of red, blue, or gray. With the exception of those who had made fortunate finds among the battlefield dead, their footwear was hard used and ranged from vestiges of tall cavalry boots to battered brogans; some even went barefoot. Their few bits and pieces of spare clothing traveled in rubber sheets, biscuit boxes, worn quilts, ancient carpetbags, or cotton haversacks—all filthy.[4]

Captain Pinckney felt "intense disgust" at the whole situation. His shabby appearance in front of the squared-away black guards shamed him. One soldier in particular insulted Pinckney by the disdainful, gingerly way he took his mildewed, lice-infested blanket before giving him a shoddy Yankee issue in return. Most of all, the captain resented having orders and insults barked at him by black men—some former lowcountry slaves freed during Colonel Montgomery's Combahee River raid—who prodded the resentful rebels into an approximate formation.[5]

When commanded to march, Pinckney shuffled forward on the beach as part of this bizarre parade. Black soldiers, on high alert for Confederate rescue parties, formed a human cage around the prisoners, with three companies in front, two in the back, and two on either side from the 21st USCT. After the first mile or so of their three-mile trek, the weakest began to drop in the sultry heat. The ailing Pinckney reeled. A sudden rain shower refreshed him just as he was about to fall, while those prisoners with hats held them skyward vainly trying to catch a few drops to allay their burning thirst. Some of the black soldiers, moved by this pitiable sight, fetched them fresh water from a nearby spring.[6]

After more than an hour of trudging across the sand, Pinckney saw what he hoped was a mirage. About seventy-five yards from the high-tide line, a stockade loomed before him. Pine fencing at least twelve feet high surrounded an open space of about an acre and a half. The top of each pole was hewn to a dagger point, its foot pounded down to the waterline to prevent tunneling. A wave of despair rippled through the captive corps when, squinting ahead, they perceived that their open-air pen was a deathtrap located between Battery Wagner (now officially called Fort Strong) and Battery Gregg (now Fort Putnam) where "the Rebel fire came strong and hot" from Fort Sumter and James Island. The rumors they had heard were true. Pinckney recalled that a "more disappointed and crestfallen set of men I have never seen." None had really believed that the Federals were actually going to put their "inhuman threat into execution," for it served no purpose. "How Confederate shells falling short of their targets and bursting upon them would advance the Union cause" no one could discern, unless the point was simple revenge. With unrestrained glee, a newspaper published in Union-occupied Port Royal described the Confederate prisoners' stockade as being "in the dangerous district, where shells fly freely, in full view of all the rebel works, and closely under our own guns." Before the compound could be built, five carts full of iron shell pieces had to be raked up and hauled away.[7]

Inside the compound 160 A-shaped tents were laid out in eight neat rows, with alleyways at right angles. Pinckney shared a tent with his friends from the 4th South Carolina Cavalry—Major Emanuel and Lieutenants Epps and Gordon. Looking up at the armed black guards from the 54th Massachusetts who loomed over them from a raised plank wall and following their every move, the men felt as vulnerable as fish in a barrel. Guards also patrolled the "dead line," a grass rope that ran about twenty feet inside the circumference of the enclosure. Crossing the line meant instant death, no questions asked. Outside the wall more sentries stood watch. Two Billinghurst Requa Battery guns, forerunners of the modern machine gun, with twenty-five rifle barrels secured on a field carriage and capable of firing off 175 rounds a minute, were fixed upon the gates but could be turned on the prisoners in case of a riot.[8]

SERGEANT JOSEPH H. BARQUET's Company H had the bad luck to be among the six companies from the 54th Massachusetts tapped for guard detail. Barquet saw himself as a liberator, not a jailor, and found tossing rotten bits of bacon to these defeated rebels an unsavory, inglorious assignment. On September 7, 1864, a year to the day after Battery Wagner fell at such a tremendous cost to the regiment, discontent blanketed the spirits of the 54th. Desperate to actually get into the fighting war to prove themselves—the real point of their enlistment—they too felt like prisoners on that cursed, unhealthy island. Day in and day out, hard labor consumed their waking hours. Maintaining the batteries put them too in the path of Confederate fire. By this juncture in the war, veterans among their ranks had few illusions about battlefield glory, but they did feel that if they must die, let it be for a purpose—in battle gaining some ground, reducing the enemy, and convincing the many remaining skeptics that black men would fight—but not with a shovel in their hand. News that the 54th would be guarding the incoming Confederate prisoners in September and thus would not be leaving the island anytime soon was decidedly unwelcome. If the soldiers did not know that the placement of the prison pen directly in range of incoming rebel fire was against the rules of engagement, they surely knew it was unsporting.[9]

Dispirited, Barquet found his job as guard straightforward and tedious. During his twelve-hour shift, he had responsibility for seventy-five sour-faced rebels. He called the roll three times a day and monitored the prisoners, making sure they policed their areas, did not leave their tents at night except for matters of necessity, or engage in unusual behaviors suggestive of escape plots. While on duty, Barquet bunked within the blown-out remnants of Battery Wagner, still redolent of an abattoir yet alive with relentless fleas—a legacy of the long-besieged Confederates—that gnawed on him all night long. Bits of metal and lead from the thousands of incoming and outgoing shells carpeted the ground. Huge Hammond calcium lights, leftovers from the siege of Battery Wagner, were mounted on the parapets and illuminated the camp at night. If more than ten prisoners ever assembled together, guards were instructed to shoot into the crowd. Since prisoners might use campfires to signal their comrades across the water, the guards had to cook and distribute the disgusting half-rations allowed their charges. This servile and demeaning task exposed them three times a day to rude epithets from the ravenous, though resentful, men.[10]

Having themselves often been hungry during their Morris Island service, few of the guards took pleasure in distributing starvation portions—a two-inch square of fatty bacon, a handful of vintage wormy hardtack, and a cup of beanless bean soup—to men who were already so thin and malnourished. They had only brackish water to drink, with no tea or coffee. One of the camp doctors attached to the 54th Massachusetts noted with discomfort that after a couple of weeks under this vindictive regime, the health of many of his prisoners was "giving way." During a tour of the stockade, though, he shrugged off those captives who called out to him: "More rations!"[11]

When Captain Pinckney "remonstrated" about the dismal quality and the ever-diminishing quantity of the food slopped on his plate by a black guard from Georgia, the man readily agreed that it was vile. "The truth is," the man confided, these prison rations "ain't fitten for a dog to eat, but they are all *these Yankees* are going to give you." Pinckney later learned that food was plentiful on the island and that, according to official protocols, prisoners of war were supposed to have access to the sutlers and to receive the same rations as their guards. In the case of Company H, that meant a breakfast of coffee, fresh beef, and hardtack; a dinner of salt beef, stewed beans, and boiled potatoes; and a supper of rice, coffee, and hardtack.[12]

Those cursing, abusive rebels received curses and abuse in return, though overall the guards from the 54th did not torment their charges for sport as in other prisons. The mostly free-born men of the regiment were less likely than other units of ex-slaves to pepper them with their "bottom rail on top this time" taunts. The 54th had seen their share of battle, death, and deprivation and generally returned civility for civility. Burnished rather than embittered by their own suffering, most men in the regiment had developed soldierly deportment, soldierly compassion, and soldierly restraint. As one Virginia prisoner observed, the black guards were "Chesterfields" in politeness compared to the white officers of the 54th. The worst of all the vitriolic Yankees, the Confederates agreed, was Colonel Hallowell, who exuded the upper-class abolitionists' distain for haughty southern slaveholders.[13]

During his various imprisonments, Pinckney had become adept at using his fine manners to smooth his way with his northern captors, but Colonel Hallowell, scion of a family of wealthy Philadelphia silk merchants, was totally invulnerable to his southern charms. Hallowell's preternatural dislike of southerners had festered into deep bitterness after the tragic encounter at Battery Wagner, where Confederate fire had horribly scarred his once-handsome face. On one occasion when he was officer of the day, the colonel intercepted a note addressed to Brigadier General John G. Foster, commander of the Department of the South headquartered on Morris Island. A colonel on General Beauregard's staff had written that if some kindness might be shown to Captain Pinckney, he would be happy to reciprocate to the benefit of a Union officer held in Charleston. Hallowell strode imperiously over to Pinckney's tent. Explaining the situation while scowling at the captain through his one remaining eye, the colonel told him condescendingly that he might be able to spare him up to five dollars' worth of tobacco.[14]

Offended by his manner and certain that this "phlegmatic, dough-faced Yankee" did not care if he lived or died, Pinckney rejected his offer of special favor. Instead, thinking a mistake had been made, he asked Hallowell to investigate why the prisoners were being fed hardtack from biscuit boxes dated 1861. When Pinckney had a lieutenant break open some of their hardtack and show the smirking colonel the writhing worms within, Hallowell laughed sarcastically. "I dare say the quartermaster is making a good thing out of feeding you prisoners," then repeated the old army chestnut that he saw no cause for complaint since they were getting both meat and bread. Pinckney recollected that he had "felt my hair stand on end at this addition of insult to injury" and invoked all his self-discipline not to strike "that infernal, low-bred" merchant's son.[15]

Pinckney had better luck winning over nineteen-year-old Captain Luis Emilio of Company E, who had been the 54th's highest-ranking officer still on his legs after the assault on Battery Wagner. For the most part, Emilio held what he considered the crass, venom-spitting Confederate officers in distain as igno-ramuses capable of supporting "any cause, however wild or hopeless." The "rabid Secessionists," he vowed, "would receive no favors at our hands." Pinckney and his lawyer friend from Charleston, Captain Henry Buist of the 27th South Car-olina Infantry, however, flattered the Spanish immigrant's son and melted his resistance. When word came down to him through the chain of command that Buist was to receive special consideration in the camp, Emilio consented to his request that Pinckney accompany him in the very special treat of ocean bathing after both gave him their oaths as gentlemen not to swim away toward nearby Fort Sumter. Before Captain Buist left Morris Island in late September on an early exchange—rumor had it that Union major general Benjamin F. Butler had been pulling strings for his brother Mason—he made a point of thanking Emilio for his kindness. The young captain was so pleased by this gesture by one of the few "agreeable gentlemen" among the prisoners that he later mentioned the in-cident in his regimental history. Little did he know, however, that he had warmly shaken the hand of one of the architects of secession. As a state legislator Buist had not only written the bill calling for the secession convention after Lincoln's election but also had risen to call the question—"Should South Carolina secede from the Union?"—thus setting the war in motion.[16]

Captains Emilio and Pinckney continued their conversations after Buist's exchange. Both men shared a love of Sir Walter Scott's romances. Pinckney, desperate for something to read other than colporteurs' tracts, gratefully ac-cepted Emilio's loan of two well-thumbed volumes by the romantic Scottish author, whose popular descriptions of knightly behavior during battle had in-fluenced many Civil War soldiers, North and South. On one occasion Emilio asked Pinckney if he had been present at the attack on Battery Wagner on July 18, 1863, or knew anyone who had been. Questions remained about the death of Colonel Shaw and the still-unknown fates of two other officers of the 54th. Pinckney located two North Carolinians, Colonel John A. Baker and Lieutenant James B. Lindsay, who had been at that fight. Lindsay, of the 31st North Carolina, told Pinckney that he had served on the burial detail and bragged, "I put that Yankee colonel [Shaw] just where he deserved to be—in a hole with six of his niggers." Pointing to his footwear, Lindsay added that he had taken them from

Shaw, "the finest boots I ever got hold of." When later confronted by Emilio, Lindsay dissembled and shrewdly became a "know nothing." The captain later chided Pinckney that the Confederates could give officer's rank to such an "extraordinarily ignorant man."[17]

Even in the dark, Confederates scavenging through the chaos of bodies slung throughout the fort would have caught a glimmer of Colonel Shaw's luxurious appointments. In a frenzy of grabbing, pulling, and tearing, the desperate men would have snatched his jeweled ring from his finger, yanked his gold watch from its chain, and tugged his supple boots from his legs. Next, off went the fine breeches; their pockets ransacked for cash. "Peeling," that postbattle ritual of completely stripping the bodies of fallen enemies down to their underclothing, was practiced by both sides. Once considered a spoil of war, this morbid practice had by 1864 become a necessity of war for desperate Confederates, and their officers hesitated to interfere. When Lieutenant Alan W. Muckenfuss of the Charleston Battalion later saw one of the looters flaunting Shaw's shimmering silk sash, he gave him a lecture about military propriety but nevertheless bought it from the man, returning it to the fallen officer's family after the war. When Shaw's sword was later found in Virginia, it too was returned.[18]

AT THE END OF SEPTEMBER 1864, Colonel Shaw was much on the minds of the men who had served under him in the 54th. For the first time in nearly a year, the 54th and 55th Massachusetts lined up with the other soldiers to receive their long-overdue wages. The paymaster had lugged in extra bags of cash containing $170,000—their current and back pay calculated at $13 a month, the same amount that white privates earned. The black soldiers' payday was a posthumous victory for the young Massachusetts officer.

Having cash in pocket put everyone in an upbeat mood. Fiddle music filled the air, and a carnival-like atmosphere swept over the island. Some soldiers indulged in marathon card playing. Others binged on a bacchanalia of tobacco and sweets bought from swindling Yankee sutlers—both black and white—who followed the troops like vultures. For some of the soldiers, though, no pleasure was as great, no victory as complete, as wiring home money via Adams's Express to anxious families who had not received a dime from them in nearly a year.[19]

During the festivities, officers from the 54th passed the hat among the men and raised $1,300 for a memorial to their fallen colonel. The Massachusetts companies gave the most; Barquet's Company H, mostly Illinois men whose own captain was never found, the least. Their grief over Colonel Shaw and the other white officers was genuine, but the soldiers of the 54th also felt keenly the loss of their own men, buried unceremoniously and anonymously in the sand; no officer proposed a monument to *their* fallen comrades. In fact, the prisoners' pen had been built over the black soldiers' unmarked graves. On at least one occasion, Confederates trying to deepen their wells by hand were horrified when they exhumed grisly bits of "black wool."[20]

The prison had been strategically located as a "breastworks" to shield from Confederate artillery those Union troops hauling guns to the satellite fortifications by day and night, which provided cover to crews at Cummings Point firing off the "Avenging Angel," a 30-pound Parrott gun that had replaced the Swamp Angel as the agent of wrath upon Charleston.[21]

During Pinckney's first nights on Morris Island, Confederate shells flying overhead panicked him. If the Federals hoped to demoralize the prisoners, they miscalculated, for the Confederate gunners on the outlying island forts had simply recalibrated their weapons and sharpened their aim. The few shells that burst over the prison pen miraculously lodged in the sand. After a time Pinckney, proud of Confederate marksmanship, felt confident enough to sit outside his tent door at night—sleep was out of the question during hours of intense activity—and watch the shells pass overhead. A startlingly loud boom would be "soon followed by a spark mounting high in the air" that would "poise itself apparently for a second while coming straight towards us, then explode either before us over Battery Gregg or behind us over Battery Wagner affording such an exhibition of fireworks as we had never seen before or wish ever to see again."[22]

Tempered by his own suffering, Pinckney grew in sympathy with the black soldiers stranded with him on this narrow island. For the most part, he believed, they were only following the "villainous" orders of the commander of Morris Island, Colonel William Gurney of the 127th New York Volunteers. To the extent that he could study the ebb and flow of the camp, Pinckney watched the white Union soldiers' interaction with the 54th troops as they pretended not to see their salutes, barked orders in a derisive tone, used vulgar forms of address, and shunted the heaviest, dirtiest, and most dangerous duty on them. One incident stood out in his mind. In preparation for yet another of their pointless, periodic long marches, Pinckney queued up at dawn to join a long line of men who also rose early to ensure themselves a full canteen of water. A black sentinel yelled from the parapet, "Disperse that crowd." When the white lieutenant near him made eye contact with the South Carolinian, he ordered the guard to fire. The shot went wide—on purpose, the grateful Pinckney believed—but ripped into a tent and wounded the sleeping prisoners within.[23]

Pinckney struck up a friendship with his guard from Company A, Sergeant Charles W. Lennox, who gained a reputation among the prisoners for his kindness and willingness to buy food in exchange for cash. Pinckney was comfortable with the black soldiers in ways that many of his prison mates or even the officers of the 54th were not, finding this dignified mixed-race barber from Watertown, Massachusetts, particularly good company, neither challenging nor deferential despite their "anomalous circumstances." During Lennox's shifts, he often stopped by Pinckney's tent to chat. The captain enjoyed hearing about the sergeant's boyhood in Massachusetts, where he received a basic education from the public school system but suffered in segregated seating at the town's only church. He also respected Lennox's expression of patriotism and desire to do his duty.[24]

Pinckney lived in fear that the Union command would study the tactics of Sir Henry Clinton's successful capture of Charleston in 1780 and emulate the British general's brazen land attack via the Stono River coupled with the warships of Vice Admiral Mariot Arbuthnot running the gauntlet of American harbor defenses. Spying a mass of vessels crossing the bar one morning, the captain approached Lennox and asked what it meant. Catching his meaning, the sergeant assured him not to "be uneasy about your city"; the ships were bound for Florida. Then leaning in confidentially, he whispered, "you know as well as I do if we had the right sort of man in command here we would go in, but we haven't got him."[25]

From his conversations with other guards, Pinckney understood how deeply affected the men of the 54th had been by their horrific experience at Battery Wagner and sought out their stories. He had been at his coastal base at Pocotaligo at the time of the battle on July 18 and possibly from there had heard the daylong booming of artillery. From their rooftops his relatives and friends in Charleston had watched the spectacle. At the distance of five miles, the exploding shells looked like fireflies at play in the night sky. Pinckney's uncle, George Parsons Elliott, joined other curious Charlestonians who visited some of the wounded black prisoners later brought into the local prison hospital. The seriously wounded men aroused Elliott's sympathy. When asked how they came to lead the charge, "all declared they had been put in front of the Yankees and were told that if they faltered they would be shot." One prisoner, either being harshly honest or canny to what his captives wanted to hear, put the 54th's situation in the most straightforward terms. He claimed that in anticipation of the second attempt against the fort that had already claimed so many lives, the Yankees had "made a breastplate out of us to save themselves."[26]

After Pinckney pressed him, Sergeant Lennox agreed to tell his own story of that fateful night when Colonel Shaw ordered the 54th into action. He described in detail the hard fighting on James Island the previous night and how, with no rest or food, they had been put in the vanguard of the second assault upon Battery Wagner. When the regiment reached the base of the looming fort and men began falling all around him, Lennox, later judged by his officers as "brave from principal," could see no hope for success. But the Union troops could neither retreat nor advance. As Pinckney recollected their conversation, Lennox said, "I saved myself by taking to that marsh on our flank where I remained until the fight was over."[27]

The sergeant apparently told the other guards about his unexpectedly pleasant conversations with Pinckney. Overhearing that iconic lowcountry name piqued Sergeant Barquet's interest, and Lennox agreed to his request to meet his fellow Charlestonian. One day in mid-October, he walked Barquet over to Pinckney's tent. If he had wanted a chance to gloat over their inversion of power, this was his moment. For nearly two decades, standing on numerous stages, stumps, and biscuit boxes, he had denounced Carolina planters for a range of sins: for perverting the course of the nation in their roles as nullifiers, then secessionists; for insisting that no state be free of slavery; and for making life in Charleston so perilous for free blacks that the delicate fabric of their community had been ripped to shreds.[28]

Feeling that every day could be his last, though, Barquet clearly had become nostalgic about his life's beginnings. For all its many drawbacks, his childhood in Charleston seemed a golden time. In retrospect, never in his life had he enjoyed the same sense of security and of belonging as he had then. Since leaving the city, he had lived in more than five different municipalities in four different states and in untold numbers of shabby rented rooms in dangerous neighborhoods.

Barquet apparently resolved to meet this deposed lowcountry aristocrat, not in anger or in defiance as some *sans culottes,* but as an equal, as a soldier and a member of Charleston's brown elite. He would be under no illusion about Pinckney's position on matters of race and slavery, but he knew that he would respect the social standing of his caste, just as Barquet recognized him as a gentleman. A constant refrain among the freemen of color, either in the "colored conventions" during the 1850s or among those enlisted in the 54th with Barquet, was "our white fellow-countrymen do not know us. They are strangers to our character, ignorant of our capacity, oblivious of our history and progress, and are misinformed as to the principle and ideas that control and guide us, as a people."[29] In the depersonalized military environment designed to strip away individualism, Barquet suffered even more from anonymity. If his visit to Pinckney was aimed at regaining this recognition, he was not disappointed.

Pinckney welcomed Barquet with a smile. He knew immediately who he was—or rather, who he used to be. "As soon as I heard Barquet's name, I located him at once," Pinckney recollected in his memoir forty years later. He saw him as an individual with a family, a heritage, a tradition, and a history, correctly guessing that the soldier was born into the "most useful class" of property-owning "free mulattos, chiefly of French, Spanish, and Portuguese extraction," who were the mechanics and butchers, tailors and barbers, dressmakers and caterers of the city.[30]

Although neither social nor political equals, the Barquets and the Pinckneys each had their place in the parallel hierarchies of Charleston, a city that their families had built together. Pinckney understood the complex caste system within the black community. Despite a bevy of laws and ordinances intended to keep blacks in subservient positions, he knew of literate men in Charleston who were store clerks, skilled carpenters, real estate investors, teachers, and entrepreneurs with substantial accumulated wealth as well as women who ran businesses and managed their own investments, even making loans to white businessmen and plantation owners.

Pinckney also knew free people of color who owned slaves. Both men grew up in a time when a cord of mutual interest was thought to link the "brown elite" and the old aristocratic white families of Charleston. Pinckney's family shared the opinion of their kinsman, Alfred Huger, that the free blacks of Charleston were "the best 'intermediate class in the world'" and would be "natural allies" of the white community as "an insurmountable barrier between the right of the master and the sedition of the slave."[31]

According to Pinckney's recollection, when these sons of Charleston met, they greeted one another like two lone travelers meeting accidentally in a foreign country and who, upon learning they hailed from the same place, shared a heartiness, even an intimacy, unthinkable at home. As southerners their interaction (though not their circumstance) was reminiscent of James Baldwin's encounter with white American writers during his first visit to Paris during the 1920s. Despite their different classes, races, and experiences, when the Americans—black and white—were thrust into mutually unfamiliar terrain, "it became terribly clear in Europe as it never had been" at home, Baldwin observed, that "we knew more about each other than any European ever could." And so it was with these two native sons stranded on the sands of what had once been a lazaretto, a quarantine station for hopeless cases, that both knew was locally called "Coffin Island."[32]

Pinckney disarmed Barquet with his warmth. Barquet disarmed Pinckney with his intelligence. Although maintaining all the traditional courtesies, the sergeant immediately turned the conversation to politics, the purview of citizens. He peppered Pinckney with questions about prominent South Carolina politicians past and present. His understanding of the principal players and political debates that dominated the public life of Charleston and had provided the background drama of both their youths "created much surprise" in the captain. Barquet explained that during his early life in South Carolina, he had been a musician with the band accompanying the governor during his annual reviews of the state's militia companies and had heard many of the noted public men speak with great passion about individual freedom and constitutional rights. His appetite for politics had been whetted during this time, along with his belief that only through the political process might his people enjoy enhanced rights. Even from remote Morris Island, Barquet continued to follow national and state contests closely, despite the door to participation still being bolted against him. The key to that door, he believed, was demonstrating that well-informed black people possessed a commitment to the common good quite beyond an interest in advancing their own agenda. That was why he enlisted. By 1864 he was losing heart.[33]

Sensing a sympathetic listener, Barquet was apparently quite forthcoming about his "many grievances" in the North. Even though he was a free man, he complained to Pinckney that "his rights were much curtailed by his color." The Black Laws in that state denied him the privileges of a citizen. Pinckney, who relished these accounts of racial discrimination in the free North, recalled that Barquet was particularly upset over the inadequacy of the public education available to his children. Overall the sergeant was quite cast down by the realization that serving in the army had not been the promised pathway to citizenship. In the autumn of 1864, he could die for President Lincoln but not vote for him.[34]

As the two Charlestonians discussed old times amid their new reality, Barquet apparently fell into a nostalgic mood. His youthful hopes of cultivating and asserting his manhood contrasted with his current status. His recent court-martial still pained him; the only real crime he could see in writing that letter to the *Weekly Anglo-African* was being clever. He told the captain nothing of that experience, though. According to Pinckney, Barquet shared with him that in retrospect he too felt his childhood in Charleston had been "the happiest years of his life" and that he "only wished he could look forward to spending the balance of it" in his hometown. When he spoke of the future, the sergeant may have been imagining that he could play a role in the rebuilding of the defeated city. Indeed, as these two middling-aged soldiers reminisced, the bombs of Federal vengeance were systematically reducing the old Charleston of their childhoods into little more than memories.[35]

Pinckney's journal only reveals one side of the conversation. What might the captain have said if he had been equally honest with Barquet (and himself)? He might have admitted to Barquet, who had also suffered so much, his heartache with the war, which he would never have mentioned to his close companions. Having raised a company of friends and neighbors with the understanding that they would serve as a home guard posted near their Santee River homes, within a year Pinckney and they had been swept up into the great maw of the Confederate army, merged into the 4th South Carolina Cavalry Regiment, and transferred away from their families, leaving the plantation district north of Charleston, and the slaves who remained, unprotected and vulnerable to the predations of Union raiders.[36]

Now, Pinckney must have wondered, had the Confederacy abandoned him? While in the camp he was often feverish as his malarial symptoms ebbed and flowed and always hungry. At night all that separated him from the cold sand were some strands of straw and his shoddy Yankee-issue blanket. Even more devastating than realizing the Confederate government was unable to negotiate his release was his father's apparent impotence to do so. Pinckney's greatest loyalty and faith had always resided in the sublimity of his noble family; now even that was shaken.

White-flagged truce ships had come and gone from Morris Island, and still no word of his long-expected exchange or any attempt to rescue the Confederate sufferers. Commanders in Charleston apparently could not enforce the most basic tenet of the prisoner-of-war conventions. Weeks passed with no mail and none of the food packages that had sustained him at Fort Delaware. Food occupied his thoughts day and night. The captain did not know that Union base commander General Foster had unilaterally decided to hold all prisoners' mail and to reroute food packages, including bread, ham, and tobacco contributed by the citizens of Charleston, to his own forces. Only a reprimand from one of his superiors for violating this prisoner-of-war convention forced Foster to reverse his policy. By time the packages found their intended recipients, most of the contents were filched or spoiled. A basket of sweet potatoes and vegetables from Pinckney's Elliott cousins at Oak Lawn on Yonges Island, though, saved him and his tent-mates from the scurvy then rampant in camp. When his mail arrived, a passing comment in a family letter informed him that his mother had died two months earlier.[37]

By October 1864 Barquet and Pinckney were not so much fighting the war as floundering in its tragic undertow, thrust together on a wispy bar of shifting sand, long an isle of dread and death. Coffin Island, a place of lost hope five miles as the seagull flew from where they had been born, both men knew, could be the place where they both met their end.

With another wartime winter coming on, the two soldiers felt adrift and stateless, like men without a country. After years of acting like a citizen—working hard, obeying the law, paying taxes, and now serving in the military—Barquet was still classified under the army rubric of "people of African descent," a person of no nationality. Pinckney too was in limbo. He had forfeited the one thing that Barquet desired most of all, his American citizenship. How long the Confederate nation might survive, he could not say. By October 1864 its fate was no more certain than his own.

Sitting together during that time of year on the Carolina coast when the sky can have an almost heartbreaking clarity, Pinckney and Barquet had called a personal ceasefire and let down their defenses. Stranded on an island of ship-wrecked dreams; hopelessness washed over them like the incessant sound of the surf. Both men felt isolated and heavy burdened with regret, forgotten by their countries, and despised by their enemies. Death felt much closer than glory.

When Barquet's shift resumed, reality returned, and he rose to leave. Not quite ready to let their roles change back to adversaries quite so quickly, the sergeant reached deep into his haversack and pulled out a piece of shortcake. He offered it to Pinckney, who "thankfully accepted, notwithstanding the source whence it came." Barquet said that he had recently built a large brick oven for baking soft bread and would be happy to break the rules and bring him some. Pinckney, having learned that everything had a price in the prisoner of war camps, proposed "a business arrangement" to compensate the sergeant for his help since the quartermaster held some US dollars in an account for him.

Barquet, however, managed to upstage the captain with his own graciousness. He waved away talk of money as any Charleston gentleman might, insisting it was "his pleasure" to help him regain his strength. Barquet walked away, head high, having won a little victory. As Pinckney watched him go, he could not help admiring "the bearing of these colored sergeants" who, he observed, carried themselves with more dignity than did their white officers, "generally a contemptible set." He understood, even then, that no matter what happened on the battlefield in the coming months, a revolution had already occurred. In Barquet he had seen the face of the future. What he could not see was what the future held for him.[38]

The two Charlestonians never met again. A plan to ship out the prisoners had already been made, and in a few days Pinckney was gone. Once the plan to invade Charleston, so long in preparation, had finally been jettisoned in order to free up Union soldiers for more-critical fields of engagement, the prisoners had lost their usefulness and became simply burdens. The 54th fell dismally back to their regular monotonous tasks with the army.

On October 20, after forty-five days of not so much living as lingering on Morris Island, Pinckney followed the unexpected order to prepare to ship out. One Virginian summed up this prison experience as just barely surviving day by day "on three crackers and two ounces of meat and some warm water" while being "abused, fired upon, shelled, cursed, starved, and rendered miserable in every form." During their internment, guards had shot and wounded three prisoners; three others died of disease. The time "under canvas" in the salt air with somewhat improved sanitation had actually helped Pinckney recover from his bout with malaria, but the poor nutrition further diminished him. Every man summoned his last bit of energy for the march back to the dock at Lighthouse Inlet. Those unable to travel by their own steam staggered along on the arms of their friends, propelled by little more than hope.[39] At last they were going home.

Only they were not. Feeling themselves the victims of a sinister joke, when they reached the landing the prisoners saw, not the white flags of exchange boats, but two old prison hulks, dismasted schooners resembling floating ogres. When the men reeled backward, their guards goaded them on like cattle to slaughter. Crushed in spirit, they collapsed in resignation once on board. After some shifting around of the sick and the "favorites," the old wrecks were underway by three o'clock in the afternoon, hauled out to sea in a most undignified manner by military transports.[40]

Crammed together once again, not knowing where they were headed or for what purpose, the prisoners began indulging in gallows humor as their vessels rose and fell with the sea. After the sadistic guards of Point Lookout, the cesspool of Fort Delaware, and then six weeks of exposure, hunger, and humiliation under fire on Morris Island, what was next—brining and skinning for shoes? Perhaps at some point, out of sight of witnesses, they would all be forced to walk the plank and save the Union troops the trouble of torturing them further. Many years after the war, these prisoners would be deemed the "Immortal 600" for all they endured without capitulating to the enemy, or in the contemporary parlance, "swallowing the pup."[41]

Cheered that at least they were heading south, when the old craft chugged into what Pinckney recognized as the channel of the Savannah River, he correctly guessed that they were bound for the dismal old Fort Pulaski on Cockspur Island. This bastion, along with Fort Sumter in Charleston Harbor, had first been conceived as part of a complex of enhanced coastal defenses that had been envisioned by his grandfather, General Thomas Pinckney, after the War of 1812. The actual work on Fort Pulaski was started in 1829 by a team of engineers that included young Lieutenant Robert E. Lee and was still not finished when it fell to General Gillmore's men in the spring of 1862. For a while after that, slaves who had escaped from surrounding plantations were held there.[42]

The pentagon-shaped fort, about two acres in size, was a single-storied structure enclosed by a moat. Heavy guns, including twelve-inch Columbiads and Dahlgrens in barbettes, were mounted on the parapet atop the casements. Carpenters were still hard at work creating cells for the prisoners and quarters for the guards when the hulks discharged their downcast cargo. About forty guns removed from their original positions were lined up on the parade ground as Pinckney surveyed this once-familiar place. His last visit to Cockspur Island had been before the war, when he and his sister had attended a picnic "given by the elite of Savannah, where music and the dance were the order of the day."[43] The old fortification, a symbol of war and men's relentless aggression toward one another, seemed now to be the true reality, and the carefree world of his youth only a momentary aberration.

At Fort Pulaski Pinckney's life improved from tortured to just bearable. Colonel Philip Perry Brown and the well-reputed 157th New York Volunteers moved with them from Morris Island and took over as their guards. The soldiers and their officers, most of whom hailed from upstate New York, had experienced the worst of the war. They had lost 98 men at Chancellorsville, then took 307 casualties at Gettysburg before having something of a respite with the Union forces at Charleston Harbor. Colonel Brown, formerly a high school principal, vowed to make Fort Pulaski "the model military prison of the United States." In contrast to the 54th's vengeful Colonel Hallowell, who frequently declared his personal preference for feeding prisoners on "greasy rags," Brown effectively doubled their rations—distributing the same quantity and quality of hardtack his own men received—and made more-or-less clean cistern water readily accessible. Determined not to go out of his way to make their lives miserable, he issued blankets, warm clothing, and adequate firewood to cook their meals. The colonel addressed the prisoners as "gentlemen" and assured them that he was quite willing to do all he could for "a brave foe." In exchange he asked that they obey his rules and maintain the good order and good sanitation of the prison.[44]

None of Brown's good intentions, however, could remedy the cold and damp of the dungeon-like brick casements with high-vaulted ceilings. Winds off the sea whistled through the embrasures now stripped of their guns. Forty-two men lived in each casement; Pinckney and Lieutenant Gordon shared an upper berth, raised off the cold brick floor, but they suffered from a frigid draught from the door. Even wrapped in every piece of clothing he owned, Pinckney shivered all night and could feel the cold penetrating deep into his bones. As winter set in with a vengeance, Pinckney, Gordon, Major Emanuel, and Lieutenant Epps squeezed together "spoon-fashion" in one bunk, sharing their body heat and whatever blankets they had.[45]

During mid-December, Pinckney and the others would lie very still during the night and listen carefully to the distant booming of artillery, trying to gauge the advance of Sherman's great blue behemoth moving irrevocably toward them. As they speculated about his route, Lieutenant Gordon began "shivering like a wet dog" at the horrid thought of his young wife and little children huddling alone in their farmhouse in Sherman's path, vulnerable to "untold depredations, outrages." Their guards remained very tight-lipped about troop movements, but Pinckney did learn one bit of cheering news. Confederates had scored a stunning victory at Honey Hill, defending the railhead at Coosawhatchie, near Pinckney's old posting at Pocotaligo. "No tears were shed," he remarked, over the report that his old nemesis from Morris Island, Colonel William Gurney, was wounded. Pinckney might have wondered, though, about his guards from the 54th Massachusetts, Sergeants Barquet and Lennox, who were in that desperate fight as well.[46]

On December 14 Pinckney "rejoiced" at the news that he was one of thirty prisoners chosen to leave the next day on a steamer scheduled to carry a hundred sick and wounded for exchange in Charleston Harbor. Rumors of exchanges had been ricocheting around Fort Pulaski. The Confederates now volunteered to return thousands of Union prisoners warehoused at the overcrowded charnel house at Andersonville without the expectation of one-to-one reciprocity. When the offer was finally accepted in early December, Federal steamers made straight for Savannah to retrieve more than 5,500 Union prisoners from a location near Cockspur.[47]

Pinckney and Captain George W. Howard of the 1st Maryland Cavalry, who too had been captured at Haw's Shop, were the only non-invalids released then. At the time, Pinckney did know specifically why he and Howard had been chosen, but he must have guessed that their connections to two equally distinguished old families had been a factor. Years later William Habersham, a Savannah rice factor and a friend of the Reverend C. Cotesworth Pinckney Jr., told him that after the city fell, he had dined with Colonel John Mulford, a well-respected Union agent for exchanges. At the end of the evening, Mulford asked what he could do for him during the occupation of the city. Habersham asked that Pinckney and Howard might be freed.[48]

With more than a twinge of conscience, Pinckney left his comrades behind and boarded the flag-of-truce ship *Laurel*, which steamed into Charleston Harbor in the dead of night on December 15. Colonel Mulford returned Pinckney's gold watch as well as the sixty-five dollars remaining in his prison account, then sent him on his way into the night with a handshake. "Buoyant in spirits" but exhausted and worn in body, Pinckney probably followed the others shuffling off to the Wayside Hospital and Soldiers' Depot. A group of volunteers operated this shelter at the railroad station so that friendless Confederate invalids were not just dumped off the transports and onto the lonely streets after their exchanges. The prisoners' arrival was quite unexpected and sent the staff into a flurry of activity. Confederate officials later questioned them closely about what they might have learned about Union movements from their guards.[49]

At first light Pinckney dashed out to examine his beloved city. Listening to the Federal guns from his prison pen on Morris Island, he had tried to imagine how extensive the damage might be, but he was unprepared for the sight before him. His shock came not merely from the destruction of those buildings that had been part of the geography of his life—the fire of 1861 had already swept away so much, including the eighteenth-century Pinckney mansion on East

Bay—but the utter and complete emptiness of the streets gave the battered lower peninsula a ghostly aura. Even the paving stones, once considered a sign of the city's growing sophistication, were gone in many places, pried up early in the war to build the city fortifications. Not just grass but now bushes grew in the streets, the only signs of life that frosty morning.[50]

So many of the people he had known—those who had animated the byways of the city, who had opened their doors to him in hospitality, who were the second or third generation living in the same home, and whose gas lamps had once illuminated the now-dark streets—were lost. Any other morning before the world had gone mad, those old folks, young folks, white folks, black folks—all victims of this terrible war—would have been moving about their houses, bacon and sausage in the pan, hominy bubbling in the pot. Shot by a bullet, struck by a shell, weakened by hunger, swept away by disease, crushed by a broken heart, or hunkering down in Columbia frightened lest Sherman come their way, what difference did it make—they were gone forever. Their shadows now haunted the town and would linger over it for a generation and more. Nothing would ever be the same as he had known it.

Pinckney headed north to Wentworth Street, an area more-or-less out of range of the Federal guns. He passed Grace Episcopal Church, where his brother was rector. In February 1861 the Reverend Cotesworth Pinckney Jr. had preached that disunion had neither been brought on by abolition or by secession but was, like the fall of Babylon, "manifestly God's *decree against our national pride*." Americans North and South, he argued, had abandoned godliness in the enjoyment of their prosperity. But now the church doors were locked and bolted after a random Yankee shell had destroyed part of the clerestory. The earnest minister had then taken his household to the safety of the family's summer place in the highlands of Pendleton, where, Pinckney would soon learn, his niece Carrie was dangerously ill with typhoid.[51]

The captain was actually searching for his nephew, Charley, who was the ordnance officer for the First Military District of South Carolina assigned to the Charleston Arsenal and had been the last man out of Battery Wagner. Young Pinckney, who was romantically attached to Lucy Memminger, was staying in her family's spacious home at the corner of Wentworth and Smith Streets, where once they had all made a parlor game of inventing a new flag for their new Confederate nation. Her father, an early fire-eater in favor of secession, no longer served as treasury secretary of the Confederacy. By the end of 1864, he had taken his wife and children to the relative safety of remote Flat Rock,

North Carolina. Lucy's brother, Major Robert Withers Memminger, a member of Lieutenant General William J. Hardee's staff, had recently raced home from Georgia, fleeing breathlessly with General Sherman's army at his heels.[52]

Pinckney's first visitor was his old nurse, "Maum Hannah," joyful at his deliverance. She learned of his release through the local "grape," even before the *Charleston Courier* published the news on December 16. After a great embrace, they reverted to their old roles. She demanded that he strip off his filthy, crawling uniform so she could give it a much-needed boiling. Pinckney gratefully obliged. While he waited in borrowed clothes, Captain Memminger secured a formal parole for him and a chit for two months' back pay from Confederate headquarters.[53]

The captain's joy at his own freedom proved short lived. Young Memminger confided the sober news that Sherman was massing a huge army on the Georgia–South Carolina border and was ready to make his move. Whether he was headed for Charleston, as many thought, or would cut through the heart of the state to more quickly rendezvous with General Grant in Virginia was anyone's guess. When Pinckney asked about Confederate plans for defense of the state, Memminger could only stare down and shake his head, though even he could not know how bad the situation really was. Sherman had assembled an invasion force of about 60,000 troops. According to General Hardee's calculation, the effective force within South Carolina's borders numbered less than 14,000 men, most of them protecting Charleston. If he counted all the various state and local militia and the dispirited survivors of the Army of Tennessee after their defeats at Atlanta and in Middle Tennessee, who might be brought to field under the command of then-retired General Joseph Johnston, the figure could go as high as 30,000, but this was optimistic. What available troops there were—the very young and the battle worn—belonged to a number of separate commands confused about their mission and with no unified head. Pinckney's former division, under Brigadier General Butler of Edgefield, was on its way back into South Carolina with about 1,500 mounted men and in severe need of more horses.[54]

Anxious to check on his Santee plantations and then to see his family, who had taken refuge in the upper part of the state, Pinckney did not linger long in Charleston. He walked about the city, stopping to buy a few Christmas presents from the limited array of blockade goods available on King Street. On his perambulations, the captain encountered a frantic friend who had been among the infirm freed from Fort Pulaski. During the night, one of the many thieves roaming at will through the streets had robbed him of his watch and every penny in his pocket. Virtually all the city police were now in the army preparing to defend the state. After recovering from his attack, his friend had reeled to the train station and spent the night there squatting next to a black man who offered to share his blanket. The soldier was to be married that day, but he had no way to get to his waiting bride because he had no money for a ticket. Pinckney, who had just cashed his own paycheck, gave the man half of what he had and sent him on his way.[55]

Pinckney slipped out of Charleston just before another devastating outbreak of yellow fever swept the city. He headed north about forty miles up to the South Santee "to see after the plantations and the negroes." He also went to inspect the family's salt-making operation. Ironically, after working for generations to purge salt from their rice fields, this vital element would save the Pinckneys. Once the Federal blockade prevented imports from the West Indies, salt became almost as valuable as gold and was traded as currency. With the rice industry destroyed, the Pinckneys and other planters along the coast broke down their threshing machines, cut their idle boilers in half to make vats, and built furnaces on the seashore. After the Federals established a presence on Morris Island, the price of salt doubled, going as high as forty dollars a bushel on the speculation that Charleston was about to fall. Before he left the Santee, Pinckney ordered two tierces (about the size of modern oil drums) of salt shipped to Columbia for safekeeping.[56]

From the Santee, Pinckney headed for Columbia by train. He stayed only long enough to secure a small rickety wagon and quite possibly the last sound horse in the capital. He picked up as many trunks and boxes belonging to family and friends as he could from the home of his cousin Harriott Horry Rutledge Ravenel to take with him farther west to his father's refuge in Cokesbury. If he tarried, he would either encounter the first of General Sherman's troops, who were ominously approaching the banks of the Congaree River, or General Hampton, who was mustering his forces to defend the capital city. At this desperate juncture Hampton would have seized the captain's plug, ripped up his parole, and ordered him immediately back to active service. Wishing to avoid either possibility, Pinckney set out under the cover of darkness and clucked his weary old horse onward to the less-traveled Winnsboro Road. Shivering in the December cold and feeling very much alone, he headed first toward the Pendleton home of his brother, Cotesworth. As a physician, he might be able to help his ailing niece.[57]

* * *

ON NEW YEAR'S EVE 1864, the Reverend Cotesworth Pinckney Jr.; his wife Annie; and their convalescing daughter, Carrie, gazed quietly into the fire trying to imagine what 1865 might bring. The melancholy silence was broken by the sound of footsteps—a man's heavy boots on the porch. Initially alarmed because Confederate deserters had become a danger in the western part of the state, they looked at one another and immediately chimed, "Tom!" Cotesworth and Annie dashed to the door. There stood "the Captain, large as life."[58]

The next day the grateful Pinckneys attended a service at St. Paul's Episcopal Church and visited their mother's grave. After supper that night the little family gathered closely around Tom, transfixed in the candlelight while he shared the details of his capture, his homesickness, his fear, his illness, his hunger and thirst, the horrors of prisons, the unexpected pleasure of eating rats, the sadistic guards, the crudeness of Yankees officers, and the kindness of a fellow Charlestonian—a black sergeant in blue—who showed him a flicker of human kindness amid an exceptionally cruel war.[59]

8

FROM LIBERATOR
TO CONQUEROR

ON THE EVENING OF NOVEMBER 24, 1864, Sergeant Barquet reflected upon the nation's second official Thanksgiving Day. The regiment, grateful that the burdensome rebel prisoners had shipped out, enjoyed a diverting day of activities with morning prayers, a military review, feasting, games, and serenades. Barquet was thankful that President Lincoln had been reelected and the nation's crusade for freedom and union would continue unabated. Then as everyone was settling in for the night, new orders arrived. The soldiers of Company H must prepare their light packs and be at the ready to leave Morris Island at a moment's notice.[1]

The troops later shipped out to Hilton Head, where they became part of an all-black brigade attached to the new 5,500-man Coast Division, composed of infantry, cavalry, artillery, marines, and sailors drawn from various seaside fortifications and placed under the command of Brigadier General John Porter Hatch. Their new mission inspired excitement, for the black soldiers were to help clear the way for "Uncle Billy" as Sherman's army ground through the nearly prostrated state of Georgia during the March to the Sea. More particularly they would be probing deeply into rebel territory, with the goal of destroying the railroad bridge crossing the Coosawhatchie River near Beaufort and disrupting the Charleston and Savannah Railroad to prevent Confederate reinforcements from flooding into the area and offering resistance.[2]

Very late on the night of November 28, concealed by darkness and chilled by the damp air, Barquet began shepherding his company aboard one of the transports making for Boyd's Landing, twenty miles up the Broad River and seven miles overland from the targeted railroad tracks at Grahamville. Hatch, anticipating that the Confederates would be in total disarray in the knowledge of Sherman's approach, expected an easy time of it. He had a superior force of well-rested, well-fed men and the element of surprise. He was surprised, though, when a dense cloud of fog descended on the area. Through a series of errors and missteps, the balance shifted in favor of the Confederates, who learned of the Federal presence by their raucous disembarkation of men and horses in the late morning of the twenty-ninth.[3]

Consequently the Confederates were waiting when the Union soldiers approached. Tipped off by a sentry, Colonel Charles J. Colcock, leader of the Third Military District, had sounded the general alarm and managed to place 1,400 men, including militiamen from Georgia, into an advantageous defensive position in the earthworks at Honey Hill, on the road to the targeted train depot. By the early morning of November 30, Colcock had formed his line and was anxiously waiting for more troops from Charleston to arrive by rail.[4]

In contrast to the long, tense night experienced by his enemy, Barquet and others in his company awoke in an abandoned cotton field at 5:00 A.M. in relative good cheer, with no premonition of what the day would bring. Once again his regiment brought up the rear, having responsibility for maintaining communications within the division. After several of the companies split off, Lieutenant Colonel Henry N. Hooper heard artillery fire and advanced with Company H as well as Company E at double time in the direction of Honey Hill. Clearly something had gone terribly wrong.

General Hatch, ordering his men to pursue what he assumed were random Confederate skirmishers, had fallen for a familiar ploy and sent them into a deathtrap at the earthworks, where wetlands and dense forests with ropes of vines blocked the Federals' escape. By the time Barquet arrived as part of Hooper's detail, a major battle was clearly underway, though smoke from a brushfire set by the rebels obscured their view. Moving his two companies to the left of the road leading to the Confederate stronghold, Hooper had the men form the best line they could, lie down flat, and conserve their ammunition by not returning the fire that kicked dirt all around them. Confusion reigned. Nothing could be done to salvage such a poorly organized and thinly supported effort. Although the Union line had reeled back in confusion at the unexpected firepower of the Confederates lodged in their nearly unassailable position, they rallied and threw themselves at the enemy with "desperate earnestness." The battle lasted all day. The unearthly, banshee-like "rebel yell" resonating through the crackle of the fire and the roar of rifles were what most survivors would remember. About 7:30 that night, the order came to fall back.

Union losses were estimated at 80 men killed, 629 wounded, and 28 missing, in contrast to the Confederate tally of 8 killed and 39 wounded. Eight men from Company H were wounded, five from Company E. Barquet would have been with those who carried out more than 150 casualties on stretchers impro-vised from muskets, tents, and blankets. The Federal dead remained on the field. Among pitiable and broken heaps were scores of hopeful young recruits from the 55th Massachusetts, determined to prove their courage equal to the 54th's. A Savannah newspaper later noted that at the Battle of Honey Hill, inexperienced black soldiers had formed the Union advance "as usual."[5]

The next morning, when birdsong once again filled the woods, Confederates returning to the scene found the road leading to Honey Hill strewn with car-nage. Artillery fire had shredded once-towering pines. On one acre of land the bodies of sixty or seventy Union soldiers lay in terrible states of mutilation, with heads partially blown off or torsos disemboweled. Bloated bodies bobbed in the creek. In one ditch alone six members of the 55th lay dead, one stacked upon one another. Confederate scavengers were touched by the wilted little sprigs of the herb "life everlasting" stuck in the black soldiers' caps for luck and surprised to find that their pockets produced a bonanza of greenbacks, their long-awaited pay yet unspent.[6]

Captain Charles C. Soule of the 55th summed up the battlefield experience of both black Massachusetts regiments in his observation that the "generalship was not equal to the soldierly qualities of the troops engaged." All that death and suffering, all that horror and pain, and still locomotives chugged undaunted down the old Charleston and Savannah. The chance to end this war—or at least combat in this theater of the war—had slipped away.[7]

Company H remained with Lieutenant Colonel Hooper for their next as-signment. On December 7 Hooper led the 54th to Deveaux's Neck in the pour-ing rain to dig rifle trenches and a gun battery from which the artillery might blast the Confederate railcars as they clattered past. The following day the troops were finally within earshot of locomotive whistles near Coosawhatchie, but a Confederate force of about 5,500 men blocked their attempts to advance. By December 10 Colonel Hallowell had arrived with about 500 men and took com-mand of the 54th and the all-black Second Brigade.[8]

Even the joyous news of Sherman's capture of Savannah on December 21, 1864, could not lift Barquet's spirits during a raw and gloomy Christmas at Gra-ham's Neck, with no feasting or other celebrations. Risk-adverse sutlers refused to venture into this dangerous territory. Rather than holiday decorations, the men made wooden "Quaker" cannons designed to trick the rebels into thinking they had artillery. All they had to look forward to were fitful nights sleeping on frosty ground with 2,000 Confederates reported in their path.

Company H joined the skirmishers that set out with General Hallowell to probe the dark and bloody ground around the once critical Pocotaligo depot. When they reached the critical railroad bridge, the Federals found only smoke and char. In retreat the Confederates torched the bridge they had defended for so long.[9]

On January 15, pickets from the 54th heard the rumble of wagons and creak of artillery caissons. Soon men in camp discerned music in the distance and even picked up strains of "national airs." Sherman's XVII Corps, under the command of Major General Frank P. Blair, was coming their way. The men were thrilled to be among the first of the eastern troops to "form a junction" with these stalwart sons of the West. The regiment spent the rest of the month shoring up their base at Pocotaligo, restoring its docks, and refitting the XVII's vast entourage of wagons, ambulances, and pontoons. Every time Sergeant Barquet turned around, something else needed to be done, from unloading supplies to building corduroy roads over soft marshy terrain. Supplies of desperately needed clothes for his regiment finally arrived.[10]

When the 54th moved its camp closer to the Salkehatchie River, Barquet had an opportunity to see Sherman's legendary men up close. They were sun bronzed and wind burned, hardy and fit. Rather than the forage caps favored by the eastern regiments, they wore slouched army hats. Their officers dressed for the business of war rather than the parade ground. The only adornments of rank affixed to their government-issued uniforms were shoulder straps and swords; not a silk sash flowed among them. No one spoke of glory, they just had a job to do. Taken as a whole, the XVII Corps gave the impression of a well-muscled merger of men, horses, and armaments moving inexorably across the lowcountry landscape. The consensus among the 54th was that Sherman was headed to Charleston to sow salt in that seedbed of secession and to make short work of the job Gillmore had not allowed them to do. The black troops were anxious to be in at the kill.[11]

When the XVII Corps pulled out, the 54th fell behind them, enjoying the pull of their draft and feeling rather invincible in their company. Sherman's men had a well-deserved reputation as pillagers living off the conquered land, destroying or consuming everything in their path. At each stop the 54th feasted like kings on their leavings and picked through all the clothing and necessaries left cavalierly behind.

On the first of February 1865, the 54th stopped near Combahee Ferry and camped close to the plantation of Daniel Heyward, who had one of those legendary lowcountry surnames with which Barquet was very familiar. They met no enemy resistance as they moved into the Combahee River plantation district; the Confederates had flown. Word spread through camp that Brigadier General Edward E. Potter's brigade, with which they had set off on this expedition from Hilton Head, was already aboard transport steamers in Bull's Bay of the Santee delta north of Charleston, the men emptying their guns at Confederate positions in Awendaw. Their brigade was to rendezvous with Potter's in the conquered city of Charleston.[12]

By February 17 the 54th was camping on the grounds of Antwerp, the Ashepoo plantation belonging to Colonel Charles Warley, a surname found among a number Barquet's relatives. The sergeant, who believed with all his heart that education was the pathway to equality and citizenship, surely despaired when he saw that black troops had broadcast thousands of volumes from Warley's library across the ground, the abandoned house, like those at Darien, Georgia, scavenged of its contents. The practice that Colonel Shaw had denounced now seemed to be standard procedure for Union forces. On February 20 a company of the 157th New York traveling with the 54th set fire to Oak Lawn, the mansion house on the plantation of William Elliott III.[13]

Although he was likely unaware of it, Barquet was marching across a countryside that was part of his own family's past. Parker's Ferry at Pon Pon on the South Edisto River was within ten miles of the Horseshoe Savannah area, where Loyalist Robert Ballingall had his plantation and where Barquet's grandmother, Margaret Bellingall—then called "Peggy"—once lived in slavery during the American Revolution.[14]

Joined by the 102nd USCT, the 54th Massachusetts pressed on with its own personal march to the sea, burning and foraging as it went. The soldiers loaded their take of the spoils on stolen draft animals and in any vehicle that came to hand, from ox carts to once-fine carriages. Grinding their way to Charleston, weighted down by civilian stores ranging from sweet potatoes and honey to geese and chickens, the joyful local "contraband" (declared free by order of General Foster, briefly head of the Department of the South) covered the road behind them as if a sluice gate had been opened during a spring flood. The mass of humanity inching along the coastal road resembled not so much a military movement as an odd and festive parade—such as would later be imagined by Italian filmmaker Federico Fellini—jauntily crossing a plain of smoldering destruction. From Savannah to Charleston, only two plantation houses would be left standing along the ninety-mile route. On February 17 news that the Confederate army had abandoned Charleston flickered through the regiment like a wave of electricity. Around the campfires late into the night, no one could talk of anything else.[15] Because of the restrictive laws passed after the suspected Denmark Vesey plot, Barquet never expected to return to Charleston when he left in 1849. Now he would be marching in as a conqueror wearing the uniform of his country.

All geared up for his triumphal entry into the capital of secession, Barquet found the bridge across the Ashley River reduced to scorched timber by the fleeing Confederates. Forced to bivouac ten miles from the city, he and his men were crushed to learn that those companies of the 54th that had remained more or less out of harm's way back on Black Island would be the first to enter the city and be compensated for all they had endured by the joyous demonstrations of those once enslaved, now free. Even the 55th Massachusetts had a victory march before them. Designated part of the Federal occupying force moving into Charleston, that regiment marched at the head of the brigade on February 21. An observer from *Harper's Weekly,* watching the 55th streaming through the streets singing the "March of John Brown's Soul," commented that "if the war itself was a revolution of citizens against their Government, it has introduced also a revolution quite as profound in the relation hitherto existing between the negro and his master."[16]

Those whites still in the city pulled their shutters and sat waiting in the dark for the parade to pass. The news of the black soldiers' burning spree on the road to Charleston had preceded them. Here, at last, they believed were the long-dreaded black Jacobins.[17]

General Hardee's Confederates regrouped about forty miles north of the city. At midnight on February 25, the last of the evacuation trains crossed the Santee River trestle north of Battery Warren, and the rebels burned their last bridge behind them. They headed toward North Carolina to meet up with General Johnston, brought out of retirement to command the Department of South Carolina, Georgia, and Florida, for what would be their last stand.[18]

When Barquet finally arrived back on his home soil, the scene staggered him. Hardee had held on to Charleston until the bitterest end, longer than General Beauregard had wanted. Anxious to leave as little for Sherman as possible, the Confederates engaged in a desperate last-minute spree of self-destruction, torching all remaining resources that might aid the enemy. Early in the war arrogant Charlestonians had engaged in a great deal of bravado about burning the city down rather than turning it over to the Yankees. The departing troops had inadvertently done just that. Ignited by accident, cotton warehouses went up like dry tinder. The first order of business for the invading army was to snuff out the flames.[19]

At nine o'clock on the morning of February 27, the 54th Massachusetts received their own heroes' welcome from the newly freed of Charleston. No homecoming of Barquet's imagination could match that which he received from the black denizens waving their hats and cheering. Another sergeant from Company H recalled that the streets "thronged with women and children of all sizes, colors, and grades—the young, the old, the halt, the maimed, and the blind" and that one "old colored woman . . . threw down her crutch, and shouted that the year of Jubilee had come."[20] As they processed through the streets, Barquet saw that the lovely old city of his youthful memory had been totally transformed. Charleston looked as if it had simply exploded. Debris covered the streets, and the skyline was a jagged cacophony of burned-out shells. Still standing, as if by a miracle, was the spire of St. Michael's Church, by which Union artillerists on Morris Island had set their sights. Although silent now, Barquet remembered its bells chiming all the hours of his youth.

Marching along familiar old Meeting Street proved a shock. Whole blocks, including the site of the Barquet home, were flattened—not by Federal siege guns, but by the Great Fire of 1861, which had consumed a swath of the city nearly a mile wide. Over 144 acres were destroyed, including landmark buildings ranging from the Pinckney family mansion on East Bay to the Catholic Cathedral of St. Finbar on the western end of Broad Street. Rather than stop at the Citadel, the military academy of South Carolina just north of Calhoun Street and where the Union occupation army had set up its headquarters, the 54th was ordered farther north up the peninsula to the Charleston Neck, following the old plank road to Magnolia Cemetery. Barquet would have the singular experience of camping among the tombs, surrounded once more by all the lowcountry names that he knew so well.[21]

The 54th's mission was to keep order in the city and the surrounding countryside as thousands of newly emancipated men and women began testing the limits of freedom. On March 1, General Hatch, who had become the military commander of Charleston, reported: "The negroes are pillaging the country lately vacated by the rebel troops. I will endeavor to get them into our lines, as I see no other way of preventing it. The men will do for the army; the women, General Saxton must try and employ." (Saxton at this time served as an assistant head of the newly organized Freedman's Bureau, designed to assist former slaves in their transition to independent living.) The regiment's first assignment was to inform the black men and women on the outlying plantations that they were legally free. While their masters had no more claim on their labor, they in turn had no more claim on their masters or a right to their land. The soldiers encouraged the new freedmen to return to the city with them.[22]

After some tedious picket duty around the 54th's base at the Four Mile House, a former tavern, Barquet shipped out of Charleston on March 12 for Savannah as part of a "negro brigade" of 2,300 troops under Colonel Hallowell. At last outfitted with new uniforms, the men looked sharp and stepped lively during a grand review that most hoped would be their last of the war. Sherman, they knew, was powering through North Carolina while Grant was in hot pursuit of Lee around Richmond.[23]

Then quite unexpectedly, the 54th received orders to return to South Carolina, this time to Georgetown. General Sherman had one more job for their brigade to do. Poised to confront General Johnston's army in North Carolina and to put an end to the war in the Carolinas, Sherman ordered General Gillmore to have the Confederates' entire stockpile of munitions destroyed, including those locomotives and cars that had been stranded around Florence, Sumter, and Camden after the rail bridges were torched. Sherman was clear: This must be done at all costs, even if 500 men had to lose their lives. No rolling stock, not even a handcar, should be available to daredevil Confederates making last-ditch attempts to reinforce Johnston once the Federals finally nailed him down. Gillmore ordered the establishment of two brigades of 2,700 men each under General Potter. Colonel Hallowell led one brigade, consisting of the 54th—675 men strong—and two other black regiments. Colonel Brown of the 157th New York, once the commandant of Fort Pulaski, led the other brigade. On April 5, 1865, they set out on their mission.

Rather than a postscript to a war already won, Potter's Raid is best understood as the first episode in the long and contentious story of Reconstruction. The 54th Massachusetts served among these shock troops of freedom, the avatars of black hopes and white fears, as they strode through Sumterville, Wateree Junction, Stateburg, and the Santee District, singing as always the "John Brown Hymn." Once liberators, now conquerors, they took whatever they wanted and went wherever as they chose.

Being liberated by black soldiers made an indelible impression upon the slaves along the Santee and transformed their view of authority in the coming transition. The narrative constructed for them by the soldiers of how their freedom came about affected their new relationship with their old masters. To these anxious, upturned faces some soldiers said that they not only were free but also would be given a land holding of their own. This promise became widely translated into the famous expectation of "Forty Acres and a Mule," a misconstruing of General Sherman's famous Field Order No. 15 of January 1865 that ordered coastal lands confiscated, divided into small plots, and turned over to the newly freed as a temporary measure to relieve the government of some of the burden of caring for the thousands of displaced people. That the old plantation lands upon which they had so labored would soon be theirs became firmly imprinted in their minds as a positive truth and holy writ, expectations that would affect the tenor of Reconstruction. When subsequent white commanders later tried to disabuse them of the notion that they would be landowners, the freed people remained obdurate.[24]

On its last wartime assignment in South Carolina, the 54th Massachusetts participated in the pillaging of the plantation district along the Santee River, for which Potter's division would be long remembered. Diarist John Snider Cooper of the 170th Ohio claimed that the 54th, encouraged by some of their company commanders, was "the worst in this business" of looting and wanton destruction of property."[25] If the black liberators shaped the attitude of the freed slaves in the postwar era, so too did the black looters shape the attitude of the planters along the Santee.

Women alone in plantation houses pulled back their drapes to watch with dread for the approach of General Potter's troops. At the first sight of hundreds of black men coming up their drive, they braced for the sound of boots on the steps. Some women were stoic, others hysterical, when at last came a pounding on the door. On the pretense of searching for rebels and arms, Potter's soldiers raced like locusts through the rooms, pocketing tobacco from humidors, thread from sewing boxes, brass casters from chair legs, backgammon boards from table tops, and silver spoons from sideboards. Soldiers rummaged through the family's clothing, sometimes leaving them only what they wore, if they were lucky. Pictures were yanked from the walls, silver stashed, and wine chugged. Feather mattresses, bedsteads, and whatever could not be carried away were cut to pieces. These "search parties" would leave in the family's carriages with their farm wagons full of smoked meat and live chickens. In their wake the grounds were as desolate as if Sherman himself had passed.[26]

The slaves identified with the victorious army, seeing themselves in some way too as victors and believing that they might treat the whites as conquered peoples. Taking cues from the soldiers, whose actions gave the imprimatur of the Federal government to looting of private houses, the slaves joined in pillaging. Sometimes poor whites did as well. The abusive way that black soldiers spoke to plantation owners of both sexes gave voice to the free people's own deeply buried anger at the deprivations of a lifetime. In one place along the upper Santee, slaves ran from house to house grabbing what they could before burning fourteen buildings to the ground.[27]

At Middleton Depot on April 11, 1865, the brigade destroyed fifteen locomotives and 140 train cars loaded with ammunition, small arms, and stores. According to Sergeant John H. W. N. Collins, the Federals captured five hundred contrabands, five hundred prisoners, and eighty head of horses while destroying a vast amount of property. They then returned toward Georgetown, burning cotton fields as they went.[28]

The 54th encountered sporadic Confederate resistance all along their way. Their last fight of the war was on April 18 at Boykin's Mill, ten miles south of Camden, against the 9th Kentucky, a mounted-infantry regiment of the famous Orphan Brigade. Although vastly outnumbered and overpowered, in what was the Confederacy's last stand in South Carolina, the Kentuckians fought with undiminished intensity from a strong defensive position in an old fort, extracting fifteen casualties from the 54th. Lieutenant Edward L. Stevens of Company H was one of the two killed and believed to be the last officer to die in the Civil War, reportedly shot by a fourteen-year-old member of the Boykin family whose father had served under Jeb Stuart.[29]

At Stateburg the 54th passed the plantation and cotton gin of the once-thriving free man William Ellison. A longtime friend of the Barquet family, Ellison had entrusted one of Joseph's brothers—"Monsieur Barquet"—in 1860 to help his children navigate the distance between the steamship landing in Manhattan and the train station from which they would depart for the Forten's school in Philadelphia for their safety. Only good luck saved Ellison's house from the invading army's torch.[30]

On April 22, while shepherding contraband onto river transports at Wright's Bluff near the present town of Summerton on the Santee, Barquet learned of General Lee's surrender. Two days later at his bivouac at Stagget's Mill, he heard the stunning news of President Lincoln's assassination. Something bitter always lingered at the bottom of the cup of victory. Rumors that the Great Emancipator's death stemmed from a Confederate plot further hardened the hearts of many of Barquet's men, possibly icing over his as well. With looting forbidden after the capitulation of General Johnston's Confederate forces in Durham, North Carolina, on April 26, Barquet walked the last twenty-five miles of his war on a meal of two ears of parched corn.[31]

On May 4, the sergeant returned once again to Charleston on the steamer *Island City* and again under the command of Colonel Hallowell, who had responsibility for maintaining the entrenchments around the defeated city as well as James Island, Saint Andrews Parish, and later Mount Pleasant. The 54th took up garrison duty at the Citadel. Every morning a large contingent of the black population gathered in Citadel Square at Calhoun and King Street, never tiring of the miraculous sight of black men marching to martial music and performing their crowd-pleasing evolutions. A number of the soldiers found sweethearts, even wives, among the town girls who came to the parade ground to see and be seen.[32]

At first, soldiers had easy access to passes and enjoyed the freedom of the city. During his idle hours, Barquet surely spent some time kicking through the rubble of his past. Adam Tunno's East Bay home had survived the shellings; a double-door storefront had been added to the old place over the years. Had the sergeant walked over to Pitt Street, he might have found his wizened aunt Hagar Cole still living in the house Tunno had bought for Margaret Bellingall and that had always been crowded with kin for more than fifty years. Hagar's only other assets were a smattering of bank shares dating back to Tunno's time that had thrown off morsels of much-needed interest over the years. She also borrowed money on the few slaves from her mother's estate to get over a bad patch, but they, of course, were all gone after the war, probably long before. After she died intestate in July 1865, eleven relatives sued for a portion of her one-third interest in the old home, sagging with age and mortgaged to the hilt.[33]

In seeing the landscape of his youthful past blown to bits, the question that must be asked, though it cannot be answered, is whether this was a final liberation for Joseph Barquet or did it fill him with a terrible sense of loss. The old capital of secession was gone, but so was the home where he had lived with his parents, brothers, and sisters. Gone too were most of the admirable men and women of the free community who had helped make him the man he had become.

IN THE LATE SPRING OF 1865, as the first Confederate penitents cautiously returned to Charleston to take the oath of allegiance and reclaim their property, the defeated whites deeply resented the black soldiers' assertion of authority as they policed the city. The black soldiers, in turn, resented the hauteur—even in defeat—of the former slaveholding class. Strong sentiment grew among the men of the 54th, particularly those from Massachusetts, that they should be recognized as the conquerors of Charleston. They wanted the capitulation of the city to be an abolitionist victory and to somehow have their sacrifice at Battery Wagner connected in the public mind with the fall of the cradle of secession. Sergeant Collins expressed the men's resentment at being whisked away to Savannah almost immediately after their triumphal entrance: "we were not allowed to remain in the city of Charleston, yet we claim the largest share in capturing it."[34]

A genuine point of pride for the 54th was seeing some of their comrades finally in officers' uniforms, although their interpersonal relationships inevitably changed as a result. Company H's Peter Vogelsang, always considered "a king" among his men, was promoted to lieutenant and made acting quartermaster. For many the true meaning of their tragic charge on Battery Wagner came clear on July 18, 1865, the two-year anniversary of the action. Frank M. Welch, a Connecticut barber who had been wounded in the assault, served as officer of the day and wore the uniform and sash of a first lieutenant. While he patrolled their post at Citadel Square on horseback, he passed the basestone laid in 1858 of the uncompleted memorial to John C. Calhoun. Admiring Welch's dignity, Barquet's friend Sergeant Lennox paused to wonder what Calhoun might have thought if he could "come out of his grave, and walk up King Street, and meet a colored man and regimental officer, and see the streets patrolled by colored soldiers, and Massachusetts ones at that! All the result of his pet doctrine, secession. Have we not some retaliation for our misfortune at Wagner?"[35]

Other men of the 54th, however, sought different forms of retaliation. They wanted not only recognition from the army but also to see fear in the eyes of the condescending Confederates returning to the city. Jacob Christy, a twenty-one-year-old former laborer from Pennsylvania who was wounded at Battery Wagner and had two brothers who were casualties of the battle at Olustee, told his sister that he and his comrades felt free to "knock them out of our way and if they don't like that, we take them up and put them in the guard house." Christy said the soldiers felt so sure that they now possessed the upper hand, "We just go into the city and take [up whole] streets just for them to say something out of the way to us so that we can get at them and beat them."[36]

Much of the racial violence that permeated the city in the first summer after the so-called peace originated from within the ranks of the occupation forces. Colonel Gurney, military commander of the city, issued a warning on May 21 to his old regiment, the 127th New York Infantry, to refrain from insulting and beating "colored people." The situation deteriorated until a riot broke out, instigated by the Duryea Zouaves of the 165th New York Infantry, inexplicably transferred to Charleston after earlier protesting against serving with black soldiers in Savannah. Their attack upon a free black civilian escalated tensions when soldiers of the 54th—who saw themselves as the special protectors of the black community—intervened. After three days, the racial violence reached a point to where General Gillmore felt compelled to bring in a white Pennsylvania regiment to restore order.[37] Black soldiers, so necessary during war, now began to be viewed by their commanders as unnecessarily disruptive to the reunification process.

Toward the end of July 1865, a curfew went into effect in Charleston. While civilians were ordered to turn in their weapons, the enlisted men were ordered to cease their insolence toward any person "of whatever color; that they do not monopolize the sidewalks, or assemble in crowds to the inconvenience of women or other passersby." Unrepentant white citizens were reminded that they were under military rule and that provoking or interfering with the troops would only delay the return to civilian government and undermine the fragile peace.[38]

General Gillmore decided to follow the precedent set by General Sherman, who had sent all black soldiers to the outlying districts after he subdued Savannah in December 1864. Gillmore ordered the 54th and 55th Massachusetts to prepare to leave for Boston, where they would be mustered out early. The other black troops, drawn largely from South Carolina freedmen, transferred to Beaufort and Hilton Head, long under Union control. On the evening of August 21, Barquet and his comrades crowded onto a troop transport heading north. Once again he left behind his old home, much transformed and draped in the mourning crepe of darkness.[39]

On August 28 Barquet disembarked at the army base on Gallop Island, an old seaside resort in Boston Harbor, and queued up for his second paycheck in two years, minus deductions for his uniform and the Enfield rifle he had lost somewhere along the way. He thus settled his account with the army, and the army its with him.[40]

On the morning of September 2, Barquet fell in for a triumphant return march through Boston. Colonel Shaw would not be leading them, of course, but the Shaw Guards, an unattached volunteer militia of black men formed in his honor, had gathered at the dock to welcome the 54th home. As the regiment wound its way to Boston Common, spectators could see for themselves the transforming force of war on the soldiers' faces. The men marched with the bearing and stride of a fighting force, bringing home the remnants of their colors and the fullness of their expectations. They were now sharpshooters and artillerymen. No bullies plotted an attack on them this time. Reaching the platform on the Common where their longtime advocate Governor Andrew waited, they performed the manual of arms with practiced flair. The speeches that day brimmed with potboiler patriotism. Predictably Colonel Hallowell's last words were admonitions rather than praise, instructing the men to return home to their families and save their money.[41] After he bade them farewell, the soldiers of the 54th dispersed and were once again civilians, very much on their own.

Barquet boarded a west-bound train for Illinois with the contentment of a man who had accomplished what few thought possible. He had survived the war and more, playing a role in a world-changing event that helped prove that bravery and patriotism had no color. He had avoided the bullets of enemies and overcome the doubts of friends, enjoying as a member of the "Famous 54th" the rare experience of a hero's welcome in both Charleston and Boston. As Barquet settled into the rhythm of the train, he may have been lulled into a false sense of finality, believing that nothing would ever be the same for the people of color in the United States—or for himself. His homeward journey, however, merely transported him from one front in America's hundred years' war for freedom to another.

9

WE HAVE LOST OUR COUNTRY

CAPTAIN THOMAS PINCKNEY's departure from Charleston in December 1864 had been like a melancholy leave-taking from the bedside of a dying relative. Confederate officers in the city confided to him that they had no hope. Once Savannah fell, the death rattle of the Queen City had begun. With the mass of Confederate troops in a desperate struggle to save Richmond, General Beauregard planned no heroic measures in South Carolina. The fall of Charleston on February 18, 1865, then, was not a shock, but news Pinckney received with profound sadness. With the interruption in the mails and the silencing of the presses, a dark curtain descended upon the city. Its people depended on rumor and their imaginations to plumb the depths of their defeat as they dwelled in a waking nightmare.

Pinckney's January reunion with his father and sisters in Cokesbury had been one of muted joy. Without his beloved mother to welcome him, the crowded little farmhouse seemed even less like a home. After the many months of longing for his family, he soon wearied of domestic life. Pouring over the letters sent to his parents by friends, relatives, and comrades who believed Pinckney had died a hero's death at Haw's Shop gave him pause. The "unusual opportunity of reading something akin to my own obituary" and knowing that "the same kind things can never be said again that were appropriate to one supposed to have laid down his life in the defense of his country" weighed heavily upon him as he considered his suffering-bystander role in the war.[1]

Driven by the need to prove himself equal to his eulogies, every day Pinckney rode the mile to Hodge's Depot, where he waited to get war news from passing troop trains. "What of General Edmund Kirby-Smith," he might ask of east-bound soldiers; "What of General Lee," of those headed west. In mid-March 1865 Pinckney learned from some men on their way to Virginia that all Confederate prisoners home on parole were officially declared exchanged and were to report to their respective commands.[2]

None of the spavined farm horses at Cokesbury could carry him to battle, so Pinckney spent the family's entire profit from their salt works, almost $3,000 in Confederate money, on a lively young stallion and dashed off "to fight Yankees." A mount was also found for his manservant, James Broughton, who dashed after him. The two went in search of the 4th South Carolina Cavalry and learned that what remained of their outfit had been attached to General Johnston's army, which was massing around Smithfield, North Carolina. The ailing Johnston, broken by his failure to defend Atlanta the past July, in effect had already retired from the army. But he gamely agreed when President Davis approached him to rebuild a fighting force with the remnants of his once-formidable Army of Tennessee and what remained of Generals Hardee's, Bragg's, and Hampton's commands. Their goal was to delay Sherman's northward-moving behemoth from joining with General Grant's Army of the Potomac to finally corner the elusive Lee in Virginia.[3]

Pinckney's months in prison camps and his own optimistic view of the world had insulated him from the true situation of the war. The captain clung to the hope that glory might yet be found on the battlefield, that the Confederacy could not fail, and that right somehow would always trump might. He waved away as treason all the fatalistic sighs from doomsayers that the end was near. As he made his way east across North Carolina, though, he encountered gangs of disheveled Confederates trudging determinedly west toward the mountains, away from the front. To his mind, these were mere deserters, ignorant cowards off to hide in the balsam, the spawn of those Scotch-Irish driven out of Pennsylvania by Indians after General Braddock's defeat in the eighteenth century. These shirkers, he believed, were categorically different from the loyal men of the Santee, descendants of steadfast Huguenots.[4]

Because of its geography, North Carolina had never developed the extensive plantation systems as had its neighbors to the north and south and was nearly the last state to secede. In 1861 Pinckney's relatives summering in Flat Rock had reported that the local mountain men and hardscrabble farmers of Henderson County had committed "conscript commotions" and refused to fight "a rich man's war" for slavery. Long-simmering class resentment continued to bubble to the surface. Just the summer before, in June 1864, an unsavory clutch of rebel deserters had stormed into the Flat Rock home of his aunt Mary Elliott Johnstone and murdered her distinguished husband, Andrew Johnstone, while he sat at his own dinner table. Only the quick action of their teenage son, who grabbed his shotgun, drove off the invaders before they committed further atrocities. Fearing reprisals, the family then fled the state. Pinckney worried about the fate of his own family's mountain home, Piedmont, that was near the Johnstone's place as well as the black family they had left in charge.[5]

As Pinckney drew closer to the front, he was struck by the "shocking condition" of that part of the state as ragged downcast men, deserters in retreat, began to outnumber those headed to confront General Sherman. Learning that one of his fellow prisoners from Morris Island, Colonel George Nathaniel Folk of the 6th North Carolina Cavalry, was camped nearby on the Catawba River, he spent the night with him to learn more about the true state of the Confederacy. Indeed, disaffection had reached crisis proportion, Colonel Folk confirmed, and he admitted that he had to resort to the most severe methods to convince those absent without leave to return to the army. As soon as deserters were apprehended, he submitted them to a "drumhead" court-martial, one of which was in progress while Pinckney was visiting that involved an attractive young "penitent" for whom the captain felt some sympathy. He learned the results of the trial the next morning when he heard shots in the near distance as he rode out of camp, a sound that greatly saddened him. The next night Pinckney spent in the home of a farmer who said that his wife was frightened of all the deserters roaming about the countryside and felt safer with a soldier in the house.[6]

On March 18, 1865, a discouraged Pinckney approached the railroad center of Smithfield and began asking the distracted officers he met along the way where he might find Colonel Rutledge's regiment. He learned that the frayed ends of Butler's Brigade—the 4th, 5th, and 6th South Carolina Cavalry—had been consolidated. William Stokes from his regiment had been placed in charge while Rutledge was away in South Carolina, trying to round up the large numbers of cavalrymen absent without leave. Some of these men were no longer fit for duty; others, repeat offenders whose first offense had been pardoned. The news of the occupation of the lowcountry by regiments of black Union soldiers had made many Santee men feel that they needed to return home to protect their families. By March desertion, disease, death, and transfers had winnowed Pinckney's Company D from the ninety-six men who trotted behind him to Virginia to less than a dozen with mounts—and his was the largest in the regiment.[7]

Exhausted, Pinckney collapsed under a tent—really a blanket thrown over a pole—belonging to his old friend Sergeant William Lucas. Before dawn Stokes—paying no attention to the captain's insistence that he needed a day to rest—sent an orderly to wake him with the command that he was needed to lead his men to the front. Bleary eyed and disoriented, he saddled a fresh young horse just impressed from a local farm and immediately regretted he had somewhere lost his martingale. At the first sound of musketry when they approached the field, the "little rascal" reared up and fell backward. Pinckney avoided being crushed by deftly slipping off one side, but when the creature scrambled to his feet, he planted an ironclad foot on the fallen rider's ankle before galloping to safety. With the sickening sound of crushed bone, Pinckney's war was over. He sent word to a no-doubt furious Stokes that he was in need of the surgeon and was helped to the rear by one of the privates from his company, who was relieved to make his exit from the field.[8]

Pinckney's depleted company stoically moved on without him. Although outnumbered three to one, the Confederates under General Johnston's leadership managed to undertake one last tactical offensive against General Sherman's army near Bentonville, about fifty miles east of Raleigh. After this battle, their war would be over too. The Confederates sustained 2,606 casualties and the Union lost 1,527 men over the next two days. Sherman and Johnston then withdrew to their respective headquarters to consider the future of their armies.

JAMES BROUGHTON AND A PRIVATE carried Pinckney to an ambulance wagon and followed him to the railroad crossroads at Hillsborough, where on a sidetrack they heaved him into a freight car fluffed with cotton bolls ready to receive the injured. Broughton had just settled the captain when a detachment of Yankee cavalry descended upon the junction like the furies. Broughton leapt upon his horse and galloped back to the safety of the Confederate camp, where he reported to Sergeant Lucas, who dissuaded him from his plan to travel more than a hundred miles back to Eldorado. The Santee District, Lucas understood, was as dangerous as a battle zone for a lone black man. Broughton would have to run the gauntlet of Yankee guerrillas lying in wait along the roads. Union officers in that area were reportedly dragooning all able-bodied male slaves to fill up their ranks and would have no scruple about seizing him. Conversely, local planters had declared all blacks not on plantations as runaways to be shot on sight and had hired agents to do this dirty work. Broughton wisely accepted the invitation to stay for the short term with Lucas's parents, who had taken refuge in Florence, South Carolina, a closer and safer destination.[9]

Back in North Carolina, Pinckney languished in the crowded freight car with nothing to relieve the pain in his ankle. He lost track of time. At one point, though, he was aroused from his fevered torpor by crowds of highly agitated men. Dragging himself to the door, he asked what had happened. "General Lee has surrendered," came the reply. "A damned lie," he retorted. Pinckney then unleashed a "philippic" against those faint of heart who could repeat such treasonous falsehood. Only after seeing the parole of a soldier returning home from Virginia could Pinckney accept that Lee had indeed capitulated to General Grant at Appomattox Court House on April 9, 1865. The death knell of the Confederate nation hit him like "a stunning blow."[10]

The looming question now was the fate of the Confederate army. From what information he had pieced together from passing soldiers, officers were not to be arrested or executed by the Federals, as he had feared, nor would their property be confiscated. After pledging their loyalty to the Union and accepting the end of slavery, Confederate soldiers could be restored to citizenship.

Pinckney's own status remained in question, though, for General Johnston had not yet surrendered his army. A few days later when he was transferred to a hospital set up at the Edgeworth Female Institute in Greensboro, he tried to find out more. Learning that gangrene was prevalent inside the building, he requested that a tent be pitched for himself outdoors, after which he took the opportunity to hobble around and ask officers billeted on the grounds what they knew. Apparently, white-flagged trains were chugging back and forth along the main rail line between Sherman's and Johnston's headquarters conveying offers and counteroffers.[11]

The generals' mutual goal was to provide not just a cessation of fighting but also the outline of a map to reconciliation. The assassination of Abraham Lincoln on April 15 complicated their task. No one knew what to expect from the new president, Andrew Johnson, a unionist Democrat from Tennessee and no friend to slaveholders. The darkened mood of the people in the North emboldened Radical Republicans in Congress to agitate for harsh retribution against the South and punishment for its wartime leaders. Both generals understood that if the Confederate soldiers did not get basically the same protections as their counterparts in Virginia, they would see no reason not to continue the fight guerrilla style or head west to join with the yet unbowed General Edmund Kirby Smith in the Trans-Mississippi Department. From his cot, Pinckney could hear cavalrymen slipping off every night for fear the Yankees would take their horses after the surrender. "Our army was melting away rapidly," he reflected poignantly.[12]

On April 26, when General Johnston formally surrendered his patchwork forces of 89,000 men scattered across South Carolina, North Carolina, Georgia, and Florida, Pinckney's division leader, General Hampton, defied him. Fearing that giving up the fight and accepting the wholesale emancipation of the slaves would only trigger "a train of horrors," he had the blessing of President Davis, who had fled Richmond and was on the run, to take as many men west as he could before the army was officially disbanded. Pinckney's regimental commander, the no-nonsense farmer Stokes, would have none of this derring-do into uncharted legal territory. Foregoing the formal surrender ceremony at Durham Station, he marched his downcast troops to Asheboro, wished his men luck, and told them simply to go home.[13]

Still recuperating, Pinckney asked Hampton's adjutant, Major Thomas Gaillard Barker, a good friend from Charleston and Flat Rock, to visit him. No longer in his tent, Pinckney had accepted the invitation of a local minister to stay in a bed set up in the parlor of the rectory, where his marriageable daughters could care for the injured officer. After listening patiently to Pinckney's detailed plan about how his friends would hide him in the woods until he was well enough to ride after Hampton, Barker explained that the division was included in the surrender, no matter where it was physically located at the time of the signing. Any of Hampton's men who persisted in acts of war against the United States would be considered outlaws and hunted down. The truth was, Barker, an early and fervent secessionist, told him quietly, "we might as well recognize the fact at once, that our cause was lost and make the best of the situation."[14]

As a gesture of good will, Sherman offered the hungry Confederates ten days' rations for their long, bitter journey home and allowed them to split up the Confederate quartermaster's stores. Pinckney, still on crutches, received a bolt of gray flannel. Captain Joseph Winthrop, a doctor friend from Charleston who volunteered to help him navigate the journey back home, got a padlock. Otherwise, the two men were penniless. Fortunately, all along the way they found people willing to give two bereft veterans a little something to eat from their own reduced pantries. Their travel south on a slow-moving train came to an abrupt end at the crossroads town of Chester, South Carolina, which had fallen prey to Major General George Stoneman on his famously destructive raid across the Blue Ridge Mountains that had targeted prisons, warehouses, and railroads. Pinckney managed to get word to his father, who sent a wagon with a mattress on the flatbed to facilitate his son's inglorious homecoming.[15]

By the time the captain returned to his family, the political architects of the Confederacy—Jefferson Davis and his cabinet—were imprisoned in Fortress Monroe, Virginia, and South Carolina's governor, Andrew Magrath, was incarcerated at Fort Pulaski. Pinckney, remembering his bitter experience there, speculated that the US government was hoping that all of the Confederate officials would contract the fever raging in their prisons and spare the nation the agony of a trial.[16]

With the death of the Confederacy, the heartsore seventy-six-year-old Cotesworth Pinckney declared himself also "weary of life" and took to his bed. The doctor diagnosed a "disordered liver" and said he could recover "if only he wanted to." But he did not. While waiting to see his younger son one last time, the elder Pinckney read a little, wrote pieces for a religious newspaper, and perhaps reflected on why God had seemingly turned his face against the Confederacy—and him. As soon as Tom hobbled through the door, the dispirited old aristocrat stopped eating and took to his room. At the very end, Cotesworth Pinckney, who had always been cold to strangers and distant with his family, let go of his "old fashioned gravity and reserve" and displayed a long-denied warmth to his children and grandchildren, "the only thing wanting to complete his Christian character." On June 9, 1865, after saying the Lord's Prayer with his son-in-law Archibald Seabrook, Cotesworth Pinckney "completed his cycle quietly," ending a lifetime of "temperance and self-denial."[17] Born with the Union in 1789, he died with the Confederacy and left a legacy of ruin. In the short term, all that his children inherited were his debts.

With transport to the Pendleton graveyard unfeasible, the Pinckneys buried their father in a simple ceremony on the Cokesbury farm. A minister from the local Methodist church performed the funeral ceremony. After sunset the "faithful negroes," carrying torches, gathered around the grave of their old master and in the flickering light chanted "a requiem of their characteristic spirituals over the grave of their old master"—and of slavery.[18]

Amid the "dreadful days" after the war, when "private sorrows mixed with public disasters," Caroline Seabrook wished she too could die. So much she had held dear had been stolen away by the war—her parents, two children, her plantation, and all the investments and cash. Worst of all, she reflected, "we have lost our country."[19]

This reality hit home most dramatically when the Reverend Cotesworth Jr., deputed by the family as an executor of their father's estate, steeled himself to publically renounce the Confederacy and take the oath of allegiance to the Union as required of all who had owned $20,000 in taxable income. Had he not done this, the family would have been rendered "quite pennyless." His daughter

Carrie, who had grown up as a child of the Confederacy, confessed, "I have shed most bitter tears over our Lost Cause & feel as if I hardly know how to bear it."[20]

In May 1865, the future of the South clarified a bit when President Johnson, who always considered secession a legal impossibility, outlined a straightforward path for reunion. The Tennessean, who had been the political voice of the yeoman of his state, had spoken of seizing the land of the slaveholding cotton nabobs who started the war and redistributing it among the loyal white farmers, but there was none of this now. To resume its former standing, any state formerly in rebellion must draft a new constitution with provisions abolishing slavery, repealing its ordinance of secession, and repudiating the Confederate debt. All men eligible to vote before 1860 would be restored to full citizenship upon application. The political rights of the freed blacks played little role in his thinking.

Less clear cut for many southerners was reconciling Confederate defeat with their previous belief that God, acting in history, had been on their side. Spiritual angst haunted the Reverend Pinckney Jr. as it had his father. Equally hard to fathom was the death of Lincoln just at the moment of Union victory. Pinckney later tried to explain to his congregation at Grace Episcopal Church, the first to open its doors during the occupation, that the darkness through which they were passing was not a sign that God had turned his face against them, but it was a test of their faith, much like the tribulations endured by the Old Testament Israelites. The one thing Pinckney could assure them with 100-percent confidence was that emancipation of the slaves had been God's will. Thus it was incumbent upon them, and upon all Christians, to treat the former slaves with "justice" and "kindness" while these men and women worked out their own destiny, whatever and wherever that might be.[21]

AT THE PINCKNEY FAMILY'S Cokesbury farm, emancipation had come in the middle of a cotton crop. Their workers were slaves when they planted the seeds and free people before the bolls ripened. Still dependent on crutches and not looking very masterful, Thomas Pinckney, as required by his pardon, called a meeting of all the hands when he returned. They were all free to leave and never look back, he told them. Always inclined to "take things by the smooth handle," he added that any who were willing to stay on and help get in the cotton crop would receive their provisions and housing as usual as well as one-third share of the harvest to split. Afterward, he promised to transport them the more than two hundred miles back to the Santee District. He had been braced for the workers to throw down their tools and take off dancing down the road, intoxicated with the promise of a new life. Instead, after he spoke, the hands were eerily quiet. After a lifetime of slavery, the concept of freedom took a while to comprehend. In the end, most agreed to see the crop in. The Santee was, after all, their home as well, and they craved reunion with their families and the land.[22]

Strangely enough, life went on more or less as usual. Caroline Seabrook described their servants' behavior as "exemplary." They performed their daily tasks "acting as if they had never heard of Lincoln." When asked about her future plans, Nancy, who had been the nurse for all the Seabrook children, vowed that "she would not leave the family for anything." Caroline knew, though, that in time Nancy would be ready to move on, and when that moment came, she would probably be content to see her leave. "Things do not work comfortably under the new system," she admitted to her cousin Harriott Horry Ravenel, "and we look forward with no small sense of relief to their going tho' we may be embarrassed for want of servants." For all the challenges involved with adjusting to the new way of life, she found it "impossible to feel any resentment against our Negroes for they came obediently out of the way of freedom [on the Santee River plantations], and only accepted it when brought to their doors."[23]

Indeed, the gift of freedom, seemingly in answer to their relentless and fervent prayers, encouraged the former slaves to believe that they too were part of God's mysterious plan and that their lives possessed meaning quite apart from relentless toil. As spring turned to summer and summer turned to fall, the freed people grew in anticipation as they watched the fragile cotton seedlings sprout and flourish. In a way the development of these plants paralleled their own transformation into people of worth in their own minds. The warming sun ignited the "squares," or buds, to set off their natural evolution into blooms that changed from cream to pale pink, maturing into red. When the late spring breezes scattered the drying petals, fibrous bolls emerged in their place as if by miracle. Their husks ripened in the intense summer heat. When the nights cooled, the plant's leaves drooped, and the bolls exploded with the "white gold" ready for picking. The eager men and women fell to their familiar prickly, backbreaking labor with a new spirit that had some kinship to joy. Every third boll they plucked for themselves; every third penny the factor would pay for this crop would go into their pockets. And that made all the difference.

"Cap'n Tom" kept his promise. In early November, with the last of the cotton picked and baled, the hands made ready to return home to Eldorado by train.

Still a bit lame, Pinckney limped about, requisitioning all the farm wagons, mules, and oxcarts he could to set off on the first leg of the journey. The crop that year had been small, but demand was high, so it fetched a good price.[24]

When Pinckney first told his sisters that he planned to stay on the Santee and attempt to restart their rice operation, they confronted him with an enfilade of opposition. The district, they had heard, had reverted to a state of nature, a war of all against all. Had he not just had a narrow escape in Flat Rock, threatened with an early grave by deserter desperados terrorizing the county?

In October Pinckney and his uncle Ralph Elliott had crossed over the Blue Ridge to survey the damage to their family homes. Upon opening the heavy door of Piedmont, Pinckney was dumbstruck to find that the locals had stripped the place bare, even patiently peeling off the wallpaper for its homespun backing. The black couple who had stayed on the place throughout the war and hidden the valuables gave him the name of the perpetrators. Summoning all his tact, he managed to regain a number of pieces from the desperately poor folk, many of whom had attended Sunday school classes taught by his father. After the leader of the gang that was trying to purge the mountain of the South Carolinians had left a warning that the two men needed to leave—or else—Pinckney and Elliott spent an anxious night at Piedmont, heavily armed and supported by young sharpshooters from another lowcountry family. While the threatened attack never came, Pinckney later rode home, reflecting on the murder of Andrew Johnstone at Flat Rock the previous year. He came to realize that "peace" meant that the old aristocratic class would be fighting a two-front struggle against deeply resentful poor whites and deeply distrustful freed blacks.[25]

Pinckney was adamant that he must "face the trials of Reconstruction" and assert his family's claim to their land. Despite her anxiety over his departure, Caroline had to smile as her brother loaded up the "rejoicing" men and women for their trip to the "Paradise" of home and family in early November 1865. In contrast to the spiritual angst of the Pinckneys over the defeat of the Confederacy, the former slaves imagined themselves as the Children of Israel: first enslaved, then liberated, and now this exodus out of the wilderness of the upcountry and back to the "Land of Promise" on the Santee. Many succumbed to the ecstasy of expectation that was escalated by the rumors that the federal government would be giving them land—even perhaps a mule—that would later make the reality of freedom all the more difficult to accept. Watching the shambolic caravan slowly disappear from sight, Caroline mused about her earnest younger brother in the role of latter-day Moses. She only hoped that when the serious work of organizing the laborers commenced, he could set aside his wounded pride and "have the humility not to lay down his commandments too stridently."[26]

Although Pinckney tried to be brave for the sake of his sisters, he left their little home shrouded in a veil of dread that weighed more heavily upon him the closer he got to the Santee River. From what he understood of the situation, the greatest danger facing him was that his "commandments," strident or not, would be ignored. He realized that with the freed people owning nothing but their labor and the planters only their land, the former slaves and the former masters would be thrust together in a hellish union. All would perish if the crops were not planted.

Naturalist Henry W. Ravenel of Aiken anticipated this dilemma when he learned that the "great experiment," or rather "torture," of emancipation was to be inflicted upon the defeated southerners "for the complacent satisfaction of Puritan philosophers." They would garner the "glory" for its success; planters, the blame for its failure. But what of the experiment's subject, "the poor negro!" Ravenel asked: "Who thinks of him? What is to become of him?"[27]

In contrast to the long-debated 1833 British policy of gradual emancipation in the West Indies, Congress ended slavery without a plan outlining how the penniless landowner and the landless worker might now live together. In further contrast with the British Caribbean policy that compensated slaveholders for their losses, in 1865 over six billion dollars simply disappeared from the balance sheets of slaveowners at the same time their debts from prewar purchases of land and slaves remained. The southern plantation economy would lose 75 percent of its value.

In freedom, workers fled the harsh, unhealthy work of the rice fields; many headed to town. Approximately two thousand laborers remained of the seven thousand men, women, and children who had cultivated 15,000 acres and produced as much as forty-five bushels of rice along the Santee Rivers and delta land before the war. By 1865, Carolina rice was in danger of losing its place in the world market, as only about 3,000 acres on the Santee were back in cultivation, with an expected yield of about half the prewar level. In the best-case scenario, planters would be shipping out about one-eighth of what they had in 1860. Disaster loomed; only the ricebirds and water moccasins thrived.[28]

The short-term solution to the labor problem that was endorsed by the occupying army in May had been for the landowners and the workers to sign contracts that outlined in a straightforward manner the mutual obligations of each party. The first contracts, all susceptible to government scrutiny, varied in their particulars, but essentially they mandated that for a six-month period from June to December, the workers would supply requisite labor and the planters would give them adequate housing and sustenance. After the harvest, all parties would share to some degree in the bounty.

With neither of his family houses habitable, Pinckney accepted Augustus Shoolbred's invitation to stay at Woodville Plantation. Their families had shared a friendship spanning three generations. Three of the four Shoolbred sons had fought for the Confederacy, and one was lost. Augustus, who was the same age as Pinckney and grew up with him, could not serve in the army because of a boyhood hunting accident and had agreed to manage Eldorado and Thomas's affairs in his absence.[29]

Augustus had tried to prepare Pinckney for what he would find and apprised him of all the postwar developments after the Union army had passed through. Working cooperatively, the freedmen had divvied up the property at Eldorado among themselves and girdled great ancient oak trees, the pride of the Pinckneys, to have more land for their plots. After extended negotiations, Shoolbred got them to agree that sharing their crops with Pinckney was the fair thing to do. They had, however, refused to return the furniture they had taken from the mansion house until Shoolbred brought in the military authorities to mandate that they drag their booty back to where they found it.[30]

Shoolbred also explained how, under the influence of the plundering Yankees, the men and women living at Eldorado had crowded onto abandoned rice barges and made their way to Hampton, home of their Rutledge relatives on Wambaw Creek, where they obviously knew Cotesworth Pinckney Sr. had hidden family treasures too big to transport inland. The Pinckneys' special concern had been to protect the general's extensive and well-chosen library from the Union officers, who had become notorious along the James River in Virginia for stealing rare-book collections and selling them northward. It pained Shoolbred to report that the former slaves, illiterate and having no use for the books themselves, had gone on a spree of wanton destruction, prying open the crates, tearing up books, and tossing them about the lawn in a way that seemed to herald the death of civilization. When later asked to explain this wanton and senseless destruction of thousands of valuable old volumes, one reply was that the white people "had gotten all of [their] sense out of them, and should get no more good from them." Augustus desperately tried to restore some basic order before Tom arrived and salvage what he could of the books strewn about haphazardly. Despite his best desperate efforts, though, torn pages and business papers, deeds, and receipts would still be stuck in branches, snagged in bushes, or lying about the ground when, heartsick, Pinckney surveyed the damage.[31]

Having reconciled himself to the defeat of the Confederacy, reining up at Eldorado and gazing upon the dilapidated mansion forced Thomas Pinckney to acknowledge what a profound personal defeat he had suffered. Once a symbol of order and harmony in the New World, the general's home had been almost totally obliterated by the formal garden now grown feral. He felt that a thousand years of darkness was descending upon the South. The lower floors of both wings of the house threatened to give way. The fences had collapsed, as much in surrender, it seemed, as in decay.[32] Had Eldorado been destroyed in some great battle or even burned in a magnificent fire, as had the family seat on East Bay in 1861, Tom might have felt less bereft, but here the home sagged, a sorry shadow of its former self, making him feel a similar personal descent from glory.

Pinckney steeled himself before going inside, as if preparing to identify the corpse of a loved one. Stepping across the threshold, he encountered a scene as bizarre as it was shocking. Much of the larger furniture—some elegant purchases from the European travels of the Pinckney brothers—had been retrieved out of the former slave quarters by Shoolbred and more or less returned to their customary places, but every piece had been transformed, reduced in ungainly ways to fit into the workers' cabins. The furniture looked like dwarfed replicas of their original, elegant forms. Every table and sofa had been broken. In sawing off the intricately carved mahogany bedposts to accommodate their low ceilings, the freedmen ritualistically cut the family's grandeur "down to size."[33]

As Pinckney walked through the halls stripped of their fine carpets, each step of his worn boots on the broad-board floors echoed in the high-ceilinged rooms. He mentally tallied the loss of General Pinckney's treasures, the tangible reminders of his family's past distinction. All weapons of any description, from the brass-barreled blunderbusses to horseman's pistols, had disappeared. The most poignant losses, however, were of the small things that had once made Eldorado a home, the little pieces of bric-a-brac, mementos from travel, and tokens of affection from family members now lost forever.[34]

For some reason, perhaps superstition, the only decoration in the whole house that remained unmolested was a towering hall mirror. This same looking glass that had once held the images of President James Monroe and Vice President Calhoun had most recently reflected the antics of Eldorado's "newly-enfranchised citizens," who had danced many a "shin dig" about the house.[35]

His own reflection may have shocked Pinckney as much as any other sight on this transformed landscape. He considered how many times over the years he had stood in that same place and wondered how closely he resembled his vaunted grandfather, General Thomas Pinckney—the Oxonian, the Greek scholar, the lawyer, the saber-wielding revolutionary, the agricultural innovator, the dreamer of a new world order, the diplomat, the trusted leader of the state and nation, the favorite of George Washington, the master of slaves, and through much effort, the master of himself.

When he now took his own measure, the Thomas Pinckney he saw in the mirror had the same body build as his grandfather, though more decidedly gaunt at the moment than the general, who loved good food and fine wine. He could make out through his long full beard the same strong facial features as rendered in the general's portraits, with his prominent nose of classical proportion befitting an architect of a new republic. In the mirror, though, Tom's eyes looked weary and dispirited, betraying his broken heart, while in the miniature done by Charles Fraser in 1818, his aged grandfather's eyes perpetually danced with excitement and expectation.

Pinckney could, though, look at himself with confidence that he had kept his famous name free from scandal, even if he had not advanced its glory. Always overshadowed by his elder brother in his youth, when Tom understood that he would never be great, he had always strived to be good. When South Carolina seceded from the Union, Pinckney had stepped forward, as had thirteen other descendants of the general. In 1861 he had stood before this mirror in his bespoke gray uniform of a Confederate cavalryman, with the modest three stripes of a captain on his sleeve and General Pinckney's sword on his belt. He might have touched the hilt and wondered, even then, whether his grandfather would have approved of his raising that sword against the flag of the United States.[36] If he had any thoughts such as this, Pinckney repressed them and never breathed a word of doubt about the righteousness of "the Cause," nor did he repine about his losses. By raising a home guard to protect the Pinckney estates and other rice plantations along the South Santee River, he may have worked out his own peace with the war. He had not placed himself in the path of glory, though. For himself, he now only expected that ultimate glory promised to the faithful.

Appearing haggard in faded and worn travel garb that his personal slaves would have shunned in an earlier year, he might have realized that he was less a reflection of his grandfather than his inverse image. In contrast to the general, whose youthful military experience and whole career actually was punctuated by heroism and wreathed in brilliance, Captain Thomas Pinckney's life as a soldier was notable for his suffering rather than for his daring, for his Christian stoicism rather than his audacity. He had been forced to surrender his grandfather's sword, the sword of another war and another cause, on the battlefield. By participating in the 1860 revolution against his grandfather's republic, he had sacrificed the authority and legitimacy that had come with that blade.

In the years ahead Thomas Pinckney would emerge as an iconic figure, celebrated in Charleston as a symbol of the Lost Cause, but that was all unforeseen in the hungry days of November 1865. At this moment the man Pinckney saw in the mirror had been stripped of all that had defined southern manliness. He had not distinguished himself in battle. His claim to his ancestral land was uncertain and might yet be denied. He had no home, no wife, and no son to carry on his noble name; he was in debt; he was the master of no man.

LEAVING ELDORADO, Pinckney set out for the workers' quarters. The last time he saw these men and women, they had been his family's slaves—now they were free. He took the same route that his mother had traveled every Saturday before the war when she visited the cabins and felt as though he was passing backward into the dark abyss of time. He could still remember how she stopped at each door, checking to see if the floor was clean, the yard swept, and the trash burning. If she was satisfied, she rewarded the tenants with sugar, tea, coffee, or soap from a pan carried on the head of one of her young maids. That memory now seemed to belong to an entirely different age, like some improbable incident in a Sir Walter Scott novel.[37] One epoch had surely ended, he knew, and another, inevitably, would begin, but at that moment his imagination could not penetrate the twilight of uncertainty in which he now dwelled.

Although Pinckney had sent word he was coming, the cabin-lined "street," usually so full of life, had the hushed feeling of a ghost town. Every door was closed tight; all was silence with no person in sight. Only the "devoted" family retainer "Maum Clarissa"—the mother of his manservant, James Broughton—stepped forward. When Pinckney asked where the men were, she replied that she could not exactly say. Disgruntled, he left her with the instruction that when he returned the next day, he expected to see each one of them.[38]

Pinckney spent a sleepless night mapping out his strategy. The success or failure of his whole enterprise rested on his ability to control his emotions. He must appear calm but resolute, prepared for trouble but not provocative. Understanding that "violent encounters" between blacks and whites had become the norm throughout the Santee District, when Pinckney set out the next morning, he strapped on his revolver and wore it in plain sight. Since his fondness for hunting was well known, he also grabbed his double-barreled shotgun and whistled for his dogs to give the impression that he was merely riding out for a day of sport rather than feeling threatened.

To his consternation, when he trotted up to the meeting place under the giant oaks, the space was empty. It seemed that the freedmen were playing some mind games of their own. Only after Pinckney called out impatiently did a few cabin doors crack open just enough for wary eyes to survey the scene. Having made the point that they now owned their own time, the hands strolled out to meet him at a leisurely pace. Only a few murmured the traditional greetings, asking after the family and bobbing their heads as of old. Some leered insolently. A couple even carried guns of their own. Most stood still, shifting their feet; anxious to see what was going to happen next. Scanning the assembled crowd, Pinckney focused on a man he knew as "Renty." Once described as a "prime field hand," he had run away to the Union fleet during the Christmas festivities in 1862. Now back and wearing a US Navy uniform, he resolutely grasped a rifle and looked his former master straight in the eye. Pinckney stared back.

Clearing his throat authoritatively, the former captain began by acknowledging unconditionally their freedom and voicing his acceptance that the old system was dead. He then announced his plan to restart his plantation operation as soon as possible. Believing Eldorado's workers the best in the Santee, he invited any who wanted to work with him to remain on the property and promised to pay them a fair wage. The mention of wages, still an unfamiliar concept for many used to barter, inspired a certain amount of murmuring.[39]

Someone called out that Yankee greenbacks were no better than "conferick" money and they would not accept them. Emboldened, another voice chimed in: "Yes, Captain, we all going to work. We going to work right here, but we ain't going to work for any white people anymore." Another chimed in, "the Union general tell us we must all go back to our homes and go to work, and we would dig the greenbacks from under the sod, and we are going to do it, but we are going to work for ourselves and for nobody else." Pinckney acknowledged their right to do precisely that. He agreed that they "were free to go and to work where and how they pleased, but that this was my plantation and not the Union general's, and that nobody could stay upon it, but those who worked for me, and upon my terms." He gave them ten days to consider their options. At that point the uniformed Renty marched with deliberation over to his cabin. He flung open the door and turned back around, shouting threateningly that this was "his home and he would like to see any man put him out of it." He then brought his rifle butt down upon the doorstep "with a ringing blow," slamming the door behind him. This initial "parlay," Pinckney noted, ended with "much dissatisfaction all around."[40]

Shaken, Pinckney returned to the Shoolbred home and waited. Ten days passed. Having no word from the hands, he returned to their quarters and engaged in another frustrating circular conversation with three men. At the heart of the matter was a crucial difference of opinion about what it meant to be free. In Pinckney's mind he owned the land, and the now-emancipated slaves owned their labor. He now had neither control over nor responsibility for them or their families. In the minds of these workers, however, freedom was ineluctably connected to owning land and the ability to control one's time. As one of the men asked Pinckney with exquisite simplicity, "what good does it do for the government to give us our freedom and not give us land to plant?"[41]

Workers on the Pinckney plantations already had a long proprietary relationship to the land that stretched back generations. Since the Pinckneys rarely sold their servants away from their families except in instances of extreme disobedience, dense multilayers of kinship bound this slave community together. According to the 1860 slave schedule, none of the ninety-seven slaves at Fairfield (then still in the estate of Colonel Thomas Pinckney) were of mixed racial heritage, while at Cotesworth Pinckney's Eldorado, only four of the eighty-five living there were classified as "mulatto."[42]

The minds of Pinckney's workers had already been poisoned against the unfamiliar concept of the labor contract by the actions of Stephen Doar, his neighbor at Harrietta Plantation, before Tom arrived back on the Santee. As the sole executor of Colonel Thomas Pinckney still living in the district, Doar assumed control of Fairfield Plantation after the war and negotiated contracts with thirty-one workers in June 1865. The hands were willing but wanted to work as they always had—in their family units moving to the ancient rhythms of dawn and dusk and the changes of the seasons. Over the centuries a task system had evolved on the lowcountry rice plantations which defined a work "day" by specific finite measures depending on the stage of the crop, such as planting or cultivating a quarter acre, pounding seven mortars of dried rice, or splitting one hundred poles into twelve-foot lengths. Speed was rewarded, for once that particular task was completed, the workers' time was their own and could be spent as they wished in hunting, fishing, raising pigs and chickens, or cultivating their family's patch of land provided by the Pinckneys.[43]

Enslaved people had understood this system as giving them a bit of control over their daily lives and once free recoiled from Doar's new and punitive approach, inspired perhaps by the attempt made on his life by his own workers. With the approval of US military authorities, Doar's contract exceeded the simple exchange of work for provisions and housing and a share of the harvest. He insisted that in freedom, rice hands would work persistently as free northern workers did. And like the northern factory manager, Doar owned ten continuous hours of their time each workday during which they must do as he instructed, including cleaning ditches or rebuilding earthen dams, with a one-hour break in the middle of the day. The Fairfield hands' deep resentment of Doar's labor regime, combined with his intrusive oversight into their personal morals and strictures against leaving the plantation, inevitably generated conflicts that resulted in arrests and corporal punishments by the military.[44]

As the wind off the South Santee grew chill and November drifted toward December, the standoff at Eldorado continued. Huddled in their cold cabins, the hungry freedmen and freedwomen, who had yearned so long for emancipation, stared "Freedom" in its face and wondered now if it was friend or foe. The harsh truth descended upon them that although they could indeed walk away, they really had no place to go. Refusing to cede what they considered their birthright claim to Pinckney land, they were quick to abuse and drive away temporary labor hired in their stead, hunkering down in stolid solidarity. Gandhian in their mastery of nonviolent resistance, centuries of suffering had taught the freed people patience. The local military commander explained to frustrated planters that using force against the workers was futile. He had learned through experience that if the freedmen felt they had been wronged, they would simply endure any punishment and make the army lose face.[45]

Leading up to Christmas, rumors flew up and down the Santee with the rapidity of river ducks that freedmen were plotting some sort of major upheaval, even a race war modeled after the white bloodletting in Haiti. This sense of impending doom seeped into the consciousness of the defeated across the region. Encountering two black men with shotguns in the countryside—not an uncommon sight before the war—caused a frisson of unease among planters and army commanders alike. So too did the habit of freedmen picking up branches and imitating military drills and the manual of arms they had seen the black soldiers do. Pinckney and other planters now routinely strapped on their revolvers in the morning and would do so for more than a year, "believing it best to let the negroes see that we were always prepared to take care of ourselves." They anticipated that unless some discreet officer backed by armed troops did not "explain to these deluded negroes the true state of affairs, . . . there was bound to be collision and bloodshed."[46]

In light of their many shared concerns about the disorganized state of their labor force and the danger of eruptions of violence, Pinckney and the other South Santee planters held a meeting to discuss how they might proceed. They agreed that despite their inherent revulsion, they must appeal to Charleston's new military commander, Major General Charles Devens Jr., formerly a Massachusetts lawyer and staunch abolitionist. After successfully managing to keep the city of Richmond from imploding into complete mayhem after the Confederate government evacuated in April 1865, he had been sent to Charleston the following July to restore order after a race riot rocked that city. Knowing they must strike as diplomatic and as conciliatory a tone as possible, the planters deputed the self-possessed and unfailingly polite Captain Pinckney to state their case. The general, however, would prove a surprise.

Despite his own personal beliefs, Devens declared enforcement of the law, rather than transformation of the moral order, his priority. Destined to become US attorney general in 1876, he belonged to the old conservative class of Massachusetts patricians who believed that, after reunion and emancipation, the Union should be generous in victory. Coming from old colonial stock himself, he saw Massachusetts and South Carolina as "ancient friends" bound together by comradeship forged during the American Revolution. He received Pinckney as a fellow aristocrat currently in embarrassed circumstances; that his father and Devens shared Harvard as their alma mater perhaps made the general more receptive to Pinckney's concerns. After listening carefully to his description of the freedmen's appropriation of the planters' houses and other property as well as their unwillingness to labor for cash or shares, the general agreed to send a company of infantrymen to the South Santee, accepting Pinckney's offer that they be quartered at Fairfield.[47]

The soldiers fanned out to the plantations across the district, delivering, in Pinckney's words, "the law and the gospel." To break the stalemate, Major General Dan Sickles, the one-legged commander of the Department of South Carolina, announced that as of January 1, 1866, all freed people must sign a work contract on the plantation where they lived or vacate the premises within ten days. Now emancipated from slavery, they must be self-sufficient. The federal government would not be transferring land to them, nor would the able-bodied unemployed receive rations from the Freedman's Bureau. Officers recommended that those who wanted to remain on the plantations sign year-long contracts with the owners and be faithful to their obligations; all others would have to find some other place to live and an alternative way to feed their families. Before the soldiers arrived to clear them out the next day, the "malcontents" at Eldorado fled. Pinckney personally banged on the door of mischief-maker Renty's cabin and was disappointed to find that the former sailor "had got the start of me," having disappeared during the night.[48]

In mid-December 1865 Pinckney explained the situation at Eldorado to his brother Cotesworth: "I have set [the freedmen] to work which they took to with considerable hesitation at first and are now going on pretty regularly though not accomplishing a great deal. In their bearing toward me I see no change. The difficulty will be only in getting much work accomplished."[49]

IN A TWIST ON THE TRADITIONAL image of returning Confederate soldiers walking up the plantation avenue to their old homes, almost every day after Pinckney's return, former slaves from the family's abandoned holdings, such as Fannymeade Plantation on Minim Island in the North Santee, lumbered up the oak-lined road leading to Eldorado, heavy laden with all their worldly goods. By December as many as two hundred had come "home" to the plantation and expected to be fed and housed as before. "If Fannymeade is not sold," Pinckney wrote, "we must operate it in self-defense by way of getting rid of the surplus population at Eldorado." Believing that his own workers had probably raised sufficient provisions to hold their own families until the spring, Pinckney worried that their "returning friends might eat them out."[50]

Pinckney also faced the immediate dilemma of how he would feed himself over the many long months needed to restore the plantation and eventually bring in a harvest. His initial plan had been to set up Eldorado as a "Bachelor's Hall," with some of his single wartime comrades from the old Santee Mounted Rifles boarding with him there. When that plan did not work out, he teamed up with Shoolbred and his two younger brothers. Avid hunters, the men decided that they would make their living with their guns. Jack, the youngest of the Shoolbreds, had swaggered home with a reputation as a "hotshot hero" with the Iron Scouts of Hampton's Legion.[51] Pinckney found a Charleston agent willing to buy their fresh game and fish. Three days a week they would roam the woods, hunting the plentiful whitetail deer and wild turkeys. Other days they would cast nets for shrimp and catch fish. Once they got the operation going, Pinckney's nephew Charley joined them. He had married his long-time love, Lucy Memminger, in 1866 and the next year came with their baby daughter, Virginia, to live at Eldorado with the "Cap'in." Whenever they had a full wagonload of meat or produce, one of the younger men—often Charley—at the end of a long workday would drive the forty miles of bad road into Charleston and arrive just as the morning market was opening. After selling their wares, he would buy as many necessities, such as wheat flour, sugar, and kerosene, as he could afford and make the long trip home. The schedule was grueling, but as Lucy observed, Charley was able to shake off his weariness easily "in Pinckney fashion."[52]

Thomas Pinckney later looked back on those days when the simple joys of peace, home, and friendship were all he could possibly want after four years of war. Although beset by worry about the future and exhausted by his daily labors, he was finally leading the life on the land he had always wanted, albeit in a minor key. Pinckney wrote in his memoir of that time, "I never made my living more agreeably in all my life." Although rice planting was, of course, more difficult with free labor, he was emancipated from the guilt of slavery and also for a while from the constant thrum of bitter sectional politics that so blighted his youthful home. His own sentiments echoed those of his brother, Cotesworth Jr., who had admitted to his congregation immediately after the war that "the sense of responsibility attached to this authority [over another human being] often pressed with overwhelming force" upon his own conscience as a Christian. In other unexpected ways Tom too had been liberated by the war, for its devastation swept away the expectation that he would somehow recapture the grandeur of his family's past.[53]

He was also liberated from his misconception that rice planting was a genteel pursuit. The only proper occupation for a gentleman, Pinckney had grown up believing, was agriculture pursued on one's own lands. The family's historical aversion to careers in business dated back to the colonial era. Charles Pinckney, a rice planter and a signer of the Constitution, insisted that in matters of government policy, finance and banking must always be "the handmaid of her *mistress,* agriculture." But as Tom soon learned, rice planting in postwar South Carolina was no longer an idyll. The independent life of the planter he had imagined proved a chimera under the new regime. In contrast to his father, who was always confident that an overseer would bring in a crop while he enjoyed European travels and long summer stays in cooler climes, Pinckney became a prisoner of the plantation. Worse, he could see that the merchants and bankers—men in control of money—would be rising to the top of Dixie's social hierarchy as they had in the North.[54]

Pinckney felt the change of status acutely when, in desperate need of credit, he had to approach two Connecticut-born tradesmen he would scarcely have acknowledged in another time. His family's very discreet longtime factor, William Bee and Company, was then tottering on the edge of bankruptcy. Everett Wheeler Edgerton, a merchant tailor, and his partner, Frederick Richards, a draper, had raked in profits in 1861 when all the local grandees engaged them to fashion their elaborate and imaginative Confederate uniforms. The free black tailors in their employ stitched night and day in their Broad Street shop. The partners navigated the shoals of war deftly, investing their first windfall in blockade-runners and then retailing the increasingly precious imported consumer goods, such as French bootees and Rio coffee, in their shop. After the war, they put their money out at interest and took a certain pleasure at having former grandees, worn hats in hand, applying to them for a loan to restart their planting operation made even more risky by the new system of labor. Edgerton and Richards agreed to underwrite the restoration of Pinckney's low-lying rice fields only if he agreed to start planting cotton on his underutilized high lands; they even pressed seeds upon him for an experimental crop. Pinckney politely agreed but deeply resented their intrusion.[55]

For all those willing to work, Pinckney offered a three-month ration of corn for free, one-third of the rice crop divided into individual shares after the harvest, and several acres of land for their personal use. Tradition in the family held that the slaves had generally stolen about a quarter of their crop anyway.[56] Pinckney's 1866 contract does not survive, but his 1868 version does. Workers agreed "to conduct themselves civilly & honestly," to faithfully obey orders, and to either perform specific tasks or to work ten hours a day. In addition to taking care of all tools and implements, laborers were expected "to be kind and gentle to work animals entrusted to their care." Any damage or injury to property would be their responsibility. All absences and advances would be noted in an account book and would be received as evidence in courts of law just as merchants' ledgers. Unexcused absence from work would result in a fifty-cent deduction from their share. After three absences or persistent disobedience, a worker could be dismissed and his share of the crop forfeited to pay for labor hired to complete his work.[57]

For his part, Pinckney agreed to furnish all tools and implements that could not be made on the plantation and to supply the necessary working animals, which he would feed at his expense. At the end of a season of "faithful performance," he agreed to give the workers half of the highland crops, typically corn and cotton. One third of the rice would be divvied up according to the level of work performed. In addition, he allowed each full-time laborer a half acre of rice land and a quarter-acre patch of high land to plant as they would. They could raise hogs and poultry provided that they kept them in enclosures and did not let them run freely about the place.[58]

During 1866, Pinckney had managed to get four of his family plantations— Eldorado, Fairfield, Fannymeade, and Eschaw Grove—up and running to some extent. As anticipated, the price of scarce commodities skyrocketed. Rice brought three dollars a bushel, nearly four times its prewar high. Pinckney imagined his greening fields as a resurrection of the lowcountry and a benediction on its future. He took immense pleasure in watching his crop mature; golden-headed stalks bending heavy laden, with rice birds swarming in anticipation. He began to dream of paying off his substantial debts. The River, however, asserted its will and withheld its grace. Great freshets of yellow water flushed out some of the rice fields so completely that when the waters subsided, not a single stalk remained. Pinckney managed to harvest little more than enough seed for the next planting, but through very strict personal economy he repaid the advance from his creditors. "Providence seems to have been against us," Pinckney concluded. Those planting Sea Island cotton fared no better as a plague of caterpillars descended upon their fields and consumed their future.[59]

Had the cotton and rice crops lived up to their promise in 1866, had the planters and workers not had to fight one another for every penny in order to survive, the postwar experiment in free labor might have proved viable, if not exactly successful. As it was, however, at the end of the harvest, acrimony accompanied the distribution of the workers' paltry shares. Even the staple corn crop proved basically a loss.

During the winter of 1866, starvation stalked the Santee delta. Some black families barely survived on green corn, pond-lily beans, and alligator meat. Stealing became epidemic—nothing was safe from looters. Iron from gins, lead pipes from cisterns, tack from barns, and cotton from the fields all found ready buyers among the "small traders" who lurked on the rivers. These men asked no questions and paid cash money that was turned into liquor, tobacco, gunpowder, and No. 7 birdshot more often than food.[60]

In the Santee District landless poor whites in 1866 also harbored many layers of resentment: toward the planters, who monopolized the best land and seduced them into war; toward the freedmen, whom they believed enjoyed special privileges and benefits from the government. As their anger deepened, violence against blacks spiked. In one incident two local men, "ignorant brutal" deserters from the Confederate army, went on a senseless and random spree against the freed people, driven by the idea that "a nigger must be licked." When federal soldiers finally apprehended them, the provost marshal at Mount Pleasant, Major Edward F. O'Brien, violated prevailing racial shibboleths by threatening that if they beat another black person, they could expect the same treatment from his soldiers, plus "a little manual labor on the public roads." If "some terrible example" was not made of "these devils incarnate," Major O'Brien insisted, "there would be no hope of peace for the freedmen."[61]

The only abundant commodity along the Santee River was blame. Pinckney attributed the failure of the Santee crops on "disorganized, unsatisfactory labor." For their part the freedmen, who had worked for six months with nothing to show, blamed Pinckney for somehow cheating them. Competing with the constant dread that planters were secretly plotting to put them back into slavery was the other feeling that their new condition was actually worse than slavery, a system in which they at least ate regularly. The contracts offered fewer opportunities for earning bonuses, and the more regimented work was "less to their taste." Sharing the risk was also a new and unwelcomed experience. Understanding how the value of their work ebbed and flowed with international markets was a remote concept. After militating to more closely reap what they sowed with an equal split of the harvest, they realized that half of nothing was still nothing.[62]

Pinckney began to suspect that the racial tensions beleaguering the lowcountry were not the natural consequence of the war or even necessarily inherent in the transition from slave labor to free, but they were being manipulated, perhaps even manufactured, by Republicans to promote their political agenda in the state and maintain the national hegemony.

The shape-shifting nature of federal policy toward the South confirmed his fears. In 1867, when the Republican Party secured a majority in both houses of Congress and enjoyed a sympathetic constituency on the Supreme Court, the Radicals attempted to wrest control of Reconstruction away from President Johnson and threatened impeachment. The Radical plan for Congressional

Reconstruction was revealed in March 1867. Ten states of the old Confederacy were put on notice that they would no longer be embraced as prodigals but punished as "conquered provinces," reorganized into five military districts with their legislatures disbanded. Since none of these states had yet passed the proposed Fourteenth Amendment, expanding the rights of citizenship for blacks, the Radicals invalidated their newly drafted state constitutions and decided to preemptively deny those liberties to many whites as well. Pinckney raged at what he saw as pure party politics that held the southern states to a higher standard on the matter of race than the Republican states of the North.

Under the Radical plan, restoration (once again) to full privileges within the Union required that each of the former Confederate states jettison its postwar constitution and draft another one. To assure that the composition of South Carolina's convention of 1868 would be different from that called in 1865 and dominated by conservative Democrats, who tried to impose "Black Laws" of the type adopted in the western states before the war, the 1867 act granted suffrage rights to black men (only in the states of the defeated South) and withdrew the right to vote from high-ranking Confederates, including Wade Hampton, despite their earlier pardons. A new round of loyalty oaths with higher thresholds essentially guaranteed that no one who fought for the Confederacy could hold elected office.

This dramatic shift in power—from the old white elite to black men (many ex-slaves, some illiterate), the so-called carpetbaggers from the North, and turncoat scalawags from the South—provoked outrage across the state. When Major M. C. Crawford, adjutant of the Freedmen's Bureau in Charleston, learned of the provisions of the Reconstruction Act, he accurately predicted that South Carolina's Confederate veterans would consider it a violation of their terms of surrender and the entire state would explode into "the most strenuous protest."[63] Humiliation of proud men still in possession of their pistols and their pride was a prescription for violence.

Caroline Seabrook argued that the family should leave the country before they were entirely crushed under the boot of the Republican government. Their neighbors on the Santee, Alexander Mazyck (a former state senator and a signer of the articles of secession) and Colonel Gabriel Manigault, refused to be reconstructed and went into self-imposed exile in Ontario, Canada, for "principle's sake." Mexico and Brazil attracted some others as "Confederados." Caroline speculated that New Zealand, with its fine weather and established Anglican church, would be an excellent place to start a "Carolina colony."[64]

Every congressional pronouncement from Washington seemed more egregious than the last. Caroline despaired that every time she thought the state had reached "the lowest depth," she learned of a "lower depth, still, threatening to devour us, opens wide." One day it seems that "we are no longer *States* but military departments," she complained. The next day she learns that the Radical Republicans dictate that her family be "put below negroes in privileges." The final turn of the screw, she feared, would be "confiscation of our small amounts of property."[65]

Actually, more than a little land was at stake in 1867, when the family prepared their appeal to the Congress for the restoration of Pinckney Island, which had come to them through the death of their unmarried cousin Harriott in 1866. The property had been seized during the federal occupation for unpaid taxes and was valued at about $17,000. When young lawyer Julian Mitchell, a Confederate veteran and son-in-law of Cotesworth Jr., returned from a fact-finding tour in Washington, he informed the family that success depended on their willingness to swear that they had done nothing to support the late rebellion. Mary Elliott violently protested having "to stand cap in hand to a dirty Yankee Congress" but was consoled that since Tom had given up his rights to the island, "our rebel captain is conveniently out of the way." Her brother and sister also detested the humiliation, but all agreed to perjure themselves in a good cause. An inquisitive federal investigator soon exhumed the truth that "the proclivities of the whole family strongly favored the rebel cause." That the family had not dislodged the freedman on Pinckney Island was a countervailing point in their favor. Since the policy of restoring property in the "insurgent States" was still in flux, their request was tabled for future consideration.[66]

IN 1867 THOMAS PINCKNEY FORESAW a dangerous situation by which the Republican Party would recruit neophyte voters "through the instrumentality of distributing government rations." Public monies could be used to organize and equip black militias at the same time Republicans worked out strategies "to disarm (as well as disenfranchise) the white men." By enacting new laws designed to pit blacks and whites against one another, he suspected, the ultimate goal of Republicans was to foment racial violence so they might intervene and continue to dominate national politics. By breaking up the plantation system through high property taxes and the disruption of field labor, they could destroy the Democratic Party's conservative southern powerbase.[67]

Pinckney looked on with stern disapproval as the newly enfranchised black men of the Santee became totally absorbed with politics. From what he could deduce, they lacked the abstract understanding of the nation as well as the practical workings of government to be conscientious citizens. Voting, in their minds, was the means to an end. On election day in one lowcountry precinct, Pinckney recalled, the new voters went to the polls with halters.[68]

Black functionaries from the Republican Party lurked around Eldorado. When they stopped by the fields to spread the word of an upcoming political event, the hands would throw down their hoes right where they stood and be off in a flash, leaving the women to finish their rows. Shoolbred, still Pinckney's operations manager, complained that the black workers thus had become "uncontrollable at best" and "constantly disorganized."[69]

The Union League, a patriotic association started in the North, recruited the freedmen to affiliate with the local Republican Party. Black soldiers, largely excluded from organizations such as the Masons, had joined the Union Leagues in great numbers and invited the freedmen to do the same during the occupation. Ironically, the appeal of the leagues to blacks mirrored the attraction of the early Ku Klux Klan among white Democrats. Former slaves relished the clandestine meetings, away from white oversight, in private homes, forests, fields, and churches and enjoyed the fraternal rituals. After the 1867 enfranchisement of black men, the leagues took on a more political character as part of the Republican machinery, and served as a substitute for the authority of their former masters. Every member had to take an oath to vote Republican. Armed guards protected every meeting, where partisan newspapers were read aloud for the benefit of the illiterate. The active involvement of the freedmen in politics encouraged state Republicans to craft platforms that appealed to their specific interests, dramatically accelerating the development of a corporate identity among the disparate classes of African Americans that would, according to one historian, have consequences nearly as great as the Emancipation Proclamation.[70]

Pinckney raged at the Union Leagues because they interfered with the restoration of plantation agriculture upon which all races in the lowcountry depended. League members threatened freedmen if they signed labor contracts with their old masters yet offered no real solutions to the problem of how the fields may be planted and the people fed. His head plowman had come to him complaining that he had nothing for his "gang of children" to eat and wanted to sign with him and go back to work, but he feared that the Union League would "make war on me." "Well," Pinckney answered, "it is your own fault; whenever you go to work you can get some rations. Your mule is in the pasture, and your plow in the barn, when you go to work is a matter between you and your own stomach." In the end Pinckney believed that his hands "were driven to work by starvation alone."[71]

In 1868, with the freedmen at the polls and the old Confederates staying home, Robert K. Scott, an Ohio native who headed the state Freedman's Bureau, was elected South Carolina's first Republican governor. Blacks won half the legislative seats, and a new constitution was adopted that gave Scott the powers of a "dictator." Believing the gauntlet had been thrown down by the Radicals, the New York–based *Nation* warned that a "civil war" was brewing in South Carolina and predicted unrest "on the Lower Santee—where the rice negroes are most numerous and most ignorant."[72]

Although in 1869 Caroline Seabrook observed that her brother's "provocations by the freedmen have been great," tensions over the contracts and living conditions never reached the level that his workers went on strike or threatened him physically as was the case on other plantations, where black troops had to be called in to put down armed violence. From childhood, Pinckney had developed a personal style of interaction with workers and "a genuine liking for the negro," as one of his friends observed, and "knew how and when to say 'No,'" which helped him win their respect. Never considering the freedmen his equal in the social realm, he never forgot their essential humanity; his thinking retained elements of his father's Christian paternalism that, ultimately, they were "all one in Christ."[73]

Outnumbered at the polls, the old planter class disengaged. Author William Gilmore Simms, an old friend of Tom's uncle William Elliott III, urged the former ruling class, which had resisted expanding black political rights, to "hold ourselves aloof" from the Republican invaders. Pinckney, for his part, emulated the dignified silence of General Lee by ignoring local politics, "choosing to let the different factions of the Republicans who were in complete and absolute control, fight it out among themselves." From 1867 to 1876, black Republicans would hold more political power in South Carolina than in any other southern state.[74]

"View on Meeting Street, Charleston, S.C., looking south to St. Michael's Church, showing the Mills House, ruins of Central [Circular] Church and Theatre in Ruins in the foreground." George N. Barnard's 1865 photograph was taken from the approximate location where John Pierre and Barbara Barquet's family home once stood. *Library of Congress Prints and Photographs Division.*

"Ruins of the Pinckney Mansion, Charleston, South Carolina, 1865."
George N. Barnard, photographer. *Courtesy of the Miriam and Ira D. Wallach
Division of Art, Prints and Photographs: Photography Collections.
The New York Public Library Digital Collections.*

"Taking the Oath," from a sketch by our Special Artist. *Frank Leslie's Illustrated Magazine,* April 15, 1865 shows Charlestonians renouncing the Confederacy to regain their citizenship and avoid confiscation of their property.
Courtesy of The Charleston Museum, Charleston, S.C.

Fairfield Plantation on the South Santee River during the 1920s.
Courtesy of The Charleston Museum, Charleston, S.C.

The John Stewart Family of Brook Hill, Henrico County, Virginia, ca. 1868.
Back row, from left to right: Lucy Williamson Stewart, Marion McIntosh Stewart
(later Peterkin), Isobel Lamont "Belle" Stewart (later Bryan), an unknown male,
Mary Amanda Stewart (later Pinckney). *Seated:* Mary Williamson Stewart and
her husband, John Stewart. On the ground below: Elizabeth Hope Stewart,
Norma Stewart, Annie Carter Stewart. *Private Collection.*

Mrs. Thomas Pinckney (Mary Amanda Stewart, 1844–1889).
Private Collection.

Captain Thomas Pinckney and his thirteen-year-old son, Charles
Cotesworth, at Blowing Rock, North Carolina, in 1889. They are accompanied
by members of the Reverend C. C. Pinckney's family. *From left to right:*
Caroline P. Means, Marguerite Pinckney, Caroline P. Mitchell and
her son Julian A. Mitchell Jr., Anne Elizabeth Pinckney.
Courtesy of the South Carolina Historical Society.

Eldorado Plantation, ca. 1890. A showplace when built by General Thomas Pinckney and his mother-in-law Rebecca Motte in 1797, the plantation house was a ruin, symbolic of the catastrophic postwar decline of the lowcountry rice culture, when it burned to the ground a century later.
Courtesy of The Charleston Museum, Charleston, S.C.

IO

CITIZEN BARQUET

BACK AT HOME IN HIS MODEST little house on Maple Street, Joseph Barquet was reunited at last with his long-suffering wife, Maria, and their children, who scarcely knew him: Horace Ward was seven; Barbary (later called Matilda), five; John Pierre, four; James, three. In early 1866 Joseph Humphries would be born; in 1867, Liston Benforth; and in 1869, Mary. Barquet had fought this war for these children's futures, but now back in Illinois he faced the grim immediacy of how to feed them all. He had a pocket full of money from his discharge but no prospects. At forty-three years old, all he could find when he first went looking for work was the hard grind of common labor.[1]

With the cheers of Charleston and Boston still echoing in his memory, Barquet received muted praise in Galesburg. He was disappointed. His family and the black community had lost ground during the war. As the black population continued to swell with the emancipation diaspora out of the South, the racial climate had shifted, like a northeast wind that suddenly transforms summer into autumn.

While the boot of the federal government was standing on the neck of South Carolina, insisting that black men and women must be allowed to control their own destinies, the people of Illinois still clung unchallenged to the proposition that theirs would be a "white man's government." The Illinois legislature had only just repealed the last of the Black Laws in 1864 after Radical Republicans clawed their way into state office. In 1866 enthusiasm for the pending Fourteenth Amendment, which stipulated race should not be a barrier to either citizenship or equal protection under the law, garnered only tepid support in the state. Resistance, however, met the proposed amendment to the US Constitution giving the vote to black men, even those who had been enslaved. Those Barquet had helped liberate in South Carolina would, as it turned out, get the franchise before he did.[2]

Barquet deeply resented that in many cases the offspring of southern freedmen, tutored by armies of northern teachers, had better opportunities to learn than his own children and determinedly renewed his campaign for expanded and equal access to public education. Even though another elementary school had been built during the war, conditions in the town's crowded segregated schools got worse every year. An "experiment" of hiring black teachers was undertaken but soon abandoned.[3]

Barquet saw the education issue as a wedge to regain his former influence among the greatly expanded black population. Black parents paid taxes as well as whites, he argued, and began organizing them to demand greater representation. He believed that breaking the racial boundaries through his military service qualified him for a leadership role in the new order he predicted was emerging in postwar America. Playing his role as liberator and conqueror to the hilt, he strutted about town, often in his uniform, enjoying the admiring glances from the black townspeople. The white leadership of Galesburg, both Republican and Democrat, began to find him an irritant.

Enlisting in the army at age forty had been Barquet's way of pursuing politics by other means, allowing him also to tap into the national network of black abolitionists. While stationed on Morris Island in September 1864, his name had appeared on the roll of "representative colored men" calling "the faithful and the true" to the National Convention of Colored Citizens scheduled for October 4 in Syracuse, New York. Frederick Douglass and other national black leaders had imagined that when millions were freed after the Union triumph, they would be consulted on how best to prepare them for freedom and eventually for citizenship. Critical to the future success of their race, convention organizers agreed, would be "strong black men" who could provide examples of a "well-ordered and dignified life" and preach the gospel of education, thrift, temperance, and sound morality among their people. Unable to attend in person, Barquet wrote to the convention "plainly and painfully" about his experiences among the southern "contrabands." The absolute first step after emancipation, he insisted, must be to "force" education upon them. He endorsed agriculture as a good pursuit for the newly freed because hard work would be repaid with good crops. Landownership, either individually or collectively, would provide "a body for the residence of the[ir] soul." Equally important, Barquet insisted, was the future of the "laboring colored men of the North." They must not be overlooked. Both state and federal governments must create good-paying jobs to nourish their "spirit of independence." With the end of slavery, black Americans should demand a better life. As their leaders, members of the convention must "follow our white brethren, holding him by the heel," continuing the revolution and "securing to ourselves and posterity a part of a common heritage."[4]

In October 1866, the Illinois State Convention of Colored Men reconvened in Galesburg after its wartime hiatus. The tone and the goals of the meeting reflected inflated expectations for the future as it took for its theme: "Equality of rights for all loyal men in America before the bar of American law." Embedded in this statement was the demand that blacks should have the vote and the rebels should lose it.[5] The overall tone of the meeting evinced a new self-understanding among the delegates. All the old prewar deference was gone, with pointed criticism of the national and state governments for their "unkind" treatments through enslavement and the punitive Black Laws. The committee on education released an explosive statement that bore the imprint of Barquet, one of its drafters, cursing the whites who "oppressed us, trampled us under foot, shot us down like dogs, treated us as beasts of burden," and "watered the soil of our fair country with the blood of our fathers, mothers, brothers, [and] sisters" despite all their own efforts to show "that we are men and American citizens."

The black veterans were particularly influential at the convention and attacked the prevailing postwar narrative that freedom had been the gift of white America. Instead, they aggressively posited an alternative theory that black soldiers had actually won the war. All would have been lost had not 200,000 "patriotic heroes," men of color, answered the call of "*their* republic." After being "robbed and peeled," they "arose from the dust, and on fields of blood and carnage . . . sustained amid the collision of arms, their long-derided assertion of their God-given manhood." When Lincoln implored them, "*Your* country's in danger, and calls for you now . . . , nobly did they respond . . . that the Republic might not perish." As references to the "great heroes" of Olustee, Battery Wagner, Milliken's Bend, and Port Hudson resonated throughout the church, Barquet probably sat a little a taller in his pew. But the harsh truth was that while black soldiers, often poorly trained and poorly led, did suffer and bravely die in those encounters with the enemy, each battle had been a Union defeat.[6]

Convention members revealed their latent fears that even winning the ballot could be futile without economic opportunity and the chance to enter the labor market on an equal footing. Otherwise, black workers would simply devolve into the perpetual "mudsill" of the economy, pariahs of society, the slaves of communities rather than individuals.[7]

On April 2, 1870, the "Hon. Joseph H. Barquet" served as master of ceremonies and delivered "eloquent" remarks at an "impromptu jubilee" celebration at which thirty-two rounds were fired in honor of the passage of the Fifteenth Amendment, barring states from denying the right to vote to any man based on race, color, or previous condition of servitude. Later in the month Barquet played a highly visible role in the "Colored Ratification Meeting" and celebration, during which the College City Cornet Band led a parade through Galesburg. One "chariot" carried twenty-nine young women waving the flags of the states in the Union. Wagons full of Sunday-school children rumbled behind them. Barquet, if not at the head of the parade, was likely among the "military marchers." In the evening blacks and whites of the town gathered in Caledonia Hall to hear "Captain" Barquet and others speak from a platform crowded with Republican politicians and graced with portraits of Grant, Senator Charles Sumner, and William Lloyd Garrison and a statue of Lincoln. At every opportunity Barquet made the point that black men had won the right to citizenship and the franchise through their military service and that he had "sharpened my trusty sword" and was ready to engage in political battle.[8]

Weary of this argument, an editorial in the *Galesburg Republican* in April 1870 countered Barquet's claims for the decisive role of the black soldier: "We do not by any means belong to that class either who believes the African the superior of the foreign-born citizen and neither do we believe in the slightest degree that the negro alone saved the republic during the late war. Had we depended upon negro prowess or intelligence we greatly fear that Mr. Davis and gentlemen of that ilk would now be making and executing laws in Washington."[9]

Acknowledging that "the colored man is a legal voter and clothed with equal political rights," the editorial suggested that African Americans could best secure their rights by staying out of politics, where they could be victims of unscrupulous opportunists, and focusing on their economic advancement. The best way to convince a doubting white public that black men were indeed ready and fit for citizenship was to "be sober upright, and industrious . . . , to go to work and stay at work," and remember that the right "to saunter on the street corners and loiter in low saloons" was not among the new constitutional guarantees. To win public confidence "the leading black men should drive the stragglers either to work or out of Knox County—toil is the inevitable fate of mankind and its decree should not be forgotten by those who are basking in the sunshine of their newly acquired freedom." The editorial closed by stating:

"We are not one of those Republicans that think a dark skin should shield vice, indolence, and general unfitness for the duties of life. . . . Let it be understood [that] black skin is no excuse for vagrancy and idleness."[10]

In May 1870 Barquet became a pawn in a political skirmish in Republican-dominated Knox County, Illinois. A Democrat on the county board of supervisors, knowing that the veteran had emerged as a gadfly constantly pressuring the white Republican leadership to endorse black candidates, had mischievously placed his name on a list of potential jurors. The Republicans fell into the Democrat's trap when they scratched off Barquet's name. An editorial in the *Galesburg Republican* railed at "the old guard of abolition" for failing to see that most stridently Democratic counties were regularly seating black jurors and winning over the new voters' support. Eventually the issue was put to rest when the Knox County Board of Supervisors swore in a black man as a petit juror, though he was not Barquet.[11]

His children's access to education continued to prove the most vexing and personal issue for Barquet. The white citizens of Galesburg, feeling that all that might be done for the black population had been done, stood firmly against integration. A petition from the town's black parents to the school board was tabled in September 1870. "Even in Galesburg," the *Republican* noted, "there is a strong opposition to blending the races." The newspaper's editor, Clark E. Carr, who had his own political aspirations, thought closing the door to education for children of color "absurd" but hedged on integration, musing that they would be "happier and probably accomplish more in their studies" by going to classes "with their own people."[12]

When Carr proposed that a public referendum be held to resolve the question of whether all races should have equal access to education, Barquet was furious and fired off a reply: "You have done us wrong!" He compared this idea to taking a vote on the Constitution. "As a part of the American people," he wrote, "we claim nothing more than what belongs to us. We have petitioned to the board of education for our children to be admitted to the public schools with other children. Our petition has been thrown under the table. . . . We do not wish to make any difficulty that cannot be met. We are citizens of this great republic; we poll as many votes as the German population and we ask for rights and nothing more than belongs to citizens."[13]

In January 1871 Barquet set about organizing the town's 319 registered black voters into a voting bloc. In March he helped set up an "equal rights league" in the Baptist church and worked out a slate of candidates, from mayor to street commissioner, that they would support. The group also raised two hundred dollars to hire a lawyer to challenge the legality of the segregated public schools of Galesburg in October and represent the city's black children at the school-board meeting the next month. That meeting dragged on until midnight, with long lawyerly speeches of "infinite pathos" warning board members that they may be personally liable for discrimination against the children of black taxpayers. Barquet gave an "eloquent" speech with frequent references to "the American eagle and the spirit of Liberty."[14]

Frustrated by long legal delays, twenty-five black children and adults, no doubt including Barquet, marched into the high school in January 1872 and demanded admission to it and the other public schools of the city. Later that year the school board accepted equality of education in principle and agreed to allow those children of "tender years" living in remote areas to attend the nearest school. But segregation persisted in Galesburg until 1874, when a state law guaranteeing equal access was passed. Just before Barquet's children became eligible to attend the high school near their home, the building somehow burned down and was never rebuilt.[15]

Barquet began to feel in subtle ways the local displeasure over his political activities. At the same time he was embroiled in the controversy over school integration in the summer of 1871, a rumor began circulating that he was planning a run for sheriff. Barquet's masonry and plastering business, which he had worked hard to reestablish, began to decline. The *Republican Register* ran a sarcastic little piece indicating that Barquet felt he was "not appreciated" and was disappointed with his reception in Galesburg since his return from the war.[16]

Barquet's most public role had been as the organizer of a "Colored Zouave Company," which sported the exotic outfits of the corps d'Afrique when it regularly performed in parades and at holiday events. The *Galesburg Republican* quipped that spring was surely on its way when "Captain Joseph H. Barquet donned his regimentals and paraded down the street in military style." The crowd-pleasing Zouaves, about forty muskets strong, won local renown for their snappy marching, skilled rifle handling, and fondness for elaborate "evolutions." But as the black citizens of Galesburg began threatening to use their new political muscle, the white citizens also became less comfortable with their demonstrations of military prowess. The planning committee for the 1871 Memorial Day celebration received suggestions that neither Barquet nor his men should march that year. Local Democrats insinuated that the Colored Zouave Company of Galesburg was in truth "an organization of black guards," a Republican political militia such as those reported as doing so much mischief in the South.[17]

In the end, after the committee decided to keep to tradition, most of the white veterans boycotted the Memorial Day parade, unwilling to march alongside the "colored troops."[18] A letter published in the *Galesburg Republican* and signed "White Republican Soldier" explained that the numbers of blacks "pushed into the ranks by their special champions" offended "scores of white soldiers." He argued that the parade honoring the war dead "was a solemn occasion" and the insistence of the "sable and tawny heroes in thrusting themselves forward" was decidedly premature and totally political. Good taste required that they should have formed a separate detachment. "Hundreds of men who followed the old flag in danger and peril did so without having negro comrades, and it is not to be expected that they will march with them now. If our colored fellow-citizens are desirous of being soldiers I am perfectly willing that they shall wheel, march and counter-march to their hearts' content, but it would certainly look a great deal better if they will perform their evolutions solely among themselves." The writer allowed "for the sake of argument, that they 'fought' nobly," but he was "not willing to have a robust and lusty colored warrior for a comrade on a hot and dusty day—no matter what the opinions of others may be."[19]

When the next Memorial Day rolled around in 1872, Galesburg's black veterans did not march. Blaming Barquet for instigating the push for integration of the parade, the planning committee replaced him the next year as organizer of the "colored" detachment. Refusing to follow anyone else but Barquet, the black veterans stayed home while the rest of the town celebrated the triumph of democracy. The month before, rumors had flitted around town insinuating that Barquet had been taking bribes to deliver black votes. A poem in the *Galesburg Republican* in April 1872 accused him of being a self-serving ward heeler who sold out his people at a bargain rate: "Here's five dollars, Captain Barkay, for your influence in the cause / Of sustaining constitutions and upholding righteous laws."[20]

The interconnections between the shunning of black veterans, the assaults upon his personal integrity, and the solid majority enjoyed by the Republican Party in both the state and Congress were not lost on Barquet. The contributions of black soldiers to the Union effort were being similarly pushed out of the national memory of the war. The further irony was that with blacks firmly committed to the Republican Party in Illinois, few were rewarded with political patronage jobs that in other places, even in South Carolina, elevated them for the first time into the middle class. For years party stalwart Frederick Douglass had waited patiently for his reward from the grateful government for his recruitment efforts to bring men of color into the Union ranks. At last in 1871, the Grant administration named him to the Commission of Inquiry evaluating the future relationship between Santo Domingo and the United States. Although Douglass celebrated his selection as a "new day for blacks," the position forced him to violate his long-held belief in the sovereignty of the Caribbean countries by taking the party line and endorsing annexation.[21]

In September 1871 Barquet served as a delegate to the National Convention of Colored Men, held in Saint Louis, that endorsed the nomination of General Grant for president in the upcoming election. By this time Barquet's public life and private life were simultaneously falling apart. The war undoubtedly had taken its toll. With the emphasis on glory and courage, few black soldiers could admit their fears and, like many other fighting men, turned to drink to bolster their courage and quell their nightmares. Just the nighttime assalt upon Battery Wagner—running over dead bodies, faces splashed with bloody gore, seeing the empty eyes of dead friends—could alone have provided a lifetime of torments. During all those months patrolling Morris Island one could never forget, for with the massive erosion, low tides would expose graves, leaving in full view a rebel skull or stumps of arms and legs "with grey rags around them." A beach walk might reveal a boot with a foot still in it and ragged bone protruding. After experiencing the terror and witnessing the horrors of the Battle of Olustee, Private Thomas Jackson of Company C, 54th Massachusetts, had a complete mental breakdown. Immediately after that battle, Barquet too had already begun to have flashbacks of the carnage. Images of the soldier who fell down on the road to be trampled by "the affrighted artillery horses" and of his comrade bleeding from a neck wound and crawling on all fours to flee the approaching enemy came to him unbidden in his moments of quiet. The accumulated mental trauma of all that he had seen, and possibly all that he had done, probably never left him.[22]

Exactly when Barquet's drinking became serious is hard to pinpoint, but the combination of political and business disappointments, his inability to sustain his growing family, and his isolation after returning home pushed him over the brink. Unlike white veterans, Barquet had few army buddies around Galesburg who shared his experiences with the 54th. Although the Grand Army of the Republic was founded in 1866 in Illinois, no branches of this fraternal organization in the state welcomed blacks until about the time of Barquet's death.

When the Galesburg census taker asked about his family in July 1870, Barquet apparently replied that his wife was "keeping house" and caring for their seven children, but according to the Chicago tally taken in that same month, thirty-eight-year-old Maria labored in the Fourth Ward as a live-in servant in the home of a white real-estate investor, William B. Warden, a native of Kentucky, his wife, and their three children. Immigrant Irish or Scandinavian women had typically performed household work in Chicago. After the Civil War, however, in an ironic imitation of antebellum southern households, upper-crust white women in the city had curiously been struck by "wench fever." Having black women in starched white uniforms opening the doors of their homes and serving at their tables became fashionable.[23]

Whether Maria had left her marriage to Joseph or whether their financial situation was just so dire that she needed to seek work in the city is not clear. In the Warden household she was allowed to have her baby—the year-old Mary—with her as well her two older children. Twelve-year-old Matilda (formerly called Barbary) performed duties as a housemaid, while fifteen-year-old Horace Ward was "at home"; the other children presumably stayed with Joseph in Galesburg. That Maria had to work in another man's home was an indignity that neither Barquet's mother nor his sisters had previously experienced in Charleston, delivering a blow to his sense of himself as patriarch, the nineteenth-century male ideal.[24]

In April 1872 Barquet left Galesburg for Chicago to be near Maria and search for work in the wake of the Great Chicago Fire six months before, which destroyed more than 18,000 buildings over four square miles of the city. Rebuilding had begun right away. The *Chicago Journal* announced: "Now is the time for carpenters, masons, and about every class of mechanics to secure steady work at good wages. . . . Let all go there who need or want work." Perhaps as many as 50,000 workers, mostly single men, flowed into the city. The *Galesburg Republican* later reported with satisfaction that Barquet had removed his family to Chicago to take advantage of this singular opportunity and to "let politics alone in his new location."[25]

Described by the *Republican* as an "excellent brickmason," Barquet found immediate success in the "Great Rebuilding," landing a job paying five dollars a day. He was soon squeezed out, though, as he had been in New York twenty years earlier, by the labor unions that were trying to use the emergency as an opportunity to make inroads into the building trades. If the great unanswered question in the South after the war was "*would* the Negro work" without coercion, in the North after the war it was "*could* the Negro work," given the resistance among unions to black membership. Immigrant laborers, especially the Irish, harbored strong animosity against blacks, fearing they would drive down wages, and were unwavering in their support of the northern branch of the Democratic Party.[26]

Barquet had always been sympathetic to the workingmen's cause and in fact had identified himself as a warrior in the ongoing struggle between labor and capital, which he believed was the next reform frontier after securing black civil rights. He applied three times to join the bricklayers' union and on each occasion was turned down because of his race. Within two months Barquet had returned to Galesburg bitterly discouraged. The Colored National Labor Union had been organized in 1869, with Frederick Douglass as its president, but by 1872 white unions dismissed this group as basically an arm of the Republican Party, and in truth, the Colored National Labor Union did little to help men such as Barquet, who had been deeply committed to free-labor ideology for all of this adult life. The *Galesburg Republican,* an antiunion newspaper critical of Barquet for his political ambitions, wrote sympathetically of his experience: "This foul prejudice becomes at once brutal and depraved when the colored man is debarred from earning bread by the sweat of his brow for his wife and children. A mob is fiendish in its instincts, even though it chooses to call itself a trade union."[27]

Rather than ply his trade at home, Barquet spent the summer of 1872 stumping across western and central Illinois declaiming for Grant's reelection. The president faced an unusual situation. Horace Greeley, lifelong abolitionist, outspoken editor of the *New York Tribune,* and nominee of the reformist Liberal Republican Party, had also been nominated by the Democrats. At a June meeting in Chicago's Third Ward, where a "large and earnest" group gathered in a meeting lead by long-time black leader John Jones to ratify Grant's renomination, Barquet complained that in the past twelve years the "Ethiopian race" had made more progress than the Caucasian had in two hundred years, but excuses were still made for denying them their rights.[28]

On August 29, 1872, Barquet and another black Galesburg man, J. D. Davis, spoke to an "immense crowd" that included many "colored citizens" who enjoyed the festival atmosphere. The Republican Party's "Wigwam," a huge auditorium, was filled with the sounds of patriotic music as well as popular songs. Barquet spoke for an hour and a half and was frequently interrupted by "the most deafening applause." The *Daily Illinois,* judging his oration "full of truth and eloquence" and "one of the best yet made in the Wigwam," recommended the team "to our Republican friends throughout the state."[29] Several days later they were back on the campaign trail, speaking once again in behalf of Grant's reelection to a large audience in the Mississippi port city of Quincy, which was evenly divided between blacks and whites. Barquet joked that it was "something new for him to make a speech" but "felt it was the duty of all, no matter how humble their origins, to do what they could for the party of principles— the party who had clothed the colored race with the stature of manhood." He claimed, "Any man who did not support that party deserved no pity if returned to the shackles of slavery" by Democrats, who had voted against the Fifteenth Amendment. Blacks, he said, would never be accused of "forgetfulness." Barquet also shared his personal insight into "the real feeling of Democrats towards the negroes" when he told how the Democrat-controlled unions had blocked him from working in Chicago after the fire because of his color.[30]

At home Barquet organized "the colored men of Galesburg" to support Grant, "the invincible soldier who gave them their freedom and the wise statesmen who preserved their rights." As he readied to head into the southern states to rally support among black voters, the Galesburg press mockingly reported: "Captain Barquet is preparing his outfit for the stumping campaign in the South. He will eloquently uphold the cause of true republicanism and free principle."[31]

By the spring of 1873, after Grant's victory, Barquet was back in Galesburg, still struggling to make ends meet. Already in a precarious financial situation, the widespread depression that settled in that year undermined all his efforts. Advertising himself as a "whitewashist," he left a slate outside Dr. Greenleaf's druggist shop for orders. The *Republican Register,* following its own advice, advised its readers, "Patronize him."[32]

Apparently some unscrupulous person, knowing of Barquet's economic woes and the esteem in which he was held in Galesburg, profited by soliciting contributions on his behalf. When Barquet caught wind of this activity, he asked the press to report that no one has been authorized to act on his family's behalf and that they had received none of the money raised in his name.[33]

Still something of a celebrity among blacks in the state, Barquet was invited to speak in Jacksonville, Illinois, at a Fifteenth Amendment celebration in March 1874. The "star of the evening," however, was Frances Ellen Watkins Harper, the courageous and popular "colored poetess" who wrote "The Massachusetts Fifty-Fourth," which was published in the *Anglo-African* in October 1863. First as an abolitionist, then as an advocate for equal rights for blacks and for women, she was a pioneer in protest poetry and was unafraid to acknowledge the problems of alcoholism and wife beating within the black community, particularly in the South.[34]

Harper was also frank about the unexpected negative consequences of expanded civil rights and the end of segregation, especially among black women teachers whose schools were closed down in black communities that had nurtured young people. Barquet would have been in great sympathy with the message of a story by Harper published in the *Christian Recorder* in 1874: "The tidal wave of progress has reached us here and I feel that the ground has suddenly slidden from under my feet."[35]

Barquet suffered from much the same sensation. His wife, Maria, was dead by the summer of 1874, the year his troubled life went into freefall. His drinking worsened, and he disappeared from Galesburg. Talk at the barbershop and the church meetings had it that Barquet had gone to work on a Mississippi steamboat. When he returned home, he was bowed by unrelieved despair. On one occasion a Galesburg policeman "collared" him for public drunkenness but, after recognizing him, released him on bond. Later that same night Barquet, still drinking, accosted and cursed the law officer and ended up in jail with a five-dollar fine. A local newspaper embarrassed him by reporting the incident. In February 1875, his son, James, pled guilty to larceny and was sentenced to two years in reform school.[36]

In 1876, the nation's centennial year, the last of Barquet's illusions fell away. After the passage of the Civil Rights Act of 1875, the official Republican Party position was that all that might be done for the nation's blacks had been done. Many Republicans had also concluded that all that could be done to reconstruct the South had also been accomplished. Reporting on the Galesburg Fourth of July celebration, the *Republican Register* noted, "Joseph Barquet (colored) made quite a good speech, pleading the right of his race to celebrate, although as the youngest child it had been placed away in the cradle."[37]

During the fall of 1876, Barquet engaged in some electioneering in the central counties of Illinois. At several stops he teamed up again with J. B. Smith. They had devised a "dog and pony show" performed for black audiences, with Barquet advocating for Republican presidential candidate Rutherford B. Hayes and Smith arguing for Democratic candidate Samuel J. Tilden. Before his hometown crowd in Galesburg, Barquet delivered what may have been his last public performance. Resorting to high theatrics, he gave a mock tongue lashing to Smith, accusing him of being a "traitor" to the party of abolition and emancipation. He had the audience in the palm of his hand and got them so riled against Smith that they booed and jeered and would not let him speak.[38]

The presidential election of 1876 proved deeply disillusioning for Barquet as well as for the rest of the nation. The carnival of corruption implicated members of both parties in fraud, manipulation, and intimidation. Tilden seemed to have won the day with the popular vote and came within a hair's breadth of having the electoral votes. The Republicans, though, were quick to challenge the legality of elections in four states. Democrats parried with their own charges, and all four states submitted two sets of electoral votes. Barquet was probably not surprised that one of the four was South Carolina.

The nation began taking sides in the electoral dispute along sectional and party lines. Another civil war was feared. Barquet was spotted in the audience in the Galesburg Opera House as one of the "colored people" observing a pro-Tilden rally in January 1877.[39] When the final resolution was reached, he was likely quite disappointed, thinking that the cause of the black man might be the real "lost cause." Democrats extracted a high price for conceding Hayes's victory. Military Reconstruction would end in South Carolina and Florida, two places where Barquet had fought and lost friends. The federal government would concede "home rule" to these newly elected Democratic state governments and retreat from its past insistence that black Americans be included in the political life of those states, be treated fairly in their labors, and be safe within their homes. The Republican Party had turned the page to confront the long-simmering issues of immigration and labor discontent that threatened the safety of American cities.

In April 1877 Joseph Medill, publisher of the *Chicago Tribune,* proclaimed the era of the freed people was over. Having been emancipated, made a citizen, and enfranchised, "there is nothing that national politics can give them as a class.... With the retirement of the Negro from politics, there will be time and opportunity" to reform the corrupt machine politics of the city. The following July the Great Railroad Strike, or "the Great Upheaval," forced the nation to focus on the longtime oppression of the northern laboring classes as local militias and federal troops were mobilized in the urban centers of America to put down violent protests.[40]

BROKEN IN BODY, MIND, AND SPIRIT—and simply broke—Barquet left Galesburg and politics for good. He moved to Davenport, Iowa, a town with a large black population. His eldest son, Horace Ward, a cook on the railroad, was based there with his wife, Catherine, a Louisiana woman, and their baby, Oscar. Eighteen-year-old James, who was operating his own whitewashing business, and eleven-year-old Mary crowded in with their eldest brother as well.[41]

On March 15, 1880, Barquet died at age fifty-seven of "Chronick Whiskey." Buried in the "free" (or pauper's) section rather than in the area designated for Civil War veterans in Davenport's Oakdale Cemetery, his children could not even scrape up enough money to get him a plot of his own. Sergeant Joseph Humphries Barquet lies in an unmarked "two in one" grave, interred over poor little George Mack, who died at the age of seven months in 1863.[42]

A note about Barquet's death in the *Daily Gazette* mentioned his creditable service with the 54th Massachusetts and encouraged "old soldiers and citizens to lend a helping hand at the funeral, as his family are in reduced circumstances." The obituary noted that Barquet's "fine abilities" had made him "quite a prominent personage among his people." He might have carved out "a good position in society" had he not been "his own worst enemy." As late as 1934 "Joe Barquette" was remembered as one of the "old-timers" of Galesburg, "a plasterer and mason's attendant" and "really a talented chap, his misfortune being an excessive love of the 'bowl that inebriates.'"[43]

Certainly Barquet's early death was attributable to more than just "Chronick Whisky." In 1873, after Barquet's prewar business partner, Andrew Jackson Perteet, was executed for losing his mind and in a blind rage killing his wife in Chicago, doctors cut out his heart and brain for study. Might something also have been learned by probing, metaphorically at least, into Joseph Barquet's heart and brain? Perhaps he just felt the hopelessness of it all.[44]

Black poet Paul Lawrence Dunbar understood the transforming effect of military service because his father, a gentle soul when he left for Morris Island with the 55th Massachusetts, was sent home after five weeks of the terror-filled ground siege in the late summer of 1863 due to a medical complaint. Unable to find any job but day labor, he was transformed into a raging, depressed abuser of his wife and children. His son reflects an understanding of one aspect of the black soldier's experience in his well-known "Robert Gould Shaw," published in 1900, a year of race riots in New Orleans and New York and the high tide of "Jim Crow" segregation legislation in the South. Dunbar, who interestingly makes the colonel rather than his men the centerpiece, ends on a downcast note and reflects on the ultimate futility of the 54th's sacrifice: "This hot terror of a hopeless fight, This bold endurance of the final pain; / Since thou and those who with thee died for right; Have died, the Present teaches, but in vain!" Although a noted poet and writer, Dunbar also became a wife beater.[45]

After running such a strong race, Barquet stumbled at the end, with the fractured heart of a man who probably concluded that his whole life had, indeed, been a "hopeless fight." Always believing the combination of military service and politics as the path to power and justice, he was devastated by the cynical realities of the postwar world. In contrast to the song written by men of the 54th that begins with the refrain, "Oh, give us a flag, all free without a slave," and ends, "And we'll stand by the Union if we only have a chance," Barquet felt in retrospect that he was never given a chance after the war was over.[46]

Joseph Barquet battled against slavery, labored for equal rights, sought education and work opportunities for his children and the children of others, fought for freedom, and then finally pushing on the door of equality, found it locked shut. He had always thought that participating in the democratic process would be the key. His greatest disappointment was that the Republican Party turned its back on the new black voters once they were no longer necessary. As a soldier, the black man had been expendable; as a citizen, merely expedient. Only in death, then, might he aspire to glory.

II

THE PRICE OF PEACE

DURING HIS RETREAT from the public sphere, Thomas Pinckney turned his attention to his personal affairs, which also were in dire need of reconstruction and restoration. Since the war's end, his days had folded one into another in a blur of exhausting activity. His worry-filled nights in the country were very long, very dark, and just as quiet as could be. Lonely and approaching forty, Pinckney soon set out to find a wife to share his life. He wanted children he could teach to hunt, swim, and fish and to whom he could pass on his noble family name and his love for the land along The River.

Traditionally, Pinckney men married beautiful women with substantial fortunes. Before the war local wags speculated about which lowcountry beauty the very eligible, but reticent, Dr. Pinckney might choose. After the war, his old fear of "being snapped up for his money" was no longer a danger. When in January 1867 the Saint Cecelia Ball was restored diminuendo, Pinckney dusted off his old-fashioned evening finery with anticipation. The most beautiful belles of the ball, much too young for a man with gray in his beard, were the daughters of banker Mitchell King. The eligible brides of Charleston close enough to his age not to cause scandal scarcely had a new ball gown, much less a dowry.[1]

With his own fortune, like his youth, lost to the war, all Pinckney had to offer a bride now was a life of rural tedium, isolation among a sea of black workers, an income dependent on the whims of The River, and his good name. As it turned out, that was enough.

Virginia's famous old marriage mart nestled in the Allegheny Mountains, White Sulphur Springs, also reopened in 1867. As soon as Pinckney had time and money for a vacation, probably 1868, he and his unmarried sister, Mary Elliott, visited the spa their parents had so enjoyed. By chance he encountered John Stewart; his wife, Mary Amanda; and their bevy of seven daughters, considerably grown since their last meeting in late May 1864, just before his capture at the Battle of Haw's Shop. The dinner he enjoyed with them at their Brook Hill home had been the last decent food he had until his release seven months later.

In contrast to the old aristocratic Charleston planter families, now so broken upon the wheel of war, Stewart and his brother Daniel had skated through the devastation remarkably well. Rather than putting antebellum profits from their tobacco brokerage into land and slaves, as had the sons of the old families, the Stewarts invested in southern railroads and other internal-improvement companies. After assiduously tracking down their many municipal bonds that had been misplaced or stolen during the chaotic evacuation of Richmond in 1865, the shrewd Stewarts thrived even during Reconstruction.[2]

The fragile beauty of Stewart's eldest daughter, twenty-three-year-old Mary, attracted Pinckney's courtly attentions. General Robert E. Lee, who knew her as a friend and frequent visitor of his daughter Agnes, described Mary as looking "very sweet." When the captain ultimately proposed, she accepted, despite not being "in love" with the kindly, well-born planter. Being a sensible person, she saw marriage as a practical matter that did not depend on "all those feelings and states" that so preoccupied her girlfriends. Still, she wrote her sister years later, "doubts and fears, very grave ones," seized her so severely on the eve of her marriage that she wanted to call it off but felt she could not.[3]

On April 20, 1870, Mary kept her promise and married Captain Pinckney in a "grand wedding" reminiscent of the glamour of an earlier time in Richmond. The many guests shoehorned into the tiny Gothic-style Emmanuel Church on Brook Road for the wedding service later enjoyed a "sumptuous reception" at Brook Hill. Stewart spared no expense as he welcomed the affiliation of his family with the noble, though genteelly impoverished, Pinckneys. The infectious high spirits among the Richmond guests, dressed in the latest fashions and buoyed by the recent end of military reconstruction and the subsequent wave of economic optimism, contrasted with the wistful Charlestonians, modestly dressed and seeing no end in sight to either the derelict Republican rule of their state or their swooning agricultural economy.[4]

Mary never revealed the sources of her reluctance, but she surely dreaded leaving her seemingly idyllic home at Brook Hill, a center of Richmond social and cultural life. The handsome colonial-era house, long in her mother's family, had been transformed by her energetic father into an architectural marvel profuse with "bays, verandas, and eclectic ornamentation." The Stewart daughters enjoyed a pleasant existence with their beautiful aristocratic mother, Mary Amanda Williamson Stewart, and rich, adoring father that resembled an expanded southern version of *Little Women*, only each sister had her own income. Their generous bachelor uncle lived with them at Brook Hill after his retirement, basking in his nieces' affections and investing money for their benefit. With their healthy bank accounts, the Stewart girls could pick and choose among the short postwar supply of suitors whose legs and arms remained intact—or they could choose not to choose. Four of Mary Amanda's sisters—Lucy, Annie, Norma, and Elizabeth Hope—never married and pursued interesting lives of culture and travel. The year after Mary's wedding, her sister Isobel became the wife of lawyer, savvy business investor, and future publisher Joseph Bryan and remained on the Stewart estate until 1883, when they moved into a mansion of their own, Laburnum, across Brook Road.[5]

The remote Santee District in the wilds of violent, unreconstructed South Carolina proved worse than Mary feared and was, she soon declared, "not a place for civilized people of any description to inhabit."[6] Plantation people paid social calls, but no "society" existed there. The desperate poverty among country people of both races unsettled her, as did the large numbers of blacks, with their superstitions and country ways, always milling around the Pinckneys' home and property. Upon the couple's arrival in the moldy old plantation house—also neither reconstructed nor restored—the humid, pollen-laden air brought Mary low with a severe attack of bronchial asthma. Pinckney nursed her at night with cups of clover tea, summoned a team of doctors, and ordered the household to be at her beck and call so that the couple might leave soon on their honeymoon trip: The Grand Tour of Europe, the gift of the Stewarts. Showing signs from the start of her future as "an invalid par excellence," Mary would soon discover that her fragile health was always better away from the Santee.[7]

When the couple's first child, Amy, was born on January 27, 1871, Mary caused quite a stir, many hurt feelings, and much tooth sucking by refusing to have a black nurse for her baby, yet she could find no acceptable white woman willing to share her exile. She still held firm after giving birth on October 26, 1872, to Thomas Pinckney Jr., the captain's son and heir. Pinckney knew that keeping his family on The River year-round was risky, but sending his children to the mountains was no longer an option since Piedmont, the family's Flat Rock home, had to be sold after the war. Besides, he could not bear to be parted from them.[8]

WITH THE RISE IN PROPERTY TAXES and the devastating economic conse-quences of the Depression of 1873, which together threatened plantation agri-culture, Pinckney felt duty bound to concern himself with state politics. In the past, the planters had traditionally paid taxes according to their own appraisal of the worth of their land, but under the Republican regime all that was changing. When the state budget trebled in 1874, the legislature shunted much of the cost to landowners. The high taxes on land felt punitive and confiscatory, like the Union troops breaking into their homes and stealing their wealth all over again. In South Carolina forfeiture of property for nonpayment of taxes climbed from 270,000 acres in 1873 to 500,000 in 1874. In about a year's time a hundred businesses closed in Charleston alone. With the collapse of the city's branch of the poorly managed Freedman's Savings Bank, 5,300 black people and 200 whites lost everything.[9]

State spending had dramatically increased during Republican rule in part because, for the first time, the legislature was expending significant public monies on schools, roads, and other improvements. The social good achieved by the Radical legislature, though, was obscured in the public mind by the venality of the mass of the legislators who were breathtakingly brazen in looting the public treasury and engaging in graft, fraud, and bribery. One legislative session spent $125,000 (nearly $1.5 million in today's money) on alcoholic spirits. Legislators appropriated furnishings bought for public buildings to their homes.[10]

Part of the problem in South Carolina was the number of Republican politicians, especially the "carpetbaggers" and blacks, who depended on public patronage for their living and dipped too freely into the public trough to make up shortfalls. The concept of public virtue and honor among the state's leaders that Captain Pinckney nostalgically remembered was long gone. Serving as governor from 1787 to 1789 as the Constitution was being ratified and being put into effect, his grandfather had been so careful about setting precedent and avoiding any appearance of favoritism that he even refused to issue any pardons.[11]

Pinckney was not alone in looking backward and thinking America's best years were in the past as the nation prepared to celebrate its centennial. Over time, growing numbers of Americans, particularly in the East, wearied of the violence and corruption that was not limited to the South but seemingly had permeated the fabric of the nation. The two terms of Ulysses Grant, who was first elected president in 1868, had solid achievements but were riddled with sensational financial scandals, theft, nepotism, and graft. Grant's willingness to pardon his friends among the wrongdoers proved particularly dispiriting to reformers. Although diehard Radicals continued to wave the "bloody flag" at election times to keep their constituencies incensed about the sacrifice of the

Union dead, sentiment among many Americans began to shift. Since the issues of slavery and secession had been settled, the time had come for the war to end.

Reconstruction, many came to believe, was perhaps the cause rather than the solution to violence in the South. Sentiment was shifting, especially in the cities, where immigrants had begun transforming urban politics and labor violence was becoming increasingly threatening, toward sympathy for members of the old southern elite thrust by law under the governance of their social inferiors. By 1876, after years of blatant postwar malfeasance among national elected officials, planners for the national centennial revived the reputations of "southern aristocrats" Washington, Jefferson, and Madison as the nation's Founding Fathers and founts of civic virtue.

The Centennial Commission organizing the national celebration to be held around the Fourth of July, however, struggled with how to incorporate South Carolina into the festivities. The unrepentant Palmetto State, so important to the creation of the Republic, was the only one of the original thirteen still brooding under the purgatory of Military Reconstruction.

As it turned out, on July 2, 1876, General Thomas Pinckney became the first South Carolinian brought back into the American creation narrative. At a special event in which the ancestors of Founding Fathers were to be recognized and asked to prepare biographies of their famous relatives, the commission had feared that South Carolinians might take this national platform to swagger and say something unpleasant about the "Late Unpleasantness." The naming of the Reverend Charles Cotesworth Pinckney—a dignified "soldier of the Cross" but not of the Confederacy—to represent his noble grandfather was raised and approved with alacrity. The committee agreed that "no more patriotic family than that of the Pinckneys ever belonged to our country." In an intimation that the road to reunion in South Carolina was not going to be easy, the steamer on which the peacemaker from Charleston was traveling to Philadelphia had an accident, and the aristocratic minister could not bless the proceedings as planned.[12]

When his grandfather got his "citizenship" back, so to speak, Captain Thomas Pinckney started his own process of reconnecting with the United States. His first order of business was to effect a personal reunion with General Pinckney's sword. Locating the young officer from Custer's brigade, James Ingersoll, who had taken his saber at Haw's Shop, he wrote reminding him of the "magnanimous offer he had made upon the field of battle" that he would return the weapon at war's end. Ingersoll, then living in Iowa, obviously had gotten wind of the value of the old sword through publicity around the centennial and fired back that "the sword was his by right of capture" and that "Pinckney should never get it again." Disgusted by this typical "Yankee cheek," the captain concluded that not much had changed after all.[13]

Pinckney understood that the nation was at a crossroads in its centennial year and that state and local elections would determine its future direction. As David Blight has so succinctly phrased the political dynamic, "the election of 1876 gave the nation a referendum on reunion."[14]

Two years before, when Pinckney attended the 1874 Taxpayers Convention, called to demand governmental reform and closer regulation of state spending, he met Governor Daniel Henry Chamberlain, a Massachusetts native and formerly a white officer in the black 5th Massachusetts Cavalry who had become involved in Republican politics after moving to South Carolina in 1866. Chamberlain supported tax reform, acknowledged South Carolina's long heritage of patriotism, and admitted that Republicans had made mistakes in their approach to Reconstruction. Despite Pinckney's past prejudice against white men who had led black troops, he believed that Chamberlain might be a northern man with southern principles and initially supported him as a good choice to navigate the state's transition out of Reconstruction in 1876. "Thinking he would give us a fair administration," Pinckney resolved to do his part for reconciliation by urging his fellow Democrats to nominate Chamberlain for governor as a fusion candidate, even in the face of criticism by many of his friends who adopted the "straight out" position, believing that any compromise with Republicans was to accept further humiliation.[15]

Pinckney little realized how difficult reconciliation would be and how profoundly Radical Reconstruction had transformed attitudes of South Carolinians until the diocesan convention of the Episcopal Church in May 1876. As a lay member from the parish of St. James Santee, he worked with his brother to create support for the admission of St. Mark's Episcopal Church to the diocese. A beautifully built, well-funded church with a white rector, St. Mark's had been founded in 1866 by members of the old antebellum "colored elite" at a time when most white churches were still closed. Cotesworth hoped that the church could serve as a bridge between the white and black communities as it had before the war. In the final tally the majority of the clergy supported affiliation with the black congregation, but the lay members blocked its admission with a level of intensity that surprised the captain. He had anticipated the argument that the inclusion of blacks in the diocese might cause some white churches to withdraw. What shocked and worried him, though, was that the majority opposed the measure because most of the congregants of St. Mark's were of mixed race, and to admit them was to somehow endorse miscegenation. This position was in part a reaction against the Reconstruction government's overturning of the state's anti-miscegenation law first passed in 1865. The Reverend A. Toomer Porter, ever the conscience of the clergy, reminded the convention that laws could be changed, but there could be no changing of the church's fundamental truth that "we are all one in Christ."[16]

An outbreak of racial violence in the upper part of the state cast doubt on Governor Chamberlain's abilities to maintain peace during the challenging times ahead, so Pinckney ended up serving as a delegate to the state Democratic convention in support of his former commander, Wade Hampton, who campaigned for restoration of home rule in the state and reform of the government. His upstate opponent, Edgefield's Martin Gary, appealed to the worst racist passions of the white electorate and argued that blacks must be kept away from the polls by all means necessary.[17] Pinckney agreed with Hampton that the way to peace and possible prosperity was to accept the political realities of the large black majority and to work out a platform that embraced the interests of both landowners and workers.[18] By promising protection, improved education, and equality before the law, black men too could be found wearing Hampton's trademark "Red Shirts."

One of the Democrat's biggest coups was winning the support of Major Martin Delany, who ended the war as a recruiter in Charleston and as one of the nation's first and highest-ranking black field officers. He remained in the city after leaving the army, holding some Republican patronage jobs, but became deeply disillusioned with the party of Lincoln in its southern translation.[19]

In October 1876, Delany ventured out to a political meeting of blacks and whites in Cainhoy, about twenty miles from Pinckney's South Santee River, to stand on a wagon bed and stump for Hampton. He argued that the fate of blacks in South Carolina would soon be in the hands of local political leaders with whom they had shared interests, and they needed to learn to work with them. His unwelcome message that northern sentiment had shifted away from the cause of the black man was first met with groans and grumbles, then the beating of drums accompanied by threats and curses from black women, with all chanting, "De damned Nigger Democrat," and finally gunfire.[20] William McKinlay, a young mixed-race teacher from a well-respected local family of tailors and businessmen, was wounded, mistaken for Delany, most assumed. The day ended with the deaths of one black and six whites, the wounding of sixteen, and the extinction of any hope for peace.[21]

The incident in Cainhoy was a harbinger of the violence and corruption that haunted not only the South Carolina elections but the national elections as well. The two had a disconcerting symmetry, for in each election both Republicans and Democrats claimed victory. In the end, after a period of what Pinckney observed as "intense excitement," Hampton was named governor over the incumbent Chamberlain in the hope that he might be able to keep the peace as the state undertook to rule itself after a decade of Reconstruction. As part of his promise to share power with blacks, Hampton appointed Delany a trial judge.[22]

After the decision was made in favor of the Democrats, Pinckney struck up a conversation with some of his downcast hands, who asked about their future. Noting the captain's confused look, they explained that they had been told by the Union League that if General Hampton won, they would be, in Pinckney's words, "remanded into slavery." They also confided to him that of the few blacks they knew who voted for Hampton, one was punished by league members with the loss of a cow; another, a horse; and a third, a storeroom full of rice.[23]

Pinckney later credited Hampton with chasing the moneychangers out of the temple of state and sending them scattering "like partridges before a hawk, two or three flying to Canada" before "the evidence of their rascalities" could be used to bring them to justice. The Republicans fielded no opposition to the general's reelection in 1878. Yet on election day, when asked to help keep order at the polls, fifty-year-old Tom Pinckney wearily strapped on two pistols and grabbed his Westley Richards shotgun. Outside the polls, white and black "details" eyed one another from their separate corners. Inside Pinckney was "disgusted" to learn that having finally gained control of the "election machinery" for the first time since the war, the Democrats were planning to ensure they maintained their advantage by using a Republican trick, the specially folded tissue "kiss joke" that expanded, once put in the ballot box, into multiple votes. Pinckney protested that it was better to lose than to cheat, even though he was convinced that the "country's salvation" was at stake.[24]

Pinckney's "miserable and uncomfortable day" at the polls was exacerbated by the palpable animosity of the black voters. The realization that his workers had come to see him as their enemy finally struck home when he overheard one of the Fairfield hands call out to friends who had begun walking home after voting: "Come back here, you men. No one is to leave this ground 'til those votes are counted, and we are to see that we get our justice." Bloodshed was narrowly avoided that day, when 549 voters cast 890 ballots at Pinckney's precinct, but shameless corruption marred the entire state's election.[25]

In 1880, Brigadier General Johnson Hagood, the former commander of Battery Wagner, became South Carolina's governor and Hampton went to the US Senate.[26] By 1882, South Carolina Democrats had adopted the longstanding New England practice of creatively redrawing the congressional districts to dilute the influence of the solidly Republican black vote. The largest concentration of African American voters was gerrymandered into a contorted frame known as the Seventh, or "Black," District; the other six districts sent white Democrats to Congress. The line just skirted the South Santee boundary. Not long afterward Pinckney wrote his cousin William Johnstone, "I can't tell you the satisfaction it is to me to be just outside of the [Black District]" since "I shall not meet my freedmen at the polls again nor be subjected to what I have been in past." Finished with politics for good, Pinckney conceded that he was willing to let others attend "the affairs of the nation . . . without comment from me."[27]

THE DEMANDS OF PINCKNEY'S plantations and his family would completely absorb and nearly destroy him during the next decade. His third child, John Stewart Pinckney, had lived only nine months before dying in July 1875. Early that fall Mary learned that another child was on the way. Tom agreed with her that since he was consumed with the work of the fields, prudence dictated that she should take their two little children and await the birth at Brook Hill to avoid another tragedy. While there, though, Amy and Tommy both became terribly ill. When he heard the news, Pinckney took the next train and rushed to their bedsides, but he was too late. The white camellias he brought from South Carolina to give to his much-adored Amy he laid on her little grave instead. He somehow managed, according to sister Mary Elliott, who traveled with him, to maintain "the strong hold of Pinckney sweetness and obedience" to God in the face of this "bitter blow."[28]

Stricken, Mary took to her bed. The Stewart house was still draped in heavy mourning when Charles Cotesworth Pinckney was born on December 16, 1875—very small but healthy—giving his distraught parents another reason for hope in 1876. After a somber Christmas, Mary remained at Brook Hill, while Pinckney returned to his "lonely house and long neglected business." About the time of the furor over the election of 1876, Mary announced that she was expecting another child. Lucy was born in June 1877 but lived only a few weeks. In May 1879 Caroline was born; by July she too was dead.[29]

Not until May 1881, when Pinckney rented a refuge for the remaining family among the pines and high ground of Summerville outside of Charleston, did Mary finally shed her mourning weeds. But it would not be for long. Later that year, during a visit to Brook Hill, nine-year-old Tommy's complaint of a sore throat turned out to be the early signs of diphtheria. Within days five-year-old Cotesworth came down with a virulent attack of measles. Both hovered between life and death. The family lost Tommy, but baby Cotesworth survived, now their only child.[30] Reflecting on her life in a letter soon after, Mary concluded that she was glad she had married her "dear husband. God bless him! . . . Life was too hard to bear alone. . . . [T]ogether you will stand and bear it."[31]

The loss of his namesake and that of his grandfather hit Pinckney with particular force. The Stewart family rallied to support him. When in October 1882 a son was born to Isobel and Joseph Bryan, they named him Thomas Pinckney Bryan. The Stewart brothers, who also knew the feeling of having no son to carry on their names, perpetuated the memories of the Pinckney boys by endowing scholarships in their names at Charleston's Holy Communion Church Institute, established by the Reverend A. Toomer Porter in 1867 to save impoverished planters' sons of the postwar generation from growing up in ignorance.[32]

At the same time, the sense of an ending lingered about Fairfield Plantation. Everyone except Pinckney realized that by 1882 his life on The River could not continue. In 1870, the year he and Mary Stewart married, Pinckney lost his rice crop, the third in a row. All Santee planters found themselves in the same situation and worse off than in any year "since the Union came in." The Stewart brothers, being canny businessmen, had probably assumed from the first that they would have to underwrite Pinckney's agricultural operations. Their well-meant injections of capital only encouraged his belief that through hard work he could somehow hold on to this one little patch of family history.[33]

When the 1872 crop also failed, the brothers covered Pinckney's losses and created a polite fiction that he would be paying them back when the market improved—a commonsensical business arrangement, all agreed, to avoid the interest rates charged by Charleston factors, themselves enthralled to New York banks, that sometimes reached 12 percent. Fierce competition from states such as Louisiana drove the price down so low that "Carolina gold" might have more accurately been called "Carolina dross." Even after a banner year in 1880,

Pinckney was still in the red and feeling "a little blue." After the ever-generous "Uncle Dan" agreed in 1881 to send the dividends due Mary directly to the captain as a salve to his pride, Pinckney wrote back a bit stiffly with his thanks for the $890 and his assurance that he would use the money "for Mary's benefit, no less than my own."[34]

To Pinckney's credit, rather than putting all of his wife's money into his failing plantation, against his own instincts he invested about half the dividends in the city's nascent textile-processing plant, the Charleston Manufacturing Company. With all of his wealth tied up in land and his income dependent almost exclusively on rice, he finally acknowledged the need to diversify. He chose this enterprise not on its prospectus but solely upon "the character of the men who had initiated it," including banker George Walton Williams, who shared Pinckney's determination that "Northern capitalists" never acquire a majority interest of Charleston business concerns.[35]

After three more years with no improvement in the prospects for rice, the now-elderly John Stewart wrote a straightforward letter to his son-in-law. The time had come to give up his Santee plantation, he told Pinckney. Having himself found an "altogether appropriate" farm for sale near the Shenandoah Valley town of New Market with lands suitable for grazing livestock or farming on shares, Stewart offered to buy it for him if he would only bring Mary and her child to live in the more salubrious climate of Virginia. Stunned by this effrontery, Pinckney replied that he honestly did not think that a change in environment would help Mary much at this stage in her lung disease. He did agree that the outlook for rice was bleak, but "I cannot see my way . . . just now" to leave the Santee.[36]

Within a year of this interchange, John Stewart was dead. In 1886, again having lost three rice crops in a row, Pinckney finally gave up—The River had won. No longer able to resist Mary's importuning, he agreed to move his small remnant family to Brook Hill. Pinckney tried to put a brave face forward as he closed the door of Fairfield forever. He managed to fool his brother, Cotesworth Jr., whose own finances flourished thanks to the marlstone phosphate discovered on his land along the Ashley River. The minister obviously was not able to penetrate very deeply into Tom's heart, for he wrote his daughter that when he found his brother packing in January 1887, he was "quite well and bright, in spite of [the] Santee and its utter failure."[37]

This "utter failure"—the loss of his independence, the separation from the land of his ancestors, and even his rivalry with The River, that check on family pride for generations—presented Pinckney with the great tragedy of his life, even as he exchanged the hardships of Fairfield for a well-appointed suite at Brook Hill with all luxuries at his fingertips.

Pinckney's dilemma over the unsustainability of agriculture was shared to greater and less degrees all over the South. For southerners, black and white, whose cultures and folkways had been so closely tied to the land and rural isolation, leaving the farms for the towns and the tyranny of the wage or cash economy meant leaving a bit of their souls behind. The flight from the land also meant the separation of whites from blacks, who became segregated in cities.[38]

Once in Richmond, Pinckney devoted the next two years to his wife and Cotesworth. The boy, the darling of his spinster aunts, quickly became absorbed into the comfortable world of Brook Hill; the fast-paced, entertaining life of the city; and the company of his Bryan cousins. Then in 1889 Pinckney lost his Mary. The Stewart family threw themselves into full-blown Victorian mourning, holding her up as the "highest type of womanhood—the Christ-like child, daughter, wife, and mother." They buried her in the graveyard of Emmanuel Church, surrounded by the little headstones of her babies. Her mother, Mary Amanda Stewart, had three stained-glass windows dedicated to the memory of her eldest daughter, her husband, and her brother-in-law, Daniel, who also died in 1889.[39]

After a trip back to Charleston with Cotesworth, the sixty-one-year-old Pinckney opted to return to Brook Hill. He had nothing to keep him in South Carolina anymore. Although some poignancy attached to the fact that his only child did not share his love of the lowcountry, father and son would both develop a great devotion to the cult of the Lost Cause, which had its most powerful expression in Richmond, a city that was looking backward to its days as the capital of the Confederacy at the same time it was leaving behind its agricultural past and becoming a modern industrial city of the New South.[40]

The epicenter of the organized crusade among Virginians to preserve and shape the memory of the Confederate war coalesced across the road from Brook Hill at Laburnum, the spacious home built by Mary's sister, Isobel, and her husband, Joseph Bryan. While serving as its president, "Belle" Bryan expanded the modest mission of the Confederate Memorial Literary Society by spearheading a campaign in 1890 to acquire the "White House of the Confederacy" and transform it into a museum dedicated to the heroism and sacrifice of the South during the war. By 1896 great numbers of "relicts" from each of the southern states, including the personal effects of Robert E. Lee, packed the rooms.[41]

Through the Bryans, Captain Pinckney met luminaries of the growing body of Lost Cause literature that by 1880 promoted the idea that Virginia was the heart and soul of the Confederacy (despite blaming secession on Charleston hotspurs and claiming to have never really supported slavery). He enjoyed the writing of Thomas Nelson Page, a local colorist whose tales, such as *In Ole Virginia; or, Marse Chan and Other Stories* (1887), romanticized plantation life in an Edenic Old South populated by chivalrous gentlemen, beautiful belles, and faithful happy slaves. Serialized in popular magazines, Page's stories helped shape the way southerners thought about their past and ameliorated the way northerners thought about the South.

The courtly Pinckney could have stepped right out of one of these novels. Like most Lost Cause proponents, Page took the position that rather than being outside of America and distinctive, southerners were in fact the quintessential Americans. Few matched this description as well as "The Captain," who was a descendant of founders and thus among the illuminati on matters of the constitutional principle of states' rights and secession, the cornerstone of Lost Cause justification. Everything about the Pinckney legend, even the devotion of the loyal manservant James Broughton, who stayed with him throughout the war, would have fit nicely in a Page tale.[42]

In the latter months of 1890, the estimable Captain Pinckney upset the decorous equilibrium at Brook Hill when he began paying court to Camilla Scott, a spinster cousin of the Stewart sisters more than twenty years his junior. In contrast to the Stewarts, the fortunes of the notable Scott family of Oakwood, Fauquier County, had been well and truly dashed upon the rocks of the Civil War. This perhaps was a bond between them. Camilla's widowed mother had been reduced to operating a boarding house near the capitol in Richmond to support her five children, who all had to pitch in with the floor-scrubbing, spittoon-cleaning, antimacassar-washing drudgery. When Pinckney screwed up his courage to tell Mary's formidable mother his plans to marry again, she fell into a paroxysm of anguish and begged him to wait.[43]

Finally, in 1892 the captain and Camilla married quietly at her brother's home in Warrenton and left Virginia for Charleston, taking up residence in a large Legaré Street house owned by a member of the Memminger family. Then in 1895, to everyone's great amazement, their daughter, Josephine Lyons Scott Pinckney, was born and later christened by her eighty-three-year-old uncle in Grace Episcopal Church, where he had been the rector for four decades. To her father's delight, she would grow to love the lowcountry with a fierce intensity that would rival his own.[44]

The joy of little Josephine, who would be warmly embraced by the Stewart clan, helped fill the cavern of Pinckney's grief that seemed to expand over the next four years. Soon departed were "Sister," Caroline Seabrook, who died in 1895, and "Brother," Cotesworth Jr., who died in 1898. That same year fire reduced Eldorado (slated to be his daughter's legacy) to a ruin. Buried among its cinders were many lifetimes of mementos, the family Bible, and the general's leather-bound books salvaged from Hampton after the war. About the same time and amid renewed feelings of defeat, Pinckney decided to lease Fairfield Plantation to a group of New York businessmen, who fashioned themselves as the Santee Hunt Club, a new generation of "Yankee marauders" content now to kill waterfowl over its fallow rice fields rather than to smite the region's rebel inhabitants. Then in 1899 the son of his nephew Charley Pinckney, twenty-eight-year-old Thomas (named Thomas Pinckney Jr.), was murdered in the streets of Charleston under suspicious circumstances involving a young woman of not entirely impeccable repute; his assailant was never found. Seventy-year-old Captain Pinckney would mourn his namesake and, as the century drew to its weary end, reflect upon the great revolution through which he had lived and how much he had lost in its wake.[45]

EPILOGUE
Lest We Forget

IN 1899, THE YEAR THAT 10,000 members of the United Confederate Veterans flooded the narrow streets of Charleston for their annual reunion, Captain Thomas Pinckney and Sergeant Joseph H. Barquet had a reunion of their own. More accurately, their separate worlds brushed up against each other one last time in the realm of memory.

Many questioned the wisdom of the Charleston City Council spending $30,000 to build Thomson Auditorium, an impractical cavernous convention hall seating 7,000 people, to house the reunion while the still battle-fatigued town remained in the throes of an agricultural depression. But as the longtime commander of Camp Sumter No. 250, an adjunct of the national Confederate veterans group, Pinckney understood its importance. The Lost Cause had become for him, as for so many Charlestonians, a great reservoir into which he could pour all the sadness and disappointments of his life. It was, after all, not about past glory, but about defeat. He took much joy in seeing old comrades at the convention, some for the first time since his capture in 1864, and even one long-feared dead. Sorrow and shock also intruded when he learned that those survivors among the Immortal 600 he had left behind at Fort Pulaski had ended the war back at Fort Delaware, the "very picture of Death masquerading in rags."[1]

The pleasure and poignancy of comparing notes with other old veterans and reconsidering their shared experiences through the lens of time convinced Pinckney that, although writing never came easily to him, he should finally heed the encouragements of family and friends to join the long gray line of Confederate memoirists. He had no tales of daring gallantry, as did those Virginians who rode with Mosby's Rangers or Jeb Stuart, but he believed that he had a story of survival that would resonate with Charlestonians. The battlefield was a universe of its own, unfathomable to civilians, but everyone in secession's city had lived through the dark night of wartime desolation, known gnawing hunger, and experienced visceral fear when black soldiers marched into town. The turning of the century, then, seemed the time for seventy-two-year-old Pinckney to pull out his old Civil War journal lest the pages turn to dust and the world forget.[2]

In early 1900, at just about the same time that Pinckney began reflecting upon his prison experience on Morris Island, the thoughts of retired New York tailor Liston Barguet turned to his brother, Joseph, as the twentieth anniversary of his death approached. Interestingly both men had changed the spelling of their surname. Joseph had started using "Barquette," suggestive of the Haitian connection, while Liston adopted "Barguet," spoken with a French inflexion. Despite the half-continent distance between them, the brothers had remained in touch. Liston supplied Joseph with clothes when he was stationed on Morris Island. In 1867 Joseph named his newborn son in his elder brother's honor.[3]

Now Liston was wondering how he might get in touch with his namesake, rumored to have joined the Buffalo Soldiers of the 10th US Cavalry, as well as Joseph's five other children.[4] He knew that growing up in the oppressive racial environment of Illinois had blighted their early lives. So too had their father's long absence during the war, then his addictions, first to politics and then to alcohol, undermined their financial security and short-circuited their education. He thought he had a way to bolster their finances a bit and, perhaps even more importantly, reconnect them with their past.

Off and on for over a decade, Liston had been pursuing a "lost cause" of his own, one that coincidentally would bring him back into Thomas Pinckney's world of the deposed lowcountry aristocracy, those defeated veterans of the Confederate war who now looked at the world quite differently than they had when the Barquets grew up among the "colored elite."

Elderly and desperate for money, as were all his kin, Liston pinned his future hopes on a lawsuit, *Rutledge v. Tunno,* that had a long, sinuous history reminiscent of Dickens's *Jamdyce v Jamdyce,* except few of the Barquets' lawyers actually ever got paid. In this case the long arm of the law reached backward to the end of the eighteenth century and the days of General Charles Cotesworth Pinckney's failed mission involving the French ambassadors—the infamous XYZ Affair—and the resultant Quasi-War with France (1798–1800). Although the United States claimed neutrality during Revolutionary France's multiyear wars with Great Britain, French privateers preyed on American merchant ships during their Atlantic crossings. One of the vessels seized, along with its valuable cargo, belonged to Charleston merchant Adam Tunno and his partner James Cox. Their firm of Tunno & Cox filed a complaint with the American government for restitution and later, along with other victims, instituted a lawsuit when the peace treaty with France extracted no indemnification for their losses. The wheels of justice ground so slowly that all the principals in these cases were dead by the time Congress passed compensating legislation in 1883. The terms of the French Spoilation Act stated that distributions may be made to those proving next of kinship according to the code of the state where the original complainants resided.[5]

In 1885 the Causton Group, which had orchestrated the legislation, engaged the law firm of Rutledge and Young to help find the next of kin of Adam Tunno and James Cox so that they might split their share of the $21,167.83 payout, which would be reduced to $14,111.87 after the lobbyists took their percentage. The principals were Colonel Benjamin H. Rutledge—Captain Pinckney's former regimental commander—and his friend Henry E. Young, formerly judge advocate for the Army of North Virginia. After minimal research, Rutledge was preparing to recommend a payout to the British relatives of the old Scottish merchant, universally reputed to be a lifelong bachelor, but Young intervened and added a complicating dimension to the case.[6]

Young remembered his grandfather, wine importer Henry Gourdin, gossiping that Tunno, with whom he had frequently done business, had a secret black family. He had learned the truth of that rumor for himself in 1867 when Charles Miller, a well-known man-about-town who "drew wine" at Charleston social events, approached him for help in sorting out the incredibly convoluted affairs of his black grandmother, Hagar Bellingall Cole, who had died intestate two years before. In establishing Miller's one-eighth interest in Hagar's Pitt Street home, he found that the house actually had been part of a trust quietly established in 1806 by Tunno to benefit Peggy Bellingall (as she was then called in the court documents), Hagar, and their future issue.[7]

When Young got in touch with Miller, he explained that Barbara Tunno Barquet, not his grandmother, was the old Scot's only child and put him in touch with Liston. After Miller described Young as a trustworthy "class" man who would do "that which is just and right" by the family, Liston asked him to represent his family's interests and was disappointed to learn that his firm had already agreed to represent Tunno's British relatives.[8]

Liston retained a New York lawyer who then contacted the scholarly judge Charles H. Simonton of the US District Court for South Carolina. One of the first southerners appointed to the federal bench after the Civil War, Simonton had an excellent reputation for fairness and dedication to the law. During his time as a prisoner of war in the execrable Fort Delaware, he had gathered a few law books and held classes on legal practice that helped launch the postwar careers of many former Confederates. The Barquets' claim to the Spoliation Fund piqued his interest and sense of justice, but he warned that the laws of South Carolina would apply in this case, which meant that while illegitimate children could receive gifts in a will, they could not make claims upon an estate. Only if Adam Tunno publicly acknowledged Barbara Barquet as his daughter might their case succeed. Simonton dispatched his clerks to dig through the county probate records to exhume Tunno's will; their whole case depended on its contents. The research returned bad news.[9]

Unfortunately for the Barquets, in his 1831 will Tunno had named Edward RoseTunno, his wealthy London-based nephew and Tory member of Parliament, as the residual legatee of his $300,000 estate, thus endorsing his brothers' children as his next of kin. Had he merely excluded Barbara, lawyers could have tried to use the ambiguity to their advantage. Instead, she was mentioned in a separate "Instrument" written in Tunno's own hand that set aside $12,500 to benefit the favorites among the slaves ("my property") and the free people ("under my protection"), including Margaret Bellingall, who was identified as "the free Black woman." Although placing Barbara in the same dependent category, he gave her a nod and distinguished her from her mother with the dignity of an honorific, "Mrs. Burguit." He also referred to Cornelia Tunno, his brother's mixed-race child with whom he had a blood connection, as "Mrs. Harrison." Tunno's lawyers clearly intended to make his estate invulnerable to all future claims from the Barquets.[10]

With this revelation and no money for lawyers, Liston's case went dormant until 1899, when out of the blue he received a letter from a stranger. Washington-based, Charleston-born Whitefield McKinlay, a rising star in the firmament of black Republicans, had a family connection to the Barquets and had heard about the lawsuit.[11] The lonely, recently widowed, seventy-eight-year-old Liston wrote back to explain the situation, adding that his life was full of "sorrow and trouble." "How strange it will be, if we receive that which is rightly ours," he mused. "We all need it. I, as much, if not more so, than any one."[12]

Liston had been perhaps the most financially successful of the Barquet brothers. His Broadway tailoring shop had been profitable enough for him to raise and educate five children and move them by 1870 from lower Manhattan to the commuter town of Mount Vernon, where their new two-story house had hot water and all the indoor conveniences of the time. But over the years, unexpected and costly problems had arisen with his brothers and his children. Admitting to McKinlay that although he once had "an elegant chance" and had made a good living, he realized in retrospect that he had been "too liberal with others, and I am now suffering for it and they are no better off in this world's goods."[13]

Initially Liston's interest in the case had been about the money. With McKinlay's agreement to help in a quiet way, though, he began to perceive another force at work. The Bible-quoting, hymn-writing tailor was as dedicated to his religious practice as an Episcopalian (and later a Swedenborgian) as his brother Joseph had been to Republican politics. He believed that he could now see in the Spoilation Fund the hand of "Divine Providence" at work righting past wrongs.[14]

Liston had never been allowed to call Adam Tunno "grandfather." But he now imagined that at the moment of his greatest need, Tunno was hovering over him like a guardian angel, embracing him at last as his grandson, and wiping away a lifetime's feeling of unworthiness. He, and perhaps all of Barbara's children, carried an inner sadness at not being publicly acknowledged by the estimable Tunno, one of the richest men in Charleston, who had no other direct descendants. In the free brown community, where respectability and kinship ties were foremost, Barbara Tunno must have felt the stigma of illegitimacy acutely as well as the inner rage at being denied her due. As a child she would have seen her father finely dressed for an evening out at the Saint Cecelia Society, heard the music floating up from John Williams's Long Room down Bedons Alley, and known she would never be invited in to dance. Her hurt became part of her legacy to the next generation. Although Tunno never claimed him, Liston did claim the old Scot, even after he had been dead for thirty years. In 1863 Liston named his first son Pascal Tunno Barguet, melding his two European ancestries together. Many years earlier his oldest sister, Margaret, had called her only child Adam Tunno Humphries.

Tunno's rejection of Barbara and her children as his kin, as part of his clan, even in death replicated on a deeply personal level the achingly painful sensation that had so tortured Liston's brother. All his life Joseph had felt denied full citizenship by the land of his birth, had loved a country that did not love him back. Liston clearly felt compelled to do whatever was necessary to assure "a triumph of justice and right."[15]

In a bit of bravado, then, Liston assured McKinlay that he had unequivocal proof to support his claim that Adam Tunno did, indeed, consider Margaret Bellingall as his wife. Having learned that before 1865 no state law barred interracial unions and that in South Carolina law intention was all that was needed to have a legal marriage, he made an assertion denying that his grandmother fit the stereotype of the wanton black mistress. Bellingall, he claimed, was a very pious woman who had been told by the Reverend Christopher E. Gadsden, rector of St. Philip's Episcopal Church, that because of her sinful living with Tunno, she could no longer participate in the sacraments. In consequence, Liston averred, "his grandfather Adam Tunno did give my grandmother a written certificate" to the effect that "he regarded her as his wife and would live with her till death did them part which he did." Gadsden "accepted the certificate and admitted her as a regular communicant."[16]

The revelation of this evidence threw the offices of Rutledge and Young into turmoil. Benjamin H. Rutledge Jr. pulled out the dusty file from the desk of his father, who had died in 1893. Charleston's legal community suddenly got interested, and a cavalcade of ex-Confederates were willing to take Liston's case. Among them was Thomas Pinckney's cousin Francis Kinloch Frost, of the Charleston firm of Smyth, Frost, and Lee, who had been recommended to Liston by his New York lawyer as "perfectly honest, and reliable and a good fighter." One of the Rutledge firm's associates, Langdon Cheves III, whose father helped design Battery Wagner and was the first Confederate killed there, became the attorney for the Tunno survivors, reduced by 1899 to two spinsters also greatly in financial need.[17]

Having spent lonely nights thinking about his Charleston years and brooding over ways his family might secure their Tunno birthright, Liston possibly conflated his memory of attending St. Philip's Episcopal Church as a member of the brown elite worshiping with the white elite and Tunno's issuing a "certificate of freedom" for Ballingall, a common requirement in the city whenever Charleston officials had one of their periodic crackdowns on free people of color. Suggestive of his state of mind, he recommended to a probably shocked McKinlay, whose hopes for a career in South Carolina politics were cut short by the Democratic "restoration" in 1876, that he contact Senator Wade Hampton, who might remember Tunno, "the state of society & etc." When an intense search of his house revealed no certificate and none of his relatives could recall any story confirming its existence, Liston became "very nervous" that his case was collapsing. Nevertheless, he wanted to press ahead and "trust in the Divine Providence that the lawyers may find some unexpected proof." Failing that, he was ready to settle with the Tunno heirs.[18]

Liston had developed his own romance of "lost" Charleston, and in his mental stroll through the past, his memory of his youth interestingly jibed with Captain Pinckney's 1900 recollections. Both men believed that the upper class of

slaveholding blacks had common interests with the upper classes of slaveholding whites and were therefore granted certain indulgences, such as the exemp-
tion of the Brown Friendly Society from strictures against blacks gathering in
any numbers. In Liston's youth, having European ancestry had been an advantage that elevated him a bit in the complex calculations of Charleston society.
What he did not understand was that by 1900 the distinctions that the Barquets
remembered as part of the social geography of their youth in Charleston, based
upon the variations in shades, ethnicities, education, wealth, and character
among the free peoples of color, had been scrubbed away after emancipation,
with "negroes" all ubiquitously placed in the same category of racial inferiority.
Whereas blacks continued to see their world as wildly diverse as a pointillist's
rendition, revealing all the subtle distinctions of their humanity with its the
full range of human successes and failures, the "color line" as drawn by whites
during Reconstruction was rendered with a single, broad brushstroke.[19]

When Liston produced neither substantial evidence nor a retainer, the Frost
firm withdrew from the case. At last George H. Moffett (the brother-in-law
of Judge Simonton), whom Liston came to think of as both "my attorney and
friend," and his law partner Claudian B. Northup agreed to take up his case
and see it to the "bitter end." In 1904 they got a ruling from Master-in-Equity
George Herbert Sass (also known as Barton Gray, Charleston's poet of the Lost
Cause), who found that when a decision about the legality of a marriage may
go either way, race could be the deciding factor. The fact that "Margaret was a
black woman," he added, "raises the presumption . . . of concubinage." If the
initial reason for their coupling was meretricious, "no amount of subsequent
cohabitation and repute will transform the connection into a marriage." From
the evidence of the will, he concluded, "Adam Tunno never intended to make
Margaret Bellingall his wife or that he ever so considered her."[20]

Fulfilling his promise, Moffett pushed the case the all the way to the state supreme court, arguing that South Carolina should bring their rules determining
next-of-kin in line with those of other states since Liston Barquet could have
won his case in New York. On July 14, 1904, Justice Eugene B. Gary (nephew of
Martin Gary, who in 1876 had advocated keeping blacks away from the polls
by violence) declined to set aside the lower-court decision. He held the opinion
that the state's provision that "bastards do not take by inheritance under our
statute of distributions" was "settled law" in South Carolina and, ever the states'
rights man, saw no need to conform to the statutes of other states. He acknowledged, however, that his decision to name Tunno's collateral great nieces and

nephews as his heirs indeed "strains the law." Left unsaid perhaps was that his decision was influenced by the fact that those claimants who were actually "of the blood" of Adam Tunno were of mixed race.[21] The judiciary of South Carolina, still deeply resentful of the loss of control over the legal system during Reconstruction, obdurately clung to their ability to defend their unique laws and define marriage once they regained that authority in 1876.

This resolution of *Rutledge v. Tunno* forms a dispiriting coda to the odyssey of Sergeant Barquet, whose life was an elusive struggle to establish his identity and that of his children as belonging to the greater American family and part of the American narrative.

IN THE SMALL GOSSIPY TOWN that was Charleston at the turn of the twentieth century, Thomas Pinckney surely heard about the Barquets' case, for many of his friends and acquaintances were involved at some level over the years. A close reader of the local press, he could hardly have missed the frequent large notices that the Rutledge firm posted calling for interested parties to the Tunno claim.

In his memoir Pinckney wrapped Barquet's story in his own and kept the soldier's name alive in the context of one of his finest moments: his display of grace and humanity toward the ailing rebel aristocrat, whom a lesser man might have enjoyed tormenting. And although they never actually saw one another again after that brief but apparently memorable interchange, Pinckney and Barquet remained in some ways bound together in the "Everlasting If," to borrow Bernard DeVoto's formulation about the alternative possibilities at Gettysburg. Their *if*, however, ponders whether their moment of comity could not somehow have been translated into future race relations. What *if* the political leaders of the North had chosen post-emancipation policies other than those that had set whites and blacks in conflict with one another, then withdrew. What *if* economic reforms rather than political revolution had been the first postwar priority or civil rights for all black Americans instead of just for the newly freed had been the goal? What *if* the northern politicians had the compassion of Barquet and realized that vindictiveness was no solution. What *if* the southern politicians had the wisdom of Pinckney to realize and pursue the possibility of a harmony of interests between blacks and whites, sharing as they surely did a mutual destiny. What *if* other choices had been made, as Pinckney wrote in concluding his memoirs, and South Carolinians "could have found a way to live without the lynching and murders that stain the annals of our fair land." What *if* Barquet had decided to return to Charleston?[22]

Even into his ninth decade, Pinckney could still be seen strolling High Battery, the city's bayside promenade, head high, tipping his hat to ladies, and gazing out into Charleston Harbor. Arrayed before him were Fort Moultrie, Fort Sumter, and Fort Johnson—all quiet now. Straining, he could see Morris Island in the far distance. Admirers spoke of Pinckney as embodying the "life and spirit of the old South," symbolic of a time and a generation "almost extinct." Likewise Morris Island and the memories of what had really happened there were moving toward extinction. Nibbled by the tides, etched by swirling currents, "Coffin Island" was by then only a fraction of its 1864 size. Battery Wagner, where so many good men died for no good reason, already had been swept away years earlier. White soldiers and black, Confederates and Yankees, at last liberated from their sandy graves, intermingled altogether in the eternal sea.[23]

On November 14, 1915, Captain Thomas Pinckney died peacefully in his bed and passed into reunion with those outside of time. A towering granite cross with a Confederate battle flag discretely etched on its base marks his grave in oak-shaded Magnolia Cemetery, located very near the place where Sergeant Joseph H. Barquet had pitched his tent fifty years earlier on the outskirts of Charleston, ready to transform the world.[24]

NOTES

Abbreviations

ARC   Avery Research Center, College of Charleston

BBR   Luis F. Emilio, *A Brave Black Regiment: The History of the Fifty-Fourth Regiment of Massachusetts Volunteer Infantry, 1863–1865* (Boston, 1894; repr., with a new introduction by Greg J. W. Urwin, New York: Da Capo, 1995)

CCP   Charles Cotesworth Pinckney

CSR   Compiled Service Records

FHL   Family History Library

JPP   Josephine Pinckney Papers (1846–1957), SCHS

LC   Library of Congress, Washington, DC

NARA   National Archives and Records Administration, Washington, DC

NYPL   New York Public Library

OR   *The War of the Rebellion: A Compilation of Official Records of the Union and Confederate Armies,* 130 vols. (Washington, DC, 1880–1901)

P-M   CCP Jr. Papers (1831–93), Pinckney-Means Family Papers (1701–1983), SCHS

RMC   Charleston County Register of Mesne Conveyance

SCDAH   South Carolina Department of Archives and History, Columbia

SCHM   *South Carolina Historical Magazine*

SCHS   South Carolina Historical Society, Charleston

SCL   South Caroliniana Library, University of South Carolina, Columbia

SFP   Stewart Family Papers (1802–1938), Department of Manuscripts and Archives, Virginia Historical Society, Richmond

SHC   Southern Historical Collection, University of North Carolina, Chapel Hill

TP   Thomas Pinckney

Prologue

1. The term "Immortal 600" was popularized by one of Pinckney's fellow prisoners from Virginia. Ogden Murray's impassioned account of their experiences at Fort Delaware and Morris Island, *The Immortal Six Hundred: A Story of Cruelty to Confederate Prisoners of War* (Roanoke: Stone Printing, 1911) complements Pinckney's narrative. See also Karen Stokes, *The Immortal 600:*

Surviving Civil War Charleston and Savannah (Charleston, SC: History Press, 2013). Mauriel P. Joslyn, *Immortal Captives: The Story of 600 Confederate Officers and the United States Prisoner of War Policy* (Shippensburg, PA: White Mane, 1996), 272.

2. TP, "My Reminiscences of the War and Reconstruction Times," 59, proof sheets, [ca. 1903], #11112, Special Collections Department, University of Virginia Library, Charlottesville (all references are from this version); Joslyn, *Immortal Captives*, 40–41; "The New Rebel Prison on Morris Island," *Port Royal (SC) Palmetto Herald*, 6 Oct. 1864.

3. The seminal book on the Carolina lowcountry's free people of color remains Michael P. Johnson and James L. Roark, *Black Masters: A Free Family of Color in the Old South* (New York: W. W. Norton, 1984).

4. TP, "Reminiscences," 59.

5. Charles Pinckney quoted in Eric Robert Papenfuse, *The Evils of Necessity: Robert Goodloe Harper and the Moral Dilemma of Slavery,* Transactions of the American Philosophical Society 87, pt. 1 (Philadelphia: American Philosophical Society, 1997), 23; Count de Mirabeau quoted in Adam Hochschild, *Bury the Chains: Prophets and Rebels in the Fight to Free an Empire's Slaves* (Boston: Houghton Mifflin, 2006), 258. See also George D. Terry, "A Study of the Impact of the French Revolution and the Insurrection at Santo Domingo upon South Carolina, 1790–1805" (master's thesis, University of South Carolina, 1975).

6. Gretchen Judith Woertendyke, "Specters of Haiti: Race, Fear, and the American Gothic, 1789–1855" (PhD diss., Stony Brook University, 2007), 21–22, 64; "Achates" [Gen. Thomas Pinckney], *Reflections, Occasioned by the Late Disturbances in Charleston* (Charleston, SC: A. E. Miller, 1822), 6, 10; Madison S. Bell, *Toussaint Louverture: A Biography* (New York: Pantheon Books, 2007), 286–87; C. L. R. James, *Black Jacobins: Toussaint L'Overture and the San Domingo Revolution* (New York: Vintage Books, 1963) 370, 373–74.

7. TP, "Reminiscences," 58–59.

8. "Colonization," *Galesburg (IL) Free Democrat*, 1 Feb. 1855.

9. Henry A. M. Smith, "Preface to Captain Thomas Pinckney's Reminiscences," SCHS; George C. Rogers Jr., *Charleston in the Age of the Pinckneys* (Norman: University of Oklahoma Press, 1969).

10. Caroline Pinckney Seabrook to Mary Maxcy Leverett, 1 July 1865, in *The Leverett Letters: Correspondence of a South Carolina Family, 1851–1868,* ed. Frances Wallace Taylor, Catherine Taylor Matthews, and J. Tracy Power (Columbia: University of South Carolina Press, 2000), 399.

11. TP, "Reminiscences," 57–59.

12. Ibid., 58.

Chapter One

1. "Deposition of Liston Barquet," Mount Vernon, NY, 29 Dec. 1902, *B. H. Rutledge, Administrator of Adam Tunno v. M. R. Tunno et al., 1-10,* Langdon Cheves III Legal Papers, SCHS. The 1819 compromise that allowed Missouri to be admitted to the Union as a slave state and Maine as a free state raised southern ire because Congress took the unprecedented step of banning slavery in certain unorganized territories, thus denying future states the historic right to choose.

2. Johnson and Roark, *Black Masters,* 51–52.

3. William W. Freehling, *Prelude to Civil War: The Nullification Controversy in South Carolina, 1816–1836* (New York: Oxford University Press, 1992), 55–61; Woertendyke, "Specters of Haiti," 21–22, 64; Michael P. Johnson, "Denmark Vesey and His Co-Conspirators," *William and Mary Quarterly*, 3rd ser., 58 (Oct. 2001): 933. For an excellent discussion of the scholarly debate over the authenticity of Denmark Vesey's plot, see ibid., 915–76. For a rebuttal by the author of *He Shall Go Out Free: The Lives of Denmark Vesey* (Madison, WI: Madison House, 1999), see Douglas R. Egerton, "Forgetting Denmark Vesey; or, Oliver Stone Meets Richard Wade," *William and Mary Quarterly*, 3rd ser., 59 (Jan. 2002): 143–52. Another book that has sparked much discussion is Edward A. Pearson, ed., *Designs against Charleston: The Trial Record of the Denmark Vesey Slave Conspiracy of 1822* (Chapel Hill: University of North Carolina Press, 1999).

4. William Pinceel (ca. 1783–1825) likely learned to craft tinplate cups and utensils from Swissborn Emanuel Pinceel, who was wounded in defense of Charleston in 1780, later a member of the short-lived Charleston Jacobin Society, and buried in the graveyard of St. Philip's Church in 1797. Although it is unclear whether he was Emanuel's child, slave, or apprentice, William named his own son Emanuel and urged him to carry on the family craft tradition. Charleston County Wills and Misc. Probate Records, 36, Book C (1818–26), 1123–25, Ancestry.com.

5. James Hamilton, *Negro Plot: An Account of the Late Intended Insurrection among a Portion of the Blacks of the City of Charleston* (Boston: Joseph W. Ingraham, 1822), 3–5.

6. Elise R. Pinckney, ed., *Register of St. Philip's Parish Church, Charleston, S.C., 1810 through 1822* (Charleston: National Society of the Colonial Dames of America in the State of South Carolina, 1979), 31, 71, 73, 91. Desverney's name is misspelled in the register as "Duvernic." His children, Rebecca and Peter Simon Antonius, were also christened in St. Philip's Church. Given the singularity of his name, he may well have some connection with French-born gunsmith Pierre Francois Desverney, who belonged, like Emanuel Pinceel, to the Charleston Jacobin Club and until his death in 1800 was well known for his red Phrygian, or Liberty Cap, and reputation as a militant "pillar of liberty" (albeit a slaveholder); the connection could instead be to his brother, Anthony, also a gunsmith. Michael L. Kennedy, "A French Jacobin Club in Charleston, South Carolina, 1792–1795," *SCHM* 91 (Jan. 1990): 9; South Carolina Inventories and Bills of Sale, 1732–1872, Book 3N (1799–1803), p. 150, SCDAH; William Cobbett, *Porcupine's Works: Containing Various Writings and Selections; Exhibiting a Faithful Picture of the United States of America,* vol. 9 (London: Cobbett and Morgan, 1801), 331.

7. Hamilton, *Negro Plot*, 3–5. Not until June 14, when another trusted slave, George Wilson, independently confirmed that a plot was afoot, did the full machinery of the city's militia and justice system move into high gear and sweep in for questioning all those who were suspected or had been accused by others. Egerton, *He Shall Go Out Free,* xix.

8. Hamilton, *Negro Plot*, 4. Pinceel received a cash reward of $1,000 and purchased more slaves. The South Carolina legislature bought Desverney's freedom from the willing Colonel Prioleau and granted him a lifetime pension "for meritorious conduct." *Charleston City Gazette,* 21 Aug. 1822. Desverney set himself up as a drayman and eventually became a slaveowner himself. Larry Koger, *Black Slaveowners: Free Black Slave Masters in South Carolina, 1790–1860* (1985; repr., Jefferson, NC: McFarland, 2011), 177.

9. "Act for the Better Regulation of Free Negroes and Persons of Color," *Acts and Resolutions of the General Assembly of the State of South Carolina Passed in December, 1822* (Columbia: Daniel Faust, 1823), 12; *Acts and Resolutions of the General Assembly of the State of South Carolina, Passed in*

December, 1823 (Columbia: D. and J. M. Faust, 1824), 61; Charleston County Index to Manumission Books, 1801–1848, (A–D), Misc. Records of the Secretary of State, 1729–1825, SCDAH.

10. "Hurricane," *City Gazette*, 30 Sept. 1822; Walter J. Fraser, *Lowcountry Hurricanes: Three Centuries of Storms at Sea and Ashore* (Athens: University of Georgia Press, 2009), 74–79.

11. Bernard E. Powers, *Black Charlestonians: A Social History, 1822–1885* (Fayetteville: University of Arkansas Press, 1994), 51.

12. In John Pierre's youth during the years before the Haitian Revolution, *gens de couleur* could not gather in any numbers, even for weddings or dances. Neither could they emulate Europeans in mode of dress or hairstyles, play European games, sit in white sections of churches, call a white man by his first name, or give one another the dignity of a "'sieur" or "dame." Free people of color could not travel to France, where they might pick up unsettling ideas of liberty, fraternity, or equality. Laura Foner, "The Free People of Color in Louisiana and St. Domingue: A Comparative Portrait of Two Three-Caste Slave Societies," *Journal of Social History* 3 (1970): 428.

13. "Deposition of Liston Barquet."

14. Powers, *Black Charlestonians,* 45–50.

15. Will of Barbara Barquet, 1846, Charleston County Wills and Misc. Probate Records, 44–45 (1845–51), 23–24, Ancestry.com.

16. "Deposition of Liston Barquet." The Naturalization Act of 1790 laid out how immigrants might become US citizens but specifically excluded indentured servants, slaves, free blacks, and Native Americans from consideration.

17. Michael P. Johnson and James L. Roark, eds., *No Chariot Let Down: Charleston's Free People of Color on the Eve of the Civil War* (Chapel Hill: University of North Carolina Press, 1984), 128.

18. "Deposition of Liston Barquet."

19. John R. Clauson, telephone interview by author, 15 Jan. 2016; Huguenot Society of London, *Proceedings of the Huguenot Society of London,* vol. 5 (London, 1898): 393; Chapman J. Milling, "The Acadian and San Domingan French," *Transactions of the Huguenot Society of South Carolina* 62 (1957): 5, 9; Donald J. Hebert, *Acadians in Exile* (Cecelia, LA: Hebert, 1980), 282; Christopher Hodson, *The Acadian Diaspora: An Eighteenth-Century History* (New York: Oxford University Press, 2012), 111–16.

20. "Affiches americanicaines," *Marronage in Saint-Domingue (Haiti)* 25 (19 June 1769): 161. Huguenot Society of London, *Proceedings,* 393; Milling, "Acadian and San Dominguan French," 5, 9; Hebert, *Acadians in Exile,* 282.

21. John R. Clauson, interview by author, 28 Dec. 2015, Newburgh, NY. British forces overcame token resistance from the French troops defending the Môle Saint-Nicolas, established a naval blockade, and occupied the strategic port for five years.

22. For an analysis of the several "waves" of refugees from the Haitian uprising, see Margaret W. Gillikin, "Saint Dominguan Refugees in Charleston, South Carolina, 1791–1822: Assimilation and Accommodation in a Slave Society" (PhD diss., University of South Carolina, 2014), http://scholarcommons.sc.edu/cgi/viewcontent.cgi?article=4049&context=etd.

23. *Negrin's Directory and Almanac for the Year, 1807* (Charleston: J. J. Negrin's, 1807), 58, 104; *City Gazette,* 26 Nov. 1807.

24. John Johnson, rector of St. Philip's Episcopal Church to James H. Holloway, 25 Feb. 1902, Holloway Family Scrapbook, ARC, Lowcountry Digital Library, College of Charleston Libraries, http://lcdl.library.cofc.edu/lcdl/catalog/lcdl:20264; Brown Fellowship Society, *Rules and Regulations*

of the Brown Fellowship Society established at Charleston, S.C. 1 November 1790 (Charleston: J. B. Nixon, 1844), ARC. St. Philip's Church attracted a large number of black Charlestonians—both slave and free—but the overlap between the Brown Fellowship Society and the church should not be overstated. Of the sixty-one society members listed from 1790 to 1816, twenty-four were included in the parish registry of St. Philip's Church, but this does not necessarily mean they were communicants. Margaret Gillikin, "Free People of Color and St. Philip's Protestant Episcopal Church, Charleston South Carolina: 1790–1822," Consortium on the Revolutionary Era, http://www.revolutionaryera.org/documents/CRE-Conference%20Paper-M-Gillikin.pdf. Before the American Revolution, the parish was a vehicle of city government, and its marriage, birth, and death registries carried the authority of civil law. Historically free people belonging to other denominations brought their children to St. Philip's Church to be baptized there as insurance if their status was challenged. Annotations of "free" or "slave" were included in the church's entries. The majority of free blacks were attracted to the nonliturgical Methodist church, which offered them more opportunities to take leadership positions. A. Toomer Porter, *Led-On! Step by Step* (1898; repr., Charleston: Home House, 2010), 196.

25. Brown Fellowship Society, *Rules and Regulations,* 12; James Holloway, letter to editor, *Charleston News and Courier,* 17 Sept. 1905, 8.

26. James Holloway, letter to editor, *Charleston News and Courier,* 17 Sept. 1905, 8. In 1843 a competing group, the Society for Free Blacks of Dark Complexion, was organized. Robert L. Harris Jr., "Charleston's Free Afro-American Elite: The Brown Fellowship Society and the Humane Brotherhood," *South Carolina Historical Magazine* 82, no. 4 (1981): 289–310.

27. James Holloway, "Centennial Fellowship Society, 1790–1905," *Charleston News and Courier,* 17 Sept. 1905, 8; J. P. Barquet (1812–15) and William Pincell (1812–15), *Index to the Compiled Military Service Records of Volunteer Soldiers Who Served during the War of 1812,* M602, roll 11, NARA. For most free blacks, militia service meant heavy "pioneer" labor on public projects (since they were not allowed to carry weapons) or even the dreaded "slave patrol." Powers, *Black Charlestonians,* 58. During the US military's transition away from the traditional fife during the War of 1812, Pinceel and Barquet were among the first buglers ready to sound the alert when danger approached. Charles E. Kinzer, "The Band of Music of the First Battalion of Free Men of Color and the Siege of New Orleans, 1814–1815," *American Music* 10 (Autumn 1992): 35.

28. David Garrigus, *Before Haiti: Race and Citizenship in French Saint-Domingue.* (New York: Palgrave Macmillan, 2006), 220; Robin Blackburn, *The Overthrow of Colonial Slavery, 1776–1848* (New York: Verso, 1988), 177; Holloway, "Centennial Fellowship Society," 8. The analogy with Jews was not strictly metaphorical. Also once considered a race apart, the Jewish peoples of France lived in ghettoes until liberated in 1791 after the French Revolution. That in 1792 to stave off an independence movement, France bestowed citizenship upon certain wealthy classes of free people of color in Saint Domingue—a first by any European nation—furthered hopes that historic barriers were crumbling.] Immanuel Wallerstein, "Citizens All? Citizen's Some! The Making of the Citizen," [2002], Fernand Braudel Center, Binghamton University, http://www2.binghamton.edu/fbc/archive/iwepthomp.htm#N_1.

29. Jehu Hanciles, *Euthanasia of a Mission: African Church Autonomy in a Colonial Context* (Westport, CT: Greenwood, 2002), 96; "A Historical Revelation," *Charleston News and Courier,* n.d., misc. clipping, Holloway Family Scrapbook, ARC, Lowcountry Digital Library, College of Charleston Libraries, http://lcdl.library.cofc.edu/lcdl/catalog/lcdl:20264.

30. Pinckney, *St. Phillip's Register,* 16, 19, 94.

31. Elizabeth Nash Eberson (ca. 1734–81) was first married to Capt. William Eberson, who died in 1766. Their daughter, Susannah Eberson Bonneau, died without children in 1777. *South Carolina Gazette; and Country Journal,* 24 June 1766; Mabel L. Webber, "Death Notices from the *South Carolina and American General Gazette* and its Continuation the *Royal Gazette,* May 1776 to June 1782," *SCHM* 17 (July 1916): 127; "Memorial of Robert Ballingall," 15 Mar. 1784, American Loyalist Claims, 1776–1835, ser. I, class AO 13, piece 48, pp. 254–56, The National Archives of the United Kingdom, Kew, Surrey, Eng., Ancestry.com.

32. William R. Ryan, *The World of Thomas Jeremiah: Charles Town on the Eve of the American Revolution* (New York: Oxford University Press, 2012), 53–54; J. William Harris, *The Hanging of Thomas Jeremiah: A Free Black Man's Encounter with Liberty* (New Haven, CT: Yale University Press, 2009), 116–17.

33. Edward Pattillo, *Carolina Planters on the Alabama Frontier: The Spencer-Robeson-McKenzie Family Papers* (Montgomery, AL: New South Books, 2011), 434; Theodore D. Jervey, "The Hayne Family," *SCHM* 5 (1904): 179–81.

34. Walter B. Edgar, *Partisans and Redcoats: The Southern Conflict That Turned the Tide of the American Revolution* (New York: William Morrow, 2003), 45–46; David K. Wilson, *The Southern Strategy: Britain's Conquest of South Carolina and Georgia* (Columbia: University of South Carolina Press, 2005), 118.

35. Ballingall Memorial, American Loyalist Claims, 254–55; Jim Piecuch, *Three Peoples, One King: Loyalists, Indians, and Slaves in the Revolutionary South, 1775–1782* (Columbia: University of South Carolina Press, 2008), 144, 186-87; Rev. Edward Jenkins, "Memo Book," typescript, 2, SCHS.

36. Ballingall Memorial, American Loyalist Claims, 256–59; Piecuch, *Three Peoples, One King,* 282; Coldham, *American Migrations,* 743-44; "In the Act Passed for Confiscation of Estates, and for Banishing Certain Persons," in "Josiah Smith's Diary, 1780–1781," ed. Mabel L. Weber, *SCHM* 34 (Oct. 1933): 196, 198; Robert Lambert, *South Carolina Loyalists in the American Revolution* (Columbia: University of South Carolina Press, 1987), 120, 241, 247, 280.

37. "In the Act Passed for Confiscation of Estates," 196, 198. That Ballingall, in the course of his duty as a justice of peace and against his personal desire, was connected to the arrest of his wife's cousin, beloved patriot Isaac Hayne, and his execution as a spy no doubt contributed to the harshness of his sentence. Henry Lee, *Memoirs of the War in the Southern Department,* vol. 2 (Philadelphia: Bradford and Inskeep, 1812), 253.

38. Robert Ballingall claimed that he had suffered losses of £2,664 and his daughter losses of £1,700 but was only reimbursed £2,070 by the British government. Ballingall Memorial, American Loyalist Claims, 256–59; Lambert, *South Carolina Loyalists,* 120, 241, 280; Alexander Chesney, *The Journal of Alexander Chesney: A South Carolina Loyalist in the American Revolution and After,* introduction by Wilbur Henry Siebert (Columbus: Ohio State University, 1921), 94.

39. Ballingall Memorial, American Loyalist Claims," 255, 266; Joseph W. Barnwell, "The Evacuation of Charleston by the British in 1782," *SCHM* 11 (Jan. 1910): 9–10, 13, 26; "Passport of Phyllis Thomas, a 'Free Black Woman,' 12 October 1782," *African Nova Scotians in the Age of Slavery and Abolition,* https://novascotia.ca/archives/africanns/archives.asp?ID=22 (original in Commissioner of Public Records, Nova Scotia Archives, RG 1, vol. 170, p. 338, microfilm 15282).

40. Ballingall Memorial, American Loyalist Claims, 254–55.

41. Lambert, *South Carolina Loyalists*, 120, 241, 280; Chesney, *Journal*, 94; Coldham, *American Migrations*, 656–57.

42. Robert Ballingall and Eliza Mary Hunter to Adam Tunno, Bill of Sale 3Q (1800–1803), pp. 319–21, South Carolina Secretary of State, Misc. Records, 1771–1868, FHC 035, microfilm 0022687.

43. Thomas M. Devine, *To the Ends of the Earth: Scotland's Global Diaspora, 1750–2010* (Washington DC: Smithsonian Books, 2011), 25, 26; Barbara L. Bellows, "The Worlds of John Tunno: Scottish Emigrant, Charleston Loyalist, London Merchant, 1746–1819," in *Citizen-Scholar: Essays in Honor of Walter Edgar*, ed. Robert Brinkmeyer Jr. (Columbia: University of South Carolina Press, 2016), 95–96; Brent H. Holcomb, *South Carolina Naturalizations, 1783–1850* (Baltimore: Genealogical Publishing, 1985), 46.

44. "Passport of Phyllis Thomas, a 'Free Black Woman,' 12 October 1782"; Robert Olwell, "Becoming Free: Manumission and the Genesis of a Free Black Community in South Carolina, 1740–90," in *Against the Odds: Free Blacks in the Slave Societies of the Americas*, ed. Jane G. Landers (Portland, OR: Frank Cass, 1996), 13; Bellows, "Worlds of John Tunno," 93–94. In 1794 Eliza Mary eloped with John Hunter, a younger son of a spendthrift laird, in Edinburgh and returned to South Carolina, breaking her father's heart. David Dobson, *Scots in the West Indies, 1707–1857*, vol. 2 (Baltimore: Genealogical Publishing, 2009), 53.

45. Ballingall and Hunter to Tunno, Bill of Sale, 319–21; "Barbary," 20 Aug. 1803, Charleston County Index to Manumission Books, 1800–1804, vol. 1 (A–D), 48, Misc. Records of the Secretary of State, 1729–1825, SCDAH.

46. Nicholas Olsberg, "Archive News," *SCHM* 71 (1970): 137; J. H. Easterby, *History of the St. Andrew's Society of Charleston, South Carolina, 1729–1929* (Charleston: St. Andrew's Society, 1929), 95, 107; Holcomb, *South Carolina Naturalizations*, 46; Nicholas M. Butler, *Votaries of Apollo: The St. Cecilia Society and the Patronage of Concert Music in Charleston, South Carolina, 1766–1820* (Columbia: University of South Carolina Press, 2004), 135. In 1802, when Tunno became a manager of the St. Cecelia, he owned the facility where their concerts were held for a time at the northwest corner of Tradd Street and Bedons Alley, known then as John Williams' Long Room and later as the Carolina Café. Ibid., 309n26.

47. From 1783 to 1787, nearly 9,000 slaves were imported into Charleston (6,000 during the years 1784–85 alone), mostly from Gambia, Martinique, Jamaica, and East Florida. Tunno also reaped large profits during the last period, from 1803 to 1807, when the slave trade was permanently banned by constitutional mandate. Adam's firm, Tunno & Cox, sold 1,446 slaves in six sales and 913 slaves in three sales in collaboration with Thomas's firm, Tunno & Price. James A. Millan, *The Final Victims: The Foreign Slave Trade to North America, 1783 to 1810* (Columbia: University of South Carolina Press, 2012), 49, 124, 128; Devine, *To the Ends of the Earth*, 141; *Charleston Courier*, 5 Jan. 1807; Olsberg, "Archive News," 137.

48. Adam Tunno Estate, Book G (1824–34), p. 556, South Carolina Inventories, Appraisements, and Sales Books, 1783–1846, Estate Inventories and Bills of Sale, 1732–1872, SCDAH.

49. US Census, 1800, South Carolina, Charleston County, Charleston, M32, roll 48, p. 134, frame 206, FHL microfilm 181423, Ancestry.com; Rita Reynolds, "Wealthy Free Women of Color in Charleston, South Carolina, during Slavery" (PhD diss., University of Massachusetts, 2007), 227 (accessed via ProQuest, http://scholarworks.umass.edu/dissertations/AAI3275800); Jonathan H. Poston, *The Buildings of Charleston: A Guide to the City's Architecture* (Columbia: University of

South Carolina Press, 1997), 102–3. Upon Tunno's death, his executors, Thomas Milliken and Arthur F. Rose, recommended that two lots adjacent to his compound and fronting Bedons Alley worth $200 and $800 apiece be conveyed to Margaret Bellingall. RMC, Book E-10 (13 Aug. 1833): 390–91.

50. For different perspectives, see Cynthia Kennedy-Haflett, "'Moral Marriage': A Mixed-Race Relationship in Nineteenth Century Charleston, South Carolina," *SCHM* 97 (July 1996): 206–26; and Amrita Chakrabarti Myers, *Forging Freedom: Black Women & the Pursuit of Liberty in Antebellum Charleston* (Chapel Hill: University of North Carolina Press, 2011), 176–202.

51. Douglas Catteral, "The Worlds of John Rose: A Northeastern Scot's Career in the British Atlantic World, ca. 1740–1800," in *A Global Clan: Scottish Migrant Networks and Identity since the Eighteenth Century,* ed. Angela McCarthy (New York: Tauris Academic Studies, 2006), 68–72; David Hancock, "The Trouble with Networks: Managing the Scots' Early Modern Madeira Trade," *Business History Review* 79 (Autumn 2005): 474–76, 484–85.

52. Mabel L. Webber, "Marriage and Death Notices from the *City Gazette,*" *SCHM* 20 (Jan. 1921): 22; Adam Tunno to Elizabeth Webb, 31 Jan. 1820, 27 Jan. 1826, Langdon Cheves Legal Papers, SCHS; Will of Adam Tunno, ibid.; Bellows, "Worlds of John Tunno," 95–96.

53. William's daughter, Cornelia Tunno, was born about 1810. With a dowry provided by Adam Tunno, she made a good match to James Harrison, son of a well-established family of shoemakers and a member of the Brown Fellowship Society. Tunno also provided two slaves for her to hire out. E. Horace Fitchett, "The Origin and Growth of the Free Negro Population of Charleston, South Carolina," *Journal of Negro History* 26 (Oct. 1941): 432; Will of Adam Tunno, Langdon Cheves III Legal Papers, SCHS. In a sign of either reconciliation or face saving, when Sarah Tunno died in 1855, she was buried next to William in the St. Philips Episcopal Church graveyard.

54. George Howe, *History of the Presbyterian Church in SC,* vol. 2 (Charleston: Walker Evans Cogswell, 1883), 329; Poston, *Buildings of Charleston,* 336–37, 340–42. The two deeds from Tunno to Bellingall for the Archdale Street and Pitt Street properties (found in RMC Books E-8, p. 56 and R-7, p. 128) were executed in 1806 but not recorded until 31 January 1812. The Tunno family clearly had a connection to Joseph Morton since Thomas served as a coexecutor of Morton's estate in 1810, and Adam later continued as a trustee, investing his money for the benefit of his grandchildren and protecting their interests after their 1822 move to Philadelphia. "Inventory of Joseph Morton," Book E (1802–19), p. 9, Inventories and Appraisements Books, 1783–1846, South Carolina Estate Inventories and Bills of Sale, 1732–1872, SCDAH; Cynthia M. Kennedy, *Braided Relations, Entwined Lives: The Women of Charleston's Urban Society* (Bloomington: Indiana University Press, 2005), 180–81.

55. Tunno would later transfer property to Barbara through a similar transaction in which his lawyers, Robert Primerose and Christopher Gadsden Morris, were the sellers of record, with the consideration being "purely nominal" so that he might give a sub-rosa gift to his "illegitimate daughter." *Liston Barquet v. Joseph P. Humphries et al.,* June 1849, Charleston District Chancery Court, SCDAH.

56. RMC, Book A-9 (1818), 46. See also *Ex Parte John Francis Plumeau and Estate of Carolina Plumeau, Re: Liston W. Barquet v. Jno. B. Humphries et al.,* 24 June 1857, Charleston District Equity Court, SCDAH.

57. "Deposition of Liston Barquet"; James Holloway, "Century Fellowship Society: Oldest Colored Organization," *Charleston News and Courier,* 17 Sept. 1905, p. 8, clipping in Holloway Family

Scrapbook, 1811–1964, ARC, Lowcountry Digital Library, College of Charleston Libraries, http:// lcdl.library.cofc.edu/lcdl/catalog/lcdl:20264; C. W. Birnie, "Education of the Negro in Charleston, South Carolina, Prior to the Civil War," *Journal of Negro History* 12 (Jan. 1927): 21, 16; Daniel Alexander Payne, *Recollections of Seventy Years* (Nashville: A.M.E. Sunday School Union, 1888), 14–15, 19–26. Bonneau was the godfather of Liston and John Pierre of Thomas Collins Bonneau. Pinckney, *St. Phillip's Register*, 68.

58. Caleb Bingham, *The Columbian Orator,* ed. David W. Blight (New York: New York University Press, 1998), vi; Payne, *Recollections,* 16, 19; Petition 1138209, Records of the General Assembly, microfilm, ND 207, roll 1, frames 160–67, SCDAH.

59. Madison S. Bell, *Toussaint Louverture: A Biography* (New York: Pantheon Books, 2007), 286–87.

60. Payne, *Recollections,* 57; Johnson and Roark, *Black Masters,* 224.

61. "Deposition of Liston Barquet." Plumeau, described as having a "white" complexion, was probably the son of Saint Domingue–born John Francis Plumeau (1816–47), a trained white accountant and "fancy store" owner on King Street. US Freedman's Bank Records, 1865–71, Item 9016, Ancestry.com; Holcomb, *South Carolina Naturalizations,* 27; James Schenck, *The Directory and Strangers Guide for the City of Charleston* (1830), 122 (accessed via Ancestry.com).

62. TP, "Reminiscences," 57–58.

63. Johnson and Roark, *Black Masters,* 46–47; John Belton O'Neall, comp., *The Negro Law of South Carolina* (Columbia, SC: John G. Bowman, 1848), 11; Brown Fellowship Society, *Rules and Regulations,* 22–23; Edward Holloway to Charles Holloway, 16 Mar. 1857, Holloway Family Scrapbook, ARC, Lowcountry Digital Library, College of Charleston Libraries, http://lcdl.library.cofc .edu/lcdl/catalog/lcdl:20264.

64. The "French Horn" of this period, made of a long tube bent in a circle with a bell at the end, still resembled its original form as a hunting horn. By 1846, one valve had been added to provide variety to its range. When John Pierre Barquet served as an official appraiser of William Pinceel's inventory after his death in 1825, he noted a "French Horn" stored in a box, estimating its value at thirty dollars. Inventory of William Pinceel, v. G (1824–34), p. 74, Inventory and Appraisments Books, 1783–1846, Records of the Charleston District Court of the Ordinary.

65. Joseph H. Barquet, Bounty-Land Warrant Application File (1855-Rejected-303.157), Unindexed Bounty-Land Application Files (1812–55), NARA; Jack Allen Meyer, *South Carolina in the Mexican War: A History of the Palmetto Regiment of Volunteers, 1846–1917* (Columbia: South Carolina Department of Archives and History, 1996), 33–34.

66. Liston W. Barquet Journal, 3 Mar. 1861, collection of John R. Clauson. In a sworn testimony in 1859, Joseph Barquet erred in saying that his deployment was December 1847. Joseph H. Barquet, Bounty-Land Warrant Application File (1855-Rejected-303.157), Unindexed Bounty-Land Application Files (1812–55), NARA.

Chapter Two

1. Thomas Pinckney's father, brother, and nephew were all named Charles Cotesworth Pinckney. To reduce confusion, his father, C. Cotesworth Pinckney (1789–1865), will be referred to in the notes as CCP, his brother C. Cotesworth Jr. (1812–99) as CCP Jr. (and sometimes in the text as "the

Reverend"), and his nephew Charles C. Pinckney (1839–1909), known as Charles or "Charley," as CCP III, although during his life he was often known as "Junior."

2. Walter J. Fraser, *Charleston! Charleston! The History of a Southern City* (Columbia: University of South Carolina Press, 1991), 209; Charles Fraser to Hugh Swinton Legaré, 30 Jan. 1833, quoted in George C. Rogers, "Fraser among His Friends," in *Charles Fraser of Charleston: Essays on the Man, His Art, and His Times*, ed. Martha R. Severns and Charles L. Myrick (Charleston: Carolina Art Association, 1983), 35. Cotesworth and Caroline Pinckney lived on the north corner of Chapel and Elizabeth Streets on what was called the Charleston Neck. James W. Hagy, *Charleston, South Carolina, City Directories for the Years 1816, 1819, 1822, and 1829* (Clearfield, UT: Clearfield, 2009), 156.

3. Legaré quoted in Fraser, *Charleston!*, 206–7; Charles P. Snow, *The Two Cultures* (Cambridge: Cambridge University Press, 1998), 40.

4. From "O God Our Help in Ages Past," written in 1719 by Isaac Watts, who drew its text from Psalm 90.

5. Theodore D. Jervey, *Robert Y. Hayne and His Times* (New York: Macmillan, 1909), 223; CCP Jr., *The Life of General Thomas Pinckney* (New York: Houghton, Mifflin, 1895), 235; *Charleston City Gazette*, 3 Nov. 1828.

6. Frances Leigh Williams, *A Founding Family: The Pinckneys of South Carolina* (New York: Harcourt Brace Jovanovich, 1978), 15, 16, 20–22, 40–41, 78–79, 99, 192, 312, 332–34. Gen. Charles Cotesworth Pinckney (1746–1825) was breveted a brigadier general at the end of the American Revolution (and later commissioned a major general in the South Carolina militia). Thomas rose to the rank of major in that conflict but will be referred to throughout by his preferred title of "general," the rank he attained (major general, actually) when, after his retirement from public life, he returned to national service during the War of 1812.

7. Jeffery Robert Young, *Domesticating Slavery: The Master Class in Georgia and South Carolina, 1670–1837* (Chapel Hill: University of North Carolina Press, 1999), 220.

8. Gen. Thomas Pinckney's first wife, Elizabeth "Betsy" Motte, was a daughter of Rebecca Brewton and Jacob Motte. She died in 1794 while the family was living England. In 1797 he married his widowed sister-in-law, Frances Motte Middleton, who brought the Eldorado plantation lands and a great deal of wealth to their union. William Mumford Baker, *The Life and Labours of the Rev. Daniel Baker, DD: Pastor and Evangelist* (Philadelphia: William S. and Alfred Martien, 1859), 153, 160–61, 164, 166, 167, 176; Mary Esther Huger, *The Recollection of a Happy Childhood by Mary Esther Huger, Daughter of Francis Kinloch of Long House near Pendleton, South Carolina, 1826–1848: With an Introduction by Mary Stevenson* (Pendleton, SC: Foundation for Historic Restoration in Pendleton, 1976), 59.

9. Harriott and Maria Henrietta Pinckney transformed their splendid old family seat on East Bay Street into "nullification headquarters" during the 1832 crisis. In 1831 Maria wrote a cogent defense of states' rights and nullification and later colluded to import a cargo of sugar into Charleston Harbor in "a practical test of the working of the tariff law" to bring the issue to a head. [Maria Henrietta Pinckney], *The Quintessence of Long Speeches, Arranged as a Political Catechism* (Charleston: A. E. Miller, 1830); Mary Elliott to CCP Jr., 3 Jan. 1833, P-M; Caroline Elliott to CCP Jr., 26 Dec. 1832, ibid.; James Louis Petigru to Hugh S. Legaré, 5 Feb. 1833, in James Louis Petigru, *Life, Letters, and Speeches of James Louis Petigru: The Union Man of South Carolina*, ed. James Petigru Carson (Washington, DC: W. H. Lowdermilk, 1920), 118n.

10. CCP Jr., *Life of General Thomas Pinckney*, 230; "Edward Rutledge Pinckney," in *Biographical Directory of the South Carolina Senate, 1776–1985*, by N. Louise Bailey et al., 3 vols. (Columbia: University of South Carolina Press, 1986), 2:1281. Col. Thomas Pinckney represented the Santee District and Cotesworth Pinckney Sr. the Charleston parishes of St. Michael's and St. Philip's. *Journal of the Convention of the People of South Carolina Assembled at Columbia on the 19th November 1832, and Again on the 11th March 1833* (Columbia: A. J. Johnston, 1833), 21.

11. Williams, *Founding Family*, 312–14.

12. Caroline Elliott Pinckney to CCP Jr., 26 Dec. 1832, P-M; James Louis Petigru to Hugh S. Legaré, 5 Feb. 1833, in Petigru, *Life, Letters, and Speeches*, 118n; "Andrew Jackson Denounces Nullification in a Presidential Proclamation," *Digital History*, ID 371, http://www.digitalhistory.uh.edu/disp_textbook.cfm?smtid=3&psid=371.

13. Mary Barnwell Elliott to CCP Jr., 3 Jan. 1833, P-M; Caroline Elliott Pinckney to CCP Jr., 26 Dec. 1832, ibid.

14. James Louis Petigru to William Elliott III, 4 Sept. 1832, in Petigru, *Life, Letters, and Speeches*, 91.

15. CCP Sr. to CCP Jr., 20 May 1834, SCL; CCP Sr., *An Address Delivered in Charleston before the Agricultural Society of South Carolina at the Anniversary Meeting on 18 August 1829* (Charleston: E. A. Miller, 1829), 14, 18, 24.

16. Lacy K. Ford, *Deliver Us from Evil: The Slavery Question in the Old South* (New York: Oxford University Press, 2009), 64, 162, 163, 165.

17. Harriott Pinckney to CCP Jr., 3 Aug. 1832, P-M. Christian conversion was contagious. Five other lawyers in CCP Jr.'s office, including his two cousins, Stephen Elliott Jr. and William H. Barnwell, also became Episcopal priests. In 1840 Elliott became the first bishop of Georgia. When CCP Jr.'s grandmother Phoebe Elliott died in 1855, she was full of gratitude that she left behind one son, one grandson, and three nephews as "preachers of the everlasting gospel." Harriet K. Leiding, *Historic Houses of South Carolina* (Philadelphia: J. B. Lippincott, 1921), 247.

18. Phoebe Elliott to CCP Jr., 7 Sept. 1832, CCP III Papers, SCL; Caroline Elliott to CCP Jr., 26 Dec. 1832, P-M. Watts's poem "Against Quarrelling and Fighting" is from *Divine Songs Attempted in Easy Language for the Use of Children*, which was first published in 1715:

> Let dogs delight to bark and bite / For God hath made them so;
> Let bears and lions growl and fight, / For 'tis their nature too.
> But, children, you should never let / Such angry passions rise;
> Your little hands were never made / To tear each other's eyes.

19. *Charleston Mercury*, 7 Sept. 1832, 2; Rebecca Rutledge to Lt. Edward C. Rutledge, 5 Oct. 1832, Rebecca Rutledge Papers, SCL. Rebecca Motte (Lowndes) Rutledge was the daughter of CCP Sr.'s sister, Elizabeth, and Rep. William Lowndes. She married her cousin Edward Cotesworth Rutledge. Their daughter, born in 1832, was Harriott Horry Rutledge Ravenel, author and wife of St. Julian Ravenel.

20. CCP Sr. to CCP Jr., 18 Dec. 1833, P-M; CCP Sr., *Address Delivered in Charleston before the Agricultural Society of South Carolina*, 14, 18, 24. See also "Review of Mr. Pinckney's Address," *African Repository and Colonial Journal* 5 (Jan. 1830): 328–36. Edward's mother, Frances Motte (Middleton) Pinckney, remained the legal owner of Eldorado but left the Santee where two of her

children had died—Edward in 1832 and Mary in 1822—and moved into the city to live with her sister in the family's King Street home, known as the Miles Brewton House. Richard N. Cote, *Mary's World: Love, War, and Family Ties in Nineteenth-Century Charleston* (Charleston, SC: Corinthian Books, 2001), 22–24.

21. Caroline Pinckney Seabrook to CCP Jr., 18 Nov. 1833, P-M; Freehling, *Prelude to Civil War*, 62; "Achates" [Gen. Thomas Pinckney], *Reflections, Occasioned by the Late Disturbances in Charleston* (Charleston, SC: A. E. Miller, 1822), 6, 10.

22. Ford, *Deliver Us from Evil*, 529; Janet Duitsman Cornelius, *Slave Missions and the Black Church in the Antebellum South* (Columbia: University of South Carolina Press, 1999), 92–93; Albert J. Raboteau, *Slave Religion: The Invisible Institution in the Antebellum South* (New York: Oxford University Press, 2004), 170; "Achates," *Reflections*, 10–12. Seabrook laid out an alternative theory to Christian paternalism in his talk to the Agricultural Society of St. John's Colleton. See *An Essay on the Management of Slaves, and Especially, on their Religious Instruction* (Charleston: Agricultural Society of St. John's Colleton, 1834).

23. Archibald H. Seabrook to CCP Jr., 25 Feb. 1843, P-M.

24. GSS, "Sketches of the South Santee," *American Monthly Magazine*, Oct. 1836, 315–17, 441; David Doar, *A Sketch of the Agricultural Society of St. James, Santee, South Carolina: And an Address on the Traditions and Reminiscences of the Parish Delivered before Society on 4th of July, 1907* (Charleston, SC: Calder-Fladger, 1908), 32.

25. CCP Jr., *Life of General Thomas Pinckney*, 210, 211.

26. Caroline Elliott Pinckney to CCP Jr., 15 Apr. 1833, quoted in Huger, *Recollection of a Happy Childhood*, 62; "Crops along the Coast," *Charleston Daily News*, 5 Sept. 1866, 1.

27. Caroline Elliott Pinckney to [CCP Jr.], 13 Mar. [ca. 1855], P-M.

28. "Thomas Pinckney," in *Men of Mark in South Carolina: Ideals of American Life; A Collection of Biographies of Leading Men of the State*, ed. James C. Hemphill, vol. 1 (Washington, DC: Men of Mark, 1907), 302.

29. The early nineteenth-century dissemination of the Pinckney family history and romantic legend was largely the work of Alexander Garden, who recounted embellished tales of the family's wartime suffering, daring, and self-sacrifice as part of the effort to build a national identity. See *Anecdotes of the American Revolution: Illustrative of the Talents and Virtues of the Heroes and Patriots, Who Acted the Most Conspicuous Parts Therein* (1822; repr., Charleston: A. E. Miller, 1828).

30. Huger, *Recollection of a Happy Childhood*, 56; Caroline Pinckney Seabrook to Charles Edward Leverett, [ca. Mar.–Apr. 1867], in Taylor, Matthews, and Power, *Leverett Letters*, 421–22.

31. "Thomas Pinckney," in *Men of Mark*, 302; John Niven, *John C. Calhoun and the Price of Union* (Baton Rouge: Louisiana State University Press, 1989), 222; Irving Bartlett, *John C. Calhoun* (New York: W. W. Norton, 1992), 70; Caroline Pinckney Seabrook to Charles Edward Leverett, [Mar.–Apr. 1867], in Taylor, Matthews, and Power, *Leverett Letters*, 421–22.

32. Huger, *Recollection of a Happy Childhood*, 59; Phoebe Elliott to William Elliott III, 29 Dec. 1841, Elliott-Gonzales Papers, SHC; *Harry S. Holmes Diary (1895–1903)*, 16 Aug. 1898, microform 51-083, SCHS.

33. Barbara L. Bellows, *A Talent for Living: Josephine Pinckney and the Charleston Literary Tradition* (Baton Rouge: Louisiana State University Press, 2006), 32.

34. "Thomas Pinckney," in *Men of Mark*, 301.

35. CCP Sr. to CCP III, 25 July 1860, CCP III Papers, SCL; Jacob Motte Alston, *Rice Planter*

and Sportsman: The Recollections of J. Motte Alston, 1821–1909, ed. Arney R. Childs (Columbia: University of South Carolina, 1999), 134; John Beaufain Irving, *The South Carolina Jockey Club* (Charleston: Russell and Jones, 1857), 83. For a room-by-room description of the elaborate decorations in Colonel Pinckney's home on Broad Street, see Maurie D. McInnis, *The Politics of Taste in Antebellum Charleston* (Chapel Hill: University of North Carolina Press, 2005), 313–16.

36. CCP Sr. to CCP Jr., 26 Mar. 1834, P-M; "Charles Cotesworth Pinckney [Sr.] and Others, Executors of Thomas Pinckney, vs. Eliza Pinckney, Benjamin Huger, and His Wife Celestine, and Others," in *Reports of Cases at Law and in Equity Argued and Determined in the Court of Appeals in Equity Court and Court of Errors of South Carolina,* vol. 2 (Nov. 1845 to May 1846) (Columbia, SC: A. S. Johnston, 1847), 212–25, 228, 231; Mitchell King to Eliza I. Pinckney, 13 June 1843, Benjamin Huger Family Papers, SCHS.

37. Eliza I. Pinckney to Celestine Pinckney Huger, 24 Feb. 1844, Huger Family Papers, SCHS. As a further insult, Colonel Pinckney left a sizable inheritance to the Hugers' son, Thomas Pinckney, if he publically dropped his father's surname. This he agreed to when he reached his majority, seeing no reason to "martyr" himself over two old men's quarrels. *Ex parte Thomas Pinckney Huger: Petition for Change of Name in the Court of Equity Charleston District, 14 May 1861,* Legal Instruments File, Huger Family Papers, SCHS; Thomas Pinckney Huger to Benjamin and Celestine Huger, 20 Feb. 1861, ibid.

38. CCP Sr. to TP, 29 Feb. 1846, P-M; Lorrie Glover, *Southern Sons: Becoming Men in the New Nation* (Baltimore: Johns Hopkins University Press, 2007), 163. After briefly attending Princeton University, nineteen-year-old Thomas Pinckney Jr. received an army commission through the influence of his uncle, Gen. Charles Cotesworth Pinckney, but soon resigned to read law in the prestigious Charleston firm of DeSaussure and Ford. He does not seem ever to have practiced. His rank of colonel came from militia service during the War of 1812. His younger half-brother, Edward Rutledge Pinckney, was dismissed from West Point, given a reprieve engineered by John C. Calhoun, then asked to leave a second time. Email, Alicia Mauldin, US Military Academy Archives, to Barbara L. Bellows, May 31, 2011, in author's possession; "Edward Rutledge Pinckney," in Bailey et al., *Biographical Directory of the South Carolina Senate,* 2:1281.

39. Paul B. Barringer et al., eds., *University of Virginia: Its History, Influence, Equipment and Characteristics, with Bibliographical Sketches and Portraits of Founders, Benefactors, Officers, and Alumni,* 2 vols. (New York: Lewis, 1904), 1:151, 2:56; CCP Sr. to TP, 29 Feb. 1846, P-M; Joseph W. Barnwell, "Captain Thomas Pinckney," *Confederate Veteran* 24 (Aug. 1916): 344.

40. CCP Sr. to TP, 29 Feb. 1846, P-M; Caroline Elliott Pinckney to TP, 3 Dec. 1846, Pinckney Family Scrapbook, JPP; Mary Elliott Pinckney to TP, 23 Jan. [1847], P-M.

41. CCP Sr. to "My Dear Cousins," 14 Feb. 1840, P-M.

42. CCP Sr. to TP, 29 Feb. 1846, ibid.

43. Galen Reuther, *Flat Rock: The Little Charleston of the Mountains* (Charleston, SC: Arcadia, 2004), 17; Alexia Jones Helsey and George Alexander Jones, *A Guide to Historic Henderson County* (Charleston, SC: History Press, 2007), 25, 130.

44. Mary Elliott Pinckney to Emmie [Emily Elliott], 18 Apr. 1862, Elliott-Gonzales Papers, SHC; Frederic Cople Jaher, *The Urban Establishment: Upper Strata in Boston, New York, Charleston, Chicago, and Los Angeles* (Urbana: University of Illinois Press, 1982), 375; Lester D. Stephens, *Science, Race, and Religion in the American South: John Bachman and the Charleston Circle of Naturalists, 1815-1895* (Chapel Hill: University of North Carolina Press, 2000), 102.

45. Stephens, *Science, Race, and Religion in the American South,* 102–3.

46. Steven M. Stowe, *Doctoring the South: Southern Physicians and Everyday Medicine in the Mid-Nineteenth Century* (Chapel Hill: University of North Carolina Press, 2004), 61.

47. Ibid., 78, 133–34.

48. Daniel J. Ennis, "Samuel Henry Dickson," in *Southern Writers: A New Biographical Dictionary,* ed. Joseph M. Flora and Amber Vogel (Baton Rouge: Louisiana State University Press, 2006), 105.

Chapter Three

1. Joseph H. Barquet, Bounty-Land Warrant Application File (1855-Rejected-303.157), Unindexed Bounty-Land Application Files (1812–55), NARA; Meyer, *South Carolina in the Mexican War,* 33–34; Jack A. Meyer, "Palmetto Regiment," 20 June 2016, *South Carolina Encyclopedia,* University of South Carolina, Institute for Southern Studies, http://www.scencyclopedia.org/sce/entries /palmetto-regiment/ (accessed 30 July 2017).

2. "Exhibit B to Master Laurens Report," *Liston W. Barquet v. Joseph Humphries Barquet et al.,* 28 June 1850, SCDAH. Joseph Pinceel Humphries had not repaid an outstanding debt of $1,300 (plus $300 interest) to Barbara's estate. John Lee, the father-in-law of both Liston and Edod, was on the verge of losing his Mansion House Hotel (the successor to Jehu Jones's Hotel) due to the sagging economy. Rather than sell Barbara's securities, he continued receiving the interest income and placed it and her other liquid assets in "cash on hand," then charged the estate a 10-percent "management fee." Ibid.

3. Julie Winch, *A Gentleman of Color: The Life of James Forten* (New York: Oxford University Press, 2002), 341.

4. Edwin G. Burrows and Mike Wallace, *Gotham: A History of New York City to 1898* (New York: Oxford University Press, 1999), 336.

5. Shane White, "'We Dwell in Safety and Pursue Our Honest Callings': Free Blacks in New York City, 1783–1810," *Journal of American History* 75 (Sept. 1988): 447, 450; Manisha Sinha, *The Slave's Cause: A History of Abolition* (New Haven, CT: Yale University Press, 2016), 321, 324.

6. William S. McFeely, *Frederick Douglass* (New York: W. W. Norton, 1995), 72.

7. Sean Wilentz, *Chants Democratic: New York City and the Rise of the American Working Class* (New York: Oxford University Press, 2004), 113, 118–19, 121, 123.

8. Ibid., 133–34.

9. *Doggett's New York City Directory, for 1849–1850* (New York: John Doggett Jr., 1849), 34; *The New York Mercantile Union Business Directory for 1850-1851, Containing a New Map of New York City and State and a Business Directory* (New York: S. W. Benedict, 1851), 138; Burrows and Wallace, *Gotham,* 701–2, 715, 808–10.

10. Edward Holloway to Charles Holloway, 16 Mar. 1857, Holloway Family Scrapbook, ARC, Lowcountry Digital Library, College of Charleston Libraries, http://lcdl.library.cofc.edu/lcdl/catalog /lcdl:20264; Johnson and Roark, *Black Masters,* 219; Payne, *Recollections,* 167. In 1856 Payne was elected president of Wilberforce University, the only historically black college founded by African Americans.

11. McFeely, *Frederick Douglass,* 149–50; William C. Nell, *The Colored Patriots of the American Revolution with Sketches of Several Distinguished Colored Persons: to Which Is Added a Brief Survey*

of the Condition and Prospects of Colored Americans (Boston: Robert Wallcut, 1855), 255. After settling in Boston, Nell helped establish the Massachusetts General Colored Association, an anti-colonization organization that opposed the movement to resettle American free blacks to Liberia or Sierra Leone.

12. Leslie Harris, *In the Shadow of Slavery: African Americans in New York City, 1626 to 1863* (Chicago: University of Chicago Press, 2002), 6; Sinha, *Slave's Cause,* 332.

13. Will of Barbara Barquet, 1846, Charleston County Wills and Misc. Probate Records, 44-45 (1845–51), 23–24, Ancestry.com.

14. *Liston Barquet v. Joseph Humphries et al.,* filed 17 Feb. 1848, Equity Court, Charleston District, SCDAH; "Exhibit B to Master Laurens Report," *Liston W. Barquet v. Joseph Humphries Barquet et al.,* 28 June 1850, ibid. On the decline of the Mansion House, see Harriet P. Simons and Albert Simons, "The William Burrows House of Charleston," *Winterthur Portfolio* 3 (1967): 189.

15. US Census, 1850, Pennsylvania, Philadelphia, Pine Ward, M432, roll 813, p. 301A, frame 74, Ancestry.com; RMC, I-16: 417; *New York Mercantile Union Business Directory for 1850–51,* 372.

16. Stephen Middleton, *The Black Laws: Race and the Legal Process in Early Ohio* (Athens: Ohio University Press, 2005), 33, 38. See Eric Foner, *Gateway to Freedom: The Hidden History of the Underground Railroad* (New York: W. W. Norton, 2015).

17. Joan D. Hedrick, *Harriet Beecher Stowe: A Life* (New York: Oxford University Press, 1994), 70.

18. US Census, 1850, Ohio, Hamilton County, Cincinnati, 4th Ward, M432, roll 688, p. 364A, frame 190, Ancestry.com; Nikki Marie Taylor, *Frontiers of Freedom: Cincinnati's Black Community, 1802–1868* (Columbus: Ohio University Press, 2005), 186, 200.

19. Ruby W. Jackson and Walter T. McDonald, *Finding Freedom: The Untold Story of Joshua Glover, Runaway Slave* (Madison: Wisconsin Historical Society Press), 22–24.

20. Barquet quoted in "Meeting of the Colored Citizens of Milwaukee," *Wisconsin Free Democrat,* 16 Oct. 1850, ibid.

21. Ibid.

22. "Whitewashing and Wall Coloring," *Milwaukee Daily Sentinel and Gazette,* 21 Mar. 1851, 3; St. Clair Drake and Horace R. Cayton, *Black Metropolis: A Study of Negro Life in a Northern City* (New York: Harcourt Brace, 1945), 45.

23. Elmer Gertz, "The Black Laws of Illinois," *Journal of the Illinois State Historical Society* 6 (1963): 463–65; Owen W. Muelder, *The Underground Railroad in Western Illinois* (Jefferson, NC: McFarland, 2008), 9; Joseph H. Barquet, "Colonization," *Galesburg (IL) Free Democrat,* 1 Feb. 1855.

24. Christopher R. Reed, "African American Life in Antebellum Chicago, 1833–1860," *Journal of the Illinois State Historical Society* 94 (2001–2): 362–63.

25. *Chicago City Directory by Hall and Smith, 1853* (Chicago: Robert Fergus Book and Job, 1854), 25; *Hall's Business Directory of Chicago, 1854–55* (Chicago: Robert Fergus Book and Job, 1855), 47; Christopher R. Reed, *Black Chicago's First Century,* vol. 1 (Columbia: University of Missouri Press, 2005), 28; Donald L. Miller, *City of the Century: The Epic of Chicago and the Making of America* (New York: Simon and Schuster, 1996), 137.

26. Reed, *Black Chicago's First Century,* 28, 71; *Galesburg (IL) Republican,* 13 May 1871, 1.

27. Joseph H. Baynet [*sic,* Barquet] to Frederick Douglass, 5 Apr. 1852, *Frederick Douglass' Paper,* 27 May 1852. On John Jones's life and career, see Charles A. Gliozzo, "John Jones: A Study of a Black Chicagoan," *Illinois Historical Journal* 80 (Autumn 1987): 177–88.

28. Charles Edward Hall, "Chicago in 1843: A Real 'Oldtimer' on the Life of Early Colored

Settlers," *(Springfield) Illinois Record,* 9 July 1898, quoted in Reed, *Black Chicago's First Century,* 53; Miles Mark Fisher, "Negro Churches in Illinois: A Fragmentary History with Emphasis on Chicago," *Journal of the Illinois State Historical Society* 56 (Autumn 1963), 553–54, 557; Reed, "Antebellum Chicago," 98.

29. Nell, *Colored Patriots of the American Revolution,* 246; Reed, "African American Life in Antebellum Chicago," 63; Frederick Douglass, "An Address to the Colored People of the United States of the Colored National Convention," *North Star,* 29 Sept. 1848.

30. "Meeting of Colored Citizens," *Frederick Douglass' Paper,* 8 Jan. 1852; Robert L. Harris Jr., "H. Ford Douglas: Afro-American Anti-Slavery Emigrationist," *Journal of Negro History* 62 (July 1977): 217. Other black abolitionists active in the early Chicago movement were John Jones, Henry O. Wagner, Abram Hall, H. Ford Douglas, James D. Bonner, Henry Bradford, Barney L. Ford, and Alex Smith. Howard H. Bell, "Chicago Negroes in the Reform Movement 1847–1853," *Negro History Bulletin* 7 (Apr. 1958): 153.

31. Joseph H. Baynet [*sic,* Barquet] to Frederick Douglass, 5 Apr. 1852, *Frederick Douglass' Paper,* 27 May 1852.

32. "Meeting of Colored Citizens," *Western Citizen,* 21 Dec. 1852; "Illinois Slave Law," ibid., 1 Mar. 1853.

33. Charles A. Gliozzo, "John Jones and the Black Convention Movement, 1848–1856," *Journal of Black Studies* 3 (Dec. 1972): 228, 234; "Proceedings of the First Convention of the Colored Citizens of the State of Illinois, Convened at the City of Chicago, Thursday, Friday, and Saturday, October 6th, 7th, 8th 1853," in *Proceedings of the Black State Conventions, 1840–1865,* ed. Philip S. Foner and George E. Walker, vol. 2 (Philadelphia: Temple University Press, 1980), 64.

34. Gliozzo, "John Jones and the Black Convention Movement," 228, 231, 232; "An Address of the Colored State Convention to the People of the State of Illinois, October 1853," *Frederick Douglass' Paper,* 28 Oct. 1853; "Proceedings of the First Convention of the Colored Citizens of the State of Illinois," 60, 64.

35. "Proceedings of the First Convention of the Colored Citizens of the State of Illinois," 60, 64–65.

36. Gliozzo, "John Jones and the Black Convention Movement," 235–36.

37. US Census, 1850, Illinois, Knox County, Galesburg, M653, roll 195, p. 1005, frame 660, FHL microfilm 803195, Ancestry.com.

38. Herman R. Muelder, *Fighters for Freedom: The History of Antislavery Activities of Men and Women Associated with Knox College* (New York: Columbia University Press, 1959), 2–3, 88–89; Paul Goodman, "The Manual Labor Movement and the Origins of Abolitionism," *Journal of the Early Republic* 13, no. 3 (Autumn 1993): 364.

39. Matthew Norman, "From an 'Abolition City' to the Color Line: Galesburg, Knox College, and the Legacy of Antislavery Activism," *Journal of Illinois History* 10 (Spring 2007): 7–8. Norman quotes an aphorism that was used to describe the town in the 1850s: "A runaway slave was as safe on the streets of Galesburg as if he were already in a free land." Ibid., 2.

40. "A Rambling Sketch of Some of Our Earlier Colored Residents," *The Home Towner,* a supplement to the *Galesburg (IL) Press,* Jan. 1934 "Struggle and Progress—African Americans in Knox County, Illinois [Knox College]," CARLI Digital Collections, http://collections.carli.illinois.edu /cdm/ref/collection/knx_strug/id/362.

41. Joseph H. Barquet, "Colonization," *Galesburg (IL) Free Democrat,* 1 Feb. 1855, 1. Barquet might be making his own play on the well-known lines from Thomas Campbell's poem *The Plea-*

sure of Hope (part 1), "Distance lends enchantment to the azure view," or he might be referencing an 1852 song satirizing Harriet Beecher Stowe's *Uncle Tom's Cabin:* "De poet says 'tis distance lends enchantment to de view, / And nigga's dat de Yankees trust will find day saying true." The song was reprinted in Clifton W. Tayleure's broadside "The Fugitive's Experience" in the *Baltimore Dispatch:* "Written Expressly for and will be sung by J. K. SEARCH (Old Bob Ridley,) in the rebuff of Uncle Tom's Cabin, at the Maryland Institute, on Monday, Tuesday and Wednesday evenings. [1852]." "The Fugitive's Experience (1852)," UTC Songs, *Uncle Tom's Cabin and American Culture: A Multimedia Archive,* University of Virginia, http://utc.iath.virginia.edu/songs/fugexp.html.

42. "Celebration of the West Indian Emancipation," *Galesburg (IL) Semi-Weekly Democrat,* 1 Aug. 1859.

43. Hermann R. Muelder, *A Hero Home from the War: Among the Black Citizens of Galesburg, Illinois, 1860–1880* (Galesburg, IL: Knox College Library, 1987), 4; James Oakes, *The Radical and the Republican: Frederick Douglass, Abraham Lincoln, and the Triumph of Anti-Slavery Politics* (New York: W. W. Norton and Son, 2007), 96.

44. Joseph F. Evans, "Lincoln at Galesburg—A Sketch Written on the One Hundred and Seventh Anniversary of the Birthday of Abraham Lincoln," *Journal of the Illinois State Historical Society* 8 (Apr. 1915–Jan. 1916), 560–64; Tom Campbell, *Fighting Slavery in Chicago: Abolitionists, the Law of Slavery, and Lincoln* (Chicago: Ampersand, 2008), 135–36.

45. "Haytien Emigration," *Galesburg (IL) Free Democrat,* 11 May 1859.

46. "Emigration to Haiti," *Galesburg (IL) Semi-Weekly Democrat,* 27 Apr. 1859.

47. John E. Baur, "The Presidency of Nicolas Geffrard of Haiti," *Americas* 10 (Apr. 1954): 439–40. In 1860 Barquet declared his net worth as forty dollars. US Census, 1860, Illinois, Knox County, Galesburg, M653, roll 195 p. 1005, frame 660, FHL microfilm 803195, Ancestry.com; US Census, 1910, Iowa, Mahaska County, Oskaloosa Ward, T624, roll 412, p. 8B, FHL microfilm 1374425, ibid.

48. Joseph H. Barquet, Bounty-Land Warrant Application File (1855-Rejected-303.157), Unindexed Bounty-Land Application Files (1812–55), NARA; An Act in Addition to Certain Acts Granting Bounty Land to Certain Officers and Soldiers Who Have Been Engaged in the Military Service of the United States, 3 Mar. 1855 c. 207, 10 Stat. 701. See also US Army, Palmetto Regiment roll books and minutes, 1846–48 (34/216/1–2), SCHS.

49. Campbell, *Fighting Slavery in Chicago,* 116, 138–39; "H. O. Wagoner," in *Men of Mark: Eminent, Progressive and Rising,* by Rev. William J. Simmons (Cleveland: George M. Rewell, 1891), 681–83; Stephen B. Oates, *To Purge This Land with Blood: A Biography of John Brown* (Amherst: University of Massachusetts Press, 1984), 170.

50. *Galesburg (IL) Semi-Weekly Democrat,* 3 Dec. 1859, 3.

51. O. Muelder, *Underground Railroad,* 8–9; *Galesburg (IL) Free Democrat,* 15 June 1860.

52. Thomas Hamilton, editorial, *(New York) Weekly Anglo-African,* 17 Mar. 1860, quoted in *The Black Abolitionist Papers: The United States, 1859–1865,* ed. C. Peter Ripley, vol. 5 (Chapel Hill: University of North Carolina Press, 1992), 73; "Abraham Lincoln: Campaigns and Elections," *The Presidency,* Miller Center, University of Virginia, http://millercenter.org/president/biography/lincoln-campaigns-and-elections.

53. Joseph H. Barquet, "Colonization," *Galesburg (IL) Free Democrat,* 1 Feb. 1855.

54. Martin Delany, "True Patriotism," *North Star,* 2 June 1848; David Blight, *Frederick Douglass' Civil War: Keeping Faith in Jubilee* (Baton Rouge: Louisiana State University Press, 1991), 155.

Chapter Four

1. Mary Elliott Pinckney to Phoebe Elliott, 14 Dec. 1860, in *A Savannah Family, 1830–1901: Papers from the Clermont Huger Lee Collection,* ed. and comp. Anna Habersham Wright Smith (Milledgeville, GA: Boyd, 1999), 65.

2. One elderly Pinckney cousin, Henry Laurens Pinckney, an influential editor of the *Charleston Mercury,* former congressman, and former mayor of the city, still remained very much in the public eye but did not enjoy cordial relations with his cousins. Not only did they not like his politics of appealing to the rising white working classes, but they also still denounced his father, Charles Pinckney, a signer of the Constitution, as "Blackguard Charley" for supporting Thomas Jefferson instead of Gen. C. C. Pinckney in the presidential election of 1800. Marvin R. Zahniser, *Charles Pinckney: Founding Father* (Chapel Hill: University of North Carolina Press, 1967), 226.

3. Mary Elliott Pinckney to Phoebe Elliott, 14 Dec. 1860, in Smith, *Savannah Family,* 65.

4. Barbara L. Bellows, "Of Time and the City: Charleston in 1860," in "Why They Seceded: Understanding the Civil War in South Carolina after 150 Years," special issue, *SCHM* 112 (July–Oct. 2011): 157.

5. Ibid., 158. *Great Expectations* was serialized in *Harper's Weekly* 24 November–29 December 1860.

6. Carrie Pinckney to "Charlie," 17 Jan. 1861, CCP III Papers, SCL; Carrie Pinckney to "Charlie," 8 Jan. 1861, ibid.

7. CCP Sr. to TP, 29 Feb. 1846, P-M.

8. Mary Elliott Pinckney to Phoebe Elliott, 14 Dec. 1860, in Smith, *Savannah Family,* 64; John S. Palmer to James J. Palmer, 16 Nov. 1860, in *A World Turned Upside Down: The Palmers of South Santee, 1818–1881,* ed. Louis Palmer Towles (Columbia: University of South Carolina Press, 1996), 274; TP, "Reminiscences," 1; Mary Elliott Pinckney to Caroline Pinckney Seabrook, [22 Jan. 1861], CCP III Papers, SCL.

9. Caroline Elliott to CCP Jr., 26 Dec. 1832, P-M; William Elliott III to William Elliott IV, 10 Apr. 1861, Elliott-Gonzales Papers, SHC. William Elliott III had long opposed the folly of disunion. Unable to support nullification in 1832, he resigned his seat in the South Carolina Senate. Lawrence S. Rowland, Alexander Moore, George C. Rogers, vol. 1 of *The History of Beaufort County, South Carolina, 1514–1861* (Columbia: University of South Carolina Press, 1996), 334–35.

10. TP to Harriott H. R. Ravenel, 12 Feb. 1857, Harriott Horry Ravenel Papers, SCHS; Smith, *Savannah Family,* 56.

11. CCP Sr. to "Charlie," 25 July 1860, CCP III Papers, SCL.

12. Alston, *Rice Planter and Sportsman,* 44–45; Robert G. Pasquill Jr., *Battery Warren and the Santee Light Artillery* (Columbia, SC: R. L. Bryan, 1987), v; CCP Sr. and Caroline Pinckney to TP, RMC, P-14 (15 Mar. 1860): 125; TP to CCP Jr., 17 Jan. [ca. 1874], P-M. In Flat Rock during the 1860 census, Thomas Pinckney reported a personal estate of $25,000, His father claimed $37,000 in real estate; his personal-estate entry is illegible. US Census, North Carolina, Henderson, M653_901, p. 825, FHL microfilm 803901, Ancestry.com.

13. CCP Jr., *Life of General Thomas Pinckney,* 230.

14. TP, "Reminiscences," 1–2.

15. "Patriotism," *Harper's Weekly,* 2 Mar. 1861, 130.

16. Pasquill, *Battery Warren and the Santee Light Artillery,* 1; TP, "Reminiscences," 1.

17. TP, "Reminiscences," 1-2.; Carrie Pinckney to "Charley" Pinckney, 8 Jan. 1861, CCP III Papers, SCL.

18. TP, "Reminiscences," 1–2; Carrie Pinckney to "Charley" Pinckney, 17 Jan. 1861, CCP III Papers, SCL.

19. TP, "Reminiscences," 1–2; Rod Andrew Jr., *Wade Hampton: Confederate Warrior to Southern Redeemer* (Chapel Hill: University of North Carolina Press, 2008), 69, 77, 79; Wade Hampton to Jefferson Davis, 8 May 1861, *OR,* ser. 4, 1:303; Wade Hampton, "The Hampton Legion," *Charleston Courier,* 3 May 1861; Caroline Elliott to CCP Jr., 26 Dec. 1832, P-M; William Elliott III to William Elliott IV, 10 Apr. 1861, Elliott-Gonzales Papers, SHC.

20. Cotesworth Pinckney Seabrook to Caroline Pinckney Seabrook, 28 May 1862, quoted in *The University Memorial: Biographical Sketches of Alumni of the University of Virginia Who Fell in the Confederate War,* comp. John Lipscomb Johnson (Baltimore: Turnbull Brothers, 1871), 350–51; Mary Elliott Pinckney to Caroline P. Seabrook, 18 Jan. 1861, P-M; GSS, "Sketches of the South Santee," *American Monthly Magazine,* Oct. 1836, 315.

21. CCP Jr. to Charles C. Pinckney, [1861], CCP III Papers, SCL.

22. TP, "Reminiscences," 1–2, 5; TP CSR, RG 109, M267, reel 29, NARA. Serving in the Santee Mounted Riflemen with Captain Pinckney were 1st Lt. Edward F. Allston, 2nd Lt. P. Bacot Allston, Lt. Alexander Watson Cordes, Sgt. George McDuffie Cordes, and Cpl. Philip P. Mazyck.

23. GSS, "Sketches of the South Santee," 315.

24. Doar, *Sketch of the Agricultural Society of St. James,* 22–23; TP, "Reminiscences," 71–72.

25. Mary Elliott Pinckney to Phoebe Elliott, 14 Dec. 1860, in Smith, *Savannah Family,* 65.

26. Mary Elliott Johnstone to Anne Elliott, 13 July [1861], Elliott-Gonzales Papers, SHC; TP, "Reminiscences," 2, 4.

27. Mary Elliott Pinckney to "Charley," 12 Jan. 1861, CCP III Papers, SCL.

28. Mary Elliott Pinckney to Caroline Pinckney Seabrook, [22 Jan. 1861], P-M; Mary Boykin Chesnut, *A Diary from Dixie,* ed. Isabella D. Martin and Myrta Lockett Avary (New York: D. Appleton, 1905), 32 (8 Apr. 1865).

29. John M. Coski, *The Confederate Battle Flag: America's Most Embattled Emblem* (Cambridge, MA: Harvard University Press, 2005), 8. The Confederate Congress's Committee on the Flag and Seal was chaired by Charlestonian William Porcher Miles.

30. TP, "Reminiscences," 4–5. The "Southern Cross" is also known as the Cross of Saint Andrew, who was crucified on an x-shaped cross.

31. William Elliott III to William Elliott IV, 10 Apr. 1861, Elliott-Gonzales Papers, SHC; Gabriel E. Manigault, manuscript autobiography, 320, Manigault Family Papers, SCH.

32. Martin Read, "Cavalry Combat and the Sword: Sword Design, Provision, and Use in the British Cavalry of the Napoleonic Era in Sword Forum International," June 2003, Military Subjects: Organization, Strategy, & Tactics, *The Napoleon Series,* http://www.napoleon-series.org/military /organization/c_swordpoint2.html.

33. TP, "Reminiscences," 2. Pinckney's Santee Mounted Rifles, along with a number of other newly organized independent companies, were consolidated into regiments, assigned a colonel and regular field officers, and uniformly armed with Enfield rifles. Pinckney's unit was increased to 160 men and divided into two companies, with Pinckney as captain of Company A and Louis

Augustus Whilden (1832–64), a neighbor from Christ Church Parish, at the head of Company B. Ibid., 3.

34. Ibid., 2–3; Bennett Baxley, *St. James–Santee Parish Historical Sketches* (St. James–Santee Parish Historical Society, 1985), 16; TP CSR, M267, roll 25, NARA.

35. Doar, *Sketch of the Agricultural Society of St. James*, 22–23; TP, "Reminiscences," 5.

36. Stephen Wise, *Lifeline of the Confederacy: Blockade Running during the Civil War* (Columbia: University of South Carolina Press, 1988), 15, 25; TP, "Reminiscences," 2, 3; Caroline (Elliott) Pinckney to "Charley," 8 Jan. 1861, CCP III Papers, SCL.

37. TP, "Reminiscences," 5.

38. Ibid., 5–6.

39. Pasquill, *Battery Warren and the Santee Light Artillery*, v.

40. Ibid.

41. Chesnut, *Mary Chesnut's Civil War*, ed. C. Vann Woodward (New Haven, CT: Yale University Press, 1981), 273–74 (2 Jan. 1862).

42. TP, "Reminiscences," 4.

43. According to CCP Sr.'s 1862 state property taxes, which he tried unsuccessfully to resubmit in 1863, the properties under his management were Fairfield Plantation, which remained in his brother Colonel Thomas's estate, as well as 929 acres and 103 slaves belonging to the estate of his aunt, Elizabeth B. Lowndes. According to his own estimation, CCP Sr.'s holdings were worth seventeen dollars for each of the 338 acres of best-quality rice land and twenty cents for each of the 1,250 acres of inferior land. At the time sixty-three slaves remained at Eldorado. Captain Pinckney paid taxes on thirty-nine slaves. E[leazer] Waterman to CCP Sr., 29 Apr. 1863, Pinckney Family Papers, 1823–64, Stuart A. Rose Manuscript, Archives, and Rare Book Library, Emory University, Atlanta. On the criticism leveled at officers, such as Captain Pinckney, who remained near home and were able to attend to their own business during the war, see Doar, *Sketch of the Agricultural Society of St. James*, 36–37.

44. Mary Elliott Johnstone to Emmie [Elliott], 26 [Oct. 1862], Elliott-Gonzales Papers, SHC; Mary Elliott Pinckney to Phoebe Elliott, 11 Dec. 1864, in Smith, *Savannah Family*, 237–38; Mary Maxcy Leverett to Milton Leverett, 2 Mar. 1864, *Leverett Letters*, 283–84.

45. TP, "Reminiscences," 83–84.

46. Mary Elliott Johnstone to Harriott Gonzales, 15 Dec. 1861, Elliott-Gonzales Papers, SHC; Mary Elliott Johnstone to Momma [Anne Smith Elliott], 13 July [1861], ibid.

47. TP, "Reminiscences," 11.

48. Ibid., 12–13.

49. Ibid., 13.

50. US Census, 1860, Slave Schedule, North Carolina, Henderson County, Flat Rock, M653, roll 923, p. 10, Ancestry.com; Mary Elliott Johnstone to Anne Elliott, [ca. 1862], Elliott-Gonzales Papers, SHC.

51. Mary Elliott Pinckney to "Emmie," 18 Apr. 1862, Elliott-Gonzales Papers, SHC; Mary Maxcy Leverett to Milton Leverett, 2 Mar. 1864, *Leverett Letters*, 283–84; TP, "Reminiscences," 67–68.

52. TP, "Reminiscences," 14. On December 16, 1862, Pinckney's Saint James Mounted Riflemen merged with the Charleston Light Dragoons and the battalions of Lt. Col. William Stokes and Major Emanuel to form Rutledge's Regiment of Cavalry, which later became the 4th South Carolina Cavalry. Gen. P. G. T. Beauregard to James Seddon, 1 Mar. 1863, in Col. Benjamin H. Rutledge file,

CSR, RG 109, M267, roll 0029, pp. 105–7, NARA, Ancestry.com. On the politics surrounding the consolidation, see W. Eric Emerson, *Sons of Privilege: The Charleston Light Dragoons in the Civil War* (Columbia: University of South Carolina Press, 2005), 44–45, 52–53.

53. Emerson, *Sons of Privilege*, 63, 137.

54. Manigault, manuscript autobiography, 377; "Colonels and Commanding Officers," Fourth South Carolina Cavalry Regiment, http://batsonsm.tripod.com/b/cav4r.html.

55. TP, "Reminiscences," 16.

56. F. K. Middleton to Alicia, 27 Jan. 1862, Harriott Middleton Family Papers, 1866–68, SCHS; Col. Benjamin H. Rutledge to Gen. M. C. Butler, letterpress copybook, 1868-1889, 303, SCHS; Col. William Stokes to Eliza Jane Stokes, 20 Aug. 1863, in William Stokes, *Saddle Soldiers: The Civil War Correspondence of General William Stokes of the 4th South Carolina Cavalry*, ed. Lloyd Halliburton (Orangeburg, SC: Sandlapper, 2010), 102.

57. TP, "Reminiscences," 17.

58. [Circular], Capt. James Lowndes, May 29, 1863, enclosures, *OR*, ser. 1, 1:14.

59. Manigault, manuscript autobiography, 376; "Report of Capt. John F. Lay, June 24, 1863, Headquarters, Dept. SC, Ga, Fla." *OR*, ser. 1, 14:298–306; TP, "Reminiscences," 14.

60. Emerson, *Sons of Privilege*, 55.

61. "Report of Capt. John F. Lay."

62. "Statement of William C. Heyward Respecting the Combahee Raid," [enclosure E], John F. Lay to Thomas Jordan, 24 June 1863, *OR*, ser. 1, 14:301.

63. TP, "Reminiscences," 16.

64. "Report of Capt. John F. Lay"; Finis, "The Raid on Combahee," *Charleston Mercury*, 20 June 1863, 1.

Chapter Five

1. Benjamin A. Quarles, *Frederick Douglass* (New York: Athenaeum, 1968), 251.

2. Gov. John A. Andrew to Francis George Shaw, 30 Jan. 1863, in *BBR*, 8.

3. McFeely, *Frederick Douglass*, 223, 224; Reed, *Black Chicago's First Century*, 144–45; Frederick Douglass, "Men of Color to Arms," *Frederick Douglass Monthly*, 21 Mar. 1863; Robert Steven Levine, *Martin Delany, Frederick Douglass, and the Politics of Representative Identity* (Chapel Hill: University of North Carolina Press, 1997), 300n80.

4. Albert J. Perry, *History of Knox County: Its Cities, Its Towns, Its People* (Chicago: S. J. Clarke, 1912), 620; H. Muelder, *Hero Home from the War*, 2, 5; *Galesburg (IL) Republican*, 20 Dec. 1873.

5. Arthur C. Cole, *The Era of the Civil War, 1848–1870: A Centennial History of Illinois* (Springfield: Illinois Centennial Commission, 1919), 225.

6. *BBR*, ix, 24; Russell Duncan, ed., *Blue-Eyed Child of Fortune: The Civil War Letters of Colonel Robert Gould Shaw* (New York: Avon Books, 1994), 326n1.

7. "Vogelsang Interview," 24 May 1886, Emilio Scrapbook, MHS, microfilm; Albert W. Mann, comp., *A History of the Forty-Fifth Regiment Massachusetts Volunteer Militia* (Boston: W. Spooner, 1908), 60.

8. George M. Frederickson, *The Inner Civil War: Northern Intellectuals and the Crisis of the Union* (Urbana: University of Illinois Press, 1993), 152.

9. Duncan, *Blue-Eyed Child of Fortune,* 24–25; *BBR,* 4, 6.

10. Howard P. Arnold, "Cabot Jackson Russel," in *Harvard Memorial Biographies,* ed. Thomas Wentworth Higginson, vol. 2 (Cambridge, MA: Sever and Francis, 1867), 457, 462; Russel to Father [William C. Russel], 13 Feb. 1863, 23 Mar. 1863, Cabot Jackson Russel Papers, NYPL; Higginson, *Army Life in a Black Regiment* (Boston: Fields, Osgood, 1870), 244.

11. *BBR,* 34; Arnold, "Cabot Jackson Russel," 463. Prior to joining the 54th, Russel served as a sergeant in the 44th Massachusetts Infantry.

12. Capt. Cabot J. Russel to [William C. Russel], 23 Mar. 1863, Russel Papers, NYPL.

13. McFeely, *Frederick Douglass,* 223, 224; [Elizabeth Cabot Putnam], *Memoirs of the War of '61: Colonel Charles Russell Lowell, Friends, and Cousins* (Boston: George H. Ellis, 1920), 35; Col. Robert G. Shaw to Francis G. Shaw, 24 Apr. 1863, in Duncan, *Blue-Eyed Child of Fortune,* 325–26; *BBR,* 25; John W. M. Appleton Letterbook and Journal, transcription by Katherine Dhalle, 4, West Virginia University Library; *The Liberator,* 17 July 1863, clipping in Emilio Scrapbook, MHS, microfilm. Women of the three committees (two black, one white) charged with designing and executing the various banners and flags for the 54th fought so much among themselves that Colonel Shaw nearly disbanded them. Duncan, *Blue-Eyed Child of Fortune,* 39–40.

14. Keith P. Wilson, *The Campfires of Freedom: The Camp Life of Black Soldiers during the Civil War* (Kent, OH: Kent State University Press, 2002), 64.

15. John W. M. Appleton to "Dearest," 29 May 1863, Appleton Letterbook and Journal, 5.

16. Duncan, *Blue-Eyed Child of Fortune,* 41; John W. M. Appleton to "Mary," 5 June 1863, Appleton Letterbook and Journal, 14; *BBR,* 37; *New South,* 6 June 1863; [Circular], Capt. James Lowndes, May 29, 1863, *OR,* ser. 1, 1:14.

17. Duncan, *Blue-Eyed Child of Fortune,* 42; Payne, *Recollections,* 57.

18. *BBR,* 44; *New South,* 6 June 1863; [Circular], Capt. James Lowndes, May 29, 1863.

19. *BBR,* 38.

20. John W. M. Appleton to his wife, 28 June 1863, Appleton Letterbook and Journal, 19; Shaw to Mother, 28 June 1863, in Duncan, *Blue-Eyed Child of Fortune,* 362–63.

21. "The War in Georgia: The Destruction of Darien," *New York Times,* 28 June 1863; Russel to [William C. Russel], 14 June 1863, Russel Papers, NYPL; Arnold, "Cabot Jackson Russel," 463.

22. Russel to William C. Russel, 21, 27 June, 5 July 1863, Russel Papers, NYPL; Arnold, "Cabot Jackson Russel," 463.

23. Robert Gould Shaw to Father, 1 July 1863, in Duncan, *Blue-Eyed Child of Fortune,* 366–67. The Militia Act of 1862 stipulated ten dollars for contraband labor for black militia and thirteen dollars for privates in the army. The 54th was recruited under the authority of the state of Massachusetts with different guidelines, such as equal pay as white soldiers, but in July 1863 Stanton ruled that the regiment's men fell under the same regulations as contraband enlisted by the Federal government.

24. Cabot Russel to William Russel, 5 July 1863, Russel Papers, NYPL; George Stephens, *A Voice of Thunder: A Black Soldier's Civil War,* ed. Donald Yacovone (Urbana: University of Illinois Press, 1998), 285n4; Appleton, Letterbook and Journal, 34; Robert Gould Shaw to Gov. John Andrew, 2 July 1863, quoted in *BBR,* 47–48.

25. *BBR,* 51.

26. Stephen R. Wise, *Gate of Hell: Campaign for Charleston, 1863* (Columbia: University of South Carolina, 1994), 61.

27. Thomas Wentworth Higginson, *Massachusetts in the Army and Navy during the War of 1861–65*, 2 vols. (Boston: Wright and Potter, 1895–96), 1:85; Quincy A. Gillmore, *Engineering and Artillery Operations against the Defences of Charleston Harbor in 1863; Comprising the Descent upon Morris Island, the Demolition of Fort Sumter, the Reduction of Forts Wagner and Gregg* (New York: D. Van Nostand, 1865), 32–33; John Johnson, *The Defense of Charleston Harbor: Including Fort Sumter and the Adjacent Islands, 1863–1865* (Charleston, SC: Walker, Evans, and Cogswell, 1890), 93; James H. Gooding, *On the Altar of Freedom: A Black Soldier's Civil War Letters from the Front*, ed. Virginia M. Adams (Amherst: University of Massachusetts Press, 1999), 51; "Operations against Charleston: The Part Taken by the Seventh Connecticut Regiment," *New York Times*, 10 Aug. 1863.

28. Wise, *Gate of Hell*, 86; Appleton Letterbook and Journal, 46; Gooding, *On the Altar of Freedom*, 36; Cabot J. Russel to [William Russel], 27 June 1863, Russel Papers, NYPL.

29. Wise, *Gate of Hell*, 86–88; Gooding, *On the Altar of Freedom*, 37, 37n6; Edwin S. Redkey, "Brave Black Volunteers: A Profile of the Fifty-Fourth Massachusetts Regiment," in *Hope & Glory: Essays on the Legacy of the 54th Massachusetts Regiment*, ed. Martin H. Blatt, Thomas J. Brown, and Daniel Yacovone (Amherst: University of Massachusetts Press, 2009), 28; Cabot J. Russel to [William C. Russel], 18 July 1863, Russel Papers, NYPL; Appleton Letterbook and Journal, 48–49.

30. Wise, *Gate of Hell*, 89; Stephens, *Voice of Thunder*, 246, 247n2; Gooding, *On the Altar of Freedom*, 38; "Vogelsang Interview," 24 May 1886, Emilio Scrapbook, MHS, microfilm; Appleton Letterbook and Journal, 50. Confederate commander P. T. G. Beauregard, not entirely sure how to process the captured black soldiers, had sent them to the jail in Charleston. One of the city's most distinguished lawyers, Nelson Mitchell, volunteered to defend them and won the black soldiers a reprieve from the threatened penalty of slavery by arguing that the Confederate civilian court had no jurisdiction over them. Wise, *Gate of Hell*, 90.

31. Higginson, *Life in a Black Regiment*, 225–26; Duncan, *Blue-Eyed Child of Fortune*, 384–85.

32. Appleton Letterbook and Journal, 53.

33. Ibid., 48, 54.

34. Duncan, *Blue-Eyed Child of Fortune*, 50; Higginson, *Massachusetts in the Army and Navy*, 1:84; *BBR*, 68.

35. [Putnam], *Memoirs of the War of '61*, 36. Colonel Shaw had apparently written Strong from James Island requesting the transfer to his brigade. "The Late Colonel Shaw," *Harper's Weekly*, 15 Aug. 1863, 525–26.

36. Wise, *Gate of Hell*, 99–101; *BBR*, 72–74.

37. *BBR*, 73–75.

38. Wise, *Gate of Hell*, 101, 115; *BBR*, 78.

39. Wise, *Gate of Hell*, 61.

40. Johnson, *Defense of Charleston Harbor*, 104.

41. Ibid.; "The Attack on Fort Wagner," *Harper's Weekly*, 8 Aug. 1863, 510.

42. Wise, *Gate of Hell*, 95; *BBR*, 77.

43. *BBR*, 78; Gooding, *On the Altar of Freedom*, 51.

44. *BBR*, 77. For various other versions, see Wise, *Gate of Hell*, 269n20.

45. *BBR*, 92, 97.

46. Ibid., 93, 95, 96, 97.

47. Ibid., 92.

48. Gooding, *On the Altar of Freedom,* 38; Gillmore, *Engineering and Artillery Operations,* 40-41; Wise, *Gate of Hell,* 103; Johnson, *Defense of Charleston Harbor,* 105; Arnold, "Cabot Jackson Russel," 465.

49. John W. M. Appleton, "A 54th Massachusetts Captain Describes the Attack on Fort Wagner," [testimony supporting the nomination of Sgt. William H. Carney for the Medal of Honor, 1899], Faces of War, http://facesofthecivilwar.blogspot.com/2012/03/54th-massachusetts-captain -describes.html.

50. Stephens, *Voice of Thunder,* 246, 249n18.

51. "Connecticut 6th Regiment Volunteer Infantry," *Stamford's Civil War: At Home and in the Field,* Stamford Historical Society, http://www.stamfordhistory.org/cw_reghist.htm#l6; Wise, *Gate of Hell,* 106, 116, 126.

52. For a discussion of how Colonel Shaw emerged as one of the most celebrated Union heroes, see Frederickson, *Inner Civil War,* 151–65. For a comparison of the mythology that coalesced around Shaw's memory and the development of the southern "Lost Cause" during the 1890s, see David Blight, "The Shaw Memorial in the Landscape of Civil War Memory," in Blatt, Brown, and Yacovone, *Hope & Glory,* 79–93.

53. George H. Gordon, *A War Diary of Event in the War of the Great Rebellion, 1863–65* (Boston: J. R. Osgood, 1882), 198.

54. Wise, *Gate of Hell,* 17.

55. Rafael de la Cova, *Cuban Confederate Colonel: The Life of Ambrosio Jose Gonzales* (Columbia: University of South Carolina Press, 2003), 210; Gooding, *On the Altar of Freedom,* 47–48; BBR, 106, 108, 125–27; Brooks Report, note 18, "Working Parties, and Health of Troops," OR, ser. 1, 14:326.

56. "Barquet," *(New York) Weekly Anglo-African,* 10 Oct. 1863, quoted in Stephens, *Voice of Thunder,* 269.

57. Ibid.

58. Gooding, *On the Altar of Freedom,* 53–54.

59. BBR, 120–23; Wise, *Gate of Hell,* 197–204.

60. Wise, *Gate of Hell,* 201, 205–7.

61. Gordon, *War Diary,* 198.

62. Wise, *Gate of Hell,* 149, 169–71; W. Chris Phelps, *The Bombardment of Charleston 1863–1865* (Charleston, SC: Pelican, 2002), 28, 31.

63. "Swamp Angel" was published in Herman Melville's first book of poetry, *Battle Pieces and Aspects of the War* (1866).

64. Joseph H. Barquet, Compiled Military Service Records of Volunteer Union Soldiers, U.S. Colored Troops, 54th Massachusetts Infantry, M1898, reel 5, NARA; Donald Yacovone, "The Pay Crisis and the 'Lincoln Despotism,'" in Blatt, Brown, and Yacovone, *Hope & Glory,* 43; Stephens, *Voice of Thunder,* 269; Thomas D. Freeman to "William," 26 Mar. 1864, quoted in *Yankee Correspondence: Civil War Letters between New England Soldiers and the Home Front,* ed. Nina Silber and Mary Beth Sievens (Charlottesville: University Press of Virginia, 1996), 47–48. Freeman speculated that two-thirds of the families of the 54th received no state aid.

65. *New York Tribune,* 8 Sept. 1865, quoted in BBR, xxi.

66. Yacovone, "Pay Crisis," 41; "Barquet," letter to the editor, *(New York) Weekly Anglo-African,* 13 Feb. 1864.

67. K. Wilson, *Campfires of Freedom*, 46–47; *New York Tribune*, 8 Sept. 1865, quoted in *BBR*, xxi.

68. Stephens, *Voice of Thunder*, 59, 76, 269; Gooding, *On the Altar of Freedom*, 82; *(New York) Weekly Anglo-African*, 13 Feb. 1864.

69. Gooding, *On the Altar of Freedom*, 93; Frederic Denison, *Shot and Shell: The Third Rhode Island Heavy Artillery Regiment in the Rebellion, 1861–1865: Camps, Forts, Batteries, Garrisons, Marches, Skirmished, Sieges, Battles, and Victories* (Providence, RI: J. A. and R. A. Reid, 1879), 132–33.

70. Frederick Douglass, *The Life and Times of Frederick Douglass: From 1817–1882, Written by Himself; with an Introduction by the Right Hon. John Bright*, ed. John Lobb (London: Christian Age Office, 1882), 602.

71. Gooding, *On the Altar of Freedom*, 97, 97n9.

72. *BBR*, 144; Gooding, *On the Altar of Freedom*, 98–99.

73. Gooding, *On the Altar of Freedom*, 98, 100.

74. Joseph H. Barquet to "Mr. Prescott," *Galesburg (IL) Free Democrat*, 17 Mar. 1864, typescript, Special Collections and Archives, Seymour Library, Knox College, Galesburg, IL.

75. "A Negro's View of Negro Troops," *Worcester Palladian*, 23 Mar. 1864, 6; "War News," *Massachusetts Spy*, 30 Mar. 1864, 4.

76. *BBR*, 162–63, 166, 168–69, 172–73; William H. Nulty, "The Seymour Decision: An Appraisal of the Olustee Campaign," *Florida Historical Quarterly* 65, no. 3 (Jan. 1987): 298; George F. Baltzell, "Battle of Olustee," *Florida Historical Quarterly* 9, no. 4 (1931): 201; Joseph T. Wilson, *The Black Phalanx: African-American Soldiers in the War for Independence, the War of 1812, and the Civil War* (New York: Da Capo, 1994), 273.

77. *BBR*, 162–63.

78. Yacovone, "Pay Crisis," 44; *BBR*, 177; Thomas D. Freeman to "William," 26 Mar. 1864, quoted in Silber and Sievens, *Yankee Correspondence*, 48.

79. "Congressional Debate Regarding Equalization of African-America Soldiers' Pay," 1864, in *Changes in Law and Society during the Civil War and Reconstruction: A Legal History Documentary Reader*, ed. Christian G. Samito (Carbondale: Southern Illinois University Press, 2009), 148; *BBR*, 192; Yacovone, "Pay Crisis," 43, 47–49.

80. "Folly Island Correspondence," *Christian Recorder*, 21 Aug. 1864; Barquet file, 54th Massachusetts Infantry Regimental Records, RG 94, M1659, frames 26–28, NARA.

81. "Proceedings of a Field Officers Court Martial which Convened at Headquarters 54th Regiment Massachusetts Voluntary Regiment, S.O. #7, 24 August 1864," in Barquet CSR, M1898, NARA. On August 7, 1864, a general order had been issued forbidding soldiers from sharing military information in letters to friends or with the press. After Barquet's court-martial, Cpl. James Henry Gooding of Company C, who had written a regular letter to his hometown newspaper in New Bedford, Massachusetts, over his initials for six months, adopted the pseudonym "Monitor." James Henry Gooding, *On the Alter of Freedom: A Black Soldier's Civil War Letters from the Front*, ed. Virginia M. Adams (Amherst: University of Massachusetts Press, 1991), xxxiv.

82. "Proceedings of a Field Officers Court Martial."

83. *The Liberator*, 26 Aug. 1864, clipping in Emilio Scrapbook, MHS, microfilm.

84. Yacovone, "Pay Crisis," 50, 38; *BBR*, 220–21.

85. "To Our Free Colored Brethren," *The Liberator*, 1 Jan. 1831, 1.

Chapter Six

1. Emerson, *Sons of Privilege*, 63; William Stokes to Eliza Jane Stokes, 20 Mar. 1864, in Stokes, *Saddle Soldiers*, 130.

2. Wise, *Gate of Hell*, 150, 172, 201, 205–7.

3. Emerson, *Sons of Privilege*, 131. The regiment's reputation was further damaged by factual errors in the local press. "Yankee Raid on the Main in the Third District," *Charleston Mercury*, 1 Dec. 1863.

4. Emerson, *Sons of Privilege*, 63.

5. TP, "Reminiscences," 18; Samuel J. Martin, *Southern Hero: Matthew C. Butler: Confederate General, Hampton Red Shirt, and U.S. Senator* (Mechanicsburg, PA: Stackpole Books, 2001), 74.

6. William Stokes to Eliza Jane Stokes, 1 Apr. 1864, in Stokes, *Saddle Soldiers*, 132.

7. Caroline Pinckney Seabrook to Emmie, 19 Apr. 1864, Elliott-Gonzales Papers, SHC.

8. Benjamin H. Rutledge Letterpress Copybook, 1868–89, pp. 304–6, SCHS; Emerson, *Sons of Privilege*, 63–64.

9. TP, "Reminiscences," 9; William Stokes to Eliza Jane Stokes, 20 Mar. 1864, in Stokes, *Saddle Soldiers*, 130.

10. George Elliott to Capt. Thomas Elliott, 9 Feb. 1863, Elliott-Gonzales Papers, SHC.

11. Harriott Middleton to Susan Middleton, 11, 17, 25 May, 1 June 1863, in *Flat Rock of the Old Time: Letters from the Mountains to the Lowcountry, 1837–1939,* ed. Robert B. Cuthbert (Columbia: University of South Carolina Press, 2017), 36–41.

12. Cotesworth Pinckney Seabrook to Caroline Pinckney Seabrook, 30 Apr., 28 May 1862, quoted in Johnson, *University Memorial*, 353, 358; Mary Maxcy Leverett to Milton Leverett, 2 Mar. 1864, in Taylor, Matthews, and Power, *Leverett Letters,* 283–84.

13. TP to Ann Mazyck Lucas, 27 May 1864, Mazyck Family Papers, SCL.

14. Gabriel E. Manigault, manuscript autobiography, 394, Manigault Family Papers, SHC.

15. Emerson, *Sons of Privilege,* 96–97; TP, "Reminiscences," 18–19; Manigault, manuscript autobiography, 395–97.

16. TP, "Reminiscences," 19; Virginius Dabney, *Richmond: The Story of a City* (Charlottesville: University Press of Virginia, 1990), 171–72. John Stewart (1806–85) was born in Rothesay, Scotland, and died at Brook Hill, which had originally been the family home of his wife, Mary Amanda Williamson (1822–1910). Stewart gave open-handed support to the Confederacy by operating a hospital on his estate, entertaining at one time or another all the Confederate high command (except the abstemious Lt. Gen. "Stonewall" Jackson), and housing Robert E. Lee's family at 707 East Franklin, where the general also lived after the war, paying his rent in Confederate dollars. Emory M. Thomas, *Robert E. Lee: A Biography* (New York: W. W. Norton, 1995), 317.

17. TP, "Reminiscences," 19; Emerson, *Sons of Privilege,* 64.

18. Rutledge Letterpress Copybook, 306, SCHS; TP, "Reminiscences," 18–19; Emerson, *Sons of Privilege,* 69.

19. TP, "Reminiscences," 20.

20. Ibid., 19.

21. Ibid., 19–20; Manigault, manuscript autobiography, 398; Lt. Col. William Stokes to Eliza Jane Stokes, 25 May 1864, in Stokes, *Saddle Soldiers,* 138.

22. TP, "Reminiscences," 20.

23. Andrew, *Wade Hampton*, 195; Gordon Rhea, *Cold Harbor: Grant and Lee, May 26–June 3, 1864* (Baton Rouge: Louisiana State University Press, 2002), 66.

24. TP, "Reminiscences," 20.

25. Rhea, *Cold Harbor*, 15.

26. Andrew, *Wade Hampton*, 195.

27. TP, "Reminiscences," 21.

28. Ibid., 20; Rhea, *Cold Harbor*, 67; Emerson, *Sons of Privilege*, 68.

29. TP, "Reminiscences," 20.

30. TP, "Reminiscences," 19, 21.

31. Emerson, *Sons of Privilege*, 76, 47; Rhea, *Cold Harbor*, 67.

32. Emerson, *Sons of Privilege*, 69; Rhea, *Cold Harbor*, 68; Andrew, *Wade Hampton*, 197.

33. Rhea, *Cold Harbor*, 71; Andrew, *Wade Hampton*, 197; Emerson, *Sons of Privilege*, 69–70.

34. TP, "Reminiscences," 21–22.

35. Ibid.

36. Ibid.

37. Ibid.; Rhea, *Cold Harbor*, 82–83.

38. Rhea, *Cold Harbor*, 82–83.

39. Ibid., 87, 89.

40. TP, "Reminiscences," 22–23.

41. Andrew, *Wade Hampton*, 199; TP, "Reminiscences," 22–23; Rhea, *Cold Harbor*, 84.

42. Andrew, *Wade Hampton*, 199; Rhea, *Cold Harbor*, 84.

43. Mary Maxcy Leverett to Milton Leverett, 20 June 1864, in Taylor, Matthews, and Power, *Leverett Letters*, 321–22.

44. TP, "Reminiscences," 30.

45. Andrew, *Wade Hampton*, 199; Rhea, *Cold Harbor*, 85–86; Emerson, *Sons of Privilege*, 74; TP, "Reminiscences," 23, 26.

46. TP, "Reminiscences," 23.

47. Ibid., 23, 26.

48. Ibid., 20, 25, 26; Rhea, *Cold Harbor*, 83.

49. TP, "Reminiscences," 27–29.

50. Ibid., 29.

51. Ibid. Pinckney refers in his memoir to an article that describes her death in prison. See "Shaft in Honor of Confederate Dead Will Commemorate Barbara Ann Duravan," *New York Herald*, 5 Sept. 1909.

52. TP, "Reminiscences," 30–31. For a copy of Pinckney's note to his father, see Pinckney Family Scrapbook, JPP.

53. TP, "Reminiscences," 31.

54. Mary Elliott Pinckney to [Ann Mazyck] Lucas, June 13, [1864], Pinckney Family Scrapbook, JPP.

55. Mary Elliott Pinckney to Phoebe Elliott, 11 Dec. 1864, in Smith, *Savannah Family*, 237–38.

56. Charles W. Sanders, *While in the Hands of the Enemy: Military Prisons of the Civil War* (Baton Rouge: Louisiana State University Press, 2005), 116–17. Their first cousin Maj. Gen. Benjamin K. Huger had been involved in working out the initial prisoner-of-war protocols in 1862 with Union brigadier general John Wool. The Huger-Wool bargain, based upon the US agreement with the

British during the War of 1812, stipulated that prisoners of war were to be kept out of harm's way, be protected from the elements, be fed rations comparable to their captors, and not be expected to perform camp labor.

57. TP, "Reminiscences," 32–33.

58. Emerson, *Sons of Privilege*, 39; Sanders, *While in the Hands of the Enemy*, 33–34; Reid Mitchell, "'Our Prison System, Supposing We Had Any': The Confederate and Union Prison Systems," in *On the Road to Total War: The American Civil War and the German Wars of Unification, 1861–1871*, ed. Stieg Forster and Jorg Nagler (Cambridge, UK: Cambridge University Press, 1999), 568.

59. Christopher G. Memminger to Edward G. Palmer, 27 July 1863, in Towles, *World Turned Upside Down*, 371. Palmer disagreed with Memminger's reply: "This state does not consider them [free blacks] citizens or else her laws prohibiting their emigration into this state would be unnecessary." Edward Palmer to John Palmer, n.d., ibid.

60. Sanders, *While in the Hands of the Enemy*, 217–18, 257 (Grant quotation).

61. Ibid., 176, 245.

62. TP, "Reminiscences," 33–36.

63. Ibid., 33; Sanders, *While in the Hands of the Enemy*, 174–76, 237, 242.

64. TP, "Reminiscences," 37.

65. Ibid., 37–38.

66. Ibid., 38.

67. Ibid., 39; Jack E. Schairer, *Lee's Bold Plan for Point Lookout: The Rescue of Confederate Prisoners that Never Happened* (Jefferson, NC: McFarland, 2008), 97.

68. TP, "Reminiscences," 40; Sanders, *While in the Hands of the Enemy*, 98, 181.

69. John Sterling Swann, "Prison Life at Fort Delaware," 26 June 1876, transcription by Neil Allen Bristow, 1998, (updated 3 June 2005), Rootsweb, http://freepages.genealogy.rootsweb.ancestry.com/~greenwolf/coombs/swann-js.htm (original in Misc. Manuscripts, MS Division, LC); Sanders, *While in the Hands of the Enemy*, 245.

70. Sanders, *While in the Hands of the Enemy*, 245, TP, "Reminiscences," 33.

71. Sidney Lanier, *Tiger-Lilies: A Novel* (New York: Hurd and Houghton, 1867), 198–200.

72. TP, "Reminiscences," 33.

73. Ibid., 42.

74. Ibid., 34–36. "Miss L. Steuart of Baltimore" was likely a relative of George Hume Steuart (1828–1903), who had been at Fort Delaware and was transferred to Morris Island.

75. Lanier, *Tiger-Lilies*, 198–99; TP, "Reminiscences," 41.

76. Sanders, *While in the Hands of the Enemy*, 181; Lanier, *Tiger-Lilies*, 199; Swann, "Prison Life at Fort Delaware."

77. TP, "Reminiscences," 44.

78. Ibid., 44.

79. Ibid., 44–45; Abram Fulkerson, "The Prison Experience of a Confederate Soldier," *Southern Historical Papers* 22 (Jan.–Dec. 1864): 133. During September 1864, typhoid killed 167 prisoners at Fort Delaware; in October smallpox, pneumonia, and dysentery claimed 377 more.

80. TP, "Reminiscences," 46; TP to CCP Sr., 20 Aug. 1864, Pinckney Family Papers, 1765–1915, SCHS. Pinckney informed his father that he was going to Hilton Head. Joselyn, *Immortal Captives*, 67.

81. Joselyn, *Immortal Captives*, 64; TP, "Reminiscences," 46; "Prison Life of Rev. Geo. W. Nel-

son," *Southern Historical Society Papers* 1 (Mar.–Apr. 1876): 243–56, available online at https://en.wikisource.org/wiki/Southern_Historical_Society_Papers/Volume_01/April/Prison_Life_of_Rev._Geo._W._Nelson; Baxley, *St. James-Santee Parish*, 16.

82. TP, "Reminiscences," 46.

83. TP, "Reminiscences," 47; Edmund M. Blunt, *The American Coast Pilot; Containing the Courses and Distances . . . together with a Tide Table* (New York, 1822), 228, 233–34.

84. TP, "Reminiscences," 47.

85. Ibid.

86. *Charleston Mercury,* 2 Sept. 1864, 2.

Chapter Seven

1. Joslyn, *Immortal Captives,* 76.

2. TP, "Reminiscences," 50; Joslyn, *Immortal Captives,* 88; *BBR,* 222.

3. *BBR,* 222–23; Joslyn, *Immortal Captives,* 79.

4. *BBR,* 222–23.

5. TP, "Reminiscences," 50.

6. *BBR,* 222; Joslyn, *Immortal Captives,* 88.

7. TP, "Reminiscences," 50–51; "The New Rebel Prison on Morris Island," *Port Royal (SC) Palmetto Herald,* 6 Oct. 1864, 6; Joslyn, *Immortal Captives,* 85, 88.

8. TP, "Reminiscences," 50; Joslyn, *Immortal Captives,* 88; Wise, *Gate of Hell,* 120, 218.

9. *BBR,* 134, 162–63, 181, 220, 222–24. Companies A, D, E, G, H, and K composed the prison detail. Federal officials claimed that the Confederates had left Union officers on the lower Charleston peninsula when they had begun their siege operations.

10. *BBR,* 223–24.

11. Charles E. Briggs to Mother [Caroline Morton Briggs], 21 Sept. 1864, Charles E. Briggs Letters, 1862–69, Massachusetts Historical Society, Boston.

12. TP, "Reminiscences," 51–53; "Co. H. meals," Oct. 1863, John W. M. Appleton Letterbook and Journal, transcription by Katherine Dhalle, n.p., West Virginia University Library.

13. Murray, *Immortal Six Hundred,* 104.

14. TP, "Reminiscences," 52–53.

15. Ibid.

16. *BBR,* xi, 226–27; "Confederate Prisoners under Fire on Morris Island," *Southern Historical Society Papers* 17 (Jan.–Dec. 1889): 37; Edmund Ruffin, *The Diary of Edmund Ruffin: Toward Independence, October 1856–April 1861,* ed. William K. Scarborough, vol. 1 (Baton Rouge: Louisiana State University Press, 1972), 586.

17. For a summary of the events surrounding the burial of Shaw, see Wise, *Gate of Hell,* 115–18.

18. *BBR,* 102; Drew Gilpin Faust, *This Republic of Suffering: Death and the American Civil War* (New York: Vintage Books, 2008), 75–76.

19. *BBR,* 227–28.

20. Ibid.; Hallowell to Saxton, 7 Oct. 1864, Emilio Scrapbook, MHS, microfilm; TP, "Reminiscences," 57. Eventually $2,832 was contributed by the 54th and about $1,500 contributed by the freedmen in the district. Realizing that at some point the army would leave and South Carolinians

would regain control of Morris Island, organizers of the memorial determined that a physical monument might be desecrated.

21. Joslyn, *Immortal Captives*, 89; Gordon, *War Diary*, 277.

22. TP, "Reminiscences," 53. Shards from Confederate mortar rounds would injure two prisoners.

23. Ibid., 51, 57.

24. Ibid., 51; *Watertown (MA) Enterprise*, 5 June 1891, 14 Aug. 1896 (Lennox obituary); Appleton Letterbook and Journal, 97; "Imprisoned under Fire: Six Hundred Gallant Confederate Officers on Morris Island, S.C. in Reach of Confederate Guns," *Southern Historical Society Papers* 25 (Jan.–Dec. 1897): 371.

25. TP, "Reminiscences," 53–54.

26. "George Parsons Elliott," in Smith, *Savannah Family*, 216.

27. TP, "Reminiscences," 56; Appleton Letterbook and Journal, 97; Lenox obituary, *Watertown (MA) Enterprise*, 14 Aug. 1896.

28. TP, "Reminiscences," 57–58.

29. Quoted in Manisha Sinha, "Black Abolitionism: The Assault on Southern Slavery and the Struggle for Racial Equality," in *Slavery in New York*, ed. Ira Berlin and Leslie M. Harris (New York: New Press, 2005), 260.

30. TP, "Reminiscences," 57–59.

31. Quoted in Powers, *Black Charlestonians*, 59.

32. James Baldwin, *Nobody Knows My Name: More Notes of a Native Son* (New York: Vintage, 1993), 4, 5; Wise, *Gate of Hell*, 2.

33. TP, "Reminiscences," 57–58.

34. Ibid., 57–58.

35. Ibid., 58; Gordon, *War Diary*, 277.

36. TP, "Reminiscences," 63–64.

37. "Relief for Our Prisoners on Morris Island," *Charleston Mercury*, 26 Sept. 1864; "Our Prisoners on Morris Island," ibid., 28 Sept. 1864; TP, "Reminiscences," 50, 63.

38. TP, "Reminiscences," 57–58.

39. Joslyn, *Immortal Captives*, 131; BBR, 231; TP, "Reminiscences," 59.

40. TP, "Reminiscences," 62–63; Joslyn, *Immortal Captives*, 137.

41. Joslyn, *Immortal Captives*, 137.

42. Fort Pulaski, named for Revolutionary War hero Casimir Pulaski, is located on Cockspur Island, about fifteen miles east of Savannah. The 1st South Carolina Volunteer Regiment (African Descent) was formed there in 1862.

43. Joslyn, *Immortal Captives*, 141; TP, "Reminiscences," 62.

44. *The Union Army: A History of Military Affairs in the Loyal States, 1861–1865*, vol. 2 (Madison, WI: Federal, 1908), 262; Helen P. Trimpi, *Crimson Confederates: Harvard Men Who Fought for the South* (Knoxville: University of Tennessee Press, 2009), 177; Joslyn, *Immortal Captives*, 131, 100, 142–43; Murray, *Immortal Six Hundred*, 58; TP, "Reminiscences," 62–63.

45. TP, "Reminiscences," 62–63; Joslyn, *Immortal Captives*, 142–43.

46. TP, "Reminiscences," 65–66.

47. "Andersonville Prison Testimony of Dr. Isaiah W. White," *Southern Historical Society Papers* 17 (Jan.–Dec. 1889): 383–88; "Exchange of Prisoners: The Latest from Colonel Mulford's Fleet 5,500 Union Prisoners Thus Far Received," *New York Times*, 2 Dec. 1864.

48. Murray, *Immortal Six Hundred,* 233; TP, "Reminiscences," 66.

49. TP, "Reminiscences," 66; *Charleston Daily Courier,* 16 Dec. 1864, 1.

50. TP, "Reminiscences," 66–67.

51. CCP Jr., *Nebuchadnezzar's Fault and Fall: A Sermon Preached at Grace Church, Charleston, S.C., on the 17th of February, 1861* (Charleston: A. J. Burke, 1861); TP, "Reminiscences," 66–67, 69.

52. TP, "Reminiscences," 66–67.

53. Ibid.; *Charleston Daily Courier,* 16 Dec. 1864, 1.

54. Andrew, *Wade Hampton,* 255–56.

55. TP, "Reminiscences," 67.

56. William P. Baldwin, *Inland Passages: Making a Lowcountry Life* (Charleston: History Press, 2004), 132–33, 135; TP, "Reminiscences," 68.

57. TP, "Reminiscences," 68.

58. "Sister" [Caroline Pinckney Seabrook] to Ria [Maria Pinckney], 4 Jan. 1864 [1865], P-M.

59. Ibid.

Chapter Eight

1. *BBR,* 234–36.

2. Ibid. In addition to the 54th Massachusetts, the brigade included eight companies of the 55th Massachusetts and the 26th and 102nd USCT, units that had originated in New York and in Michigan. Brig. Gen. Edward E. Potter's brigade also included the 56th, 127th, 144th, and 157th New York; the 25th Ohio; and the 32nd and 35th USCT.

3. *BBR,* 237–38.

4. Ibid., 237–41; de la Cova, *Cuban Confederate Colonel,* 236.

5. *BBR,* 244–58; "General Foster's Expedition—Casualties in Massachusetts Regiments," *The Liberator,* 16 Dec. 1864.

6. *Savannah Republican,* 3 Dec. 1864, quoted in "The Battle of Honey Hill, S.C.: Rebel Account of the Action," *The Liberator,* 30 Dec. 1864; *BBR,* 245, 250–53.

7. *BBR,* 250; Charles Soule, "Battle of Honey Hill," in *The New Annals of the Civil War,* ed. Peter Cozzens and Robert I. Girardi (Mechanicsville, PA: Stackpole Books, 2004); 460. The best account of the Battle of Honey Hill is found in Stephen R. Wise and Lawrence S. Rowland, with Gerhard Spieler, *Rebellion, Reconstruction, and Redemption, 1861–1893:* vol. 2 of *The History of Beaufort County, South Carolina* (Columbia: University of South Carolina Press, 2015), 301–39.

8. *BBR,* 254, 257–59.

9. Ibid., 265–66.

10. Ibid., 265–66, 269.

11. Ibid., 269–70.

12. Ibid., 272.

13. Ibid., 278; de la Cova, *Cuban Confederate Colonel,* 247.

14. Suzanne Cameron Linden, *Historical Atlas of Rice Plantations of Ace River Basin* (Columbia: SCDAH, 1995), 31–33.

15. *BBR,* 278–79, 280.

16. Ibid., 283–84; *Harper's Weekly,* 18 Mar. 1865, 172. The first black troops into Charleston were Companies B and F of the 54th Massachusetts and the 102nd USCT.

17. Robert J. Zalimas, "A Disturbance in the City: Black and White Soldiers in Postwar Charleston," in *Black Soldiers in Blue: African-American Troops in the Civil War Era,* ed. John David Smith (Chapel Hill: University of North Carolina Press, 2002), 361–62.

18. BBR, 284; de la Cova, *Cuban Confederate Colonel,* 247.

19. BBR, 282.

20. Ibid., 284; John H. W. N. Collins, "Letter from the 54th U.S.C.T," *Christian Recorder,* 15 Apr. 1865.

21. BBR, 284.

22. OR, 47(2):641.

23. BBR, 285, 287.

24. John David Smith, "Field Order No. 15," in *Encyclopedia of the Reconstruction Era,* ed. Richard Zuczek, vol. 1 (Westport, CT: Greenwood, 2006), 248–49.

25. John Snider Cooper Diary, n.d., quoted in Leonne M. Hudson, "The Role of the 54th Massachusetts Regiment in Potter's Raid," *Historical Journal of Massachusetts* 29, no. 2 (Summer 2002), n.p., n29, *HJM* online archive, Westfield State University, http://www.wsc.mass.edu/mhj /pdfs/Hudson%20Summer%202002%20complete.pdf.

26. "From the Diary of Harriet R. Palmer," 8 Apr. 1865, in Towles, *World Turned Upside Down,* 456–58.

27. "Partial Letter of Alice Gaillard Palmer," Apr. 1865, ibid., 455–56.

28. John H. W. Collins, "A Soldiers Letter," *Christian Recorder,* 30 Apr. 1865.

29. J. Wilson, *Black Phalanx,* 278; BBR, 303.

30. BBR, 306; Johnson and Roark, *Black Masters,* 270–73, 310.

31. BBR, 308.

32. Ibid., 310–12.

33. De la Cova, *Cuban Confederate Colonel,* 225; RMC, Deed Book Q, 14:5 (2 Aug. 1860), 14:35 (Satisfied, 19 June 1868); Koger, *Black Slaveowners,* 202–3.

34. Collins, "Letter from the 54th U.S.C.T."

35. William C. Nell to Charles W. Lennox, 20 July 1865, quoted in "Colored Soldiers No Longer Wanted to Guard Rebels," *The Liberator,* 25 Aug. 1865.

36. Jacob Christy to "Dear Sister," Apr. 1865, in Robert Ewell Greene, *Swamp Angels: A Biographical Study of the 54th Massachusetts Regiment: The True Facts about the Black Defenders of the Civil War* (Washington, DC: BoMark/Greene, 1990), 311; BBR, 378.

37. "Ill-treatment of Colored People in Charleston," *Christian Recorder,* 10 June 1865; Zalimas, "Disturbance in the City," 372–75.

38. Zalimas, "Disturbance in the City," 376.

39. Ibid., 363; BBR, 314, 317. Lt. Gen. U. S. Grant disagreed with Gillmore's plan, arguing that, with more than 11,000 freedmen newly enlisted by the summer of 1865, the policing force should all be black and the 3,000 white soldiers so long in service returned home.

40. BBR, 317; Barquet CSR, reel 5, NARA.

41. BBR, 319–20.

Chapter Nine

1. TP, "Reminiscences," 30, 69.

2. Ibid., 70.

3. TP, "Reminiscences," 70–72; Andrew, *Wade Hampton*, 279–80.

4. TP, "Reminiscences," 72.

5. Ibid., 77; Mary Elliott Johnstone to Anne Elliott, 13 July [1861], Elliott-Gonzales Papers, SHC; Ralph Emms Elliott to Anne Elliott, 15 June 1864, ibid.

6. TP, "Reminiscences," 70–72.

7. Ibid., 72–73; Emerson, *Sons of Privilege*, 102.

8. TP, "Reminiscences," 72–73.

9. Ibid., 70, 73, 74; *(Augusta, GA) Daily Constitutionalist*, 18 Mar. 1865, 3; *Charleston Courier*, 16 Mar. 1865, 2.

10. TP, "Reminiscences," 75–76.

11. Ibid.

12. Ibid.

13. Andrew, *Wade Hampton*, 296–98, 300; Stokes, *Saddle Soldiers*, 199.

14. TP, "Reminiscences," 75–76; Joseph W. Barnwell, "Captain Thomas Pinckney," *Confederate Veteran* 24 (Aug. 1916): 343–44. Pinckney's official records indicate that he was included in the April 26 surrender at Durham Station and was exchanged with the sick and wounded. TP CSR, RG 109, M267, roll 381, NARA.

15. TP, "Reminiscences," 76–77.

16. Caroline Pinckney Seabrook to Mary Maxcy Leverett, 1 July 1865, in Taylor, Matthews, and Power, *Leverett Letters*, 397.

17. Caroline Pinckney Seabrook to "Catherine," 3 Oct. 1865, Elliott-Gonzales Papers, SHC.

18. TP, "Reminiscences," 69; Will of CCP Sr., Pinckney Family Scrapbook, JPP.

19. Caroline Pinckney Seabrook to M. M. Leverett, 1 July 1865, in Taylor, Matthews, and Power, *Leverett Letters*, 377; Caroline Pinckney Seabrook to Catherine, 3 Oct. 1865, Elliott-Gonzales Papers, SHC.

20. Caroline Pinckney Seabrook to M. M. Leverett, 1 July 1865, in Taylor, Matthews, and Power, *Leverett Letters*, 399; Carrie Pinckney to Mary Elliott Pinckney, 8 May 1865, P-M.

21. CCP Jr., *New Year's Sermon Delivered at Grace Church, Charleston, SC, January 7, 1866* (Charleston: Courier Job Press, 1866), 4, 11, 12, 14, 16.

22. TP, "Reminiscences," 82.

23. CPS to Harriott Horry Rutledge Ravenel, 28 Sept. 1865, Harriott Horry Rutledge Ravenel Papers, SCHS.

24. TP, "Reminiscences," 82.

25. Ibid., 76–78.

26. Ibid., 82–83; Caroline P. Seabrook to Harriott Horry Rutledge Ravenel, 28 Sept. 1865, Harriott Horry Rutledge Ravenel Papers, SCHS.

27. "Henry William Ravenel, 1814–1887: Private Journal 1863–1865," 99 (17 May 1865), *Henry William Ravenel—Plants & Planter*, Center for Digital Humanities, SCL, http://ravenel.cdh.sc.edu/viewer/transcript/Carolina/5101.

28. "Crops along the Coast," *Charleston Daily News*, 5 Sept. 1866, 1.

29. TP to the CCP Jr., 11 Dec. 1865, P-M. James Shoolbred, a prosperous Scottish merchant from Auchtermuchty, came to Charleston as the first British consul in 1790, just two years before Gen. Thomas Pinckney left the city to become the first American minister to the Court of Saint James. He married a Pinckney cousin, Mary Gibbes "Polly" Middleton (1785–1808), who had inherited Woodville. His son, Dr. James Gibbes Shoolbred, had died in 1860, leaving the plantation and its 103 slaves to his wife and children. Suzanne Cameron Linder and Marta Leslie Thacker, *Historical Atlas of the Rice Plantations of Georgetown County and the Santee River* (Columbia: SCDAH, 2001), 746; Will of Dr. James Gibbes Shoolbred, Charleston County Wills and Misc. Probate Records, 48–49 (1856–62), 618–19, Ancestry.com.

30. TP, "Reminiscences," 83.

31. Ibid.

32. TP to the Rev. C. Cotesworth Pinckney Jr., 11 Dec. 1865, P-M.

33. TP, "Reminiscences," 83–84.

34. Ibid., 83–84.

35. Ibid., 84.

36. CCP Jr., *Life of General Thomas Pinckney*, 230.

37. TP, "Reminiscences," 87.

38. Ibid., 84.

39. Ibid., 84–85.

40. Smith, "Field Order No. 15," 248–49; TP, "Reminiscences," 85; TP to Honorable James L. Orr, 8 Jan. 1863, TP CSR, M267, roll 381, NARA.

41. TP, "Reminiscences," 85; Scott Strickland, "Traditional Culture and Moral Economy: Social and Economic Change in the South Carolina Lowcountry, 1865–1910," in *The Countryside in the Age of Capitalist Transformation: Essays in the Social History of Rural America*, ed. Stephen Hahn and Jonathan Prude (Chapel Hill: University of North Carolina Press, 1985), 148.

42. US Census, 1860, Slave Schedules, South Carolina, Charleston County, St. James Santee Parish, M653, roll 1232, pp. 23–24, 39–40, Ancestry.com.

43. Phillip D. Morgan, "Work and Culture: The Task System and the World of Lowcountry Blacks, 1700 to 1880," *William and Mary Quarterly*, 3rd ser., 39 (Oct. 1982): 566, 578, 595.

44. Ibid., 566, 573, 592–93; Julie Saville, *The Work of Reconstruction: From Slave to Wage Laborer in South Carolina, 1860–1870* (New York: Cambridge University Press, 1996), 24.

45. Saville, *Work of Reconstruction*, 40; TP to CCP Jr., 11 Dec. 1865, P-M; Lt. Col. A. J. Willard to Capt. George W. Hooker, 7 Nov. 1865, Registered Letters Received P-Y (May–Dec. 1865), Records of the Assistant Commissioner of the State of South Carolina, Bureau of Refugees, Freedmen, and Abandoned Lands, 1865–70, M869, reel 8, NARA.

46. TP, "Reminiscences," 84, 86; Stephen Hahn, "'Extravagant Expectations' of Freedom: Rumour, Political Struggle, and the Christmas Insurrection Scare of 1865 in the American South," *Past and Present* 157, no. 1 (Nov. 1997): 122–23; W. E. Towne to Gen. R. Saxton, 17 Aug. 1865, Registered Letters Received, P-Y, May–Dec. 1865, Letters Received by the Asst. Commissioner of the State of South Carolina, Bureau of Refugees, Freedmen, and Abandoned Lands, 1865–70, M869, roll 8, NARA.

47. TP, "Reminiscences," 84, 86; *Dedication of the Equestrian Statue of Major-General Charles Devens . . . July 4, 1906* (Worcester, MA: Worcester County Memorial Devens Statue Commis-

sion, 1907), n.p.; Charles Devens and Arthur Lithgow Devens, *Orations and Addresses on Various Occasions, Civil and Military* (Boston: Little and Brown, 1891), 2, 275, 283. Devens was a founder of the Military Order of the Loyal Legion of the United States, formed by an elite group of Union officers fearing an undermining of the Republic after Lincoln's assassination, "in historic memory of the Society of Cincinnati," an organization of which Gen. Thomas Pinckney served as president. David S. Heidler and Jeanne T. Heidler, "Charles Devens Jr.," in *Encyclopedia of the American Civil War: A Political, Social, and Military History* (Santa Barbara CA: ABC-CLIO, 2000), 594.

48. TP, "Reminiscences," 86.

49. TP to CCP Jr., 11 Dec. 1865, P-M.

50. Ibid. Fannymeade Plantation was in neighboring Prince George County.

51. Ibid.; Ulysses R. Brooks, *Butler and His Cavalry in the War of Secession, 1861–1865* (Columbia, SC: State, 1909), 130.

52. Lucy W. Pinckney to "Rye," 23 Apr. [1867], P-M; Elise P. Rutledge, "Register of St. John's-in-the-Wilderness, Flat Rock," *SCHM* 63 (Apr. 1962): 181.

53. CCP Jr., *New Year's Sermon Delivered at Grace Church*, 11, 12, 14; Barnwell, "Captain Thomas Pinckney," 344; TP, "Reminiscences," 87.

54. Barnwell, "Captain Thomas Pinckney," 344; Pinckney quoted in Jaher, *Urban Establishment*, 337.

55. TP, "Reminiscences," 87–88; *Charleston Courier*, 20 June 1864, 8 Feb. 1866; "The Edgerton Database," Rootsweb, Ancestry.com, http://freepages.genealogy.rootsweb.ancestry.com/~edgerton /EverettWheeler1805.htm; Edmund L. Drago, *Avery Center: From Education and Civil Rights to Preserving the African American Experience*, rev. and ed. W. Marvin Dulaney (Charleston: History, 2006), 32; "Charlie" to Dr. Liney, 5 Dec. 1863, in "Beleaguered Charleston: Letters from the City, 1860–1864," ed. Martin Abbott and Elmer L. Puryear, *SCHM* 61 (July 1960): 174.

56. TP, "Reminiscences," 87; Freehling, *Prelude to Civil War*, 63.

57. TP Contract, 15 Apr. 1868, reproduced in Martin L. Abbott, *The Freedmen's Bureau in South Carolina, 1865–1872* (Chapel Hill: University of North Carolina Press, 1967), 142–43.

58. Ibid.

59. TP, "Reminiscences," 87.

60. "Report of Business Transactions for the Month of August 1866," Bvt. Maj. Edward F. O'Brien, S.A.C., to Bvt. Maj. A. Mc. L. Crawford, bureau adjutant of Charleston, 5 Sept. 1866, Reports of Conditions and Operations, July 1865–Dec. 1866, Records of the Asst. Com. for the State of South Carolina, M869, roll 34, NARA; "Court of General Sessions," *Charleston Daily News*, 2 July 1866, 8.

61. "Report of Business Transactions for the Month of August 1866."

62. TP, "Reminiscences," 87–88.

63. Eric Foner, *Reconstruction: America's Unfinished Revolution, 1863–1877* (New York: Harper & Row, 1988), 183–84, 200; Bvt. Maj. M. C. Crawford to Bvt. Maj. E. L. Deane, asst. atty. gen., Freedmen's Bureau, Headquarters District of Charleston, 17 Oct. 1867, Letters Received by the Asst. Commissioner of the State of South Carolina, Bureau of Refugees, Freedmen, and Abandoned Lands, 1865–70, M869, roll 8, NARA.

64. Doar, *Sketch of the Agricultural Society of St. James*, 39; Caroline Pinckney Seabrook to Rev. Charles Edward Leverett, [Mar.–Apr. 1867], in Taylor, Matthews, and Power, *Leverett Letters*, 421.

65. Caroline Pinckney Seabrook to Rev. Charles Edward Leverett, [Mar.–Apr. 1867], in Taylor, Matthews, and Power, *Leverett Letters*, 421.

66. Mary Elliott Pinckney to Caroline P. Seabrook, 18 Jan. 1867, P-M; Julian Mitchell to CCP Jr., 31 Jan. 1867, ibid.; Sen. Edwin D. Morgan (Committee on Finance), "Report [on Petition of Heirs of Miss Harriott Pinckney]," Committee Rpt. 94, 7 Apr. 1868, in *Index to the Reports of Committees of the Senate of the United States for the Second Session Fortieth Congress, 1867-68, in One Volume, from No. 4 to No. 189, Inclusive* (Washington, DC: Government Printing Office, 1868), available online at https://archive.org/stream/reportscommittee03senagoog#page/n346/mode/2up.

67. Foner, *Reconstruction*, 183; TP, "Reminiscences," 93; Saville, *Work of Reconstruction*, 144.

68. TP, "Reminiscences," 96.

69. August Shoolbred to Maj. Gen. Edward R. S. Canby, n.d., quoted in Saville, *Work of Reconstruction*, 168.

70. "The Rebellion on its Last Legs," *The Liberator*, 6 Jan. 1865; Saville, *Work of Reconstruction*, 150–51.

71. "Report of Business Transactions for the Month of August 1866"; TP, "Reminiscences," 86–87.

72. Walter B. Edgar, *South Carolina: A History* (Columbia: University of South Carolina Press, 1998), 388; "This Week," *Nation*, 10 Sept. 1868.

73. Archibald H. Seabrook to CCP Jr., 29 Mar. 1869, P-M; Langdon Cheves to Harriott Middleton, 27 Aug. 1868, Harriott Middleton Family Papers, 1866–68, SCHS; Barnwell, "Captain Thomas Pinckney," 344.

74. Simms quoted in Charles J. Holden, *In the Great Maelstrom: Conservatives in Post–Civil War South Carolina* (Columbia: University of South Carolina Press, 2002), 49; TP, "Reminiscences," 87, 97; Edgar, *South Carolina*, 388.

Chapter Ten

1. US Census, 1870, Illinois, Knox County, Galesburg, roll M593_240, p. 101A; image 32125, FHL microfilm 545739 "List of Black Heads of Households in Galesburg," *Annewalt & Lawrence's Galesburg Directory, containing a Catalogue of Inhabitants—A Full Report of Religious, Educational, Benevolent, Social, and Political Institutions—An Index of Business, and the Advertisements of Enterprising Business Men; to which Is Prefixed a Sketch of the City* (Burlington, IA: Merchant Printing, 1867), "Struggle and Progress—African Americans in Knox County, Illinois [Knox College]," CARLI Digital Collections, http://collections.carli.illinois.edu/cdm4/item_viewer.php?CISOROOT=/knx_strug&CISOPTR=382&CISOBOX=1&REC=7.

2. *Proceedings, Illinois State Convention of Colored Men, Galesburg, October 16th, 17th, 18th 1866* (Chicago: Church, Goodman, and Donnelly, 1867), 2, 12, 26; Cole, *Era of the Civil War*, 336.

3. H. Muelder, *Hero Home from the War*, 12.

4. "A Call for a National Convention of Colored Citizens of the United States," *The Liberator*, 9 Sept. 1864; Sgt. Joseph H. Barquet, *(New York) Weekly Anglo-African*, 5 Nov. 1864; Edwin S. Redkey, ed., *A Grand Army of Black Men: Letters from African-American Soldiers in the Union Army, 1861–1865* (New York: Cambridge University Press, 1992), 215–16; Michael Vorenberg, *Final Freedom: The Civil War, the Abolition of Slavery, and the Thirteenth Amendment* (New York: Cambridge University Press 2001), 158–60.

5. *Proceedings, Illinois State Convention of Colored Men, Galesburg, 1866*, 1.

6. Ibid., 26.

7. Ibid., 2, 12, 24, 26.

8. Foner, *Reconstruction*, 270; "Impromptu Jubilee," *Galesburg (IL) Republican*, 2 Apr. 1870; "An Evening Meeting," ibid., 1 Apr. 1870; "Colored Ratification Meeting," ibid., 16 Apr. 1870; ibid. 23 Apr. 1870; ibid., 18 Mar. 1871.

9. *Galesburg (IL) Republican* 9 Apr. 1870, 1.

10. Editorial, ibid.

11. Ibid., 14 May 1870.

12. Ibid., 23 Sept. 1870, 28 Jan. 1871.

13. "A Letter from Captain Barquet," ibid., 28 Oct. 1871, 8.

14. Ibid., 16, 30 Mar., 18 Nov. 1871.

15. Ibid., 13 Jan. 1872; William L. Steele, *Galesburg Public Schools: Their History and Work, 1861–1911* (Galesburg, IL: Board of Education, 1911), 44–45; H. Muelder, *Hero Home from the War*, 15; *Galesburg (IL) Republican-Register*, 28 Feb. 1874.

16. *Galesburg (IL) Republican*, 22, 29 July 1871, quoted in H. Muelder, *Hero Home from the War*, 10, 18.

17. *Galesburg (IL) Republican*, 13 May 1871, 16 Mar. 1872.

18. H. Muelder, *Hero Home from the War*, 19.

19. *Galesburg (IL) Republican*, 4 June 1871.

20. Ibid., 18 May 1872, 50; ibid., 3 June 1871; "Town Talk: 'An Indignant Candidate,'" ibid., 13 Apr. 1872.

21. Charles A. Church, *History of the Republican Party in Illinois, 1854–1912* (Rockford, IL: Press of Wilson Brothers, 1912), 108; Merline Pitre, "Frederick Douglass and the Annexation of Santo Domingo," *Journal of Negro History* 62 (Oct. 1877): 394.

22. Redkey, "Brave Black Volunteers," 30; William S. Marston to "Mother," 14 Apr. [1864], William S. Marston Letters (1862–64), SCHS; Joseph H. Barquet to "Mr. Prescott," *Galesburg (IL) Free Democrat*, 17 Mar. 1864, [typescript of article], Special Collections and Archives, Seymour Library, Knox College, Galesburg, IL.

23. Leslie A. Schwalm, *Emancipation's Diaspora: Race and Reconstruction in the Upper Midwest* (Chapel Hill: University of North Carolina Press, 2009), 98; US Census, 1870, Illinois, Knox County, Galesburg, roll M593_240, p. 101A, image 32125, FHL microfilm 545739, Ancestry.com; US Census, 1870, Cook County, Chicago, Ward 4, M593_200, p. 136A, image 74584, FHL microfilm 545699, ibid.

24. US Census, 1870, Cook County, Chicago, Ward 4, M593_200, p. 136A.

25. "Plenty of Work," *Chicago Journal*, n.d., quoted in *Galesburg (IL) Republican*, 29 Oct. 1871, 6; Richard Schneirov, *Labor and Urban Politics: Class Conflict and the Origins of Modern Liberalism in Chicago, 1864–1897* (Urbana: University of Illinois Press, 1998), 53; "Local Variations," *Galesburg (IL) Republican*, 27 Apr. 1872, 1.

26. "Local Variations," *Galesburg (IL) Republican*, 27 Apr. 1872, 1; Karen Sawislak, *Smoldering City: Chicagoans and the Great Fire, 1871–1874* (Chicago: University of Chicago Press, 1995), 173–74.

27. *Galesburg (IL) Republican*, 29 June 1872.

28. "First Ratification Meeting of the Campaign—The Colored Men in the Field Fighting for Grant," *Chicago Post*, 12 June 1872, 6.

29. "Speeches by J. D. Davis and Capt. J. H. Barquet," *(Springfield) Daily Illinois State Journal*, 30 Aug. 1872.

30. "Republican Rally Saturday Night," *Quincy (IL) Daily Whig,* 3 Sept. 1872, 2.

31. *Galesburg (IL) Republican-Register,* 13 July 1872, 1; ibid., 20 July 1872, 8; *Galesburg (IL) Republican,* 13 July 1872; ibid., 20 July 1872, 8.

32. *Galesburg (IL) Republican-Register,* 24 Apr. 1873, 1.

33. Ibid., 23 Aug. 1873, 1, quoted in H. Muelder, *Hero Home from the War,* 18.

34. *Galesburg (IL) Republican-Register,* 28 Mar. 1874; Eleanor Alexander, *Lyrics of Sunshine and Shadow: The Tragic Courtship and Marriage of Paul Laurence Dunbar and Alice Ruth Moore: A History of Love and Violence among the African American Elite* (New York: New York University Press, 2001), 29; James Smethurst, "Those Nobel Sons of Ham: Poetry, Soldiers, and Citizens at the End of Reconstruction," in Blatt, Brown, and Yacovone, *Hope & Glory,* 170.

35. Quoted in Schwalm, *Emancipation's Diaspora,* 202.

36. *Galesburg (IL) Republican-Register,* 5 Sept. 1874; ibid., 31 Oct. 1874, 20 Feb. 1875, quoted in H. Muelder, *Hero Home from the War,* 18.

37. *Galesburg (IL) Republican-Register,* 1 July 1876, quoted in H. Muelder, *Hero Home from the War,* 19.

38. Norman, "From an 'Abolition City' to the Color Line," 18.

39. *Galesburg (IL) Republican Register,* 6 Jan. 1877, quoted ibid., 19.

40. Schneirov, *Labor and Urban Politics,* 69, 112.

41. US Census, 1880, Iowa, Scott County, Davenport, roll 364, p. 582C, frame 44, FHL microfilm 1254364, Ancestry.com.

42. List of Internments, Oakdale Memorial Gardens, Davenport, IA.

43. *(Davenport, IA) Daily Gazette,* 15 Mar. 1880 (viewed online); "A Rambling Sketch of Some of Our Earlier Colored Residents," *The Home Towner,* a supplement to the *Galesburg (IL) Press,* Jan. 1934," "Struggle and Progress—African Americans in Knox County, Illinois [Knox College]," CARLI Digital Collections, http://collections.carli.illinois.edu/cdm/ref/collection/knx_strug/id/362.

44. Norman, "From an 'Abolition City' to the Color Line," 18; "Execution of Perteet: Wife-Murderer Acknowledges His Crime," *New York Times,* 20 Dec. 1873.

45. Paul Laurence Dunbar, "Robert Shaw Gould," *Atlantic Monthly,* Oct. 1900, 488; Alexander, *Lyrics of Sunshine and Shadow,* 18, 24.

46. Allen Flint, "Black Response to Colonel Shaw," *Phylon* 45 (1984): 210–11.

Chapter Eleven

1. Susan Middleton to Harriott Middleton, 27 Feb. 1863, Cheves-Middleton Papers, SCHS; Mary Elliott Pinckney to Caroline Pinckney Seabrook, 15 Jan. 1867, P-M; TP to CCP Jr., [ca. 1867], ibid.

2. "Description and Finding Guide," Stewart Family Papers, 1802–1938, Department of Manuscripts and Archives, Virginia Historical Society, Richmond.

3. Robert E. Lee to Mary Lee, 29 Mar. 1870, in Capt. Robert E. Lee, *Recollections and Letters of General Robert E. Lee by His Son* (New York: Doubleday and Page, 1905), 388–89; Mary Stewart Pinckney to "My Dear Child" [Norma Stewart], 8 May 1882, Stewart Family Papers, Virginia Historical Society.

4. *Richmond Whig,* Apr. 22, 1870. The Stewart brothers purchased the land and underwrote the construction costs for Emmanuel Church, a project dear to the heart of Mary Williamson Stewart.

5. In 1871, when Isobel, called "Belle," married Bryan, he also relocated his law practice from Fluvanna County to Richmond. Another sister, Marion McIntosh, married at thirty-five years old to the Rev. George William Peterkin, who had ridden during the war with Stonewall Jackson and became the bishop of West Virginia. "Bishop George William Peterkin, Husband of Marion McIntosh Stewart," The Peterkins, Brook Hill: Family, History, Community, http://brook-hill.net /peterkin.

6. Mary Stewart Pinckney to Emmie, 25 Mar. [1871], Elliott-Gonzales Papers, SHC.

7. Mary Elliott Pinckney to Emmie [Emily Elliott], 2 June [1870], ibid.; Lucy W. Pinckney to "Rye," 23 Apr. [n.y.], P-M; Caroline P. Seabrook to Emmie, [n.d.], ibid.

8. Mary Amanda Pinckney to Emmie, 25 Mar. [1871], Elliott-Gonzales Papers, SHC; Reuther, *Flat Rock,* 17.

9. "Thomas Pinckney," in *Men of Mark in South Carolina: Ideals of American Life; A Collection of Biographies of Leading Men of the State,* ed. James C. Hemphill, vol. 1 (Washington, DC: Men of Mark, 1907), 303; Edgar, *South Carolina,* 394, 397.

10. Edgar, *South Carolina,* 394–95.

11. CCP Jr., *Life of General Thomas Pinckney,* 98.

12. *The National Centennial Commemoration Proceedings on the One Hundredth Anniversary of the Introduction and Adoption of the "Resolutions Respecting Independency," Held in Philadelphia on the Evening of July 2, 1876, Pennsylvania Academy of the Fine Arts, and July 1, 1876, at the Hall of Independence* (Philadelphia: Printed for the Committee by Collins, Printer, 1876), 88. Years later Pinckney expanded the essay into his book-length biography of the general.

13. TP, "Reminiscences," 24. Pinckney's former division commander Matthew Butler, who was elected the US Senate in 1876, agreed to ask a colleague from Iowa to track down Ingersoll, a native of that state. After reading Ingersoll's reply, Butler added his own message: "You see the mean dog has no idea of keeping his word with you and I understand this [note] to indicate that he is open to an offer of money, which is the only way you will ever recover it." Ibid., 24–25.

14. David W. Blight, *Race and Reunion: The Civil War in American Thought* (Cambridge, MA: Harvard University Press, 2001), 135.

15. TP, "Reminiscences," 87. Daniel H. Chamberlain (1835–1907) was governor of South Carolina from 1874 to 1877.

16. George B. Tindall, *South Carolina Negroes, 1877–1900* (Columbia: University of South Carolina Press, 1952), 196. Among the founding families of St. Mark's Episcopal Church were the well-respected Dereefs and Holloways, who for generations had had long-term relationships with St. Philip's Episcopal Church through the Brown Fellowship Society. Ibid.

17. TP, "Reminiscences," 88.

18. Ibid., 96.

19. *BBR,* 314; Frank A. Rollin, *Life and Public Services of Martin R. Delany* (Boston: Lee and Shepard, 1883), 139, 140, 157, 209–13.

20. TP, "Reminiscences," 96.

21. *Charleston News and Courier,* 18, 24 Oct. 1876; Alfred B. Williams, *Hampton and His Red Shirts: South Carolina's Deliverance in 1876* (Charleston: Walker, Evans, & Cogswell, 1935), 274; TP, "Reminiscences," 93.

22. TP, "Reminiscences," 90, 91.

23. Ibid., 91, 93.

24. Andrew, *Wade Hampton*, 440; "How the Democrats Won in South Carolina," *New York Times*, 16 Nov. 1878; TP, "Reminiscences," 94–95; William A. Dunning, *Essays on the Civil War and Reconstruction* (1897; repr., New York: Harper and Row, 1965), 372–73. Generally when the excessive number of votes was discovered, a partisan of whichever side was perpetrating this particular fraud would be blindfolded and, with ceremony—and in theory unable to tell one ballot from another—would draw out just enough votes to make the numbers jibe with the number of registered voters. Ibid.

25. TP, "Reminiscences," 94–96; "How the Democrats Won in South Carolina," *New York Times*, 16 Nov. 1878.

26. John Schreiner Reynolds, *Reconstruction in South Carolina, 1865–1877* (Columbia, SC: State, 1905), 229; Wise, *Gate of Hell*, 116.

27. TP to William Johnstone, 9 Aug. 1882, SFP.

28. Mary Elliott Pinckney to Maime, 4 Dec. 1875, P-M.

29. Ibid. The children of Thomas and Mary Pinckney were Amanda (27 Jan. 1871–14 Nov. 1875), Thomas (26 Oct. 1872–28 Oct. 1881), John Stewart (22 Oct. 1874–9 July 1875), Charles Cotesworth (16 Dec. 1875–20 Aug. 1934), Lucy (18 June 1877–12 July 1877), and Caroline (4 May 1879–23 July 1879). "Pinckney Genealogy," typescript in Pinckney Family Scrapbook, JPP.

30. TP to John Stewart, 31 May 1881, SFP.

31. TP to "Ria," 26 Oct. 1881, P-M; TP to Daniel Kerr Stewart, 4 Mar. 1882, SFP; Mary Stewart Pinckney to Daniel Kerr Stewart, 27 Mar. 1882, ibid; Mary Stewart Pinckney to "My Dear Child" [Norma Stewart], 8 May 1882, ibid.

32. TP to Daniel Kerr Stewart, 14 Jan. 1882, SFP. The Stewart brothers suggested that Pinckney choose the recipients of these scholarships. One went to the son of Pinckney's cousin William Johnstone, who as a teenager had shot his father's murderer in Flat Rock during the war. The other went to the son of Robert G. Johnson, one of Pinckney's "most trusted troopers," who had come to work for him on shares after the war. Ibid.

33. John S. Palmer to Harriet Palmer, 29 Nov. 1870, in Towles, *World Turned Upside Down*, 678.

34. Edgar, *South Carolina*, 394; TP to Daniel K. Stewart, 27 May 1881, SFP; TP to John Stewart, 16 June 1881, ibid.; Mary Stewart Pinckney to Daniel Kerr Stewart, 31 Dec. 1881, ibid.; TP to Daniel Kerr Stewart, 14 Jan. 1882, ibid.

35. TP to Daniel K. Stewart, 6 Feb. 1881, SFP.

36. TP to John Stewart, 1 Apr. 1884, ibid.

37. CCP Jr. to "Ria," 6 Jan. 1887, P-M.

38. In the 1930s Pinckney's daughter would observe how the "personal compact" between blacks and whites, who shared a mutual commitment to the land and a shared interest in its successful harvests, had expired in "a new free world." Josephine Pinckney, "They Shall Return as Strangers," *Virginia Quarterly Review* (Oct. 1934): 544, 556.

39. Thomas Condit Miller and Hu Maxwell, *West Virginia and Its People*, vol. 3 (New York: Lewis Historical, 1913), 772; *In Memoriam: Mary Stewart Pinckney* (Richmond: Whittet and Shepperson, 1889), 3. The Stewart family made generous contributions to complete Mary's last project, St. James Episcopal Church and Chapel of Ease at McClellanville, which has a large stained-glass

window to her memory. Anne B. L. Bridges and Roy Williams, *St. James Santee, Plantation Parish: History and Records, 1685–1925* (Spartanburg, SC: Reprint Company, 1997), 289–93.

40. Eventually Cotesworth would present his joyful father with two grandsons, Thomas and Charles Cotesworth, little echoes of the founding brothers. And years later one of them would hunt down General Thomas Pinckney's purloined sword and restore it to the family's possession, where it remains to date.

41. Marie Tyler-McGraw, *At the Falls: Richmond, Virginia and Its People* (Chapel Hill: University of North Carolina Press, 1996), 211–12; John M. Coski, "The Museum of the Confederacy," *Encyclopedia Virginia*, last modified 18 Jan. 2012, accessed 21 July 2012, https://www.encyclopedia virginia.org/Museum_of_the_Confederacy.

42. Thomas L. Connelly and Barbara L. Bellows, *God and General Longstreet: Essays on the Lost Cause and the Southern Mind* (Baton Rouge: Louisiana State University Press, 1982), 35–36, 43.

43. Camilla Scott was born in 1854. Her mother, Heningham W. Lyons, was the daughter of James Lyons, a sociable Richmond lawyer and politician who once owned Laburnum. His house burned, but Joseph Bryan later bought the property for his own family's home. Camilla's father, Robert Eden Scott, a Fauquier County lawyer whose murder by Yankee "renegades" in 1862, lack of a will, and loss from fire of the family home Oakhill sent his third wife and her five children into a spiral of desperate poverty for years. Camilla never shook off the shame and anger she and her sisters experienced. When she married Captain Pinckney, she eventually succeeded in having him buy one of the most elaborate Victorian mansions in the city, where the family of three lived. Bellows, *Talent for Living*, 16–20, 24–25.

44. Lise Rutledge Ravenel to Willie Childs, 5 June 1892, Lise Ravenel Childs Papers, SCHS; Mary Lyons to Sallie L. Taliaferro, 13 Mar. 1891, Sallie L. Taliaferro Papers in William Booth Taliaferro Papers, Special Collections, Swem Library, College of William and Mary; Bellows, *Talent for Living*, 16–21.

45. Bridges and Williams, *St. James Santee*, 311–16; Bellows, *Talent for Living*, 21–22; "Death of Mr. Pinckney," *Charleston News and Courier*, 1 Mar. 1899, 6. Hunt-club members, many of whom had southern roots, elected Pinckney an honorary member along with former president Grover Cleveland, the one Democrat in a long line of Republican presidents from 1860 to 1912. Henry H. Carter, *Early History of the Santee Club* (Syracuse, NY: Gaylord Brothers, 1908), 10.

Epilogue

1. "The Thomson Auditorium," *Charleston News and Courier*, 1 Nov. 1898; TP, "Reminiscences," 26, 30, 98–99; John Sterling Swann, "Prison Life at Fort Delaware," 26 June 1876, transcription by Neil Allen Bristow, 1998, (updated 3 June 2005), Rootsweb, http://freepages.genealogy.rootsweb. ancestry.com/~greenwolf/coombs/swann-js.htm (from original in Misc. Manuscripts, MS Division, LC); Joslyn, *Immortal Captives*, 272.

2. TP, "Reminiscences," 26.

3. Joseph H. Barquet to "Mr. Prescott," *Galesburg (IL) Free Democrat*, 17 Mar. 1864, typescript, Special Collections and Archives, Seymour Library, Knox College, Galesburg, IL.

4. Joseph's daughters, Mary Dudley and Matilda "Barbary" Smith, participated in Liston's law-

suit (see below for details). None of the names of his known sons appears on the list of plaintiffs, but a "George Barquet," also of Chicago, is so identified; perhaps one of them had changed his name. Joseph, a porter, lived with Horace Ward, a cook, and his family. John Pierre had a family of six children and worked as a hotel cook in Oskaloosa, a coal-mining area of Iowa with a substantial black population. James was dead. Liston Benforth Barquet did serve with the 10th US Cavalry and remained in the army until 1896, when he cashed out, still a private, and disappeared from the public record and family contact. "Deposition of Francis Plumeau and Caroline Eudora Watson (Barquet) Watson," Langdon Cheves Legal Papers, SCHS; US Census, 1900, Iowa, Mahaska County, Oskaloosa, T624, roll 446, p. 14A, FHL microfilm 1240446, Ancestry.com; US Census, 1900, Illinois, Cook County, Chicago, Ward 2, roll 246, p. 18B, FHL microfilm 1240246, ibid.; Record for Liston B. Barquet, Buffalo Soldiers, Returns from Regular Army Cavalry Regiments, 1866–1916, M744, roll 98, no. 34, ibid.; Liston Barquet to Whitefield McKinlay, 28 Jan. 1903, Whitefield McKinlay Papers, Carter G. Woodson Collection of Negro Papers and Related Documents, Manuscript Division, LC.

5. *Rutledge v. Tunno et al.,* Supreme Court of South Carolina, July 14 1904, *Southeastern Reporter* 48 (16 July–10 Dec. 1904): 297, 299; Greg H. Williams, *The French Assault on American Shipping, 1793–1813: A History and Comprehensive Record of Merchant Marine Losses* (Jefferson, NC: McFarland, 2009), 146, 210, 216, 339, 355.

6. *Rutledge v. Tunno et al.,* 400.

7. *In Re Adam Tunno,* 9 Feb. 1900, Langdon Cheves Legal Papers (1875–1932), p. 52, SCHS; Philip N. Racine, ed., *Gentlemen Merchants: A Charleston Family's Odyssey, 1828–1870* (Knoxville: University of Tennessee Press, 2008), xv. Young earlier succeeded in winning all of Hagar Cole's other children or grandchildren a portion of her one-third interest in the house that sold at auction for $800. Hagar's descendants who benefited were Isabella Simons, Eliza Lesesne, Owen D. Chatters, Mary Cole, Sarah McKinlay, Charles Miller, Edward Warley, Alexander Forester. Still pending, though, was a mortgage held by a cousin, George McKinlay (brother-in-law of Mary Louisa Barquet and father of Whitefield McKinlay), that had to be satisfied. RMC, Book Q 14 (2 Aug. 1860), 35; William Cole, "Bill for Partition," 26 June 1867, Charleston District Equity Court, Hager Cole File, Papers of Rutledge and Young, SCHS.

8. Liston W. Barquet to Whitefield McKinlay, 21 Sept., 18 Oct. 1899, McKinlay Papers, LC.

9. "In Memorium: Judge Charles H. Simonton," *Annual Reports of the City of Charleston* (1905), 7–13; Liston Barquet to Whitefield McKinlay, 21 Sept. 1899, McKinlay Papers, LC.

10. Will of Adam Tunno, 1831, Charleston County Wills and Misc. Probate Records, 38–39 (1826–34), 1001–5, Ancestry.com. Tunno's nephew, Edward Rose Tunno, educated at Cambridge University and the Inns of Court, had previously inherited a massive fortune at the death of his father, John, Adam's eldest brother. Tunno's bequest was to repay in part a debt he incurred when he took over John's Charleston business after the American Revolution. Barbara L. Bellows, "The Worlds of John Tunno: Scottish Emigrant, Charleston Loyalist, London Merchant, 1746–1819," in *Citizen-Scholar: Essays in Honor of Walter B. Edgar,* ed. Robert H. Brinkmeyer Jr. (Columbia: University of South Carolina Press, 2016), 96.

11. Born in Charleston in 1852, Whitefield McKinlay was the son of Mary Elizabeth Weston (daughter of wealthy miller Anthony Weston) and tailor George McKinlay, whose brother Archibald had married Mary Louisa Barquet. After Archibald's wife died, leaving him with a daughter also named Mary Louisa, he remarried and took his family to Toronto about 1860. By 1895,

Mary Louisa (who had returned to Charleston during Reconstruction) had been widowed by one husband, Congressman Alonzo J. Ransier, and apparently abandoned by another. In desperate economic straits, she appealed to the McKinlays for help. Whitefield contacted Liston in 1899 because she kept insisting that her uncle in New York knew of a lawsuit that would bring all her family justice and economic salvation. Johnson and Roark, *No Chariot Let Down*, 111n2; Willard B. Gatewood, "Aristocrats of Color: The Black Elite, 1880–1920," *Journal of Southern History* 54 (Feb. 1988): 7; Canada, *Census Returns for 1861*, Ontario, Toronto, York Township, roll *C-1090, p. 14*, *Ancestry.com*; Committee on House Administration of the US House of Representatives, "Alonzo Jacob Ransier 1834–1882: United States Representative 1873–1875, Republican from South Carolina," *Black Americans in Congress, 1870–2007* (Washington: US Government Printing Office, 2008), 108; A. Reid McKinlay to Whitefield McKinlay, 28 Dec. 1895, McKinlay Papers, LC.

12. Liston Barquet to Whitefield McKinlay, 21 Sept. 1899, McKinlay Papers, LC.

13. Liston Barquet to Whitefield McKinlay, 1 Oct. 1899, ibid.

14. Liston Barquet to Whitefield McKinlay, 21 Sept. 1899, ibid.; Liston W. Barguet Journal, 2 Mar. 1861, John R. Clauson collection.

15. Liston Barquet to Whitefield McKinlay, 28 Mar. 1900, McKinlay Papers, LC.

16. Liston Barquet to Whitefield McKinlay, 20 Dec. 1899, ibid.

17. Liston Barquet to Whitefield McKinlay, 23 Feb. 1900, ibid.; Langdon Cheves III, *In Re Adam Tunno*, 9 Feb. 1900, Langdon Cheves III Legal Papers, SCHS.

18. Liston Barquet to Whitefield McKinlay, 2 Sept. 1899, 23 Mar., 28 Mar., 13 May, 20 Oct. 1900, 28 Jan. 1903, McKinlay Papers, LC.

19. Gatewood, "Aristocrats of Color," 9.

20. Liston W. Barquet to Whitefield McKinlay, 12 Jan. 1903, McKinlay Papers, LC; Sass, *Rutledge v. Tunno* (1904), 404–6. Among the other "surrounding circumstances" leading to Sass's decision was that Bellingall's name never appeared on Tunno's many real-estate transactions as a waiver of dower rights, as wives were bound to do. Ibid., 408.

21. Moffett, *Rutledge v. Tunno*, 409–11; Gary, *Rutledge v. Tunno*, 412.

22. Bernard DeVoto, "Fiction and the Everlasting If," *Harper's Monthly* (June 1938): 42–49; TP, "Reminiscences," 96. Pinckney's reminiscences were never published. At age seventy-seven he did not want to put more time into expanding his memoir by two-thirds as his prospective publisher (probably his cousin A. E. Gonzales, a founder of the *Columbia State* newspaper) had requested. About 1904, he passed his proof sheets to Myrta Lockett Avary, a well-known Virginia author, who rewrote his account in a much more sensational fashion and included it as the chapter "The Devil on the Santee (A Rice-Planter's Story)" in her collection *Dixie after the War: An Exposition of Social Conditions Existing in the South, during the Twelve Years Succeeding the Fall of Richmond*, published in 1906. A. E. Gonzales to James Henry Rice, 8 Dec. 1922, Elliott-Gonzales Papers, SHC; TP to "Hat" [Harriott Horry Pinckney Ravenel], 16 Aug. 1911, Harriott Horry Ravenel Papers, SCHS.

23. Paul Rea, "Thomas Pinckney: First President of the Charleston Museum," *Charleston Museum Bulletin*, Nov. 1915, 53–54; Joseph W. Barnwell, "Capt. Thomas Pinckney," *Confederate Veteran* 24 (Aug. 1916): 344.

24. Barnwell, "Capt. Thomas Pinckney," 342.

INDEX